Price's Lost Campaign

Shades of Blue and Gray Series

Edited by Herman Hattaway, Jon L. Wakelyn, and Clayton E. Jewett

The Shades of Blue and Gray Series offers Civil War studies for the modern reader–Civil War buff and scholar alike. Military history today addresses the relationship between society and warfare. Thus biographies and thematic studies that deal with civilians, soldiers, and political leaders are increasingly important to a larger public. This series includes books that will appeal to Civil War Roundtable groups, individuals, libraries, and academics with a special interest in this era of American history.

Price's Lost Campaign

The 1864 Invasion of Missouri

Mark A. Lause

University of Missouri Press   Columbia and London

University of Missouri Press, Columbia, Missouri 65201
Printed and bound in the United States of America

First paperback printing, 2013
5 4 3 2 1 17 16 15 14 13

Cataloging-in-Publication data available from the Library of Congress.
ISBN 978-0-8262-1949-7 (hard cover: alk. paper)
ISBN 978-0-8262-2033-2 (pbk: alk. paper)

∞™ This paper meets the requirements of the
American National Standard for Permanence of Paper
for Printed Library Materials, Z39.48, 1984.

Design and composition: Jennifer Cropp
Printer and binder: Thomson-Shore, Inc.
Typefaces: Minion, Adobe Jenson, and Rage Joi D

I would dedicate this work first and foremost to my wife, Katherine L. Allen, whose lifelong patience and support has always made her a part of anything I have ever accomplished, and, in this project, to the years of family members, teachers and school chums who have patiently borne part of the burden of my obsession with the 1864 Missouri campaign.

Contents

Price's Lost Campaign

Introduction

By the fall of 1864, the American Civil War had entered its final and most desperately brutal months. Trench warfare mired the vast armies in Virginia while the hellish turn of events in Georgia aimed at breaking the morale and spirit of the civilian population. In futile desperation, large Confederate armies shook free of the Federal death grip for a final rampage through the Shenandoah Valley, Tennessee, and Missouri. The last of these, "Price's Raid," is not only the least discussed but frequently also remains unmentioned in single-volume accounts of the war.

Certainly, one can ascribe much of the negligence to the ponderous parochialism accorded the Trans-Mississippi, reflecting the wartime priorities of both Washington and Richmond. After settling their respective claims in Missouri during the first year of the war, both governments contented themselves with self-fulfilling assumptions that marginalized the region's role and siphoned off the manpower from west of the river to Mississippi, Tennessee, or Georgia (which, in turn, suffered neglect in the interests of the war in Virginia). For this reason, in most accounts of the war, Missouri tends to wink out of existence after the first year, or makes periodic cameos as a sideshow of guerrilla warfare in which the brutality takes center stage rather than the military role of those brutalities within the wider conflict.

Nevertheless, the numbers involved justify no such inattention. The Confederates enumerated over 12,000 at the inception of the operation with perhaps 2,000 to 3,000 partisans already active in the state. They claimed to have acquired between 5,000 and 9,000 more men along the way.[1] Even allowing for exaggeration, as many as 15,000 or more may have marched at some point with Price's army, though he never had a force near this large at the same time—and, in the end, lost many more men than he gained.

The Federals mobilized massive numbers to meet the incursion. Starting with only about 11,000 garrison troops across the entire state, they called more from Kansas and Illinois. They rushed several thousand more recruits into uniform and diverted another 9,000 veterans who had been on their way to Georgia.

Before the campaign was over, they also mobilized over 24,000 Enrolled Missouri Militia (EMM) and perhaps 10,000 Kansas State Militia, which included an indeterminate number of exempts and resident aliens placed under arms. This brought into action a total of around 65,000 to 70,000 Unionists.

The fall 1864 campaign in Missouri put into motion numbers comparable to the contemporary operations in Georgia. However, the final, desperate Confederate gamble in the far west covered five times the distance as General William T. Sherman's march. One veteran described "the last campaign beyond the Mississippi; a campaign in which a part of the Union troops and most of the confederates marched over 1500 miles." It began "in a torrid heat and end[ed] in snow and zero cold; a campaign begun for politics and ending with dramatic coincidence on the day on which politics were finally swept out of the war."[2] The campaign began with one of the most numerically lopsided engagements of the entire war and ended in the largest battle of the Trans-Mississippi war.

Then, too, how then did movements of 80,000 to 90,000 men over 1,500 miles become remembered as a "raid?" Those Confederate "raids" accorded pride of place in Civil War history—those of Generals J. E. B. Stuart and John Hunt Morgan—involved no more than a fraction of Price's numbers. In fact, the intentions of the Confederates arriving in Missouri also far exceeded those of a "raid." They hoped to displace the Federals in control of the state, not merely to disrupt their functioning. Price's army aspired to capture of one of the nation's largest and most vital industrial centers as well to retake a state capital wrested with some difficulty at the war's start. They anticipated that Federal military occupation and the ascendancy of Radical Republican policies unsanctioned by regular elections had prepared Missourians to embrace a Confederate liberation.

Interestingly, incredulous Federal officials began discussing the operation as a "raid." They did so because they entirely underestimated the size of the Confederate force entering the state and avoided drawing attention to their unpreparedness by redefining it. Interestingly, the less stringent standards of a "raid" suited the Confederates who failed to attain any major goal worthy of an incursion by such numbers at such a time in the war. In the end, history represents a consensus among those with a vested interest in how we remember the past and the power to shape that memory.

Of course, the Confederate goals did shift during the campaign, suggesting three distinct phases. From September 19 through October 7, the Army of Missouri sought to seize St. Louis and Jefferson City, reoccupying the state. Armed rebels moved to within striking distance of St. Louis and Jefferson City at a time when both were defended by significantly smaller Federal forces. Price's army not only failed to seize these strategic goals, but actually failed to make such an attempt. Leaving aside what became of the campaign after Jefferson City, this study focuses on the earlier phase of the campaign, which most clearly places Price's Missouri expedition alongside those of Generals Jubal Early in the Shenandoah Valley or John Bell Hood in Tennessee.

In addition, Confederate accounts of the campaign are unbelievably weak. The Richmond *Daily Dispatch* reported that Union troops were shooting old men in their homes, drowning children in rivers and, of course, that "The females have been insulted and outraged, and then compelled to wash the filthy clothes of the Yankee soldiery upon pain of death on refusal." It also reported that "the drafted militia desert and fly to the Southern army. A short time since two regiments of militia were organized and armed by the Federals at an inland post" but "turned themselves, their arms, and everything belonging to the post, over to the Confederate general." The *Charleston Mercury* reassured beleaguered southern readers, increasingly resentful of the sacrifices imposed on them, that Price "conscripts all the Union sympathizers that he finds, and large numbers of volunteers are joining his army. Many drafted men are escaping from St. Louis and joining Price, and Rosecrans has issued orders to shoot every man going in that direction." Obviously, such newspapers had no correspondents with Price's army and, had they done so, they would have had to be sprouting wings to file such stories in early October.[3] In reality, the Confederate papers depended entirely on the northern papers for the news and had no qualms about simply inventing filler that would be politically soothing to the readership.

Too, the Richmond press had no problem extrapolating its romanticized view of the war in the east west to Missouri, just as the governments there and in Washington easily moved recruits from the west to the east. Certainly, no man had a greater claim to paternity of the Confederate cause in Missouri than the former congressman and governor, General Sterling Price. The postwar founders of the Lost Cause later hung a lithograph in the Missouri Room of the Confederate White House in Richmond depicting "Old Pap" Price as the state's version of Robert E. Lee. It gave Price a youthfully athletic form mounted in the Washingtonian pursuit of national independence at the head of a well-uniformed army arrayed under the "Stainless Banner" of the Confederacy.[4]

Such a romanticized view of the 1864 campaign dissolves with the first serious look. In reality, the lithograph in Richmond depicted Price leading troops two years earlier in northern Mississippi, an event in which luck played no small role in sparing his forces. Two years later, the general rarely pulled his three hundred pounds into the saddle, preferring to ride in a buggy picked up along the way. He spent an increasing amount of his time in an ambulance nursing recurring bouts of malaria contracted in the Mexican War or, charged his critics, a perpetual hangover.

Certainly, many Missouri admirers of the Lost Cause will bristle at any attempt to understand Price in realistic terms. In doing so, they opt for the eastern version of what happened in their state rather than the perspective of its local founding father, Major John N. Edwards. Edwards called the 1864 campaign "the stupidest, wildest, wantonest, wickedest march ever made by a general who had a voice like a lion and a spring like a guinea pig."[5]

That contrast between the image and the realities of the campaign and its commander cut to the core of the contradictions of Confederate Missouri. Price's Army of Missouri claimed to have the goal of liberating the state from a Federal occupation, but nobody actually saw it as that simple. For three years, volunteer forces pushed each other back and forth between the Missouri and the Arkansas Rivers. Periodic incursion of several thousand regular Confederate troops into Missouri captured smaller Federal garrisons, paroled prisoners, and recruited secessionists into Confederate service. They also seized supplies, cut the telegraph, destroyed the railroad, and generally wrought havoc. This shaped particularly harsh measures by the Federals to keep control of the state and protect their supporters and by the Confederates to wage a guerrilla war against the authorities. Preemptive and retaliatory violence left both sides largely demoralized and discouraged.

The Civil War was the first modern war not simply in technology but in the politically motivated brutalization of an entire society. Three years of such warfare shaped the assumptions and aspirations of too many of Price's erstwhile liberators of Missouri, many of whom had slipped home to recruit or to visit family and friends. Too many of them knew the extent to which other Missourians—eagerly as well as grudgingly—cooperated with the Unionist "Hessians" and "Tories." Far too many marched back into Missouri with Price eager to settle old scores under a leadership itself too weak or dispirited to exercise the responsibilities of command.

The Federal understanding of the campaign reflected another aspect of modern war, that of a notoriously inglorious bureaucratic dogmatism. As in more recent conflicts, what was actually experienced in the field proved remarkably incapable of rattling the administrative assumptions that defined both the war and the Napoleonic model of individual commanders.

Either way, the most powerful figures of the Civil War generation from both sides shaped simplistic images of rustic honor and drums-and-bugles glory. The postwar drive for political legitimacy found this fertile soil for a Homeric view of our epic past, purchased at the price of a clear understanding of our collective experience. Hopefully, we have reached the point where a serious study of the 1864 Missouri expedition can provide us worthwhile new insights into modern warfare.

A project pursued for so long incurs debts so broad as to defy their thorough acknowledgement. At a minimum, I would like to thank the Langsam Library at the University of Cincinnati, particularly Milkaila Corday of its Interlibrary Loan service, but also the various manuscript collections touching the subject in Missouri, especially the State Historical Society of Missouri at Columbia and the Missouri Historical Society at St. Louis; the excellent staff of the University of Missouri Press, particularly Clair Willcox; Debbie Upton for excellent work copyediting the text; and Douglas R. Niermeyer of the Missouri Commandery of the Military Order of the Loyal Legion, who freely shared information and insight. I hasten to recall, as well, the many people over the years who have shared stories about the 1864 campaign, the earliest being my grandmother, Mrs. Olivia M. Alfermann Lause, whose own grandfathers witnessed and participated in these events.

Prologue

The Sacred Soil of Missouri

The State, the Army, and the Department

For decades before the Civil War, Americans had wondered at the large earthen embankments and pyramids along the Mississippi and Missouri valleys. Finding the contemporary native peoples ignorant about these often very extensive monuments and works, the whites speculated about Vikings, Phoenicians, or even the biblical Lost Tribes dwelling briefly in an alternative Promised Land; some sort of an earlier, populous, and civilized race of Mound Builders left their monuments before being apparently assailed by relative newcomers, the Indians. By the time they had become Missourians, most whites hardly had little time to speculate before they carted away the rubble, pottery, and bones to make room for their own civilization. Literate and confident in their own society's abilities to avoid the mistakes of the past, they regarded their achievements as irreversible progress. In the 1850s, as St. Louis carted off the last of these enigmatic "fortifications," William Pidgeon's *Traditions of De-Coo-Dah* explained to the civilized whites warring on the Native Americans that these formations represented earthen defenses raised by an earlier civilization destroyed by the savage predilections of those indigenous peoples.[1]

The would-be civilizers of Missouri made it part of the United States. The new republic embraced ideas of liberty that included the freedom of those who could afford it to seize Indian lands and own Africans to work it. By 1861, the inconsistencies and contradictions threatened its survival, and the war that followed turned the state into an embattled terrain of deserted towns and smoldering ruins largely populated by widows, orphans, and refugees. What emerged institutionally by 1864 were two Missouris—an Army of Missouri and a Department of Missouri—waging war over an uncertain future.

Missouri and the Civil War

Kentuckians, Virginians, and Tennesseans settled and populated what became Missouri in the generation after its acquisition as part of the 1803 Louisiana Purchase. They displaced the remaining native peoples and followed the Missouri River west with plans for slave-based tobacco, hemp, and cotton plantations. The most coherent and well-connected political force in the state, these planters and aspiring planters established their predominance around the Great Bend where the generally eastbound Missouri River turned sharply south before turning east again, as well as in "Little Dixie" in the north-central part of the state. Their request for a statehood that sanctioned human slavery required the Missouri Compromise of 1820, inaugurating a nationally escalating series of conflicts between states that shared the "peculiar institution" and those that did not.

Sterling Price embodied Missouri's southern identity.[2] Born and raised on a Virginia tobacco plantation, he studied law and, in 1831, at twenty-two, joined his family between the towns of Fayette and Keytesville in the Great Bend, where they grew corn, wheat, and oats as well as hemp and their most reliable crop, tobacco. Price married and farmed until marketing his tobacco drew him into the business world of Chariton County, which he represented in the Missouri General Assembly as a Democrat. After serving as speaker in the assembly, he won election to the U.S. Congress in 1844, but left for the army with the outbreak of the war with Mexico. Another congressman, Jefferson Davis, faced serving under his father-in-law, Zachary Taylor, and tried to swap assignments with Price, who earned no points with Davis by passing up the opportunity and opting for service with other Missourians.

Missourians fought a distinctive war with Mexico. By August 1846, the first wave of Missourians had moved over the Santa Fe Trail and organized the New Mexico Territory, before moving on, as Price's new Second Missouri Mounted Infantry arrived to garrison the territory. In January 1847, the Pueblo Indians rose up, encouraged by those Mexican officials ousted by the *Yanquis*. The rebellion killed several prominent whites, including Governor Charles Bent, before Price's wrathful Missourians bottled the insurgents in the Catholic church at Pueblo de Taos. After blasting them with cannons and killing 154 of them, they tried some of the leaders for treason, even executing one of them, inspiring one observer to note "a great assumption on the part of the Americans to conquer a country and then arraign the revolting inhabitants for treason." In February 1848, Price led the Missourians south through El Paso del Norte (present-day Juarez) to Chihuahua, where the authorities assured him that the war had actually ended and even evacuated their garrison to prevent bloodshed. Just to make sure, Price pursued them to Santa Cruz de Rosales and overran them on March 16, killing some 250 of them with minimal American losses.[3]

Back in Missouri, the wartime acquisition of these vast new territories divided the state's dominant Democratic Party. When the bombastic U.S. senator Thomas Hart Benton defied the pro-southern bloc, it split Democrats in the legislature into Benton and anti-Benton factions. Price returned to his estate—now called Val Verde—as a known "Southern Rights" man, but also as a war hero who had done nothing to tarnish his older Bentonian credentials. In 1852, he defeated Thomas L. Price, a Jefferson City Benton man for the Democratic gubernatorial nomination, won the general election, and presided over the state's subsequent "Border War" with antislavery settlers in the Kansas Territory.[4]

Still, even the large-scale slaveholding farmers wisely ignored cotton and mostly abandoned tobacco in favor of the corn and wheat needed to feed a growing network of communities watered by the commerce of the two greatest rivers in North America. Railroads increasingly supplemented the rivers, and the southern interior of the state yielded lead, iron, and mineral wealth. The railroads, the waterfront, and the industries required infusions of capital and people from the North, the eastern seaboard, as well as legions of Irish and the "Dutch," an inaccurate description of the Germans, émigrés from the *Deutschland.* The term also covered the Swiss, Austrians, and even Bohemians, also politically peppered with the radical veterans of the 1848 revolutions, as were groups of Hungarians, French, Italians, Poles, and others. By 1860, commerce and the beginnings of industry built a vigorous population of 1,182,012, although fewer than one in five lived in a community larger than 2,500 and only one in twenty adults labored in manufacturing.

A statistically representative Missouri community of five hundred grew at a convenient crossroads or river ford. Although men still outnumbered women, the natural proportions of birth had almost restored a balance. Over a third of the residents had not passed the age of fifteen, only a quarter beyond twenty-five years. Some of the dozen people over forty-five probably remembered raising the older buildings, the larger of which likely doubled as an inn, a tavern, a stagecoach stop, and a public hall. Usually, neither the religious denominations in town nor any traditional authority enjoyed the kind of hegemony needed to provide the necessary cemeteries and schools. A small number of civic-minded and practical lawyers, doctors, and entrepreneurs—often linked by family, marriage, friendship, church, or other associations—managed community affairs. This likely included one or more men of the original families, their rough pioneering ways having possibly ripened into a certain genteel eccentricity. A few of these gentlemen accounted for almost all of the town's fifty-one slaves. Those local elites preferred to leave the mundane matters of paving roads, dredging rivers, or securing railroad contracts to local developers capable of negotiating with the generally Democratic state government.

Rather anomalously for a southern state, Missouri's local elites were hardly of one mind, even on a subject such as slavery. Not only had the Democratic Party split, but a certain level of antislavery sentiment seeped into the state with the capital and people coming from the outside. Parts of the state even experienced local versions of the third-party movement that swept the non-slaveholding states. The Republicans who eased their way into power in St. Louis constituted an urban-based new party espousing the value of "free labor" contested for power within a slaveholding agricultural state. As the sectional crisis intensified nationally, Missouri's internal struggle became more complicated.

The Democratic government that took power in 1860–1861 seriously misunderstood those local elites and the voters that generally followed them. Later apologists argued that, of the 165,518 Missouri voters who cast ballots in the 1860 presidential election, the Republican Abraham Lincoln won only 17,028, of whom "nearly all lived in St. Louis, Franklin, and Gasconade counties."[5] However, Stephen A. Douglas, the regular Democrat, carried the state with 58,801, and John Bell, the Constitutional Unionist got almost as many (58,372), with only 31,317 voted for the "Southern Rights" Democrats. Crudely, one in ten voters favored Lincoln and the electoral success of the northern states, while fewer than two in ten even saw the threat of secession as useful and more than seven in ten favored almost any kind of compromise. This overwhelming desire for compromise to save the Federal Union elected the governor and most of the legislature as regular "Douglas Democrats." Yet, that state government, basing its claim to a mandate on the 1860 election, rejected the results of the very same election in choosing Lincoln. Disgusted, the Virginia-born St. Louis sign painter Frederick W. Benteen attributed secession and war to "a number of politicians who had been defeated in the national election and were sore on that account."[6] When seven southern states declared themselves out of the Union, Missourians elected a state convention in February 1861 that flatly rejected any course so irreversible.

War came to Missouri not as a conflict between the Union and the Confederacy, but between the federal and the state authorities. The state government refused to raise its quota of volunteers to "coerce" the South and called out the Missouri State Guard (MSG), which seized the U.S. arsenal at Liberty and opened Camp Jackson within striking distance of the much-larger St. Louis arsenal. Unionists there, who bypassed the state government to fill Missouri's quota on their own, seized the camp on May 10, after which former governor Sterling Price took command of the MSG. When an uncomfortable truce fell apart in June, the Unionists moved against the state government, driving it into exile and the remnant of the state convention established an unelected Provisional government. As the Federals forced the MSG into the southwest,

Confederate forces entered the state and, with the MSG, defeated the Union army at Wilson's Creek, after which the MSG turned back into central Missouri that fall to capture Lexington. Under the MSG's protection, part of what was left of the state legislature reassembled at Neosho and voted for secession. Yet, renewed Federal offensives the following winter drove them into Arkansas where a victory at Pea Ridge in March 1862 ended the prospects of a Confederate Missouri. Richmond subsequently transferred Price and virtually the entire MSG—now assimilated into the Confederate army—east of the river.

Sharing the low priority the Confederates accorded the Trans-Mississippi war, the Union government transferred most of the volunteers raised in the state to fight east of the river as well. Because of the state's weakened defenses, Confederate regulars periodically returned to the state even after Pea Ridge. Recruiters regularly raised large new units and piloted them back to Arkansas, often cooperating with the guerrillas, and Federal authorities tended not to distinguish between them when captured. Columns of several thousand Confederate entered southwestern Missouri and rampaged through parts of the state from July through October 1862. The following year saw the January 1863 attacks on Springfield and nearby communities; a spring incursion through the "Boot Heel"; and, a fall cavalry raid far into western Missouri.

Meanwhile, Price and the Missouri Confederates made insistent demands, even as they gained prestige east of the Mississippi. When the secessionists sought to retake Kentucky in the fall of 1862, Price led a small army to distract the Federals in northern Mississippi by capturing Iuka in the northeast corner of that state. On September 19, General Ulysses S. Grant attempted to trap "Old Pap" Price in a pincers movement, the arms of which were expected to move together once they heard the sounds of battle beginning. However, that curious convergence of factors that muffled the sound of the artillery and gunfire created what contemporaries called an "acoustic shadow," a piece of good fortune by which Price avoided the fate of most Confederate generals who faced Grant.[7] Yet, Price repeatedly demanded an opportunity to retake Missouri, at one point banging his fist on the desk of Confederate president Jefferson Davis and threatening to resign and return west on his own. Price got his reassignment, and, on July 4, 1863, led a futile attempt to seize Helena, Arkansas, on the Mississippi River in an effort to draw Union troops away from Vicksburg or establish another Confederate bastion on the river.

Union victories in the field acquired vast amounts of ostensibly Confederate territory, while the transfer of recruits to the east left the Federals with weakened garrisons to secure what it held. The result made general the kind of guerrilla warfare that originated in the antebellum Kansas troubles. Much of the state's river and creek bottoms, as well as its bluffs and ridges, had escaped the plow or the axe, and provided small bands with relatively hidden, alternative routes of movement over long distances. The limited number of available Union soldiers made the interception of guerrillas seem almost impossible, even if sympathetic civilians had not provided them food, supplies, or intelligence. Moreover, the standard-issue, long-range single-shot musket poorly countered the hit-and-run tactics, and the experienced "bushwhackers" carried two, three, and even four pairs of revolvers on their person or horse. At any given point, no more than a few thousand partisans operated in bands of a hundred or so under officers such as William Clarke Quantrill, "Bloody Bill" Anderson, or George Todd.[8] Yet, their hit-and-run tactics occupied much larger numbers of the enemy.

More important, that kind of a war made the nearest tree line almost anywhere in the state a possible front line. It militated heavily against taking prisoners, leaving witnesses, or distinguishing between enemies and civilians, who might find themselves in the wrong place at the wrong time. Eager to deceive the enemy, Missouri's guerrillas frequently wore blue uniforms to get close enough to make effective use of revolvers and knives, and it scarcely mattered that the practice confused friend as well as foe. Confederate sympathizers faced enough problems under the Federal occupation, and more than one of them pleaded their Unionism to guerrillas wearing blue with fatal results. Dependent on systematic terror, some guerrillas decorated their gear with scalps and even human skulls.[9] Then, too, the nature of such fighting attracted apolitical thieves and murderers.

Although poorly documented, these small, localized acts of violence meant that Missouri hosted what eventually became at least 1,162 engagements. Virtually every community in the state contributed men to the war, and most directly experienced some of its violence. Hostile armies had pushed each other back and forth between the Missouri and Arkansas Rivers several times, bringing escalating guerrilla activities in their wake. The process stripped the countryside of its potential fighting men, its livestock, and its crops. Every campaign swelled the numbers of refugees clustered about the garrisons, leaving much of the state for small groups of brigands. Outside of St. Louis, Jefferson City, and Kansas City, almost no county south of the Missouri River survived the war with its courthouse intact and its records secure or unmoved.[10]

Each stage in the escalating conflict confronted Missourians with often-difficult choices that shattered the bonds of family and friendship as well as community. Most tended to follow their local elites, while leaving incorrigible minorities virtually everywhere. Many took the path of least resistance less from opportunism than the simple pragmatic concern to support the side most capable of governing stably. Indeed, more than elsewhere, Missouri's war actually divided individuals against themselves. One slave recalled, "when de Rebel sojars come by our place old mastuh had de table set for den, and treat 'em fine—'cause he's a rebel—den when de Yankee's come along he give dem da bes' he had, and treat 'em fine 'cause he's a 'Yankee.'" A later writer interviewing Missourians as to their wartime experiences paraphrased a frequent response: "Me? Why I fought in both armies." By 1864, the Unionist militia in Osage County included an entire "Reb Company" that had reconsidered their initial stance.[11]

The inconsistencies may have seemed less obvious from their perspective, of course. They had defended their homes and the state against an armed threat in 1861 and would do so again after 1862, albeit against different threats, those posed by guerrillas and raiders. Among Confederate Missourians, time, distance, and wishful thinking blurred their view of these shifting political realities.

The Army of Missouri

Still, the fall of Vicksburg closed the Mississippi River to the Confederacy, effectively ending the ease with which the Confederacy drew on the west for troops, while Washington continued to drain its manpower. Federal demands to transfer troops east fell on a succession of compliant department officials often eager to win their own transfers east by appeasing the War Department. This brought some of the worst Union defeats west of the Mississippi.

From September 22 to October 26, 1863, Confederate colonel Joseph Orville Shelby demonstrated the weakness of the Union military occupation. In the tradition of Generals J. E. B. Stuart and John Hunt Morgan, he mounted a fast-moving, modest column reported to fluctuate between 800 and 1,200 men. They planned to take what they needed from the population, requisitioning horses, wagons, and food, and to stay in the field by keeping on the move. Their hit-and-run actions aimed not to occupy and hold territory, but to demonstrate the inability of the Unionist authorities to protect the people and their property. They rode through the heart of western Missouri as far as Marshall and returned after covering close to 1,500 miles.

In the spring of 1864, the regional fortunes of war more than embarrassed the Union. In conjunction with the Red River campaign into western Louisiana, Federals pushed through devastated southern Arkansas with Price falling back to extend its long and vulnerable lines of supply. His April counterattacks sent the hungry bluecoats reeling in retreat as ragged rebels plundered the clothes and food they needed from the captured stores. That month saw the Confederate massacre of southern blacks and whites on the Mississippi at Fort Pillow, Tennessee, but Price's forces similarly treated Arkansas "Tories" and black Federals who fell into their hands, adding to the 2,400 Union casualties.

Nevertheless, early that summer, Richmond woke to the roar of Federal guns, booming desperate arguments about the Confederacy's need to do something to stave off impending defeat. Generals Grant and William T. Sherman won great victories in Virginia and Georgia but their almost 100,000 casualties left them howling for more soldiers, even as their control of the Mississippi rendered meaningless any similar demands from Richmond. On the west bank, Confederate generals Richard Taylor and John B. Magruder discussed seizing and briefly holding part of the Mississippi to permit crossing their remaining forces to the east. In short order, they realized that if they had not been able to hold part of the river when they had it, taking it would be quite unfeasible.

They recognized that an 1864 reelection of Lincoln over Democrat George B. McClellan would amount to a popular mandate to prosecute the war and nobody believed the Confederacy could elude defeat for another four years. Trans-Mississippi commander General Edmund Kirby-Smith had failed to influence the elections two years earlier when he invaded Kentucky, but the subsequent course of the war hardly made them less desperate. As to Missouri, should Lincoln be defeated, the absence of any Confederate presence on what it claimed as its twelfth state would weaken its hand in any negotiated peace settlement.

Missouri Confederates used Shelby's "Great Raid" to argue for the permeability of the Union defenses, but what they proposed would be no mere raid. Price would reorganize the entire cavalry corps of the Department of Arkansas into a mounted, mobile strike force that would be more than a dozen times larger than that Shelby, Morgan, or Stuart had taken on a "raid." He would then turn command of the department to Magruder, leaving him in Arkansas and the Indian Territory with about 25,000 men, mostly infantry. Once the cavalry expedition had regained ground in Missouri, Kirby-Smith had an entire Louisiana infantry brigade earmarked to follow Price north and consolidate its gains, with Magruder's infantry to follow. Fueled by the pace of his new recruits, Price's horsemen would continue into the heart of the state with the foot soldiers of the Trans-Mississippi in their wake.[12] While starting with a mounted strike force, the strategy involved taking and holding strategic points.

Then, too, the forty-three-year-old head of Missouri's secessionist government-in-exile Thomas Caute Reynolds lobbied tirelessly to carry the war back into the state. After his election as lieutenant governor in 1860, the former lawyer and diplomat negotiated with southern political leaders on behalf of the state, but returned to a law practice in his native South Carolina after the Federal military—without the nicety of an election at the time—established a Provisional government. In December 1862, Missouri's elected but deposed governor died, and the constitution required an election within eighteen months, but Reynolds argued successfully that, since the Confederacy could hold no election in the state, he should fill the term. Reynolds reestablished a Confederate state government in exile at Marshall, Texas, and sent another Missouri delegation to the Congress in Richmond. He also had a tact that eluded Price in dealing with Jefferson Davis.[13] Back in Missouri, he pointed out, the impending 1864 election would deliver a death blow to Confederate claims there, because the victory of the "Conservative" Thomas L. Price—Sterling Price's old rival from 1852—or the "Radical" Thomas Clement Fletcher would be a mandate for Unionism and dissipate even the most tenuous claims to legitimacy by Reynold's organization.

That summer, the newly promoted brigadier general Shelby once more demonstrated the continued ease with which a large mounted Confederate force could cross the Arkansas River. The thirty-four-year-old Kentucky-born proprietor of a Waverly hemp factory and ropewalk had made considerable money in land and slaves. A leader in the bushwhacking war against Kansas Free Staters, he rose far and fast in the ranks, raising a regiment, then a brigade, of his own in Yankee-occupied Missouri. Shelby had repeated this incursion behind Federal lines in both his spectacular 1863 raid and in his summer 1864 ride into northern Arkansas. According to one account, he had predicted certain defeat back east and advised Kirby-Smith that with "fifty thousand soldiers such as yours you can seize St. Louis, hold it, fortify it, and cross over into Illinois. It would be a diversion, expanding into a campaign—a blow that had destiny in it."[14]

On August 28, Old Pap Price took the 4,000 members of the cavalry corps of his Department of Arkansas and turned that department to Magruder. Learning from his enemy's earlier carelessness with its supply train, Price led his mounted force on a 350-mile detour upriver on August 31, skirting Little Rock on September 2 as Shelby made a diversionary attack on DuVall's Bluff. On September 13, Price's column reached Batesville and joined Shelby at Powhatan two days later.[15] From September 16 through 18, Price organized a new Army of Missouri.[16]

Riding with them came some additional unattached units and a party of distinguished observers, such as Governor Reynolds. Expelled for supporting secessionism, former U.S. senator Trusten Polk had left his family securely and prosperously back in St. Louis, but now hoped to return a conqueror. On their way, they encountered the thirty-eight-year-old Virginia-born former mayor of St. Joseph, Brigadier General Meriwether Jefferson Thompson, who had recently been paroled but, upon hearing of the invasion, hurried from Alabama to join it. Prior to his capture, he had led partisan "Swamp Rats" in southeastern Missouri, but through his ruthless hit-and-run tactics he had striven to respect the standards of conventional warfare, and actually hanged four of his own men for stealing horses.[17] The new army lent Confederate Missouri the kind of substantive presence it had long lacked.

Price's new army had 12,176 men in three divisions. In addition to Shelby, who had 3,351 in his, the army had talented men commanding the two other divisions. The largest division with 5,069 men went to the Kentucky-born Arkansas politician Brigadier General James Fleming Fagan, a veteran of the Mexican War, who had fought from Shiloh to Helena. Price passed over more experienced cavalry commanders to select Fagan, based on his leadership of the mounted rear guard covering Price's retreat through southern Arkansas the previous spring. Command of the remaining division of 3,756 men fell to thirty-one-year-old Brigadier General John Sappington Marmaduke, the native Missourian, son of a governor, and graduate of Yale and West Point. Before the war, he officered operations against Indians and Mormons, rising to division command by late 1862, and leading two 1863 incursions back into Missouri.

The Army of Missouri had as experienced and talented a leadership as any. Only five years in age separated Fagan, Marmaduke, and Shelby, who came to share ardent, if not initially eager secessionist politics. In 1862, two of them had fought at Shiloh in April, and all three of them fought at Prairie Grove in December. From July 1863 through April 1864, the three of them served under Price at Helena, Little Rock, and Jenkin's Ferry. Their leading brigade commanders, as well as many of the regimental officers, had similar records.[18]

Still, no amount of combat leadership and battlefield competence could compensate for the logistical problems involved in the campaign. Price and Kirby-Smith agreed that, after Price's fast-moving cavalry had seized part of Missouri, an entire Louisiana infantry brigade would move north in support, followed by another 25,000, but Magruder "would not move unless Price actually secured and held part of Missouri and Kirby-Smith would not press the matter to risk infantry without this." Among the men Price already had, though, Shelby reported that over two-thirds of his men in one brigade and a fifth in another had received no arms. In a region where adult white men carried arms in peacetime, this probably did not mean that these men had no weapons, but that the military authorities had not issued the arms they had. Without having the same firearms, the army would need to manage an unworkably wild variety of ammunition to keep those weapons firing. Most seriously, Price never arranged to mount the entire command and even those few on foot—fewer than two hundred in Shelby's division—would slow cavalry to the pace of infantry.[19] This shortcoming seems remarkable given that every argument for the prospects of the campaign's success turned on speed and the element of surprise.

However fast it might move, Price's army could not outrun the nature of the war in Missouri. By this point in the war, Confederates of the border states generally clung to an abiding faith that made absolutely no sense to those who did not share it. As one Federal veteran complained, Missouri had chosen not to secede, "yet not one of its State-righters 'followed his State according to his true allegiance.'" Instead, they "followed its enemies and fled to other countries, where, under various fantastic theories, they persuaded themselves that they were holding the offices of Missouri—the 'true' Missouri." In their eyes, those who had opposed secession "were not the true sons of Missouri."[20] In the most practical sense, Price's soldiers proposed to move into a Missouri eager to enforce the secession that its residents had rejected three years earlier, when such a course had a much better chance of success.

Nor could the Army of Missouri outrun its own experience in warring on those who were "not the true sons" of the South. Of the five Missouri brigadiers in Price's army, Colonels Thomas R. Freeman and Sidney D. Jackman had been guerrillas in southeastern Missouri, and David Shanks had also served behind the lines. Among those regiments, John Q. A. Burbridge, with the help of Colton Green of St. Louis, had raised MSG units in northern Missouri and kept their ties to the partisans there. So had Moses W. Smith, Alonzo Slayback, and Benjamin Elliott. The Boot Heel still remembered the activities of Sol Kitchen, William L. Jeffers, J. A. Schnable, and Timothy Reeves (also spelled Reves) while Robert R. Lawther had commanded guerrillas in central Missouri, and, prior to the 1864 campaign, John Truesdale Coffee and William O. Coleman were known primarily as guerrillas. In fact, Slayback, William C. Kelly, and Caleb Perkins began the 1864 campaign as recruiters behind Union lines, contributing to the estimated 1,500 Confederates raised that summer in preparation for the invasion. Perkins and Dewitt Clinton Hunter had been in the most brutal guerrilla bands in the state, those of Captains Quantrill and Anderson, with Hunter even participating in the Baxter Springs massacre a year earlier.[21]

In the field, the first armed clash of these troops took place on September 8 at Glass Village, Arkansas. Part of Brigadier General William L. Cabell's brigade of Arkansans stumbled onto an unfortunate little detachment of the Federal Third Arkansas Cavalry, resulting in eight Federal casualties. Of the five prisoners, two had fled conscription into the Confederate army to fight voluntarily for the Union. The Confederates sentenced them to summary execution as "Tories."[22] This rather ominously presaged the character of the Confederate liberation of southerners from military tyranny.

The Department of Missouri

While Confederate Missouri assumed the form of an army marching into the state, Unionist Missouri had taken ponderous form, as an administrative department within a broader hierarchy of military administration. Reorganized in May 1864 as part of the new Military Division of West Mississippi, the Department of Missouri had a jurisdiction matching the geographic borders of the state with the addition of a prisoner-of-war camp at Alton, Illinois. The department included the Districts of St. Louis, Rolla, Central, Southwest, and North Missouri. Each district contained subdistricts with a headquarters that coordinated the work of various garrisons and outposts that protected key strategic sites, including county seats, towns, railroad stations, or bridges. The department entailed no less than an experiment in the military government of an American state.

The telegraph reflected the innovativeness of the military department and its potential for uniting the state. The wire went everywhere the railroad did and more. When the main line of the Pacific Railroad ended in Warrensburg, the telegraph extended a spur to the river at Boonville and long lines to Kansas City and through Pleasant Hill and Weston to Forts Leavenworth and Scott in Kansas. That along the North Missouri Railroad extended a line south from St. Joseph to Weston, which provided a second line between St. Louis and the west. Beyond the end of the southwestern branch of the railroad at Rolla, the "Wire Road" or "Telegraph Road" marked its course to Springfield, and south from there to Cassville and, depending on how well it could be kept repaired, to Fayetteville in Arkansas. So, too, the telegraph line on the Iron Mountain Railroad continued beyond Pilot Knob through Cape Girardeau to Sikeston and New Madrid with another line from Cape down to Bloomfield. The garrison at Pilot Knob had also extended a line to Patterson.[23] This provided a society warring with itself over the survival of the ancient practice of human slavery an almost instant state of communications.

The grand old man of the Trans-Mississippi war—the New York-born fifty-nine-year-old General Samuel Ryan Curtis—proposed an extensive telegraph system as the best protection against an unanticipated invasion. Early in the year, Curtis, the commander in Kansas, planned to run lines south from Fort Scott through Fort Gibson in the Indian Territory to Fort Smith, Arkansas, and down the Arkansas River. To any extent the scattered Union garrisons could maintain the wire, it would transform into a genuine defensive line. By the fall, Little Rock had wires running to Lewisburg up the Arkansas River to the northwest, DuVall's Bluff to the east, and Pine Bluff to the south, all between forty and fifty miles from the capital, and the line at Fort Smith and Van Buren sometimes made it to Fayetteville. However, the War Department in Washington dismissed elaborate projects such as Curtis's as being more costly than what was actually at risk. The nature of the wartime command structure assured a certain number of such colossally poor choices.

Beyond this, the idea of military rule was anathema to the very republican tradition the Unionists sought to preserve. To be sure, the Provisional government of Hamilton R. Gamble had exercised its mandate from that state convention that deposed the secessionists. For three years, though, this civilian authority rested less on the demonstrable consent of the governed than on the military power of the Federal occupation, which had the lives, liberties, and properties of the people of the state in its unaccountable charge. An innovatively bureaucratic military structure evolved to look after the collection of taxes and the administration of justice. Even those who defended the need for military rule acknowledged the scale of its corruption and fraud that amply vindicated traditional American fears of such institutions. As early as 1861, commanders closed newspapers not to protect military secrets or even to silence critics of the government but to muzzle questions about specific commanders and decisions. Local army provosts charged with raising additional forage and funds did so largely through confiscating the property of those identified as enemy "sympathizers," though no mechanism permitted the accused to confront their accusers and some leading secessionists never seemed to be called to account.

Perhaps because of the lack of statewide elections, political questions went unresolved and divided Unionists into two increasingly hardened factions. The conservative "Claybanks" sought to keep the focus on the preservation of the United States, while the radical "Charcoals" advocated measures such as the abolition of slavery left untouched in Missouri by the Emancipation Proclamation. The ultimate authority would rest with the army until the 1864 election provided a government with a popular mandate to resolve such questions.

The Lincoln administration had no luck in finding a general who could not only command troops but also avoid warring on one or another of these political factions. Three years earlier, General John C. Fremont had helped inspire the Radicals by using his authority to declare martial law and a virtual end to slavery. Still, Radical Unionists in Missouri, such as A. W. Reese, ultimately came to see Fremont as

> a military dandy and popinjay who hedged himself in with orderlies and lackies, and allowed no intelligence to reach him except such as "came through the proper channels;" in other words till all the "red-tape" in the Department had been exhausted.[24]

Fremont's successors, though, generally opposed emancipation and allied themselves with the Conservatives.

The last of these was Major General William Starke Rosecrans, a hard-drinking and tough-talking little engineer of forty-five years whose biographer located his career at "the edge of glory." "Old Rosy" graduated fifth in his class from West Point but left the army for industrial ventures, suffering an 1859 accident at his Cincinnati kerosene plant that left him badly burned. Taking an Ohio brigade into western Virginia at the start of the war, he rose gradually until September 19, 1862, when, with General Grant in charge, he clashed with Sterling Price's Confederate army at Iuka. He then took command of the Army of the Cumberland, which he marched from Nashville toward Murfreesboro along Stone's River, where Confederates ambushed him on New Year's Eve. His masterful and virtually bloodless Tullahoma campaign in the summer of 1863 had backed the Confederates all the way into northern Georgia. Then, on September 19, 1863, exactly one year after Iuka, a reinforced Confederate army unexpectedly turned on the Federal army along Chickamauga Creek, just as it had at Stone's River.[25] This time, though, the Confederates overwhelmed Rosecrans's line and his shattered, badly bloodied army trudged back into Chattanooga, as the Confederates occupied the heights above them.

Back in Chattanooga, Rosecrans suffered something very like a nervous breakdown. The assistant secretary of war Charles A. Dana had actually seen Rosecrans crossing himself as the Confederates poured over his position, hardly conveying the confidence to his men that might be expected of a veteran commander. Later, Rosecrans telegraphed Washington that "our fate is in the hands of God, in whom I hope." "We must put our trust in God," he told officials, "who never fails those who truly trust." Horrified, Lincoln thought his general was "confused and stunned like a duck hit on the head." Fearful that Rosecrans might do something rash, the government hurried Grant to replace him and extricate the army. Grant found that Rosecrans had solid plans to break the Confederate hold on the town, leaving him to marvel at Rosecrans's failure to implement them.[26]

After a brief period without command, Rosecrans got the Department of Missouri, fully aware that his career teetered at the brink and convinced that caution would be the key to his survival in the post. For the Lincoln administration, perhaps his most important asset in this post would be his Catholicism. This he shared with virtually all of the Irish, a sizable portion of the Germans, and even some of the transplanted southerners in the state. At the war's onset, the slaveholding Archbishop Peter Richard Kenrick—the younger brother of Bishop Francis Patrick Kenrick of Philadelphia—had urged Catholic neutrality, but remained personally "inclined to the southern cause." Like the secessionist state government, he had viewed the Federals as an army of conquest and refused to permit priests to accept appointment as army chaplains, even as one of them, a personal friend of the archbishop, took just such a post with the Confederacy. Most Catholics shared none of the archbishop's affection for secession, but remained unmoved by the Protestant reformism of the abolitionists. As well, local military intervention against secessionist clergy raised deep concerns over "ecclesiastical liberty."[27] A Catholic Federal general seemed likely to help assuage the friction between the government and an important component of more conservative Unionists.

Still, Roman Catholicism never represented as clearly reactionary a force as either the secularists or the church hierarchy imagined. Notwithstanding the stance of the archbishop, the parish priests found neutrality impossible and often had very different predispositions, particularly given the anti-Catholic, anti-immigrant proclivities of many of the armed secessionists. The secessionists in Ripley County, led by Reeves, a Protestant clergyman, made it impossible for Father John Hogan to remain at St. Benedict's in Doniphan. By July 1861, Father Van Luytelear also fled southern Missouri for the safety of a new St. John the Baptist, a church later known as St. John Gildehaus. The following year's "unequal contest" in western Missouri drove Father Russe to seek safety among the secularists of Hermann. The war also coincided with the arrival of Father Alexander Mathauschek at the German Catholic parish in Washington, when he was to minister to early Polish settlers around St. Gertrude; contemporaries described "his bearing, especially on horseback was that of a cavalry officer."[28] Particularly in eastern and central Missouri, many of these priests actively aided the Federals, several of whom were their own parishioners.

Many of the Germans, regardless of their religious opinions, had also yet failed to assimilate fully the white supremacist assumptions slavery required. When one group of soldiers down from St. Louis stopped at Farmington, black children not only brought them food, but began waving switches to keep the flies away from about them. "We don' need that," said one of the bluecoats. "Come on and eat with us."[29] It speaks volumes about the real treatment of slaves that such a simple expression of basic fellow feeling by a white soldier would be remembered for almost seventy years.

Republicans nationally watched these developments with some trepidation. Horace Greeley's *New York Tribune* noted that radical Unionists there had divided among themselves over how independent of the Lincoln administration they wanted to operate. The *Tribune* fretted that the Radicals' gubernatorial candidate Thomas C. Fletcher opposed the renomination of Lincoln, and the *Westliche Post* declared that it would strike from its ticket "every man who may profess a preference for Lincoln." "The history of the past few weeks ought to teach the radical Unionists of Missouri how much is at stake at the ensuing election. If they fail to elect their State ticket, it may cost thousands of both sections into which the party is now divided, not only their property, but their lives."[30]

In military terms, Rosecrans's assignment left him powerless unless he mastered Missouri's chaotic militia system. While the earlier MSG had fought on behalf of the secessionist state government, it confronted not only regular and volunteer units but also local Home Guards and a "Three Months' Militia." Soon, the Unionist Provisional government had established a "Six Months' Militia," which did not last half as long before the state, with Federal cooperation, started the Missouri State Militia (MSM) in January 1862. July required periodic military service of every able-bodied man who had taken an oath of loyalty and could bear arms in an Enrolled Missouri Militia financed by the Provisional state government.[31] Although the mobile operations of the state's Federal military virtually absorbed the MSM, the EMM remained the largest single component of the state's defense.

One account confidently estimated that, in 1864, the EMM, with other militia units, fielded 50,000 men in arms to meet Sterling Price's invasion. On paper, the EMM had roughly seventy-five "regiments" with many other units, but these were not the standard in size, and political geography had defined their jurisdiction. Participation in the EMM reflected an adult male population in flux due to ongoing recruitment drives, the natural movement of civilians, the political shuffling in command, and the absence of regular mobilizations to update the records. The most basic information available to the Department or the state authorities or even the local officers seems never to have been more than piecemeal and what official sources exist acknowledge that the actual size of the EMM "has not been ascertained."[32]

Certainly, the military record of the militia was remarkably good. Although the regular Federal officer caste, like their Confederate foes, disparaged the "green" militia said to scatter at the first shots or surrender on demand, that same command structure often left it untrained, indifferently officered, ill equipped, or even unarmed. In fact, even the most "green" unit included some discharged veterans of the toughest fighting that had taken place in the western and Trans-Mississippi volunteer service. Wiley Britton, that astute participant and chronicler of the region's war, thought much of the EMM prone to panic under artillery, but remarkably competent in dealing with guerrillas. Britton rightly added that the army's repeated failure to keep Confederate regulars out of the state left its officers continually fretting over the reliability of the militia. Even so, the EMM demonstrated in the January 1863 Confederate attack on Springfield that with the back to the wall in defense of their communities, the militia's men could go toe to toe against tough veteran units and emerge victorious.[33]

Politically, however, the militia system satisfied nobody. Franklin County slaveholders complained that the local EMM enticed slaves to run away, sheltered them, and helped to recruit them to the Union army. Upriver at Boonville, EMM companies formed with the understanding that they would fight guerrillas but not Confederate regulars. Fearing that Radicals might overreach their authority in dealing with secessionists and their property, including slaves, Conservative officials often removed them and crippled the militia. Still farther up the Missouri, at St. Joseph, Unionists complained that Democratic "Copperhead" officers of the "Paw Paw" EMM maintained order by disarming Radical Unionists. Radicals, concerned about arming those who would not fight the Confederates, veered away. Even in a crisis, the authorities balked at calling out the militia.

Rosecrans tried to reorganize the EMM into a tighter and more predictably reliable force in June 1864 with his General Order No. 107. It authorized "township committees of public safety" to "choose and organize, out of the Enrolled State Militia of your locality, one or two companies of about 100 men each, selected for courage, energy, and willingness to serve for the protection of your respective counties." In essence, the plan sought to distill from the EMM a more coherent "Provisional Enrolled Missouri Militia" to "restore civil law and order" against the guerrillas. In practice, the areas that had been least threatened had found the older methods sufficient and those most threatened found the new ones inadequate.[34] So, the Provisional EMM seems to have added yet another layer of militia organization.

Rosecrans's subordinates, with the cooperation of state authorities, used the militia, as needed, to supplement his own department's districts and subdistricts. Command of the District of St. Louis belonged to possibly the most-hated man in the state, a thirty-five-year-old Ohio native and Kansan, Brigadier General Thomas Ewing Jr. Ewing, the first chief justice of the Kansas Supreme Court, left for the war and had charge of the District of the Border at the time of the guerrilla massacre of civilians at Lawrence, Kansas, in August 1863. In response, his General Order No. 11 drove what population remained in several Missouri counties into refugee camps. His subsequent responsibilities blanketed southeastern Missouri, including the Mississippi River and the Iron Mountain Railroad.

The pragmatic system, which grew in response to the guerrilla threat, represented the best possible use of the very limited number of available men. Garrisons grew company by company, as the need arose, which fragmented the regimental organization. The District of St. Louis, for example, made do with only 1,500 effectives in the First Subdistrict, the city, Colonel Hugo Wagelin with posts at DeSoto, Pacific, Ste. Genevieve, and Potosi. Colonel Hiram M. Hiller's Second Subdistrict rested on a garrison of 400 at Cape Girardeau, and spread across the Boot Heel with about 250 at New Madrid and other outposts such as Bloomfield. Major James Wilson's Third Subdistrict usually had only about 150 at Pilot Knob, or even only a few score at Patterson and Ironton. As of the close of August, only 550 of the EMM on active duty supplemented those roughly 2,100 men, but these belonged not to local post commanders but to Brigadier General Edward C. Pike, the EMM's division commander back in St. Louis. It worked well in dealing with guerrillas, though the arrangement invited a piecemeal destruction by an invading army.

The department's four other districts were in somewhat similar shape and in the hand of military administrators as much as battlefield commanders. To the west of Ewing's jurisdiction, the fifty-one-year-old Brigadier General John McNeil had the District of Rolla, the vital provisions base at Rolla that supplied most of the Federal operations as far south and west as New Mexico. A Canadian born hatter, he had worked in Boston before opening his own shop at St. Louis and entering the legislature. At the war's start, McNeil led one of radical Turner-based German regiments at St. Louis that had helped clear the city of the secessionists, and then saw service in Louisiana.

The state had three other district commanders. A forty-eight-year-old former mayor of Toledo, Brigadier General Egbert Benson Brown had lost the use of one arm in leading the successful defense of Springfield, and now ran the Central District from the Missouri River halfway to Arkansas and west to the Kansas line.[35] Brigadier General John Benjamin Sanborn, a thirty-eight-year-old New Hampshire lawyer, had led troops at Vicksburg before taking the District of Southwestern Missouri, a post previously held by both Brown and McNeil and running to the Arkansas line. Finally, thirty-six-year-old New York native Brigadier General Clinton Bowen Fisk, a former insurance broker who had helped secure St. Louis, had the District of North Missouri, the vast expanse above the Missouri River. Through the summer, a disturbing increase in the outbursts of guerrilla activities particularly plagued Fisk's district.

These district commanders had military experience and no small amount of administrative abilities. Yet, they rarely remained in place long enough to develop an intimate understanding of their specific district's peculiarities in terms of troops, militia experience, and political conditions. By the late summer of 1864, they saw themselves as merely caretakers of a state only weeks away from an elected civilian government.

Yet the state showed signs of having suffered politically from the absence of political argument and deliberations over the previous three years. Frustration with the apparent slowness of the Lincoln administration in moving on such matters as slavery and suffrage sparked a nationally serious split among Republicans that threatened to outlast the president's renomination at the party's June national convention. As the party's leadership merged into a broad Unionist presidential campaign, Missouri Radicals toyed with the idea of running an independent ticket. Charles E. Moss had taken up editing the *Radical Democrat* in the interests of running John C. Fremont, even though rumor even placed Fremont in the Democratic camp for George B. McClellan and the Fremont boom ultimately fizzled. Still, the June 1864 National Convention of the Lincoln forces had to choose between two Missouri delegations and, after picking the Radicals, had the odd experience of having selected those pledged not to vote for Lincoln on the first ballot.[36] In the end, all agreed to renominate Lincoln, though not without reservations.

William L. Avery, the secretary of the western branch of the Union National Committee, described the renomination process in Missouri to Lincoln's confidant, John G. Nicolay, as simply a jockeying for power. "The peculiarities of the canvass here would be ridiculous, if not fraught with so much danger to the country." The "peculiarities" Nicolay enumerated underscored all sorts of the combinations between individuals and cliques among "conservatives" with "radicals."[37]

Not entirely out of the picture, the Democrats remained an important factor in Missouri, though they fueled Radicalism by attempting to build a political party around hostility to the war policy. Claiming to speak for the soldier, the Radicals unstintingly—and surely, at times, unfairly—excoriated the failure of the Federal authorities to suppress the rebellion. The authorities permitted soldiers "when properly off duty, to attend such meetings, but are under the same bonds to keep the peace as civilians," but, when overenthusiastic Democrats reportedly chucked rocks at soldiers, it sparked the Lindell Hotel riot of September 15, which ended the rally in short order. One Democratic paper complained authoritatively that "the story of Price's advance on Missouri is without foundation, and that it was invented by the Lincoln Government as an excuse for filling up the State with soldiers."[38] Through the early fall, they tended to tell many voters what they really wanted to hear and believe.

Indeed, many shared the views of Congressman James S. Rollins, who complained bitterly about conditions in the state to Edward Bates, who passed his letter to Lincoln. "In Missouri the prospect for peace and quiet as it respects the rebellion is better than it ever has been: — there is not a regularly authorised, or organized band of Confederate soldiers in the State: there never will be again!" There were bushwhackers, who "belong properly to no side, they act from no other motive than a love of plunder. The military are very rapidly disposing of these fellows, — by Christmas, there will be few of them left." Rollins wrote, "The chief cause of difficulty now in our state is owing to the action of this political party known as 'Radicals.'" Radical silence would "encourage a healthy Union Sentiment — in six weeks Missouri would be as quiet and as loyal as Pennsylvania."[39] In short, the Democrats attributed the problems of the war to the Republicans and the Republicans remained divided.

Both sides prepared to act within a landscape of their imagination. Confederate authorities stepped off into land where the residents were eager for secession, and the Federals would mobilize citizens as a matter of military administration rather than politics. In reality, the nineteenth-century realities of blood and iron would blight such landscapes. The components of Price's army had passed through a porous line of 35,000 Federals in Arkansas. Through the summer of 1864, recruiters in Missouri raised almost 69,000 Union volunteers, but transfers east reduced this to 25,000 and, by August 31, left a mere 11,000 scattered through the department. By September, the ranks of the new twelve- or six-months regiments remained unorganized and mostly unsupplied, untrained and, sometimes, even unarmed.[40] How such widely distributed troops would challenge the passage of over 12,000 concentrated Confederate veterans remained to be seen.

Only three years after St. Louisans had carted off the last of its prehistoric "fortifications," Euro-Americans turned their nightmare of the past into a present reality and raised earthen defenses on the same landscape to fight a real war. Their civilizations had taken two mutually exclusive directions, and their protagonists wielded picks and shovels to raise vast earthen works along the banks of the Mississippi, the Missouri, the Gasconade, the Meramec, and other rivers to protect themselves, their supplies, their communities, and their access to the rivers and railroads from a usually unseen enemy. Civilized Missouri—not a fantasized "De-Coo-Dah"—prepared to wage war on a new scale of savagery matching anything that took place among the ancient residents of the land.

One

The Beginning

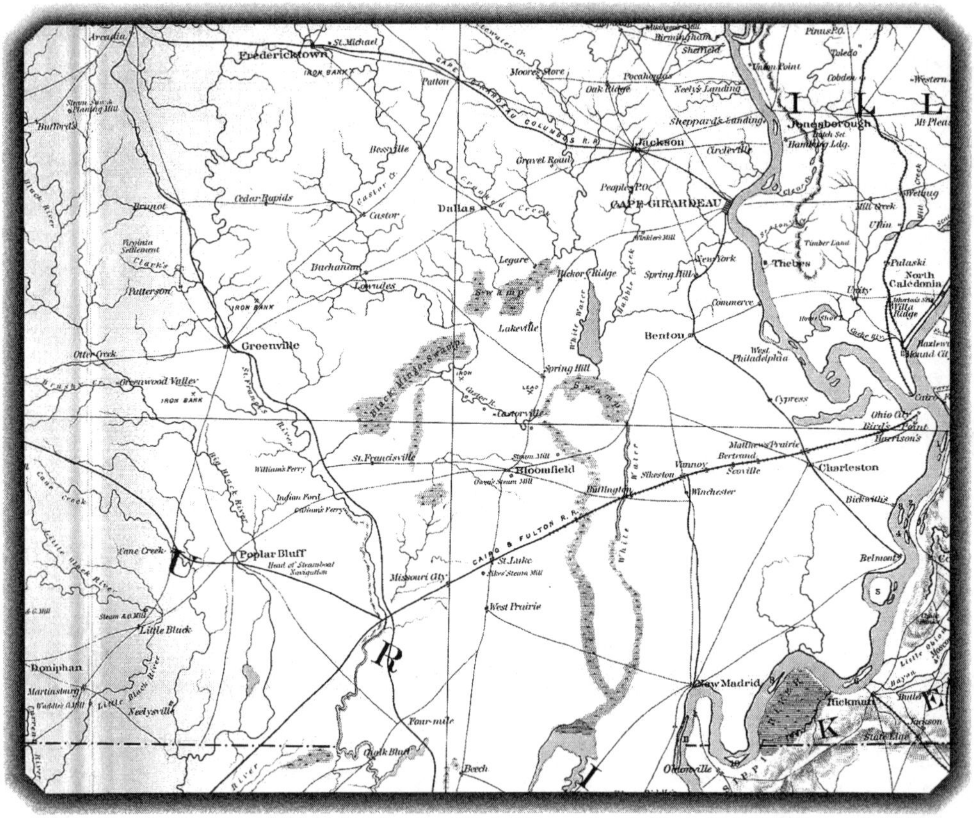

Detail from *The War of the Rebellion: A Compilation of the Official Records of the Union and Confederate Armies*

1

Of Conquest and Liberation

From Arkansas into Missouri

On Monday, September 26, a column of blue-clad riders galloped down the gravel road between Shut-in Gap toward the village of Arcadia disrupting lunch for a small group of pickets watching from a roadside shade tree. Although the others mistook the riders coming toward them as militia on their way to Fort Davidson, Sergeant Azariah Martin, a Kentucky-born twenty-five-year-old Confederate volunteer, insisted otherwise. Only the previous winter, Union troops had found Martin wounded in the military hospital at Cotton Plant, Arkansas. Paroled, he had returned home, enrolled in the state's militia to fight guerrillas, and, finally, joined the newly organized Forty-seventh Missouri. Martin had only worn the Federal uniform for three weeks when he saw the men in blue and insisted, "They are rebels! I've seen too many rebels to not know rebels when I see 'em!"[1] No enemy column that size would be entering the valley without a big fight in the works.

Although the Confederate movement of September 1864 aimed at one of the largest cities in America, it moved through some of the most-isolated and sparsely populated terrain in the region. The invaders scattered to permit easier foraging through the countryside. This also disguised the scale of their forces, which seemed to appear piecemeal at various points in southeastern Missouri near the Arkansas line. Yet, the expedition could not risk concentrating to deal with the fortified enemy garrison in the Arcadia Valley. The first attempt to test Union strength in the area is what surprised Sergeant Martin and his comrades.

Opening Moves

The Federal authorities had an ample forewarning. In early September, Arkansas rumors of an imminent invasion reached General Cadwallader Colder Washburn at Memphis. On September 2, he proposed to hold at Cairo units of

General Andrew Jackson Smith's Sixteenth Corps on their way from Louisiana to Georgia. Grant and others in the national command chose to err on the side of caution, permitting advance detachments of Smith's men to wait at Cairo.[2] The arrival of these troops in St. Louis would minimize the dependence of the Department of Missouri on the militia, but Smith's men turned up only in drips and drabs themselves.

Other indications of Confederate intentions turned up. The Federal authorities in southwestern Missouri intercepted a September 7 letter from Confederate colonel Frank Gordon to his wife, stating that General Jo Shelby would be leaving for Missouri the next day, and detailed a plan focused on central Missouri, whereby 12,000 Confederates under Price would "march by way of Rolla direct to Jefferson City."[3] Although it included the correct size of Price's force—which Gordon and Shelby may have mistakenly expected the Federals to learn from scouts—the disinformation as to their route caused no end of confusion for weeks.

However, while Federal commanders accepted such information about the route, they remained utterly incredulous about the numbers involved. They rightly questioned rumors of 20,000 and upward, doubting the presence of so many thousands "where there is scarcely subsistence for as many hundred, is simply preposterous." Remarkably, General Frederick Steele of the Federal District of Arkansas contributed almost nothing to understanding the enemy force that had passed through his chain of garrisons. Although Steele had an army several times larger than either Price or the threatened Unionists in Missouri, he diverted roughly 4,000 of Smith's men to his own purposes on September 8. Until September 17, Steele used General Joseph A. Mower's division of Smith's corps not to probe the forces to his north but to bolster his own positions on the Arkansas River. When Steele finally did send Mower's men looking for Price, they moved as infantry in pursuit of a largely mounted Confederate column and never got within a hundred miles of Price.[4] In short, those military organizations with the most men and resources siphoned off what was destined for those with the least.

Mid-September brought the first of Smith's men to St. Louis. A former slaveholder and Indian fighter, Smith had actually mustered Sterling Price into the U.S. Army many years before. The previous July, he had bested Confederate general Nathan Bedford Forrest at Tupelo in Mississippi, but, as an old regular army man seemed to have been regarded as a political ally of the most conservative currents. The Democrats in St. Louis apparently "sent one of their number to pump him" for some political statement, after which a group of them came by for a serenade "to draw out the General in a speech. But lo and behold he gave the Cop[perhead]s a terrible scathing and defended President Lincoln warmly."[5] Smith arrived with every authorization from the army to operate independently from General William S. Rosecrans, but he readily placed himself and his men at the service of the department.

Despite rumors of a drive on Rolla, reports of the presence of Confederate regulars centered on General Thomas Ewing's district, specifically Major James Wilson's subdistrict headquartered at Pilot Knob. Wilson's own father had supported secession, and he had a brother fighting for the Confederacy. That September, his long absence in the army likely contributed to his divorce.[6] The national cause that had demanded so much from him would now require much more.

Only a few years before the war, the Iron Mountain Railroad reached from St. Louis to Pilot Knob and the riches of the Arcadia Valley in Iron County. The town of about six hundred grew at the shadow of the mountain from which it took the name. With the war, Federal authorities had established a garrison and a large earthen Fort Davidson to protect the railroad and the raw materials.[7] The outpost straddled the most direct route from Fredericktown to St. Louis.

Through the summer, the guerrilla operations in or near the Arcadia Valley became larger and more audacious. On September 13, forty to fifty of them attacked fourteen men of the Third MSM Cavalry near Caledonia. The Federals killed one and wounded several, having two wounded themselves. That same night, partisans "plundered the stores at Iron Mountain and destroyed the papers and machine in the telegraph office." Matters were worse farther from the garrison, which reported sharp increases in refugee populations, with the Western Sanitary Commission counting "over 1700 persons, mostly women and children" at Pilot Knob.[8] On Friday, September 16, Major James H. Wilson, Ewing's subdistrict commander at Pilot Knob, got orders to locate any of the rumored Confederate forces.

By then, Wilson had expanded his force to a few hundred men, but they still had to cover a jurisdiction that ran as far as Arkansas. Most of the men came from his own Third MSM Cavalry—then fighting a bitter war of reprisals with guerrillas—but he had numerous bits and pieces of different units. These included about half of the available Forty-seventh Missouri; Captain Amos P. Wright's company of the Second MSM Cavalry; Captain Patrick F. Lonergan's of the First MSM Infantry; and Captain Robert L. Lindsay's of the new Fiftieth Missouri. Despite the newness of units such as the Forty-seventh and the Fiftieth, their ranks included many veterans. Captain Hugh M. Bradley had been in Wilson's own Third MSM before joining the volunteers, and thirty-four-year-old James S. McMurtry had served in the militia and done an earlier stint with the Thirty-first Missouri, which had fought at Vicksburg. Lindsay's company garrisoned Mineral Point, and the Forty-seventh had a company in blockhouses on the railroad back to Potosi with another at Fredericktown, twenty miles southeast of Fort Davidson.[9]

Some thirty-five miles to the southwest, members of the Third MSM Cavalry and the Forty-seventh Missouri staffed the garrison at Camp Benton near Patterson. Connected by telegraph, these companies under Captains Morgan Mace, James S. McMurtry, and Pinckney L. Powers sat nearest the state line. The town's founder, a Virginian named William Patterson, had remained loyal to the Union, but John Kemper, the storekeeper who had laid out the town, had long since gone back east to join Robert E. Lee's army. When local secessionists laid a suspected trap by inviting a Union officer and former preacher to address their congregation, the officer accepted the invitation, but began his sermon by drawing a revolver and announcing that he "would shoot the first person who attempted to leave before he got through without his permission." In such places, unfriendly as well as friendly eyes always watched the soldiers of either side.[10] On Sunday, September 18, Captain Robert McElroy sent Lieutenant Erich Pape on a sixty-mile ride south with less than ninety men.

What actually happened when Pape's men reached Doniphan, the seat of Ripley County, will probably forever remain confused. Antebellum southern hegemony always required the ruthless suppression of anything that threatened not only slavery but the political dominance of the slaveholders. Secessionist attempts to coerce or burn out their enemies in Missouri usually did much to strengthen Unionist sentiment among whites who had earlier had little interest in black slavery, but the tactics seem to have succeeded in Ripley County. There, the secessionists drove out the Unionists, and, when the Federals drove the Confederate regulars out of the state, much of Ripley County went into hiding.

Many who remained provided substantive support for local partisans under Timothy Reeves. The previous summer, a local storekeeper named Kittrell, who also kept a boardinghouse just outside of Doniphan, had sold food to some soldiers of the Third MSM Cavalry that nearly killed them. This earned a stern warning from the Federals that the further mistreatment of soldiers would forfeit the courtesy and rights of noncombatants. Thereafter, he set his dogs on exhausted and sickly paroled prisoners from the Fifty-fourth Illinois trudging north toward Ironton. Finally, in December, Reeves's guerrillas captured the better part of a company of the Third MSM Cavalry, which responded by striking hard and fast against Reeves's band.[11]

Contemporary secessionists complained of their victimization by Union soldiers, and later admirers of the Lost Cause spun elaborate tales of what they call "the Wilson Massacre." Supposedly, Federal soldiers opened fire on civilians at a Christmas dinner, killing "around 100," 65 of whom had been civilians, women, and children, and took 112 locals into custody, many of whom died before reaching those authorities. (Another such postwar story told of "a Negro Arkansas Home Guard unit" that overran a hospital, slaughtering "a reported 150 and wounding an undetermined number.") Nevertheless, even in the more isolated nooks and crannies of the Civil War, atrocities on a much smaller scale were documented.[12] Regrettably, such doubtful stories distract from the historical reality that there had been incidents enough to justify escalating retaliations, at least in the minds of those fighting it.

Around 5 a.m. Monday, September 19, Pape's column galloped into Doniphan, their new Colt revolving rifles blazing. They captured two pickets and surprised about forty Confederates under Rector Johnson's guerrillas working in advance of Shelby's division. With the Federals in pursuit, the Confederates crossed the Current River, destroyed the bridge behind them, and waited along the bluffs opposite. According to a Unionist account, one group of Federals formed at the river, while the other began to ford, stopping to water their horses in midstream to display their disdain for the enemy. The horsemen then finished chasing Johnson's men the eight miles into Arkansas. Back in town around noon, Sergeant James C. Steakley, who had not eaten all day, asked at the house of a Widow Low for a meal. As they spoke at the door, fires broke out at Kittrell's hotel and two other buildings, and she turned to Steakley and his men, pleading "for God's sake" not to burn her house. They assured her that they would not, and Pape quickly reassembled his men to ride the eight or nine miles back north. They stopped at 4 p.m. to eat and interrogate their two prisoners, who readily acknowledged belonging to a northbound army under Sterling Price.[13] At about 5:30 that afternoon, the troopers continued on about a dozen miles to the Vandiver farm near Ponder's Mill on the Little Black River.

In the end, the history of Doniphan and Ripley County suffered most from politically motivated after-the-fact exaggerations. Although genuine atrocities were real and numerous enough, former secessionists later claimed that the Federals burned the town and "every house and farm building" all the way back to Ponder's Mill, but contemporary sources are relatively clear. Since the secessionists had already burned the homes of known Unionists, it had already left little. A Union sergeant acknowledged seeing orders from Pape's superiors to burn out the local secessionists, probably not merely in retaliation but to root out the base for the guerrillas and end attacks on Federal soldiers. Confederate Samuel Hildebrand arrived later and found "every house but one" burning in Doniphan—one suspects it was that of the widow who had fed the Union soldiers—so he ordered that one torched himself. As to Pape's burning everything over the dozen miles north from Doniphan, another Confederate observer, Dr. William McPheeters, took that road and counted "three houses, or rather the smoldering ruins of three residences, burned on yesterday by a company of Yankee cavalry."[14]

Camped that night on the Vandiver farm, some Federals heard "the steady tramp" of large numbers of men around them, but Pape could not imagine such numbers. At sunup, they found themselves surrounded by dismounted Confederates three ranks deep in places. Using their Colts to good effect, the Federals charged and broke the rebel lines several times before falling back to their camp to reload. With the last of these, a number of mounted men in blue uniforms rode back into camp among them, and these turned out to be Confederates, which left the men "all mixed up together, rebels and our men." Steakley and seventeen others cut their way out, but Second Lieutenant William Brawner and "several others" fell wounded. While some Confederate reports mention prisoners, the ruthlessly straightforward Hildebrand said that the rebels had lost two killed and four wounded, but "captured sixteen Federals and shot them." They certainly shot and left for dead Sergeant Simon Branstetter when he tried to surrender.[15] While one Federal account indicates that all but about a dozen of the Unionists eventually turned up, Confederates report more Federal casualties, including executions, the most likely explanation being civilians in the wrong place and the wrong time.

The news these survivors carried to Patterson convinced McElroy that he had no chance of resisting the kind of numbers that seemed to be bearing down on him. He telegraphed his report to Wilson who ordered Patterson evacuated and sent Sergeant Edward Wilkinson and ten men with a wagon to aid with the operation. Around noon Thursday, September 22, McElroy led his little column east toward the St. Francois River. Back in the town, Hildebrand's advance rushed the rear of the column; he "captured eleven negroes and seven white men in Federal uniform and shot them." Later, on the road, Colonel Benjamin Elliott's Confederate cavalry caught McElroy's column, capturing five from the Forty-seventh and two from the Third MSM Cavalry, while Wilkinson lost his wagon, its teamster, and three of his men. In the aftermath, the Confederates executed Brawner and two newly captured Federals who had been on the Doniphan scout.[16] McElroy's survivors moved all night and reached Fort Davidson the next afternoon.

There, Wilson, in turn, had been dutifully telegraphing Ewing the news that a Confederate force had reentered Missouri. He passed on the rumors that thousands foraged near the state line to accumulate rations for five days, but could not resist adding, "I cannot believe the report to be true."[17] Protected by the rugged terrain and official incredulity in the Union command, the Confederate advance moved north.

The Invasion's March

Price's army entered Missouri in three diffuse divisions, with Shelby on the left to the west, General John S. Marmaduke on the right to the east and General James Fagan's Arkansans up the center. From the Federal perspective, it was as if these larger numbers materialized out of almost nothing, because the smaller Confederate columns and detachments began to converge as they reached more populated areas with farms, which provided more forage. As they pressed north, the diffused Army of Missouri began to take form, with Shelby and Marmaduke both focusing on Fredericktown, the other of Wilson's major outpost.

Marmaduke's advance first passed through the subdistrict of Federal lieutenant colonel Hiram M. Hiller at Cape Girardeau on the Mississippi River. A year and a half earlier, Marmaduke had 5,000 men in the area, with plans to take Bloomfield and Fredericktown simultaneously, isolating and capturing Cape Girardeau, before turning on Pilot Knob. The Federals there—then under John McNeil—had withdrawn to the Cape and withstood what amounted to a half-hearted Confederate attack in April 1863. Paradoxically, the very success of the Union forces in holding such places led to the transfers that left Hiller, like Wilson, with only a few hundred in his entire command.

Hiller informed St. Louis that, despite good communications with New Madrid and Charleston, his line to Bloomfield had simply gone dead. There, Captain Lewis Sells of the Second MSM Cavalry stumbled onto four hundred of the enemy as far north as Kennett with a thousand more on the state line at Chalk Bluff. The news caused "great excitement at New Madrid." Whatever his own doubts, Hiller proved much more credulous than Wilson, and arranged to call out the Fifty-sixth EMM, raised two "companies of citizens," and asked St. Louis for arms and ammunition for a thousand men. Within hours of the time the rebels overran McElroy's force near Patterson, Confederate colonel William L. Jeffers's Eighth Missouri Cavalry stormed into Bloomfield, knocking Sells's little scouting party back up the Sikeston road. Sells's men backed across the Whitewater River, fighting a furious running rear guard action before reaching Sikeston, the tiny community opposite the rail terminus across the Mississippi at Cairo.[18]

Chaos and panic swept over Hiller's entire subdistrict. By the time Jeffers's rebels took Jackson only ten miles northeast of the Cape, Hiller estimated, with surprising accuracy, that he faced 3,000 rebels, with another 7,000 in the vicinity. Ewing sent gunboats to the Cape, but remained as dismissive as ever of the reported numbers and issued bizarrely unrealistic orders for Hiller to retake Bloomfield and Chalk Bluff "even with a mere picket."[19] Since other sources indicate that Rosecrans thought Cape Girardeau might be the most likely initial target of the invasion, it is noteworthy that he (and Ewing) chose to keep Hiller in the dark about their suspicions.

The dutiful Hiller tried to implement Ewing's orders. When the Confederates left Jackson, he sent Captain Adolph Tacke with twenty-five men from the Fifty-sixth EMM to reoccupy the town. The thirty-one-year-old Tacke had served his apprenticeship as a millwright before joining the Prussian army and emigrating to the United States. Having a few years in the state, he left his milling business to enter the Fourth Missouri as a private and had since commanded a company of militia. His handful of mounted men retook the town about 5:30 p.m. on Saturday, September 24. As they sat down to supper, though, Jeffers's rebels—joined by Lieutenant Colonel J. F. Davies's Battalion Missouri Cavalry—reappeared. Tacke's experience and coolheadedness enabled his detachment to escape.[20] However, with Hiller's undersized force bottled at Cape Girardeau, the Confederates veered off to rejoin Marmaduke's northbound division.

This unexpected reversal of authority proved disastrous for civilians, especially African Americans. Decades later, though, Hannah Jones recalled her brutalizing life as a slave near the Cape. Her master did not own slaves to raise crops but "just raised niggers on his plantation" for sale south, and encouraged the men to take multiple wives. When Price's men arrived, they found the men gone, "just leaving us nigger women and chillun. Dey burned down frame and log huts just de same." They found some of the men, though, for "Dey killed three of us niggers in our camp dat morning."[21]

On Thursday night, September 22, the first of Shelby's men turned up ahead of Marmaduke's at Fredericktown. Half a century before, the key institutions of the community had coalesced around the square, including its Masonic lodge and a newspaper, the first in the state to advocate Free Soil principles. After sending men into both armies, the community had watched as the Union forces drove the MSG from its doorstep in October 1861, but three years later, the small garrison from the Forty-seventh Missouri abandoned the town to join Wilson at Fort Davidson some twenty miles northwest. On Friday morning, the rest of Shelby's division began arriving, and the town experienced some looting. One soldier gunned down a woman who refused to give him a dress she was holding. Federal scouts still flitted about the area seeking some idea of the enemy numbers until Sunday, September 25, when a patrol found itself swapping gunshots with several hundred Confederates eight miles west of Fredericktown.[22] By then, much of Price's army had arrived.

Meanwhile, Shelby's division had headed north from Fredericktown to Farmington, some eighteen miles northeast of Pilot Knob. Bypassed by the Iron Mountain Railroad, the seat of St. Francois County found its population stalled at about five hundred, but clung to prosperity, heavily dependent on enslaved workers. Decades later, one of them recalled both the physical brutality of the beatings and the sale of her family members. Even in so small a place, there existed a "nigger-breaker."[23] Union control of the town had changed all of this, but the return of the Confederates would temporarily restore the old order.

The slave children who carried lunch to whites in baskets remembered the passage of Price's army on the weekend of September 24–25. Ordinarily, they stopped in a corner of the town graveyard on their way home to consume the leftovers, but that morning, mounted Confederates came up the road from Fredericktown. Several of the more exuberant amused themselves by leaping over the rail fence and chasing the terrified black children. Decades later, the slave children recalled that, when they saw large numbers of soldiers, they hid, often under the houses. Said one, "I can jes remember how afraid us chillum was of de soldiers." Elsewhere in Farmington, one of Shelby's armed men strode boldly into a farmyard, stole eggs, and tried to stash them in his boots. As he climbed back over the fence, the eggs broke and he had to pour out their contents before putting his feet back into them. As he walked off down the road, one particularly brave black woman "ran out to de fence and hollored, 'goody, goody.'"[24]

It took the Confederates two attempts to take Farmington. Lieutenant Christian Hiber of the Sixty-eighth EMM put together a makeshift defense of the town around a core of about a dozen soldiers from the Forty-seventh Missouri. When the first Confederates showed up on Saturday, Hiber pulled his men into the courthouse, where their "gallant defense" ultimately drove the rebels from town. However, on Sunday morning, some fifty to sixty noisy Confederates returned, and surrounded the courthouse. They drove the Federals upstairs and set fire in the lower story of the building, forcing the defenders to surrender. Shelby's men finished torching the Court House, conscripted all the men not in hiding, and "sacked the town," before 150 of them went into camp at Big River Mills on the road to Mineral Point. Hildebrand recalled little violence against civilians there, beyond killing "a German, named Abright, who ran when we approached, refused to halt."[25] A local farmer got news of the Confederate presence to Federal troops, most likely one of those small groups posted along the Iron Mountain Railroad, which yet remained untouched.

Farmington also represented the first well-reported case of what Unionist civilians regarded as large-scale Confederate kidnapping. Rosecrans's aides rightly described it as "Price is carrying out the conscription law of the South, taking every man who can bear arms from sixteen to sixty, and paroling only those in the State and U.S. service." As everywhere else in the South, it proved "a merciless conscription."[26]

Meanwhile, St. Louis headquarters seemed so persistently unable to trust its people in the field that Ewing decided to go see the situation for himself. On Saturday, he accepted Smith's offer of some 1,300 men with some artillery and planned to take them down the Iron Mountain Railroad toward Pilot Knob. They arranged to meet Ewing Sunday morning, with Smith to bring the rest of his infantry on a later train.[27]

At dawn Sunday, September 25, Ewing left Jefferson Barracks to find less than half of what he expected, but thought that would be enough, particularly with the rest of Smith's men to follow. Their train steamed south, crossed the Meramec, and stopped briefly at Pevely, a tiny village twenty-seven miles from the city noted for its dairy products. There, he listened to more rumors about a large enemy force to the south. They continued to DeSoto, only forty-two miles from the city. Already, it might have occurred to Ewing that the reputed size of what he faced seemed to grow as he got closer to it. Although DeSoto had less than two hundred residents, it was the major center in Jefferson County, focused on the railroad, and protected by the county's Eightieth EMM, which, recalled one veteran, had "no duties to perform except to guard bridges and steal chickens."[28] At DeSoto, Ewing also began to encounter the recruits of the Forty-seventh Missouri.

Command of the regiment belonged to thirty-seven-year-old Colonel Thomas C. Fletcher, the founder of DeSoto. Having helped to launch the Republican Party in the state, he had represented it at the 1860 national convention that had nominated Lincoln. He subsequently led Missouri troops from Vicksburg to Atlanta before coming back to raise the Forty-seventh. The project involved such friends as Franz Dinger from Iron County, as well as Amos Maupin, John W. Maupin, and Judge James Owen from Franklin County. With the first rumors of an invasion, Fletcher had rushed the organization of his regiment and personally hurried to Cape Girardeau to consult and reassure Hiller.[29]

In Fletcher's absence, Lieutenant Colonel Amos W. Maupin commanded the Forty-seventh. A slaveholder born to Kentucky parents of Virginia antecedents, he had worked as a blacksmith and wagon-maker before serving as the sheriff of Franklin County, just west of St. Louis. An orderly man, Maupin had seen no need to uproot either slavery or the Federal Union and had been crucial to thwarting secessionists at Union, the county seat. His townsman, Major David Murphy, had left teaching school there, raised the state's first Federal company from outside of the city, and established an illustrious record as an artillerist before joining the new regiment, through which he later passed to command of the Fiftieth Missouri.[30]

Radical Unionism grew directly from the dynamics of the conflict. It began by driving conservative slaveholders into alliance with abolitionists and even German revolutionaries in order to overthrow the secessionist state government. Only a few years earlier, though, Maupin had protested the efforts of the local EMM to encourage his own slaves to run away. The exigencies of war and the presence of common mortal enemies brought him to where he was about to fight shoulder to shoulder not only with the Germans but also with blacks.[31]

From DeSoto, Ewing dispatched scouts toward Farmington, but did not wait to receive their report. In fact, the Confederates actually held the town and it would be some time before Captain Hiram A. Rice with a hundred men would brush the remaining Confederates from the town.[32] Ewing's southbound train also shed detachments along the track to guard its bridges, sometimes relieving and boarding previously posted squads.

Sixty-one miles from St. Louis, at Mineral Point, the train stopped for the night. Despite the stories from northbound refugees, Ewing wrote his wife that he still did not "fully credit" rumors of a large rebel presence. He even telegraphed Rosecrans that he had encountered nothing and had not yet firmly decided whether it would be worthwhile to continue on to Pilot Knob.[33] On Monday morning, though, Ewing and his remaining four hundred men continued south, blissfully unaware that thousands of Shelby's Confederates were sometimes only a few miles off from the rails.

Somewhere on this last leg of the trip, Fletcher joined Ewing. With an escort of only three cavalrymen, the Radical candidate for governor then backtracked west to join those of his regiment at Pilot Knob. Despite rumors of his capture and death, Fletcher arrived in fine fettle, assuring Dr. Seymour D. Carpenter, the district medical officer, that Shelby could only have a few thousand men in the area, adding, "We'll lick the hell out of them in short order."[34]

Meanwhile, events had robbed General Smith of the luxury of such ignorance. As agreed with Ewing, Smith boarded the rest of his infantry on a later train to take south. When it got to DeSoto, though, the scouts Ewing had sent toward Farmington had returned with the news that Shelby's advance had already gotten that far north. Smith sent more scouts that direction and ventured to place a stronger garrison at Mineral Point, from which he hoped to scout as far as Cadet Station. However, Smith told Rosecrans that the Confederate presence north of Pilot Knob could threaten St. Louis, so his own main force would "probably go no farther than DeSoto."[35] To the south unfolded one of the greatest dramas of the entire war.

Fort Davidson and the Arcadia Valley

Unaware of these developments, Ewing detrained at Pilot Knob station around noon on Monday, September 26. Between noon and 1 p.m., after making his way to nearby Fort Davidson, he sat down to bacon and hard bread—"hardtack" as they called it in the east—washed down by coffee. As he ate, he listened to more reports about the scale of the enemy presence in his district. The sixty-five men just back from Patterson reported a large force there and stories that Marmaduke and Price were present as well as Shelby.[36] However, rumor was that the nearest concentration of Confederate troops was at Fredericktown to the southeast.

In reality, Ewing's vast district had shrunk to what he could see. To his east, Pilot Knob itself rose several hundred feet above the plain while Shepherd

Mountain loomed to the west and southwest. Three main roads led back north. One toward Potosi hugged the western side of Cedar Mountain, with the railroad and Middlebrook Road running between Cedar Mountain and Rock Mountain, with the Farmington road running northeast between Rock Mountain and Pilot Knob. The roads and the rails converged in this pastoral setting at the industrial village of Pilot Knob, with its two hundred residents. South from there, the road ran past the fort, through the quarter-mile Ironton Gap between the base of Pilot Knob and Shepherd Mountain, to Ironton, the county seat a bit over two miles from the depot. Less than a mile farther sat Arcadia, the oldest of the nearby settlements, which had grown largely around a Methodist high school. It had just reopened under the protection of the Union garrison, though it was about to have an unscheduled holiday. Near there were the ruins of Fort Curtis, earlier Federal defenses in the valley, and the junction with a gravel road running east out of the valley through the Stout's Creek Shut-Ins toward Fredericktown. From the upper valley near the fort, Knob Creek meandered south running through Ironton Gap and joining Stout's Creek, which left the valley through the Shut-Ins, four miles southeast of the fort.[37]

The Federals built Fort Davidson the previous year to defend against guerrilla raids on the industrial works at Pilot Knob. However, the surrounding mountains made it a potential death trap against large numbers of regulars with artillery. The fort itself had six sloping earthen sides, each about a hundred feet long and four to six feet high, reinforced inside by two-inch planks and capped by a two-foot firing parapet. Just northeast of its center was the magazine, a forty-by-twelve-foot underground chamber roofed by wooden planks and fifteen feet of earth. As an extra measure, the Federals had surrounded the fort with a moat ten to twelve feet wide and six feet deep, and dug two rifle pits reaching to the north and south from the moat. The garrison had also stripped the timber from the facing slopes of Shepherd Mountain and Pilot Knob.

Ewing realized that he and his roughly 1,450 men had a very good arena for getting the measure of any force that might move on Fort Davidson. Properly used, the narrow gaps and shut-ins could minimize any numerical advantages such an enemy might have and might even allow his men to use the entire valley as a kind of natural fortification. The closest Confederates of which he knew were at Fredericktown and their entrance into the Arcadia Valley from the southeast would be through the Shut-Ins. The terrain in the valley produced a series of strong fallback positions, including Ironton and the Ironton Gap, before withdrawing into Fort Davidson. After telegraphing what he now described as "apparently credible rumors" to Rosecrans, Ewing added laconically, "I can hold the fort against 4,000 to 5,000 cavalry and four pieces of artillery."[38] Ewing could not imagine that he faced considerably more than that.

Ewing believed his own force strong enough for anything he needed. More than half of his men had probably faced guerrillas, but an open battle with Confederate regulars would be a different matter. Captain William J. Campbell's Iowans had spent two and a half years fighting from Tennessee to Louisiana, but these accounted for less than a tenth of Ewing's force. Civilians who volunteered to bear arms during the emergency represented another extreme. Fletcher particularly warmed to those "loyal citizens who came to us and took arms, and fought by our side in sight of their homes." The candidate even took responsibility for distributing to them "some very inferior muskets and plenty of ammunition." (The War Department badgered Fletcher for payment over decades to come.)[39]

A disproportionately large portion of the civilians at Fort Davidson was African American. An anonymous memoir of the fight said that Captain Lonergan formed "a company of negroes" that "did some good fighting." Sources variously described Charles Thurston or Solomon Lax as commanding about fifty black volunteers, and another described a "Captain" Jim Fares, who died at the makeshift hospital in the dirt cellar of the nearby Immanuel Lutheran Church. A number of these blacks formed an artillery crew, with some last-minute training by Charles W. Purcell of the Sixty-eighth EMM and a former officer of the Third MSM Cavalry who turned up to help in the emergency.[40] Perhaps none of the fort's defenders had a more clear idea of what was at stake or risked more than these black Missourians.

By the time Ewing turned up, Price had already authorized Fagan's Arkansans to move from Fredericktown into the Arcadia Valley.[41] After moving to the St. Francois, only a few miles short of Shut-In Gap, Fagan sent Colonel William F. Slemons's brigade to probe into the Arcadia Valley. At about 1 p.m., just as Ewing finished his lunch back at the fort, Slemon's men startled Azariah Martin and the other Union pickets about a mile and a half east of Arcadia, where the Fredericktown road joined that running north to Ironton. They sent Private John D. Gourley back to the fort to get reinforcements, but as the column of Confederates continued to appear, the scale of the force they faced required more immediate action. Martin, who knew that the Confederates would shoot him as a deserter if they took him, offered to get word through himself and took off at a gallop cross country to notify the small garrison at Ironton. Indeed, the rest of the pickets soon followed in his wake.[42]

At this point, Ewing had already realized that any attack would likely be from Fredericktown and had sent Lieutenant John A. Rice with a patrol of the Second MSM Cavalry to monitor what the Confederates might be planning. On their way to Arcadia, they rode directly into the advance of Slemons's rebels, who turned back to meet the main body of Confederates. When Slemons's main force rode into play, it simply brushed aside Rice's squad, which fled to the ruins of old Fort Curtis and wisely opted to keep a low profile for the present.

By then, the pickets had reached the rest of Ewing's force. At Ironton, Martin found others from his regiment lolling northeast of the courthouse, and shouted, "Rebels coming! Rebels coming!" Then, he continued toward Fort Davidson, running into eighty-three men of the Third MSM Cavalry at Ironton Gap just north of town. Some escorted him to Major Wilson at the fort where Martin dutifully reported and rushed off to join his company in the south rifle pits. Although used to false alarms, Wilson sent his regiment by column of two to retrace Martin's course.

Wilson's men had hardly passed through Ironton before they ran directly into two or three hundred of Slemons's brigade down the gentle slope from town. Both formed lines and began exchanging volleys without doing much appreciable damage, but the Confederate force grew as more of Fagan's men arrived. At around 2:30, the reinforced rebels charged across the fields of the Russell and McFarland families—locally called "Russellville"—threatening to cut off the Federals from Ironton. The unnerved Unionists broke ranks, remounted, and made for the safety of their fort.

Back at Ironton, Captain Franz Dinger and the thirty-one-year-old Lieutenant George J. Tetley agreed to join this withdrawal. As Dinger's wife, Amelia, scurried into the cellar of their house, the captain took his men on double-time back through the courthouse in hopes of falling back to Ironton Gap nearer the fort, but a misunderstanding left part of the company with Tetley back in the courthouse. Four or five times their number of rebels stormed into the town, and blasted away at the scattering Yankees. In the clear view of the entire square, the closely pursued Private William Rector of the Third MSM Cavalry dismounted and raised his hands in an effort to surrender but an unnamed red-shirted rebel gunned him down only to die himself in an outraged hail of lead fired from the courthouse.

As this happened, the iron whistle of the town foundry at Pilot Knob wailed a warning, just in case anyone in the valley had not heard the shooting. Wilson himself reformed about three hundred men from the Second and Third MSM, as well as the mounted recruits for the Forty-seventh and Fiftieth Missouri and started back toward Ironton, meeting Dinger and his men, who about-faced to return to town. Meanwhile, at the fort, the long roll drummed the Iowa infantrymen into formation to come forward with Lieutenant Morgan Simonton's two guns of the Second (New) Missouri Light Artillery. Wilson's horsemen pushed the Confederates from Ironton, where an argument broke out between Dinger and Tetley over their respective handling of the fight. Facing more pressing matters than the history of the engagement and still hoping to drive the Confederates back through Shut-In Gap, Wilson pressed beyond town to battle lines of the dismounted Arkansans, where he waited for his infantry and artillery to arrive.

The afternoon went well for the Federals. At about 3 p.m., Wilson faced an impressive Confederate battle line running from near the abandoned works of Fort Curtis on the west to the southern bank of Stout's Creek on the east. However, he had Simonton's artillery at the center of a strong infantry formation with cavalry covering the flanks, concentrating on his far right. Skirmishers from the Third MSM Cavalry advanced in two ranks, one firing and falling to reload, as the second moved forward to fire. At a crucial point, Lieutenant Rice's previously isolated patrol from the Second MSM Cavalry emerged from the ruins of Fort Curtis to open fire on the Arkansans' left, opposite to where Wilson had his mounted reserve. The Confederates backed to the woods, which broke up their formation, and then remounted to retreat to Shut-In Gap. The mounted portion of Wilson's command soon followed.

Around 5 p.m., Wilson's three hundred men tried desperately to dislodge about five hundred of Slemons's rebels on the timbered hillside overlooking the road through Shut-In Gap. As Wilson prepared to raise his saber and order a withdrawal, a Confederate ball grazed the left side of his head, knocking him from the horse. Stunned, bleeding, and in pain, he remounted and tried to disengage his force back in an orderly way. The withdrawal stranded Lieutenant Erich Pape and his flankers on a small bluff east of the gap, but their luck from Doniphan and Patterson still held. Sent by Wilson, Lieutenant Warren C. Shattuck showed up to guide them to safety, though this required them to charge through the Confederates from behind.[43] After doing this, they rejoined Wilson's men as they rode back through the lower valley. Darkness fell on any chance of keeping Price's army out of the Arcadia Valley.

Neither nightfall nor the end of the combat brought much rest.[44] Campbell's Iowans had advanced to an apple orchard on a ridge where they waited dutifully until Wilson's horsemen returned from the Shut-In Gap. In the lull, Wilson exchanged pleasantries with Campbell and discussed the unexpectedly still growing number of enemy campfires flashing alight in the darkness beyond them. As the rebels at Arcadia fired skyrockets to guide their reinforcements into the valley, the Union officers decided that the rumors may well have been true and that a small army was pouring into the valley. At 8:30, Wilson and Campbell asked Ewing for permission to fall back to a more defensible position near the Ironton Gap. When the still skeptical Ewing offered to return Simonton's artillery, Campbell quipped that these would only be something more to be lost. At about 10 p.m., Captain Charles S. Hills of Ewing's staff rode out to see the situation himself, and promised Wilson to return with an order for withdrawal. An hour later, Wilson moved his force back to Ironton.

When the order came to fall back, Wilson placed the infantry, both Iowans and Dinger's company of the Forty-seventh on his right near Ironton and his cavalry on the left. As the rain added to the chill of autumn in the night air, the men took turns in the shelter of the courthouse. As Fletcher noted, "the gallant Major Wilson" had been "everywhere," and his work left little real doubt about the truth of their situation.

The need for better information was evident when Dr. Carpenter had passed on a rumor that the Confederates had 100,000 men in the valley! Joseph A. Hughes, a Wayne County recruit in the Forty-seventh, volunteered to climb to the top of Pilot Knob and signal the fort as to the extent of the enemy campfires. After his signals caused considerable confusion, James Lindsay, probably the enlisted man in the Fiftieth, followed him up the mountain. To avoid confusion, Lindsay returned in person to tell his superiors that the valley was "full of men, horses, wagons and artillery."

Speaking for many who expected not to survive capture, Fletcher urged their immediate evacuation, but found himself in a decided minority. Eager to fight to the end was Dr. Carpenter, who "had not yet smelled the powder, felt as bold as Ajax," and Murphy, then supervising the civilian construction of four firing platforms on the fort walls, had smelled little but powder for three years and agreed with Carpenter.[45]

Scouts confirmed that the roads remained open to the north. Ewing realized that if General Smith and more infantry had not arrived yet, they would likely not do so, but he still believed that a strong Federal force must have gotten as far south as Mineral Point or some place near enough to assist them. By 10 p.m., Ewing had the base supplies and those civilians eager to flee ready to transport to Mineral Point. Later records indicate that they sent through at least one locomotive and probably two wagon trains. Charged with protecting one of the latter, Lieutenant M. P. Tate and thirty-five men of the Forty-seventh had orders to abandon the wagons if attacked and withdraw to the west of the road.

The need to learn the size, strength, leadership, and intentions of this unexpectedly large Confederate army required them to stay, but probably none of the Federals realized the full implications of their decision. Most immediately, as Carpenter prepared to retire with Ewing into a tent pitched in the powder magazine, he commended the strength of "the bomb proof," to which Ewing clarified that it was, in fact, not bombproof, and, if hit, would certainly blow them to pieces. After a citizen ventured into the darkness to look for the wounded and found Confederates between himself and the fort, he decided to embark on a four-day hike to Cape Girardeau.[46]

In the longer run, Murphy expected that they would soon be defending the fort itself. In preparation, he organized "a body of colored men" to construct gun platforms. Captain William C. Montgomery's battery had brought six guns supplementing what was already available at the fort, and Murphy's work crews worked by oil lamp to get the salvage timber from the roof of the powder magazine to mount four of Montgomery's cannons, using ropes to prevent their recoil. By the time they finished, they had five of the eleven available guns focused on the Ironton Gap through which the Confederates would surely come.

Tuesday morning, September 27, began with a fog, veiling everything in the Arcadia Valley. For those trained in the classics the situation of that small, stubborn Federal force bracing itself for the onslaught of thousands became reminiscent of Leonidas and his comrades at Thermopylae. The analogy cast Ewing and his Spartans holding that mountain pass against the countless Persian legions of Xerxes. It also placed the Federal authorities back in St. Louis in the positions of the Athenians, cleverly planning the ultimate victory. In fact, the defenders at Fort Davidson hoped to buy knowledge, not time for their comrades to prepare a defense of St. Louis, not that such motives would have mattered.

In reality, Rosecrans had little sense of what he should have been preparing at St. Louis until the time for preparations had come and gone. As late as Thursday—while fighting went on at Ponder's Mill, Patterson, and Bloomfield—he thought "a formidable invasion" merely "probable." Friday, he thought that only a fraction of the 8,000 rebels north of the Arkansas River could have ventured into Missouri. On Saturday, he dismissed as a rumor the idea that it would be large enough to be commanded by Sterling Price. During Monday's battle in the Arcadia Valley, Rosecrans conceded Price's presence as a "probability." By Tuesday, Rosecrans reverted to discussing a force under Shelby of no more than 6,000 men.[47] Indeed, Unionists in the field risked a great deal to get accurate information to a Federal high command seemingly incapable of processing it in any accurate and timely fashion.

2

September 27

From Pilot Knob through Potosi to Centralia

By late Tuesday afternoon, one soldier looked out over the field around Fort Davidson to see a sight "not to be forgotten by those who were there. The dead, the dying, the wounded, piled up here and there with the fragments of destruction all around."[1] The scene cut particularly deep because of the remarkable natural beauty of the seemingly timeless terrain that framed its strange isolation, and because everyone knew even greater violence and destruction awaited them.

The close-ranked assault on the fort belied the underlying nature of this campaign. The heroism of its Unionist defenders owed less to their military training and discipline than their abject fear of falling into Confederate hands. That assault brought ample reminders of what created that fear when Price's army executed prisoners at Potosi and Confederate partisans slaughtered soldiers and civilians at Centralia. No line of march or battle defined the campaign as well as the sweeping assault on Federal authority and order across the entire state.

The Assault on Fort Davidson

Tuesday in the Arcadia valley began when the Arkansans began their drive to push the Federals into the fort. The thirty-seven-year-old Virginian brigadier general William Lewis Cabell had helped design the distinctive rebel battle flag, but left administrative posts for the western field command of a brigade that already fought in Arkansas and the Indian Territory; his 2,500 men constituted Fagan's largest brigade. Near Ironton, he relieved that of Colonel William Fergusen Slemons and 2,000 of his men through a light rain to form a line of battle running for three-quarters of a mile, advancing on the town.[2]

Major James Wilson immediately saw the hopelessness of his situation and decided to fall back to Ironton Gap. Lieutenant Morgan Simonton's two guns fired half a dozen rounds before limbering and hurrying back to rejoin Wilson's two hundred horsemen on the Federal left, the eastward end of the south-facing Federal line. On the right, Captain William J. Campbell moved his Iowans on the double-quick up an alley and out of the town toward the Ironton Gap. When some civilians tried to join them, Campbell turned them back, suggesting that their cellars would prove safer than Fort Davidson. Meanwhile, Wilson's mounted Federals quickly folded into Ironton and followed Iowans as a rear guard.

The Federals reestablished a second position straddling the quarter-mile span of the Ironton Gap. Campbell sent the company of the Forty-seventh Missouri that had been with them back to the fort, hurried his men across Knob Creek, and scrambled up the slope of Shepherd Mountain. Those under Captain William V. Lucas had Campbell's left, nearest the road, while Lieutenant Smith Thompson took the right flank. At this point, Sergeant Edwin T. Langley and eighteen more Iowans, who had been on duty near Mineral Point, turned up after realizing that they had been cut off from St. Louis.[3]

Wilson dismounted his cavalry, forming a similar line to the east of the Ironton Gap, extending toward the southern slope of Pilot Knob. Although he had a certain portion of his men minding the horses, his remaining two hundred formed a strong defensive line around an old brewery called the "Halfway House." Behind them to the north, others covered the village of Pilot Knob with its railroad terminus and the Farmington road. Nearby, Simonton's guns unlimbered.[4]

Ewing's command prepared to do what they could to protect the gap from the fort. Of the Forty-seventh, Amos W. Maupin had three companies in the south rifle pits and Thomas C. Fletcher two companies in the north rifle pits, both supplemented with members of the Fiftieth. From the parapets of the fort, David Murphy readied his impromptu artillery crews drawn from the civilian volunteers, the First MSM Infantry, and the Third MSM Cavalry, manning guns that supplemented Captain William C. Montgomery's battery.

The Confederates had vastly greater numbers to manage and, as the Arkansans repositioned themselves, Ewing got breakfast rations to his entire command. The Confederates placed guns near Ironton Gap but their shells generally overshot, landing in or near Pilot Knob and forcing Dr. Seymour Carpenter to move his hospital back to a safer position, and Simonton wisely pulled his section of artillery nearer the fort. Around 9 a.m., Cabell's rebels had gotten into position to advance on the gap. When they did so, Campbell's Iowans clambered to their right up Shepherd Mountain and Wilson's men shifted left, opening the way for Murphy's big thirty-two pounder from the southeast corner of the fort to blast the Arkansans. Several times, the Union line opened like a curtain for their artillery at the fort to drive back Cabell's brigade.

By about 9:30, Campbell decided to shift farther up Shepherd Mountain to thwart any Confederate attempt to move up the slope from the west. He drew his line farther uphill to cover that eventuality and found a large number of rebels had already started for the summit. Moving his men on the double-quick up a timber road he tried to outrace them, but found his force backed down the denuded eastern slope of the mountain, and headed toward Fort Davidson.[5]

Cabell's line reached and broke around the south end of Pilot Knob as well, driving Wilson's men from their position. The Federal artillery from the fort raked its slopes with canister and bought enough time for Wilson to rally his troops back near the village and the depot, that last hope for immediate relief from General Andrew J. Smith's infantry.

Ewing's purpose remained getting an accurate measure of the enemy's size. For this reason, Campbell's men turned back to Shepherd Mountain and Wilson's men started up Pilot Knob, with Captain Dinger's company of the Forty-seventh joining Wilson to hold the village and the roads behind them. At 10:15 a.m., though, the Confederate press toward the summit of Pilot Knob drove off the two Federal observers who had spent the night up there.

Around this time, General Sterling Price himself reached Ironton with the division of General John S. Marmaduke. Marmaduke, Captain T. J. Mackey, and Lieutenant Colonel Lauchlan A. Maclean of Price's staff rode up Shepherd Mountain to survey the situation. Once back, they discussed placing artillery there, overlooking the fort, would force Federal capitulation. Supposedly, Marmaduke and Fagan, whose men had been pushing the Federals all morning, argued against such a time-consuming project.[6]

However, Price did attempt to use his intimidating numbers to get what he wanted with minimal loss. At about noon, according to Fletcher, the Confederates approached the fort with a flag of truce demanding its surrender. When Ewing gave a "polite but emphatic refusal," Price's staff waited another hour, then sent a second offer coupled to the warning that the Confederate command "would not be responsible for consequences in case of our refusal." Referring to the previous spring's massacre of a Federal garrison in Tennessee, Ewing quipped, "They shall play no Fort Pillow game on me." With his officers now unanimously agreed, he flatly refused this second request.[7] Clearly, the Confederate threat had exactly the opposite effect of that intended and made placing themselves voluntarily into the hands of Price's men an unacceptable option.

Rebel muskets on Shepherd Mountain drove Maupin's men from the south rifle pits. Union riflemen and First Lieutenant John Fessler's artillerists turned a merciless fire their direction. Meanwhile, some of the Confederate cannons got the range of the fort, one shell cutting the "fine gray horse of Col Maupin cleen in too." Warned about the threat of artillery on Shepherd Mountain, Murphy scoffed, "I'll knock hell out of it in a minute."[8]

Murphy waited patiently as the Marmaduke's men pulled two guns up the timber road to the peak and fired on the fort. At that point, he began targeting his reply with a well-practiced expertise that eluded most artillerists in the region. One shot broke the axle of one Confederate cannon, forcing its abandonment. Others drove off the second piece. Confederate cannoneers at the south end of the mountain—just beyond the view of the fort—tried to use its flagstaff to measure its distance, but Murphy's guns then targeted the smoke and drove back those guns as well. In the end, the Confederate artillery proved no match for the Federal guns and gunners.

Price later chose not to report these events and implied that he had chosen against putting artillery on the mountains overlooking the fort. He made this implausible even more improbable with the strange story that civilians from town informed him that the Federals had impressed local men into service at the fort and that he did not want to fire on innocent civilians. One historian called this a "fantasy," and it speaks volumes that any general officer even tried to explain his decisions in such a way.[9] In fact, Murphy's guns fired at real artillery on Shepherd Mountain and the disabled gun was found there.

Unsure of immediate Confederate intentions, Ewing decided to send the Iowans back up Shepherd Mountain to keep Marmaduke's men from repeating their effort. At 1:15 p.m., they pulled a half-shaved Captain Lucas from the post barber and headed back up the slope with signalmen to direct the Federal guns with even greater accuracy. Once there, though, Campbell found so many rebels that he realized his feeble force would never hold them. Leaving his men with orders to fire one volley and withdraw, if attacked, Campbell hurried back to warn Ewing personally to expect a full assault from that direction.

From Shepherd Mountain on the west, Campbell's men knew that over 1,100 men of Brigadier General John Bullock Clark Jr.'s brigade of Marmaduke's division waited just up the slope from them. A Harvard graduate, Clark had risen rapidly from a lieutenancy in the MSG, but it still left him eclipsed by his father, a hard-drinking, tough-talking Missouri congressman expelled during the secession crisis. The battle provided Clark an opportunity unprecedented in his already impressive wartime career.

Meanwhile, they could also see Cabell's 2,000 men to the south preparing for another advance. To the east across the valley, over 1,700 in the brigades of Slemons and Thomas H. McCray prepared to move against Wilson's two hundred horsemen near Pilot Knob. Even to the north, five hundred men from Colonel Thomas R. Freeman's brigade and Lieutenant Colonel Alonzo W. Slayback's battalion, detached from Shelby's division, came from around Shepherd Mountain, and Colonel Archibald S. Dobbin's brigade waited near the Potosi road as a reserve. In all, Price had committed roughly 5,000 men to the attack.

Perhaps at this point, Ewing finally realized the extent of their dilemma. He sent Captain Henry B. Milks with twenty men to check on their route of escape to the north. On their way, they ran into five hundred of Freeman's rebels, moved into position, fired a volley, and scurried up Shepherd Mountain, drawing off some of the Confederates, though cutting themselves off from the fort.

Around 1:30 p.m., the Confederate onslaught on Pilot Knob began in earnest.[10] Wilson had moved his feeble detachment from the Iron Furnace to the gap, and began moving up the northern flank of the Pilot Knob. Fully as convinced as Campbell that his force would never be able to hold them, he sent Lieutenant W. H. Smith and Warren C. Shattuck to arrange for Ewing to cover the retreat of his men to the fort. Ewing sent Sergeant C. B. L. Rowland with twenty-five of the Forty-seventh Missouri to form ranks in the open field and cover the flight of Wilson's men from Pilot Knob and to the safety of the north rifle pits. As expected, the overwhelming wave of Confederates with field guns and canister drove Wilson's men from their pathetic defensive toeholds. Lieutenant John A. Rice led a small group beyond the iron furnace and through a livestock pen before being forced to surrender. However, after only ten minutes as prisoners, he and his mean escaped into chaos of the ongoing fighting. Lieutenant George Tetley got others back to the safety of the north rifle pits, as did Shattuck.

On the crumbling left of the Union line, Wilson found himself surrounded with about sixty-five of his remaining men. Blasted by Confederate fire, he emptied three revolvers as he led his men in a breakout charge. With his numbers falling rapidly, he attempted to reform in a hollow near the road from the summit, but fell back again to a mill. There Wilson, Dinger, and about fifteen others made a desperate stand before the two officers and five of their men fell into Confederate hands.

Others avoided this fate. On his way back to Wilson, Lieutenant W. H. Smith and twenty other mounted Federals found themselves cut off from the fort. Thinking fast, he led a mad dash up the Middlebrook Road; Confederates pursued them north for five miles, but they would eventually make their way to St. Louis. Also cut off was the now-superfluous telegraph operator, John H. Byrne, a thirty-five-year-old former militia enrollee from St. Louis, who managed to fade into the background until he could slip off north on roughly the same route. However, the Confederate advance on the fort from the east had to contend with the Union artillery once it had a clear shot. It took about five minutes to drive them into the bed of Knob Creek.[11] Still, periodic gunfire from that direction rattled through most of the afternoon.

At about 2 p.m., the brigades of Slemons, McCray, Cabell, and Clark formed a long semicircular line from Pilot Knob on the east through the Ironton Gap to Shepherd Mountain on the west. From left to right in Clark's command—the only Missourians in the line—the regiments of Colonels William L. Jeffers, John Q. Burbridge, Robert R. Lawther, Lieutenant Colonel Robert C. Wood, and Colonel Colton Greene had only 1,200 yards down the slope, across the plain, and to the fort. One of Clark's batteries fired a signal shot that buried itself into the mud between the feet of forty-nine-year-old Captain William P. Adair of the Forty-seventh Missouri, who "ripped out an oath." Clark's advance immediately encountered the Iowans, who fired their volley, as ordered, and fell back to the fort. The terrain slowed and broke up Clark's advance even more effectively, leaving it to emerge at the foot of the slope after an hour with a gap of 150 feet between the regiments of Burbridge and Lawther. Despite an impressive rebel yell in the face of heavy Union fire, Clark's Confederates dived for shelter into the banks of Knob Creek, which also looped that direction near the fort.

Ewing's Federals coiled more tightly into Fort Davidson. The enfiladed remnants of the Forty-seventh Missouri filed from both the south and north rifle pits into the fort, but Simonton's artillery horses bolted, leaving two cannons abandoned northwest of the fort. Back on Shepherd Mountain, Milks's men continued to evade Freeman's Confederates, but their appearance at the edge of the timber cut drew "friendly fire" from the fort. Milks sent runners to identify themselves to Ewing and inform him that they would attempt to get back after nightfall.

Then came a concerted assault. As the Arkansans advanced toward Fort Davidson from the south, Clark's brigade reemerged to approach the west wall. Less than twenty yards before them, terrified Federals crouched behind the parapet four, five, and six deep, those in the rear reloading and passing the weapons forward. Some Confederate shells overshot the fort to land near the new hospital site, one striking an ambulance and spilling the Union wounded onto the field. One of the luckier shots severed the rope used for the drawbridge into the fort, which left it immobilized a few feet above ground level. Ewing told Campbell to "get twenty men—volunteers—to stand at the gate till the death!" Other Iowans helped drag barrels into a makeshift barricade.[12] After falling back some distance, Cabell's brigade dressed ranks for another try and fire from the exhausted and unnerved Federals began to slacken.

At this point, the schoolteacher Murphy may well have saved the fort. The officers moved among them with threats and words of encouragement, but Murphy did much more. The schoolteacher-warrior had just lost his wife while he had been to war and may well have valued his own life less than he might have earlier. In any event, when a Confederate shell decapitated one of the artillerists, members of the barely trained crews began to freeze. As Fletcher wrote, Murphy "mounted the redoubt and proceeded to address the audience in our front as it lay in concealment, daring and defying them to come on, and in a voice so loud that it woke the echoes of the mountains, reflecting upon their courage and parentages. Out of admiration of his daring they refused to shoot him, as they could easily have done." When Ewing urged him to take cover, Murphy replied "there was never a prettier place in this world to die than right here." His gunners—all of the fort's defenders—cheered wildly. As Cabell's line moved forward a second time, they found Murphy on the parapet, cursing, taunting, and even throwing rocks, conduct that kept the makeshift crews at their essential guns.[13]

When the Arkansans wavered and fell back to the creek bed, a handful of Iowans and artillerists rushed into action. Leaving the cover of the walls, they manhandled Simonton's two guns to the drawbridge, dropped some loose planks as runners, and pulled the guns into the fort. At about this time, the Confederates of Freeman and Slayback advanced from the north, moving down the road to within 200 yards of the north rifle pits. Forty MSM cavalrymen dashed forward and began a short, sharp, and bitter skirmish that drove the rebel horsemen back toward Cedar Mountain.[14]

Then, from the south, Cabell's brigade made one last desperate heroic charge. Some thirty yards from the fort, Federal fire shot Cabell's horse from under him and his men moved him to safety. This time, though, the first of his men not only reached but leapt into the shelter of the moat. Campbell realized that, as their numbers increased behind the lip of the parapet, they would be in an excellent position to rush over the wall itself. He began shouting this warning and started toward Ewing when an artillerist reminded him that the magazine had some of those new dart-like hand grenades. Joined by roughly a dozen black civilians, Campbell hurried off and returned with plenty of them. He and his men helped to throw them into the moat. The blasts cleared the immediate vicinity of the wall "as if by magic." With only half an hour of daylight left, those of Cabell's army remaining on the field crawled off or, perhaps, stayed permanently.[15]

Fighting sputtered on. As Confederate sharpshooters continued to fire on the fort from Knob Creek, Sergeant Henry C. Wilkinson organized a response from fifteen to twenty of the best shots in the fort. These rested the barrels of their best rifles on the parapet, patiently waited for a rebel to shoot, and fired below the smoke, which ended much of troublesome sniping. The Federal artillery also kept the Confederates at bay, one shell passing through a log house and ripping the leg off Major George W. C. Bennett of the Tenth Missouri Cavalry. Determined to clear Knob Creek of the closest sharpshooters, twenty members of the Forty-seventh Missouri reoccupied the south rifle pits, then climbed out into formation and advanced only to face some five hundred to a thousand shots, which sent them scurrying back to the safety of the fort. (Some sources indicate that Fessler also used his artillery to disable yet another rebel cannon on Shepherd Mountain, but this may well be conflated with the earlier incident.) The heavy shelling of the day had inadvertently ignited an $80,000 pile of charcoal at the Pilot Knob furnaces, and its glow lit the whole darkening valley.[16]

The outcome had been better than any of the Federals might have hoped. Had the issue turned on the numbers of troops involved, the Confederates would have likely overwhelmed Fort Davidson. The Union artillery, though, well managed by experienced officers, kept the Confederate big guns at bay, and rebels had nothing like the Colt revolving rifles of the MSM Cavalry or the hand grenades the Iowans had used to clear the moat of attackers.

The losses at Fort Davidson were devastating.[17] Price later ungenerously—if not simply contemptibly—blamed the failure of the assault on "the Arkansas Jakes," but those present on both sides agreed that the Confederates "came up in fine style," and left evidence of their courage scattered about the fort. One observer recalled that, for twenty-five feet from the moat, one could walk around two-thirds of Fort Davidson from the south to the northwest on the bodies of the dead and wounded Confederates. Dr. Carpenter claimed to have made something of a count and thought the enemy casualties to be "over 1000." Another told Fletcher he had counted 1,468 Confederates on the ground, though some placed the losses around 1,500. The Confederates buried some 500 of their dead, and Federals later interred another 125, these in addition to those buried in the course of the fighting. However, the most knowledgeable historian of the battle, Bryce Suderow, estimated some 800 casualties, which jibes with reports of about 200 killed with 600 to 800 wounded.

Remarkably, the reported estimates of Union casualties proved no more reliable. Contemporary accounts run from a dozen to 22 killed, with 40 to 65 wounded, and one historian apparently combined these numbers to suggest 77 killed. In addition, there were between 67 "missing (prisoners)" to 129 generally.[18] The actual numbers ran much higher, and not all the missing men were prisoners. Many individuals and entire groups, like those under Lieutenant Smith, found themselves cut off and made for Cape Girardeau, St. Louis, or other places in Federal hands. Finally, of course, regardless of the estimates at this point, neither side had finished adding to them.

Well into the night, the Confederates prepared for a final assault the next day.[19] The valley echoed with the sounds of the rebels in Ironton building ladders to throw against the fort's walls. Price sent couriers north to recall Shelby's division to the Arcadia Valley. Some of the women from town approached the fort to tell Fletcher that Confederate colonel Slayback would attempt to negotiate the safe surrender of the fort's defenders. One Union officer described a general appreciation of Slayback as "a gallant and brave man, generous and Noble Hearted," but very few, if any, of the Federal officers thought a Confederate victory could or would restrain those among them intent on murdering prisoners. Ewing consulted his officers, including Milks, who had returned to the fort from a harrowing day on Shepherd Mountain. Fletcher frankly said that he fully expected one or another member of Price's army to execute him and others, and Campbell flatly refused to surrender. Long before midnight, Ewing came to the conclusion that their only real hope lay in evacuation.[20]

Evacuation would require the defenders to leave the protective walls of their fort, detonate the magazine, and destroy everything of value they could not take with them. When Dr. Carpenter reminded Ewing about the proximity of so many of the Confederate wounded, the commander said simply, "War is not a benevolent institution!" At 10 p.m., Carpenter, Dr. James R. McCormack, and others took water and whisky to the Confederates lying to their front. They also organized teams, quietly triaged the wounded, and moved about fifty of them to nearby houses, surely saving their lives.[21]

Late that night, the officers at Fort Davidson began waking the exhausted soldiers with whispered orders. Each got a hundred rounds of ammunition and as much bacon and hardtack as they could carry. The horse details returned with 250 mounts, but the infantrymen took so many of them that it left much of the cavalry dismounted and the artillery to abandon their caissons and make do with only a hundred rounds. In the darkness, the soldiers placed straw and blankets over the boards and carefully lowered the drawbridge. They also placed blankets and tents over the wheels of the artillery, and put sacks of hay over the horses' hooves to muffle their movements. At 1 a.m., the Unionists filed from their fort.

Once outside, they moved with an incredible discipline and silence. Slayback's Confederates were north of Pilot Knob on the road to Caledonia and Potosi. The Federals crept through the town, then moved along a small side road that joined the Potosi road north of Slayback's position and under the shadow of Cedar Mountain. Only nine hundred yards north of the fort, they passed within fifty yards of the campfires of Dobbin's brigade, the Federals later recalling the facial profiles of enemy soldiers against those fires. Those Confederate pickets who saw the movement supposed it to be their own troops. After all, they expected Shelby's men to turn up at some point in the northern part of the valley.[22]

In Wilson's absence, Milks had command of both the Third MSM Cavalry and the subdistrict headquarters, and he dutifully stayed behind. Lieutenant James Copp, Lieutenant John W. Hendrick, Sergeant W. H. Moore, and nineteen enlisted men waited with him. They had orders to give Ewing's column a good head start and to blow the magazine of Fort Davidson to pieces at 3:30 a.m. Milks, Copp, and Moore descended into the magazine and broke open enough of the powder to create a large pile in the center of the chamber. Failing to find a fuse, they poured a trail of powder back through the fort and across the drawbridge. Then, they made a hurried search for any deep sleepers, rousing five but missing at least two others in the darkness. They also placed sixteen of their dead and fatally wounded on the roof of the magazine to provide the nearest they could to an honorable burial. When the time came to ignite the powder trail, the mistiness of the night kept extinguishing the fire. Finally, after going back to check on the trail, Moore emerged in a hurry, gasping out to his comrades that he had actually lit the powder where it entered the dry shelter of the magazine.[23] Milks and the last of Ewing's men lost no time in mounting up and taking off.

Back on the road, Ewing had sent those hundred men "who had seen the most service" forward as an advance under Captain Pinckney Powers. Sergeant Wilkinson later recalled that, at one point, Powers turned to him in the saddle, and said, "There will be a bright light back yonder directly." Almost immediately, Wilkinson turned to see a column of red and white flame erupting hundreds of feet into the night sky miles behind them. By all accounts, the magazine went around 4 o'clock in the morning.[24]

The blast shook the earth around as far away as twenty miles. It toppled trees near the fort and threw into the air shells that exploded there like fireworks with yellow, blue, white, and red. At the makeshift hospital at Pilot Knob, the concussion knocked Dr. Carpenter to the floor. There, too, Reverend D. A. Wilson warned a black man named Tom injured while helping in the fort that the Confederates would likely kill him when they arrived, unless he escaped into the night. The explosion showered dirt and ruble on Milks and his detachment, which had been a mere 150 yards from the fort at the time of the blast. Even closer, nobody had woke up Private Thomas Long of the Third MSM Cavalry, who found himself clawing his way through several feet of dirt into the night air, where he found that a local cobbler-tailor had also surfaced. The civilian slipped away to his home, while Long searched desperately among the unburied dead for a rebel uniform of the right size. He wound up spending two days in the chaos of Price's army before getting a chance to slip off and make his way to St. Louis.[25]

Over in the Confederate camp, Dr. William McPheeters felt the blast "shaking the whole earth." Some recognized it as the magazine but thought it an accident and expected the badly shaken Federals would surrender at daylight. At the home of Willie Lawson in Arcadia, Price remained unaware of the blast until 8 a.m. The encircling mountains, the densely wooded terrain, the temperature fall, the prospect of rain, and other factors probably created the same sort of "acoustic shadow" that had served Price two years before at Iuka.[26] This time, though, the strange anomaly served his enemies.

North of Fort Davidson: Potosi

Ewing and his column sought safety by following the earlier evacuation of their supplies and refugees north to where they had hoped to find Smith's infantry. Unknown to any of them, the locomotive Ewing had sent north from Pilot Knob under Captain Herman Garven had barely made it through. Along with long lines of wagons moving north, the train carried the supplies and between 1,700 and 2,000 refugees, black and white. The engineer made poor time because of the frequent stops along the way to pick up those troops Ewing had earlier dropped off at the depots and the bridges, including 250 men left at the Big River bridge near Irondale. Just below Mineral Point, the train stopped to make emergency repairs to the line. "By this time the woods were filled with Confederates, and picket firing began."[27]

Shelby's men, including his own old "Iron Brigade" under Colonels David Shanks and that of Sidney D. Jackman rampaged across the area. After seizing Irondale, Colonel Benjamin Elliott's regiment turned to the railroad, destroying the large bridge on the Big River, the North Big River bridge, and smaller bridges nearby. Where the rail bed itself showed signs of weakness, Shelby's men lined on either side of the railroad, each man opposite a tie and, at the signal, they uprooted the entire rail bed, throwing the material down the embankment. The Federals had only two small veteranized cavalry regiments, the Thirteenth Missouri and the Seventh Kansas, operating out of Pevely, and could get "no definite information of the whereabouts of the enemy." Reflecting what it had been told, the *New York Tribune* reported, "Whether this invasion is intended as a real serious demonstration, or merely as a feint to cover operations elsewhere, remains to be seen."[28] The prudent course required the Federals to keep between this enemy force of indeterminable size and St. Louis.

Official reports and press accounts tell us little of the frequent skirmishes across the district. The newspapers claimed that the Confederates lost fifty men in a fight at the North Big River bridge, while the Federals lost "but seven." Samuel Hildebrand's autobiography recalled meeting only four Federals from Fort Davidson near Big River, noting that he "shot them and threw their bodies in a mineral hole."[29]

The delay of the northbound train from Irondale caused real problems at Mineral Point. There, "the first lady operator" in the Military Telegraphic Corps west of the Mississippi waited for the operator from Irondale to relieve her. A few years before, Louisa Volker accompanied her father, who exchanged his St. Louis grocery for a Mineral Point tavern. The telegraph operator at the time, Clinton S. Barrett, probably taught her how to operate the equipment and she took over when he went on to Pacific. With the first news of the invasion, Volker stayed on the job at Mineral Point. For two full days, she relayed the messages north and south and waited to be relieved by the Irondale operator.[30]

The northbound refugees fared poorly. Shelby's men reportedly captured thirty-six wagons near Hopewell and "fifty empty wagons" elsewhere, though these may be muddled versions of the same event. Decades later, Robert Bryant remembered the trip he took from Pilot Knob with his father George Bryant. "De government gave de old man a team to make it to St. Louis. Me and my mother and my brother who was deaf and dumb went with dem but da soldiers captured us and de old man jumped off de mule and high tailed it to the woods. My mother got out of the de wagon and took my brother to de woods too. De soldier rid up to de wagon and said, 'Little boy, you don't need to be afraid, I'm after your father.'" This had an effect on Robert far different than probably intended, for he "started to get out of the de wagon and fell down under de mule and dare I was on de ground. I got up and made for de woods and got in a hole where de hogs was a-wallerin'." He recalled that it would be three days before his mother found him, and that blacks warned one another of nearby Confederates by tossing rocks onto their roofs.[31]

Even as the Confederate ranks converged on Fort Davidson, Shelby's men stormed into Potosi, roughly ninety miles short of St. Louis. Earlier called Mine-a-Breton, the community had a history that went back a century. A prosperous lead-mining community, it had already produced a number of prominent citizens including Moses Austin before Texas and the California Gold Rush imploded its population. Although alerted by developments at Farmington, an attack on Potosi seemed unlikely to most residents, including the former county surveyor, Lieutenant Colonel Irwin K. Walker of the Thirty-second EMM, whose martial bearing inspired some confidence. If the Confederates moved north, there seemed to be better routes, and the locals believed that the proximity of Smith's infantry would protect the town. In its latest contribution to the war effort, Potosi had raised much of two companies for the new Fiftieth Missouri; one of which remained in town, bolstered by members of the EMM. They occupied the Washington County courthouse "made of brick, the windows being battened up with solid oak planking four inches thick, having loop holes to shoot through."[32] Such precautions had served Missouri towns well against mounted raiders lacking artillery.

Donald M. Palmer arrived in Potosi around noon Tuesday, to rumors that the Confederates were on their way. He had ridden eighteen miles the previous day to sell his horse, and his partner, Thomas B. Shaw, brought "a load of rosin and turpentine" to Potosi. The two young Yankees watched in terrified amusement as many civilians fled north despite the assurances of "a lawyer by the name of B——, and an Eastern man" who "rigged himself up in a very fierce military jacket and cap" and extorted all to a last-ditch defense of the town. Palmer recalled that despite the *nomme de guerre*, this "General B——" "suddenly disappeared" himself, later turning up in Illinois. Having had "considerable experience in the past summer" evidently in the militia, Palmer "merely did what I thought was my duty" when he joined their ranks at the courthouse. By most accounts, these totaled about thirty soldiers and 130 "armed citizens."[33]

When "an ex-provost marshal" with a rank of lieutenant suggested a scouting party, Palmer and Shaw volunteered. Promising not to abandon his men, the officer led from town, but just beyond its limits, they rode directly into "the entire rebel advance, charging into town enveloped in a cloud of dust, but through which could be seen the glitter of arms, and even at the distance we were, could be plainly heard their demonic yells." The squad wheeled about and galloped back into town where Palmer dismounted "a little quicker than I ever got off a horse before in my life." As the bullets whistled "pretty thickly" around them, he saw their bold commander and another man galloping up the main road to St. Louis "as fast as horse-flesh could carry them."[34]

The fight was brief but terrifying. Behind the protection of the courthouse walls, they "kept up sort of an unsteadying firing, on both sides," but Confederates by ones and twos slipped nearer the Federals and took cover. They heard "a deep sound" from the rebel artillery that had wheeled into place near the railroad depot, and the shells soon rained "a shower of bricks and mortar, laths and plastering" upon the defenders. Palmer recalled that the fourth shell "burst inside," followed by another. Then, he thought "the whole ceiling suddenly vanished from sight and then I felt myself falling." Unwounded but dazed by the concussion, he noted that other shells actually landed in the courtroom.[35] Promised treatment as prisoners of war and respect for property in the town, the Federals surrendered.

The white flag, however, only began "the reign of terror in that town which lasted for ten days." Confederate artillery fell silent, but the shooting continued until one of the Confederates who entered the courthouse went to the door and unleashed "a terrible volley of oaths" that silenced it. Once inside, the rebels made "a general demand for money, watches, revolvers, &c." One took Palmer's revolver, another his watch and chain, and a third "cursed me at a terrible rate" for being too slow about turning over his pocketbook. "I had no idea that we would be robbed in the way that we were," he later, "or I would have attempted to hide some of my things." The Confederates then murdered the first two prisoners who stepped out of the courthouse, "both shot through the lungs." As young Ike Jamison turned to go into the street, the rebel who had just robbed him shot him in the back. On the street, the prisoners found that the invaders had already gunned down a civilian for having taken a shot at them. For undetermined reasons, Confederates also killed at least five more civilians, two of whom were known locally as secessionists. Once outside, they forced the prisoners to "trade" their coats, hats, shirts, pants, boots, and shoes, leaving the line of prisoners to assume the trappings of the most ragged of the rebels. Even in the tension of the exchange, the prisoners could not suppress a "hearty laugh" at their transformation.[36]

Marching their prisoners out of town, the rebels "separated the citizens from the soldiers." A Federal officer had agreed to claim Palmer and Shaw as his soldiers, but the guards engaged in "so much talk of killing the militia" that the two civilians decided to take their chances. As if to confirm their judgment, "a former citizen of Potosi" accompanied by a Confederate colonel called for Colonel Walker, Lieutenant F. M. Jamison—"a brother to the one shot at the Court House and a fine young fellow"—and others. As their captors led them off, each of the EMM officers "seemed resigned to his fate." As to the enlisted men, in addition to the two gunned down at the courthouse, four more would be executed. The surviving prisoners, cold and hungry, eventually collapsed into the muddy ground and slept fitfully.[37] Their captors gave no sign of what they might do with them.

Some civilians, however, proved eager to collaborate with the Army of Missouri. The Confederates had long learned to disregard as southerners those soldiers and civilians who bore arms against them, while that self-selecting lot that came out to greet them as liberators became essential to maintain their faith in "the Cause." One diarist understood that, from a Confederate perspective, Price's legions were "*everywhere* received with the greatest enthusiasm by the 'rebs' in Mo. His march was in *triumphal style* and was, in fact, a continual *ovation*, from the Arkansas line to Mo. river." At Potosi, Judge Ambrose Ransom, who had settled in nearby Franklin County over forty years earlier, rode out to greet the Confederates. Shelby's men were welcomed by a government purchasing agent named Simms, who had made a decent living selling horseflesh to the Union army.[38] From the Confederate perspective, this had to happen enough to sustain their sense of self, against the backdrop of murdering prisoners.

Centralia

Through the summer, thirty-six-year-old General Clinton Bowen Fisk of the District of North Missouri found himself overwhelmed by the rising tide of guerrilla activities. From his headquarters at St. Joseph, he had functioning subdistricts at Macon, Mexico, and Hannibal, along the line of the North

Missouri Railroad, with other key garrisons at Savannah, Columbia, and Glasgow. However, large-scale guerrilla operations sapped Federal garrisons, exposing the moribund state of the EMM and the disorganized provisional militia companies.

On September 20—a full week before the assault on Fort Davidson and the attack on Potosi—newly recruited Confederates had materialized outside of Keytesville, demanding the militia's surrender there. After the surrender, the secessionists entered the town and killed Robert Carmon and William Young, the former the sheriff and the latter "noted as a Union scout and spy. Both were over sixty years of age." Another Unionist scout named Cunningham stumbled into a nearby house to get water, only to find it occupied by a squad of bushwhackers "dancing and having a generally jolly time."[39]

General Fisk fumed about the surrender, which would not be the first or the last such scandal in northern Missouri. "Cowardice and treason combined caused the loss of Keytesville," he wrote. "The fiends murder none but radical Union men, while conservatives of undoubted loyalty are spared in property and person. The radicals are hunted from their homes, and their substance appropriated and destroyed." Then, too, Fisk frankly acknowledged that his most reliable support came "chiefly from the radical portion of the community, it is with great difficulty they are restrained from depredations" against those who had targeted and victimized them.[40]

By 1864, George Todd and "Bloody Bill" Anderson had broken from the band of William C. Quantrill to build their own guerrilla groups, but they periodically cooperated. On September 23, three days after Keytesville, Sylvester F. Gosline of Boone County reluctantly hosted the *debut* of several new guerrilla bands. Captain James W. McFadden and seventy men of the Third MSM Cavalry stopped for the night on their way with fourteen wagons of supplies from Sturgeon to Rocheport, a Missouri river town described as "our capital" by guerrillas. Seven miles short of their goal, they stopped at Gosline's Lane, a narrow little side road. George Todd's hundred guerrillas caught them loitering along the road and in the apple orchard. Those Federals near their mounts escaped toward Sturgeon or Columbia while those without horses fled into the adjacent cornfield. The guerrillas butchered eleven soldiers and three teamsters, seizing 18,000 rounds of ammunition and other supplies. Todd's band continued into Howard County, joining others under the twenty-five-year-old Kentuckian Captain William "Bloody Bill" Anderson. Together, they moved north, attacking Allen on the North Missouri Railroad near the present town of Moberly.[41]

The Federals actually had nothing in the area that could have handled such concentrations of what were usually small groups of partisans. Confederate sympathizers informed the guerrillas of the units at Sturgeon, Mexico, Columbia, and Paris. Major A. V. E. Johnston's three companies of the new Thirty-ninth Missouri—some in service hardly a week—gathered a collection of "old brood-mares and plow-horses, with some indifferent mules" and set off in a painfully slow pursuit as Anderson's men galloped away. The guerrillas moved up Young's Creek toward Centralia, a village founded by Democratic congressman James S. Rollins, among others. Its dozen buildings included two hotels, a few stores, the school, and the depot.[42]

Tuesday morning, September 27, a farmer arrived at Centralia warning of a large guerrilla force gathering nearby, predicting that "Hell will be to pay in this country, now!"[43] Shortly after, Anderson and eighty men approached the town from the southeast. They looted every house and pillaged the depot where they found a barrel of whiskey to ease their rounds. At about 11 a.m., the stagecoach from Columbia rolled into town and right into the arms of the guerrillas. The passengers included Sheriff James Waugh and Congressman Rollins on his way to the Democratic district convention at Mexico, but they gave their names simply as "Mr. Smith" and "Mr. Johnson" and bluffed their way into the background, escaping with mere robbery.

The train arrived in the middle of this. As the engineer saw the situation in town, he began to slow with the intention of reversing back to Mexico, but, when he remembered the gravel train not far behind him, decided to attempt to run through the town full throttle. The guerrillas opened fire and threw ties and other debris onto the track, forcing the locomotive to a screeching halt. Arch Clement then jumped aboard and warned the two dozen uniformed men to surrender. Unarmed except for two cavalrymen with their revolvers, the soldiers surrendered and the guerrillas began robbing the 125 other passengers. Afterward, they robbed and stripped the uniformed men, including a civilian in a blue blouse and kepi, who was also a German and "thought to be a Jew." Anderson moved them into line south of the tracks. "What are you going to do with the fellows?" asked Clement. "Parole them, of course," answered Anderson. About two dozen guerrillas then opened fire on the unarmed and helpless men. One took five bullets, but still managed to knock his assailants aside and crawl under the railway platform before his assailants dragged him out and finished him with a shot to the head. The guerrillas torched the depot and ordered the engineer to start the train down the track. He complied but managed to save the locomotive by setting the pumps and lowering the fire to where it would run out of steam in a couple of miles.

By then, somebody had told the guerrillas that Congressman Rollins and Sheriff Waugh were in town. To find them, Anderson soon began terrorizing what was left of the population, but the two men remained hidden until the guerrillas left the town. Only a year before, Rollins had scoffed at the idea of any serious threat to Unionism in the state, as a mere political ploy by the

Radicals, but he would be neither the first nor the last forced to rethink their assumptions by the military campaign.

At 3 p.m., Major Johnson and his men finally arrived at Centralia to find the guerrillas gone. Later Confederate apologia told of their swearing vengeance against the entire town and of a beautiful girl who pleaded with Johnson not to pursue the guerrillas, but the people who were there only recalled his disbelief that hundreds of the enemy lurked in the woods south of town. Certain that guerrillas would not operate in such numbers, Johnson left a detachment in the town, and took two full companies in search of Anderson's men. Leaving thirty or more of his men to hold the horses, Johnson took about ninety forward with fixed bayonets on their single-shot muzzle loaders against what he did not realize was a far better armed and mounted force three or four times the size of his force. At about a hundred yards, the mounted guerrillas charged, their revolvers repeatedly blazing against the Federal force.

The contemporary press called it "the most atrocious affair since the massacre at Lawrence," while a local chronicler described it as "the wildest and the most merciless, and in proportion to the number of the force vanquished, the most destructive of human life" in the war. Few of those in Johnson's line and only some holding the horses got away. Anderson's guerrillas lost three dead, one mortally wounded, three seriously and several slightly wounded, but they butchered 108 of the Union soldiers. The *Louisville Daily Journal* reported "most were shot through the head, then scalped, bayonets thrust through them, their ears and noses cut off and thrust into their mouths." Other accounts describe bodies stripped, several scalped, and one "mutilated in a revolting manner not to be described," his privates severed and placed in his mouth. Those not savaging the dead and wounded rode into town, where they bullied and assaulted civilians, killing at least one local Confederate sympathizer.[44]

What befell Johnson and his men demonstrated how far the war had grown beyond the question of how the southern states should respond to the 1860 elections. In the wake of the massacre secessionists across the state had to brace for the retaliations it invited. Some, along the Iron Mountain Railroad, were "said to be selling their property and taking to the bush, fearing that the outrages of Anderson's gang of guerrillas will be avenged."[45]

So ended the first grand days for the "liberation" of Missouri.

In a large sense, the campaign fundamentally reshaped the terrain of war. The detonation of the magazine at Fort Davidson literally remade the field over which the Napoleonic ranks had moved so splendidly. The explosion had covered many of the dead and wounded near the fort, and the pragmatic Confederates left "many buried where they fell." In the end, "all down the Valley, in many a nook and corner and out-of-the-way place are the bones of heros [*sic*], forgotten even by friends."[46] The civilians of Potosi or the mutilated bodies of Centralia changed the contours of the conflict even more fundamentally.

Some certainly resisted this. Jeff Thompson had reached Pilot Knob just as the assaults were beginning. Once there, he fell in with Governor Thomas C. Reynolds, who shared a similar approach to these problems. Through the campaign, Thompson "made speeches to many of the Regiments, begging them to restrain themselves both in pilfering and murdering prisoners, for their own sakes." Later, as the ranking officer taking a town, he struggled valiantly to keep his men in order, but found the very idea "something so new to most of the soldiers, that their officers could not control them by ordinary means."[47] It was less a matter that the perpetrators of Potosi or Centralia disagreed with Thompson than that they just did not even recognize his concerns. Then, too, the war in Missouri never bore much resemblance to the gentlemen's affair that opened in the east three years before, which is not to say that some tried to fight the war by such rules.

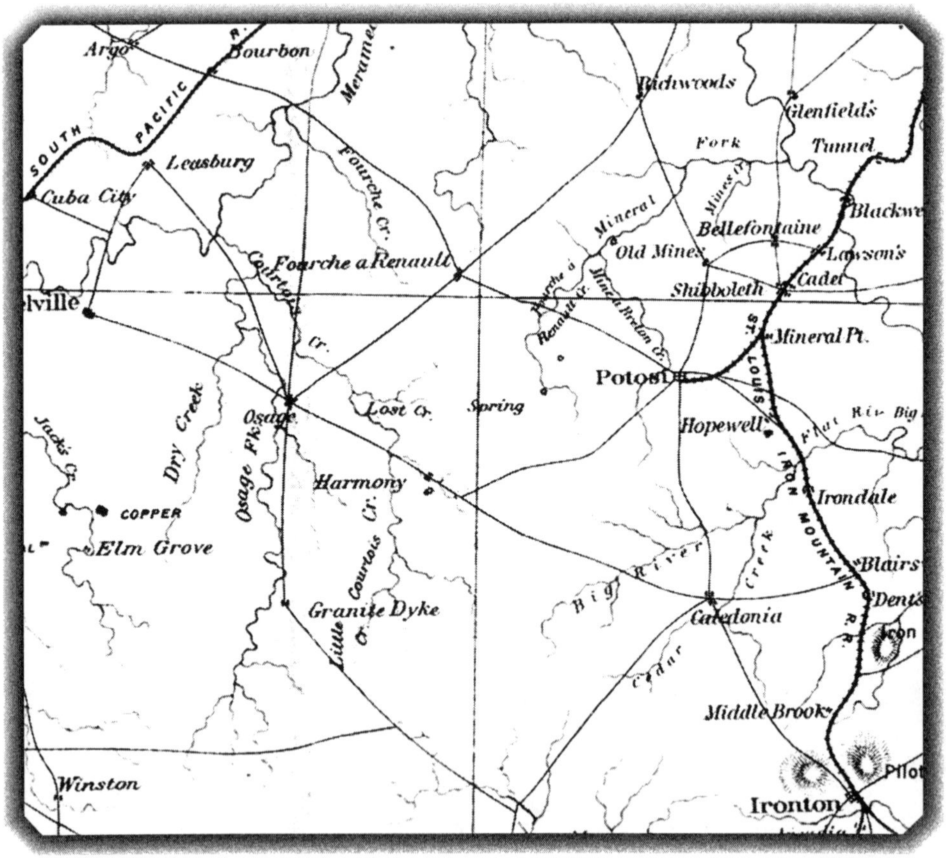

Detail from *The War of the Rebellion: A Compilation of the Official Records of the Union and Confederate Armies*

3

Sounding the Alarm

The Road to Rolla

Late Thursday, September 29, the engineer George Curry rolled his locomotive into Pacific west of St. Louis with unmistakable news from an unexpected direction. His trip had taken hours longer than it should have, with a particularly harrowing stop to restore the track where the Confederates had removed half a dozen rails. During these makeshift repairs, a lost second lieutenant separated from General Thomas Ewing's force boarded the train. As they neared Sullivan, they passed an estimated four hundred mounted Confederates riding toward St. Louis through the nearby woods. Gambling that this was only the advance and that the track ahead remained intact, Curry had poured on the steam and cannonballed past them.[1] Once at Pacific, the crew and passengers hurried to the telegraph office to wire Federal headquarters that Confederate general Sterling Price, indeed, brought an unexpectedly massive army in the state and that it seemed to be heading right for St. Louis.

General Thomas Ewing and his little force had abandoned the safety of Fort Davidson before it became a death trap. They hoped that Price's Confederates had better things to do than pursue them cross country toward the Federal base at Rolla. Nevertheless, both sides found themselves in a bizarre cat-and-mouse chase, stumbling through the dark over the rugged Ozark terrain. In the end, Ewing and the Unionist survivors found themselves again pinned down, this time at a little train station on the southwestern branch of the Pacific Railroad.

The Flight

The eruption of Fort Davidson's magazine briefly illuminated Wednesday's predawn skies before fading into an even more intense darkness. The Federals groped their way up the road toward Potosi in hopes of making a relatively short dash to join General Andrew J. Smith's infantry at Mineral Point. None of the twenty men in Captain Hiram A. Rice's advance knew the way, so Captain Patrick F. Lonergan sent forward a local man, James A. Shields of the Third MSM Cavalry, to pilot them.[2] Captain Charles S. Hills of the Tenth Kansas, one of Ewing's acting aides-de-camp, also rode near the head of the column.

After a hard march through the night and into the early morning, they reached Caledonia, only twelve miles short of Potosi, itself only a few miles west of Mineral Point. There, Ewing's advance encountered a Confederate patrol, killing one, wounding another and shooting the horse from under a third. Upon hearing the gunfire, Ewing galloped into town to find Hills's men trying to question a taciturn prisoner. Iowa captain William Campbell saw they had no time to waste and it was, after all, Missouri, so he sent some enlisted men to get a rope and began tying the noose in it as he repeated the question. The prisoner immediately identified himself as one of several thousand of General Jo Shelby's cavalrymen on their way south to rejoin Price for a concerted assault on Fort Davidson.[3]

The revelation chilled them more deeply than the wet autumn night. Between them and St. Louis stood not Smith's Federal infantry but a Confederate cavalry division. "If you want to fight, there's the road," Campbell told Ewing pointing north. "If not we must take some other road, and that quickly." Their only real option ran west toward Rolla and the hope that Price's army would not be distracted by their escape. As more local civilians joined the column, one of them pointed out the way, and the ragged line slipped through Caledonia and up the side road toward the northwest.[4]

To the Confederate commanders, Ewing's force seemed to have vanished into the fog of war. Shelby had told the wives of his prisoners from Potosi that they would parole the prisoners; however, his men subsequently took the unfed prisoners on a miserable twelve-mile forced march through the rain. They allowed some to retrieve partly eaten apples that had been stolen, tasted, and discarded by their guards. Shelby and his staff did not expect Ewing's men to be coming north from Fort Davidson because they never seem to have heard the explosion of the magazine. For whatever reason, Shelby's exhausted and wet troops formed a battle line up the road from Caledonia waiting from 10:30 to 2:30 for the main body of Price's army to drive the Federals north into their position.[5]

Meanwhile, south of Caledonia, General John S. Marmaduke's division waited for Shelby's southbound march to turn the Federals back their direction. Back at Pilot Knob, their unexpected victory left Price's army generally stunned. Dr. William McPheeters and other officers made courtesy calls on Dr. Seymour Carpenter, telling him that "they would be dining in St. Louis." Carpenter found Major James Wilson wounded, coatless, and barefoot among the Federal prisoners. Confederate general Jeff Thompson had ridden over to reassure

Wilson and the prisoners that they were in the hands of Confederate regulars, but other Confederates conveyed the impression to Wilson that he would be killed. Confederates boasted of having made "a complete smash of the records and arrangements for Lincoln's draft." While the battle had inflicted as much as $25,000 in damages to the iron works, Price's men accounted for most of the $50,000 to $60,000 looted from the stores. With a flourish, the general had ordered captured flour and other provisions "distributed among the women and children," but, when he rode off, his men carted off the booty for themselves.[6] Their desire to eat their fill may have been a factor in delaying well into the afternoon the pursuit of Ewing by Price and Marmaduke.

Meanwhile, Ewing's bone-weary footsore column slogged on through the rest of Wednesday. At some point, Captain Henry B. Milks and the mounted volunteers who had exploded the fort's magazine caught up with them. Ewing appointed him "chief of cavalry" and assigned him to organize a rear guard that would also keep as tight as possible the sleepless ranks of the dismounted soldiers, militia, and refugees.[7] Still, nothing could keep exhausted stragglers from dropping out of the ranks, and some surely decided that they stood a better chance leaving a smaller trail by slipping off into the woods.

Ewing did not call a stop until they climbed into Webster, also called Palmer, a tiny village "nestled under the hills," some thirty miles from Fort Davidson. Many collapsed along the road into a fitful sleep "with our muskets in hand." Captain William V. Lucas recalled ravenously tearing into his hardtack and bacon, "the first food we had had in about thirty hours." The younger and more adventurous negotiated the steep hill to the northwest in search of food. One found "the best cream there that he had ever tasted," while others "shot down the first cattle in the vicinity," variously remembered as fat yearlings or "some poor old cows," the men roasting the meat on "ramrods held in the blaze of our camp-fires." Through the night, stragglers tumbled into the encampment, as did several women claiming to be on their way back home toward Caledonia. Ewing indulged them, apparently oblivious to the likelihood that they would pass on any information to the Confederates, though his intentions later became apparent.[8] Shortly after the women left for Caledonia, Ewing called his officers together.

A civilian named Wingo offered escapees from Fort Davidson a vital new option. If mounted Confederates pursued them, Ewing's men would have to cover fifty-five miles of gently rolling terrain and open country to reach Rolla. Wingo, however, offered to lead them through over some thirty-five miles of back roads and trails northwest to Leasburg, Harrison Station on the branch of the Pacific Railroad. There, they might be reinforced by Colonel Isaac S. Warmouth's Sixty-third EMM, and would have the options of moving up or down the tracks to St. Louis or Rolla, perhaps even by train. This route generally followed the ridgelines between and adjacent to the Huzzah and Courtois Creeks, which meandered through deep walled valleys toward the north, converging just about a mile before flowing into the Meramec River. The retreating column would be vulnerable where they periodically plunged into those valleys and over several treacherous and bone-chilling fords, but most of the terrain was such as to deny the Confederate the use of their larger numbers. However, to make sure Rosecrans would get news of the invasion's scale, Ewing sent the trusted Captain Hills north into the pitch-black woods with orders to reach the railroad and follow it northeast toward St. Louis.[9]

Between midnight and 1 a.m., Ewing roused his exhausted column from a well-earned sleep. Some three miles back down the road, Sergeant Azariah Martin again did picket duty. After having been fed by a generous local family, they had waited for their relief. Around midnight, Martin recalled, they decided that something had gone wrong and trudged back up the ridge to town, where they "found the last of our men marching out."[10] They brought up the rear of an exhausted line of soldiers, militia, and civilians on a trek already epic in its misery.

Survivors recalled a drizzling rain through most of the overcast night and the thick growth of forest shrouding them in even deeper darkness. Those at the head of the column needed a lantern to find their way and left short candles or small fires to keep others on the course, even using a bugle when the rain fell too intensely for fires. Soldiers carried their weapons "with the locks under their armpits to keep the priming dry." In the twists and turns, most lost all sense of direction and time. The trail tumbled them into the valleys and plunged them through cold rain-swollen fords. The shorter marchers sometimes found themselves up to their arms, and the worst crossings required holding hands or linking arms to form a human chain. At one such ford, they lost control of a cannon and abandoned it. Repeated immersions shrunk shoes, swelled feet, and strained muscles painfully. Those with mounts kept the column moving by loaning their mounts for long stretches to the worst sufferers. Ewing had ordered his men not to stop until daylight, but straggling became such a problem that the column halted regularly, and participants caught short naps where they could. After several hours put them eight or nine miles beyond Palmer, Ewing called a long rest stop. The soldiers and refugees foraged as best they could in the dark, at least one group feasting on a turnip patch near the road.[11]

Meanwhile, Shelby's Confederates did not set off in immediate pursuit of Ewing. Rather, they countermarched from Caledonia to spend much of Wednesday around Potosi and Mineral Point, where telegraph operator Louisa Volker and her sister remained behind to protect their father's house as best they could. Most of the men there had long fled the kind of Confederate conscription imposed at Potosi, but Volker hid all evidence of her employment, slipped a pistol in her pocket, and waited. The Confederates arrived and burned the depot, the tank, and the engine house, and they plundered the Volker home of its blankets, clothes, and food. Not until 5 p.m. did the last of Shelby's men leave, taking the road west from Potosi. Volker noted that they killed several blacks, leaving three of the bodies "where they fell until the hogs had nearly devoured them."[12]

Marmaduke's division set off late Wednesday afternoon, pursuing the trail directly from Caledonia to Palmer. Based on the erroneous belief that the Federals camped at Palmer—perhaps passed on by the Caledonia ladies—the Confederates lost more time in a pointless effort to surround the town. Finding no Federals there, Marmaduke's men took the most obvious escape route, the road to Rolla.[13] Only later did they backtrack and catch the scent.

Even Palmer was not too small to have victims. Captain Andrew J. Harris had led the local men in Warmouth's Sixty-third EMM. He had sent Lieutenant Joshua Mason to get supplies at Fort Davidson, from which he had returned as part of Ewing's column. Probably in hopes of getting the local people out of the area to safety, Harris remained behind. Marmaduke's men captured them along with Sergeant David C. Mason, the North Carolinian Solomon Gilliam, and two others, killing the lot of them. A local physician, recalling the murders, noted that Mason had earlier been a member of Wilson's regiment "and you know them Cossacks had it in for the 3 M.S.M. Cav." A woman a mile and a half east of the village reported the rebel shooting of a Federal straggler around 1 p.m., the man lingering into the night before dying, after which "we wimon of the neighborhood buried him nere where he fell."[14]

At the main body of the Unionists, Ewing had sent mounted volunteers to retrace their steps back to Palmer. The last anyone had seen of his hand-grip with documents that might be useful to the rebels had been on an artillery caisson back at the village. Milks sent Corporal William H. Cameron with ten volunteers from his Third MSM Cavalry. The squad stashed their cumbersome Austrian rifles near a roadside tree, hurried back up the trail, and encountered three or four mounted men. Cameron's men chased them into the darkness until they rode into a line of mounted figures, "about 16 or 20 strong." The man on their left stepped forward and, as one corporal questioned him, Sergeant James C. Steakley realized they were talking to Price's scouts and tried desperately to get Cameron's attention. At this point a mounted civilian with the Confederates blurted that they were rebels holding him prisoner and spurred his horse past the astonished bluecoats, who wheeled to follow him. Half a century later, Steakley wondered whether the rifles they had left in the woods were still there, "for when we came back we had no time to stop or even to think of them."[15]

The people in Ewing's column—then more than twelve miles from Palmer—looked up when a lone rider, perhaps the civilian who had just escaped them, galloped past the Federal ranks. "The Rebels are coming," he shouted as he galloped on. When Cameron's squad rejoined the column, Milks and Lieutenant Erich Pape formed an impromptu rear guard of sixty-one available horsemen. Hoping to scatter the Confederate reconnaissance before it reached the column, the Federals charged through them, blazing away with their revolvers and causing as much confusion as they could before returning. Milks reported that sixty of the sixty-one returned and the missing man turning up later that day, but Steakley noted that Lewis Lincoln, the civilian brother of one of the militiamen, had participated in the action and fell in the skirmish.[16] For those making the reports, though, civilians did not enter into the count.

Accounts of what happened on that long trudge from Palmer to Leasburg are very sparse and muddled. Much of it took place in the dark and over rugged ground. The dense woods and narrow road made it difficult for the Confederates to deploy enough men for an effective attack or for the Federals to organize a defense if they had done so. What fighting took place often involved only parts of the forces involved, and writers in different parts of the column may or may not have been involved in skirmishing at any point. Worse, when the fighting began, it seemed almost constant. Certainly, though no serious assaults began until the column dipped into the valley to cross the Courtois Creek and, then, the Meramec River.

At that point, overworked, hungry, and exhausted muscles plunged into thigh-deep chilling waters with some strong currents. Colonel Thomas Fletcher had stopped there to use his personal mount to lead the most sickly and feeble of the enlisted men across; Private James Brown wrote, "All honor to all such officers of any rank." After he crossed, Campbell turned back to see "a long, steep hill cut on the south side of the ridge, with a deep gorge or ravine to our left; passed over a small stream skirted with small timber." The road turned west along the valley with the farm on the right as it turned up "a low range of hills to the north west."[17] Then he heard the firing behind him and knew that the Confederates were trying to press the mounted rear guard as it descended into the valley.

Campbell turned to Captain William C. Montgomery of the artillery and said, "We have got to fight here or they will flank us." Montgomery hurried his cannon into position on the ridge as Campbell organized his infantrymen into a rear guard. "Will I give them a broadside?" asked Montgomery. "No, Captain," replied Campbell, "one gun at a time and give them 'hell' and they will give us a wider berth." The Federal fired "a dozen or so" shells at the unprotected mounted Confederates attempting to follow the narrow route into the valley. This toppled quite a number of rebels with their mounts into the gorge before them and caused a "wild panic on that hill for a short time." This encounter likely inspired the recollections of John M. Cooper of the MSM Cavalry: "we give them hale clumba" with the Union guns. When they no longer saw an enemy in sight, they limbered the guns and moved on.[18] The Confederates avoided renewing the attack where the terrain funneled them, which allowed the Federals to hurry on, making it to the bluffs on the far side of the Meramec River.

From these bluffs, the horrified Federals watched from the relatively open ground as their pursuers emerged from the river valley and reformed. Confederate colonel Robert Lawther's Tenth Missouri Cavalry led this, the strongest attack thus far, folding Milks's rear guard back into the column, later claiming to have captured twenty-five, killed two, and to have lost only one killed and two wounded. A anonymous participant wrote that it nearly "stampeded" the Federals, some of whom agreed that, for the first time, the column assumed a "mob feature" as "refugees—men, women, and children, white and black" broke into a panicked and undirected flight that delayed the movement of soldiers to the rear. Murphy seized officers, soldiers, and armed civilians and physically pushed them back into line. Milks later noted that his own efforts to calm the panic delayed his own entry into the fight. "The ball opened," he recalled, "before I had gone far."[19]

The Federal rear guard strengthened. Major Henry H. Williams, another of Ewing's aides-de-camp, sent three companies of the Third MSM Cavalry, the rest of the Forty-seventh Missouri, and Lieutenant Philip Smiley's section of the artillery unlimbered on the ridge. Nevertheless, Campbell recalled how new Confederate units—perhaps the first of Shelby's men—turned up proving to be "more aggressive, and began to crowd my skirmishers." As Smiley saw the Union reinforcements balking and falling back, he thought they were the Iowa skirmishers, so he pulled out his guns, leaving the skirmishers on their own. At this point, as Campbell described it, "the band of colored men came to our assistance, fifteen or twenty of them. Their leader said: 'Captain, where shall we take position?' Said I: 'You are brave men, form on my left.' They fought well, I will never forget them." Fortunately for them, the Confederates had seen the artillery move and did not expect to be greeted with such a concentration of fire. With the blacks on his left, Campbell folded the company on his right back at an angle and turned back the threat on both flanks. He then ordered an about-face, quick-time retreat of the rear guard, black and white, toward higher and more open ground and reformed. The Confederate advance once more hit another unexpectedly strong volley, after which "we about faced and made all haste" back to the main body of the rear guard some quarter of a mile back.[20]

There, Fletcher and Amos W. Maupin had stabilized the line of the Forty-seventh—with Private Brown among them—to the right and left, anchoring the position. Campbell and his men ran "past the two guns that had unlimbered while we were holding the eager cavalry back." As they "cleared the battery, both guns sent shells into their midst," and the Union artillerists worked their field-pieces "for all that was in them." Unable to bring their superior numbers to bear, the rebels quickly lost enthusiasm, but the available rear guard could not remain long without exposing the retreating column behind them in more open terrain to any enemy cavalry that might have gone around them via another ford. The Iowans watched as Smiley's guns "limbered up and passed us on a gallop, and we followed as fast as our wearied condition would permit."[21] This bought another few miles of peace for the column.

The most diligent efforts to unravel the details of these desperate encounters remain smudged, reflecting the blurred memory of those who felt "almost constantly engaged." Once they had crossed the Meramec, the Federals made their way north in rapid bursts with "occasional halts to rake the woods with grape and canister." The quicker rebel cavalry would easily overtake the Union column, but any Federal rear guard would have to keep on the move continually. "Six distinct charges of that kind were repulsed that day; whenever we drove them back, we limbered for the rear and went quick time." Fletcher, too, counted "half a dozen or more pretty severe skirmishes," in which the Federals admitted to having lost four killed and eight wounded, but had "emptied many saddles" and inflicted "considerable loss" among the Confederates riding into waiting Federal guns.[22] Again, the time they bought with these "seesaw tactics" depended entirely upon a timing that became increasingly problematic, and their success would be measured in only fractions of a mile unmolested closer to Leasburg and the railroad.

Certainly, by 3 p.m., it took the entire of Ewing's available fighting force to hold the Confederate onslaught. Separated from their company by the initial attack, Peter Schrumm and two other men rejoined it as it formed in a field to hold the rebels in the adjacent woods while the militia held the road and the Iowans its right. Although, all saw the vast numbers of rebels covering the landscape to the south less than a mile away, the Iowans advanced coolly "like Spartans of old" and "proved themselves all heroes." Meanwhile, two hundred yards to their front, Confederate colonel William Jeffers ignored his orders to advance, saying "I'll be damned if we'll charge them! They are all there in a nest." As the rebels balked, an exuberant Campbell shouted, "Damn them! We can whip them alone!"[23] After thwarting that last effort, the Federals again fell back quickly.

That engagement with Jeffers bought a respite. The column reached "a wide flat bushy ridge like what we call 'Flat Woods.'" Thereafter, the road followed this very gradually sloping ridge until it reached a moderate crest before rolling down into Leasburg. James W. Nations of the Fiftieth Missouri reported that, after this stand, "we were not further annoyed until late that evening, when within a mile or two of Leasburg." As Ewing's column crossed the crest of that low ridge and began the few miles down that long, modest slope to Leasburg, dusk already loomed. By then, Shelby had arrived and dispatched Colonel John Q. A. Burbridge's Fourth Missouri Cavalry and Lieutenant Colonel Robert C. Wood's battalion southwest to Cuba to destroy the railroad to Rolla.[24]

Leasburg

The residents of Leasburg probably heard the gunfire through the day, as it grew louder and closer. Their new village consisted of "probably a dozen little residences scattered over a square of about ten acres" with open fields and considerable brush beyond. Earlier known as Harrison Station, it renamed itself for Samuel Lea, the community's first merchant, postmaster, and innkeeper, as well as its first resident. Doubling as a depot, Lea's two-story frame hotel of probably ten rooms had "a platform extending to the track" south of the hotel and running through a deep cut, from five to fifteen feet as you continued east. As the embattled Federals came into view several miles south of town, small detachments led by Lieutenants Warren C. Shattuck and James A. Blain arrived at different times to locate some military authority only to find that Warmouth's EMM had gone to Rolla.[25]

To the south, Ewing's column faced its greatest danger "just at dark and within a mile of Leasburg." Shelby's division, which had taken the road west from Potosi rather than from Caledonia, had likely provided those "new rebels" the Federals began encountering just after they crossed the Meramec River, but it seems to have borne the brunt of the attack before Leasburg. Private John M. Cooper of the Third MSM Cavalry recalled that a large number of newly arrived horsemen "made a valiant charge on us," being a "last attempt to ride us down." It mortally wounded Lieutenant James Braden and severely wounded color-bearer E. H. Tyler. Although "the flag fell to the ground" briefly, the Federals held their own until the "darkness put an end to the struggle." Cooper, Henry Gains, George Rhoads, and others found themselves "surrounded by the rebels and taken we was stripped of our boots and clows and you bet they got our pocket bucks the first think." Shortly afterward, though, the Confederates bedded down and Cooper and Gains, watching their guard fall asleep, lit out into the woods, where they evaded recapture.[26]

Blain, in charge of the men at Leasburg, listened as the sounds of the day's closing skirmishes rattled to the south and watched as small groups from the column trudged into Leasburg. In hindsight, the "many hatless and without arms" coming into the town likely fled the column for fear of its being overwhelmed. These panicked sources probably informed Blain that the Confederates had broken Ewing's line and captured the artillery. As if to confirm this, Blain remembered that "a party of the enemy charged into the place but did not see us." Despairing, he thought there was little more his few men could do and decided they should ride due north toward Hermann on the Missouri River, "the nearest post that we believed we could find safety." However, about the time Blain's men left town, so did the rebel scouts, and the ever-reliable Major David Murphy turned up with another Union advance party.[27]

Murphy quickly recognized the potential of the railroad cut. Under his supervision, the men began seizing cordwood and railroad ties to transform the cut into a strong defensive line. If they had only a hundred rounds when they left Pilot Knob, the artillery must have been nearly out of ammunition. Still, they wheeled two cannons into position with support about a hundred feet south of the railroad in "an old long frame building open partly on one side, and at one end, which appeared as if it had been a cattle shed." The rest of the artillery—possibly with very little or nothing to fire—parked at the northeast corner of the village, ostensibly protecting their left flank.[28] What filed into Leasburg may have been as little as six hundred.

Within minutes, a train on its way from St. Louis "pulled into the cut and stopped." It included "two car-loads hard tack" and two of ammunition, but Ewing feared allowing it to continue would risk its capture by the Confederates. Murphy recalled that the thirty-one-year-old engineer, George C. Curry—also an enrollee in the Twenty-third EMM—understood the significance of the situation immediately. He offered the grateful Ewing a chance to get the particulars of the invasion through to St. Louis, and wasted no time, backing his locomotive into a siding and uncoupling the eight or nine cars. These included "two car-loads of hard tack" and two of ammunition and at least one passenger car that disgorged its contents safely into the cellar of a nearby store.[29] Curry's train then barreled off back northeast toward St. Louis.

Almost immediately another train pulled into the station. Ewing quickly commandeered it, uncoupled the cars, and sent a group of picked men to the locomotive to scout the tracks toward Rolla, in the hopes of reaching the headquarters there and returning with reinforcements. In a short while, though, the train steamed back into town with the news that the rebels had already seized the next station. Surveyed only seven years before as the tracks extended through the highlands of Crawford County, Cuba had contributed troops to both armies. Here, too, though Shelby's Confederates had gone beyond destroying railroad property to loot the town's store and the home of Stephen Sweetin, an officer of the Sixty-third EMM. The train-bound Union scouts had gotten close enough to see the flames in the night before deciding to come back. They then steamed back toward St. Louis, but found that, in the short while since Curry's locomotive had gotten through, the next station that direction, Bourbon—little more than the depot and a log cabin—had suffered a similar fate.[30] The locomotive chugged back into Leasburg to share the fate of its disappointed soldiers and refugees.

Although the rain continued, Ewing's men made the most of their position at Leasburg. He sent a number of couriers, including officers such as Lieutenant Colonel Maupin, to get word to Rosecrans. Those who stayed, however, at least had cover and shelter and were not on the move. They also tapped into the cargo they found on the cars, including "ammunition, hardtack, bacon, picks, shovels and several barrels of whiskey." In the absence of a Confederate attack, most worked through the night to improve the defenses and making emplacements for two pieces of artillery. Thanks to the train cars, each of the defenders now had "piles of cartridges" at the ready.[31]

Even in the darkness, the men would need those cartridges. Scouts reported the "whole force of the enemy" gathering south of the town, though they actually faced parts of Marmaduke's and Shelby's divisions. Captain Lonergan sent about two hundred men into a large two-story log structure about six hundred feet to the front of the cut, but Captain Morgan Mace found it indefensible and pulled them back to the cut. At about 9 p.m., "a sort of Goliath" approached a flag of truce to challenge any Federal officer to single combat, but Ewing sent him packing before he got a good look at the works. On the far left, the corporal of the guard neglected to send new pickets to replace a black civilian and Azariah Martin, who began fretting when the black man began started shouting his protests, and called out himself, "I guess somebody had better relieve the nigger!" A muzzle flashed not fifteen feet away with a voice promising, "Damn you. We'll relieve you and the nigger, too!" The two pickets stumbled back through the darkness, Martin falling and playing dead as the Confederates "ran right over me" and a bullet struck the sole or heel of his boot, jerking his foot sharply. Brown recalled this dash on the works as "sometime soon after this spiteful firing on our big kitchen fire."[32] In fact, the Federals probably fared far better than the hungry Confederates out in the woods and fields.

Exhausted, though they were, Ewing's men remained "as determined as ever not to be captured." Schrumm later claimed that they had been "promised that if we got to Leasburg, we should get on a train and go to Rolla." As the hour grew later, Federals tried packing themselves onto the freight train. Around midnight, their noisy efforts to fit the horses aroused the officers inside the hotel. "Boys," said Ewing, "for God's sake get back to your places behind the defenses, or we are likely to be massacred." Disappointed, the men filed out to spend another "short night" in search of sleep.[33]

Friday morning, the town's first schoolteacher—also Leasburg's first *bona fide* abolitionist—woke to hear the Confederates outside asking where he lived. Moses Harmon had cut his foot with an axe while a child, and been repeatedly turned down for Federal military service, though he had helped raise the first Union regiment at Rolla. A former student at Arcadia, he become a Methodist preacher with radical views on labor, land, and women's rights as well as slavery. His presence had long annoyed the local secessionists, who happily planned to settle old scores by having him "subscripted" into Price's army. However, his family covered for Harmon, who slipped away into hiding.[34]

In midmorning, the Confederates marched into position "along the rising ground in full view and safe distance of us." Captain William M. Price rode toward the cut with another officer on foot and an enlisted man with a flag of truce. Ewing sent Lieutenant Charles H. Cummings with a similar escort through "the gateway besides the hotel" to stop the Confederates about 150 yards from the Federal defenses and hear its demand for the surrender. Later, Confederate major William C. Kelley confirmed to Union sergeant Samuel B. Rowe that this had been no more than a ruse to get a look at the defenses. After they returned and spoke to Marmaduke and Shelby, the latter decided that the losses storming the position would gain little, particularly since Ewing's men "would probably not be an active factor in further resisting the raid." Instead, they decided to "leave a small force to make a show of siege, and go on and join Price's column." One account says that Federal officers seriously considered surrender, but Ewing's response, in the end, was to raise "Old Glory" over the railroad cut. They had lost the post flag at Pilot Knob, so he told one of the Iowa officers to get their regimental colors and "Put up your old flag!" Amid the cheering, the artillerymen fired a few rounds until Ewing, still concerned about ammunition, ordered them to wait for a target.[35] Few seriously doubted that they would soon have one.

Tensions built through Friday. Part of the Forty-seventh Missouri returned to that "loghouse" south of the cut with fence rails stripped from a nearby potato patch to seal the worst gaps between the logs, and settled in. Back at the patch, a "large elderly man" from town helped the Unionists butcher a pig killed in the previous night's shooting, but an alarm sent them running back to the cover of the cut, where an exhausted young soldier, half-asleep on his musket, saw an unidentified man bounding toward him and mortally wounded the citizen. There could have been more accidents like this, had not Ewing dumped the whiskey found on the train alongside the tracks. Out of sight of the officers, some filled their canteens from the puddles that collected, while others actually stretched on the ground and drank out of the horse tracks. One, who reportedly had too much and showed himself too often, got a bullet in the forehead. However, an Irish soldier told a German that he "would rather live an' lick Price than to have a whole bar'l, so I would."[36]

On Friday afternoon, Murphy called a break in the work on the fortifications to introduce Mrs. Lea and others from the town. They presented and officially raised a new flag, replacing the Iowa colors and providing the veterans of Fort Davidson once more with a common banner. Shortly after, a lost party of rebel couriers rode to within one hundred yards of the cut. "We are General Marmaduke's men," they called; "Who are you?" Murphy replied by inviting them into the works, but the men continued to inquire who held the cut until the Union adjutant asked whether their own self-identification as Marmaduke's men might be "a Yankee trick." With both sides calling each other barefaced liars, the rebels meandered off.[37] Friday passed without the expected assault.

Still worried about a night attack, Ewing asked Campbell for a volunteer to sneak out between the lines and torch "two large barns with many hay-stacks near them," which would illuminate any enemy advance. As the officers cautioned the men to fire at nothing in front until ordered, Corporal Earl J. Lansom left instructions about the care of his wife and child should he not return. He then stripped to his pants, shirt, and stockings "and vaulting from the rifle pits, disappeared in the darkness." After half an hour, Ewing and other officers waiting hopefully saw a light in the upper part of one of the barns followed by the sound of musketry. Then, "through the mellow light which had begun to fall around us came bounding the intrepid corporal." Gasping for air, Lansom tumbled into the cut. He joined the other Federals, who had not slept well for nearly a week, and passed yet another nervous night aggravated by "quite a heavy rain."[38]

Rolla

Back in St. Louis, the news that Price's army was advancing their way put headquarters into something of a quiet frenzy of denial. On Wednesday, Rosecrans still spoke of an enemy concentrated at Fredericktown. He admitted Price's presence in a Thursday night telegraph to General Samuel R. Curtis, but deflected its importance with the hopeful delusion that "the rebels will go to Rolla."[39] In short, it had taken ten days to convince Rosecrans of the invasion's scale, but he still could not pinpoint that invading army to within a hundred miles nor say anything reliable about their intentions.

Yet, it seems hard to imagine that Rosecrans actually believed Price would move on Rolla, given his correspondence with Brigadier General John McNeil, commanding the district there. On Wednesday, Rosecrans noted that sparse rains had left the Gasconade "almost a dry river" and the upper Osage "merely a succession of pools," which left almost nothing between the Confederates and Rolla. However, three-quarters of McNeil's little force consisted of 1,200 green recruits and 300 of the Sixty-third EMM in which he had little confidence. Colonel Albert Sigel of the Fifth MSM Cavalry supervised civilians as well as soldiers working on Major Charles Biehle's Fort Wyman and the Star Fort under Captain William Dette, a German born architect, both officers being from the First MSM Infantry. At a minimum, McNeil needed several hundred to garrison Salem, Steelville, and Waynesville, and fortifying Rolla could easily consume everything that was left, and Sigel ordered those outposts not to attempt to hold out against a large force but to "annoy them as much as possible in your retreat" toward Rolla. Earlier Rosecrans had wanted McNeil to protect the southwestern branch of the Pacific Railroad as far as the Moselle bridge near Pacific. McNeil pointed out that the EMM in Franklin and Gasconade Counties could cover that part of the line easier, adding that they had to be in better shape than the Sixty-third EMM.[40] Rosecrans, however, had remained concerned about the emancipationist politics of the militia in Franklin and Gasconade Counties, and chosen to leave them disorganized for a year.

Brigadier General John Benjamin Sanborn of the District of Southwest Missouri at Springfield responded to the rumored threat on Rolla with remarkably good sense. On Tuesday, Sanborn had left a small garrison, mostly EMM, to protect Springfield and set off up the Wire Road. The passing of 1,500 of his available cavalry seemed so large a movement that slaves along one part of the road wondered whether the soldiers would drain their spring by filling their canteen. When Sanborn's men arrived, they passed through McNeil's lines and continued toward the northeast, where reportedly large bodies of Confederates had turned up at Waynesville and Mount Vernon. At 1 a.m. Saturday, a resident of Cuba brought Sanborn's men a "verbal message from General Ewing" that put the rescue effort in operation. Sanborn sent forward detachments of the Second Arkansas Cavalry and the Seventh Provisional EMM to support a probe by a large new regiment of Illinois cavalry.[41]

Colonel John Lourie Beveridge of the Seventeenth Illinois Cavalry got orders from McNeil to relieve the "closely beleaguered" force at Leasburg. The New York–born Evanston lawyer had risen to command of the Eighth Illinois Cavalry at Gettysburg where it had helped to secure the "high ground" on the first day essential for Union victory in the next two days.[42] A man of considerable nerve, Beveridge had detachments of his new regiment scouting east of Rolla as far as St. James and Steelville.

The desperation of the soldiers and civilians at Leasburg simmered into Saturday morning, the first day of October. At about noon, Captain Milks shouted from the observation post on the roof of the hotel, "Troops approaching from the north!" For an instant, the battered survivors of the ordeal must have held their collective breath for news of its fate. Then Milks called down, "They carry the stars and stripes!" The exhausted and filthy defenders of the makeshift fort below suddenly realized that they had survived the ordeal. An Iowan recalled that they "cheered, clasped one another in their arms, shook hands, leaped about and genuinely acted like crazy men."[43]

As the flag of the Seventeenth Illinois Cavalry came into clear view, Lucas broke into song:

Yes, we'll rally 'round the flag, boys!
We'll rally once again!
Shouting the battle cry of freedom!

The rest of the little post at Leasburg, soldier and civilian, hoarsely shouted the refrain of a battle cry that had never conveyed greater meaning.[44]

Some of Beveridge's horsemen may have tried to catch the spirit with three rousing Illinois cheers, but most were simply too exhausted. They had forsaken food and sleep to reach Leasburg, and their first words as they tumbled from their mounts were requests for rations. After a brief repast, the cavalrymen, joined by some of the Third MSM, scoured the countryside and found "only a few stragglers," which could only have meant that the rebel army had moved up the tracks toward St. Louis.[45] Despite the joy of having survived, those with families and homes in the apparent path of the invasion had new cause for worry.

The Illinois Cavalry escorted the veterans of Pilot Knob and Leasburg into Sanborn's lines at Knob View. There, they mingled with a detachment of the Second Arkansas Cavalry, a number of whom had also had Confederate service. Then, Ewing's infantry boarded a train at St. James for Rolla while the rest marched to safety, even as Sanborn's horsemen continued northeast to repair the track at Cuba, retrieve the train stranded at Leasburg, and find the actual whereabouts of the Confederates.[46]

After the war, Confederates frankly acknowledged the courageous determination of the Unionists in the Arcadia Valley, the escape from Fort Davidson, the retreat to Leasburg, and the resistance there. Years later, Marmaduke asked Lucas how many Federals they had been fighting. When the latter guessed that the Confederates had engaged "less than five hundred," Marmaduke muttered that it "seems impossible" because Ewing had "traveled as fast as cavalry and fought with such confidence that I believed he had at least two thousand." Shelby later concurred that Ewing's read guard had been "the finest body of men for that work I ever saw." He had thought the Union column generally had "3,000 to 4,000 men." In his mind, only the presence of larger numbers could have justified such a "bold dash in the face of so large an army as confronted him."[47]

The Confederates themselves inspired the heroic determination of Ewing's command, by making surrender an unthinkably risky option. From General Ewing through Sergeant Martin to the lowliest privates—and to the civilians, black and white—Unionists knew that an indeterminate portion of them simply would not survive capture by the Confederates. The justifications for such concerns littered the roadsides, fields, and town squares from Patterson to Potosi to Palmer to Centralia.

The losses of the chase to Leasburg and the skirmishing there blurred into those of Pilot Knob. Press accounts reported "all the artillery" made it, although participants talked of losing one cannon at a deep ford. Even the highest estimate of Federal casualties are that the missing amounted to "about 300, mostly prisoners," and the official account mentioned only eighty-nine casualties. "We think it was something over this," wrote one anonymous participant. McNeil's estimate that Ewing brought into his lines 700 probably included civilian refugees, including the train passengers discharged at Leasburg, while Lucas's figure of 500 probably reflected military effectives. Given that Ewing had started with about 1,450 at Fort Davidson, his actual overall casualty rate made the encounter one of the most costly of the war.[48]

As to the Confederate casualties at Fort Davidson, modern scholars have revised the initially high estimates of 1,200 to 1,500 down to 800 to 1,000. Confederates had even less constraints about giving a Missouri count and misreporting their losses. Shelby later said that "there were not less than 700 Confederates killed and wounded" in the reckless assaults on Ewing's column after it left Caledonia.[49] If so, even the lower estimates for the fighting in the Arcadia Valley would have added to 1,500 for the entire venture.

These mounted excursions from Rolla made it abundantly clear that the Army of Missouri was not moving their direction. Lieutenant Colonel Joseph A. Eppstein took "all available men" of his Fifth MSM Cavalry as a "corps of observation" along the road running from Jackson Mills to Bennett's Mills, placing a strong force at Lake Springs only twelve miles east of Rolla. Friday night brought "a slight encounter" with "a small party of Shelby's flankers, in which the enemy left three dead on the ground; no casualties on our side." Over the next few days, Eppstein reported that the men on his left clashed only with "a small band of prowling marauders" and that those under Captain August Benz at Salem encountered rebel recruits on their way south.[50] Had the bulk of Price's army wanted to move on Rolla—or Jefferson City—it was simply going the wrong direction.

In fact, those Confederates that had been at Leasburg had swept northeast toward St. Louis. On its way from Leasburg, George Curry's locomotive had steamed past about four hundred horsemen closing on Sullivan Station, and scouts operating from Rolla followed Shelby's men there. The community's namesake, Stephen H. Sullivan, had laid out the town in response to the new railroad and it then boasted little more than a hotel and a school. Its founder lived long enough to see and remember how Shelby's men arrived on Friday, "about the middle of the afternoon and surrounded the town; made all the male persons prisoners; burned the railroad depot, ties, cord wood, water tank and a lot of bridge timber; tore up the track, telegraph, etc., but did not burn any private property." The Confederates reported destroying "vast quantities of lumber and cord-wood burned, with 3 passenger and 5 box cars." Sullivan himself noted the shooting and killing of "several" civilians and prisoners of war, including John Jesse, Abner Moody, and Samuel Hays Jr. A local man, Hays was enrolled in the Seventy-third EMM, while Moody, from nearby Stanton, had served in the Tenth Missouri Cavalry. After Shelby's division moved on, Marmaduke's followed in the night.[51]

Shelby's advance continued to St. Clair and the Virginia Mines, the most lucrative local source of lead. The settlers of 1849 had called their town Traveller's Repose for its pastoral stagecoach accommodations, but, on the eve of the war, citizens renamed it St. Clair for a resident railroad engineer. Despite the presence of locally prominent secessionists, the Confederates not only destroyed the depot and the water tank, but seized horses and forage and ransacked the stores. The next day, the footsore, wet, cold, and hungry Private Palmer arrived, having had only an ear of corn generously passed on by a rebel soldier. After shivering through the autumn night, he encountered his old comrades from Potosi as not only unparoled but "perfectly despondent" prisoners.[52]

The determination and heroism of the Federal soldiers, militia, and civilians at Leasburg gave Unionists much to celebrate. They had rallied to the colors against an invading army almost ten times their size, engaged the largest part of that army, endured a record march to escape, and, somehow, most remained in the land of the living. Such was the stuff of legend, and the more pressing the wartime realities, the greater the need for legends.

The Confederates, in turn, spun tales of their own. Later Price claimed that he had decided to bypass St. Louis for Jefferson City while at Pilot Knob. As one county history put it, "so much time was wasted [at Pilot Knob] that St. Louis could no longer be taken. Time was given for General Smith to reach St. Louis from Cairo with his corps." Pilot Knob had been "a defeat attended by severe loss, and if it ever had been the purpose to make an attempt on St. Louis, as the troops were led to believe, it had to be abandoned."[53] Yet, the end of September placed two of Price's three divisions less than two days from Jefferson City, and had he wanted to move on the state capital after the Arcadia Valley, Price could have been there at the start of October. Regardless of the losses to that point—likely well offset by recruitment and conscription—Price still remained committed to the reestablishment of Confederate Missouri and neutralizing the most important Unionist center in the state, St. Louis.

Two

The Primary Goal

4

The Mysteries of St. Louis

Myths and Realities in the City's Defense

A traveler familiar with antebellum St. Louis would have had seen many differences during a wartime visit. Armed uniformed soldiers or armed militia guarded the depots, blockhouses at the railroad bridges, and all the major roads. A train passenger coming from the west toward Jefferson Street saw a giant earthen fort covering more than a city block looming out the right window. Fort Number Seven was one of ten linked by additional earthen redans roughly along Jefferson, not far from where the city had carted off the Indian mounds a few years before. Several blocks beyond the fort, the train neared Eighth Street and the same window offered a view of the old McDowell Medical College on Gratiot, now a military prison for suspected spies and saboteurs.

It took a single lifetime for St. Louis to grow from a frontier outpost to one of the largest cities in North America. The scale and speed of this expansion posed difficulties with which Americans were neither experienced nor exceptionally talented. The nature of this explosive growth also drew together a large, diverse, and rapidly industrializing population from across the western world, creating issues unaddressed and opportunities mostly unexplored. The civil and military authorities found it administratively and logistically convenient to rest the defense of the city on a militia, but commercial and industrial considerations shaped a policy that balked at the systematic arming and mobilizations of wartime St. Louisans. In part as a result, Confederate enemy emissaries, spies, and saboteurs had been moving in and out of St. Louis with remarkable ease for over three years. In the fall of 1864, an entire army threatened to do the same.

The City

Newness was an inescapable reality for St. Louis. When U.S. officials first counted the inhabitants, only 1,600 residents lived there, but the newly acquired city grew tenfold over the next thirty years to reach 16,469 in 1840, and it repeated the feat over the next twenty years to reach 160,773 by 1860. The original outpost started in the interior of a great eastward bend in the Mississippi River below the mouth of the Missouri. Jefferson Street did run roughly north-south largely spanning the bend, roughly containing the city on the west, while streets to the east turned whichever direction suited the mood of the municipality at the time they were built.[1] Without a guide, newcomers usually got lost, and the explosive growth of the city made everyone a newcomer at some point.

Where the waters proved inadequate, the metropolis extended artificial rivers of commerce. Bellefontaine Road ran north and northwest, through miles of sparsely settled, wooded marshlands toward Spanish Pond. Natural Bridge Road continued fifteen miles northwest to the old village of Bridgeton and the newer one of Normandy, before reaching the St. Charles Rock Road, running northeast through Florissant toward the Missouri, west over the Meramec River at Fenton Ferry, with a branch to Creve Coeur Lake and the village of that name. Other roughly north-south roads west of the city included Old King's Highway and Hall's Ferry Road. To the west, Manchester Road ran not only to the village of that name but also to Chesterfield and Ballwin, an important center for wagon manufacturing.[2] Rugged hills slowed growth to the south and southwest. Originally settled from Ste. Genevieve almost a century before, Carondolet perched on a two-hundred-foot bluff overlooking the Mississippi some seven miles south of the city. It earlier ceded much of its commons for Jefferson Barracks, but wartime gunboat production transformed what was left of village into a small industrial city.

The Meramec River formed the southern boundary of St. Louis County. In the south-central interior of the state, the Bourbeuse from the west and the Big River from the south fed the Meramec, which reached St. Louis County at Pacific. At that point, it veered south sharply before cutting east again to the Mississippi below St. Louis. Graveled "rock roads" or macadamized roads forded the river, linking the city to points south and southwest. Gravois Road connected these important crossings from Lemay Ferry to Fenton Ferry, still known by that name despite having a new bridge. The large loop of the river to the southwest of the city provided what some called "Rebel Bend," the easiest route for secessionists to or from the city to the south.

Most recently, railroads extended their tentacles from the city into the state. In addition to the southbound Iron Mountain Railroad to Pilot Knob, a northbound eighty-six-mile branch of the North Missouri Railroad went by way of St. Charles and Warrenton to Mexico where it joined the main line connecting Hannibal on the Mississippi with St. Joseph on the western border. Most dramatically, though, the much-touted Pacific Railroad ran almost due west, creating new suburbs and the possibility of commuting as it passed through the important manufacturing center of Cheltenham at almost six miles, Webster Groves at ten, and Kirkwood at nearly fourteen. Nineteen miles from the city, Meramec Station marked the intersection of rails with Gravois Road leading down to it.

The railroads created the small seeds of modern suburbs. A few dozen of the more pioneering of the urban middle class had settled on the heights northeast of Glencoe Station, with Eureka—home of the brother of Confederate general Joseph E. Johnston—only four miles on and, after another two, Allentown. At the edge of the country—thirty-seven miles from the city—mining investors had founded "Franklin" only twelve years before, but, two years before the war, the advent of the westbound railroad promising to reach California renamed it Pacific City. From there, the main line continued west, while a southwestern branch ran seventy-seven miles to Rolla.[3] The war made the latter an essential line of supply for virtually all Federal operations as far off as the Indian Territory, Texas, and New Mexico.

Although a slaveholding city, St. Louis had seen numerous clashes over the issue of slavery. It began with the controversy in some St. Louis papers over the attempt of the territorial authorities to seek a statehood that legally established the institution of slavery. At one point, a mob responded to the stabbing of a white law enforcement officer by chaining a black man to a tree and burning him alive. When the white abolitionist Elijah Lovejoy excoriated them for such conduct, they drove him and his paper from the city, followed him to Alton, and murdered him. Only a few years before, Dred Scott won a ruling in favor of his freedom from the St. Louis court only to be reversed by the state, and ultimately the U.S. Supreme Court, which decided in 1857 that no black had any rights a white man need lawfully honor. The ruling made slavery theoretically legal everywhere and scared residents of the non-slaveholding states into the new Republican Party.

The railroad, the industries, and the anomaly of slavery turned St. Louis into a true peculiarity. Its business community of St. Louis came largely from the northeastern states, and Germans already constituted a third of the city. Mostly recent immigrants, they saw themselves as refugees from the lack of economic opportunity, personal freedom, and national unity in central Europe. A sixth of the city—half of its unskilled work force—was Irish. Largely skilled workers, the Germans constituted a natural constituency for the "free labor" ideology of the Republicans, while the Irish tended to feel African American competition in the labor market as a real threat. When war erupted, most of the city remained Unionist, and much of it took an active hand in breaking the political power of the secessionists and had no interest in doing so while maintaining slavery.

With the wartime absence or silence of the secessionists, the local balance of power shifted quickly toward Radical Unionism. Having been at odds with the state authorities when they had been secessionists, the metropolis found itself straining against the conservative policies of the Unionists' Provisional state government under Governor Hamilton R. Gamble, which sought to placate slaveholding Unionists and keep control over the revolutionary dynamic of the war. In January 1864, Gamble died, and his moderate ally, General John M. Schofield, gave way to Rosecrans. In many respects though, Rosecrans proved even more conservative than his predecessors on slavery and much else.[4]

Rosecrans understood that, notwithstanding the war—and partly because of it—the business of making money still trumped almost everything. The city—at least that part of it that mattered to the authorities—grew rich in the wartime economy. Entrepreneurs could sell the government arms, horses, food, or any item that could then be condemned by a friendly officer, bought cheaply at a government auction, and resold through the same process. Those who could not master this practice simply forged requisitions. Particularly in St. Louis, such possibilities gave rise to what one historian aptly called "the most unblushing frauds." Indeed, when ordered to fortify the city, military officials chose sites so as not to interfere with the principal routes in and out of the metropolis. As a later congressional investigation found, the fact that the projects were largely complete did not prevent one local capitalist from presenting the government with an after-the-fact bill for $151,000, and it did not keep his friends in the army from paying it. The Radicals' appreciation of General John C. Fremont did not inhibit his closing of the abolitionist *Missouri Democrat,* not for its radical abolitionist politics but for its exposing corruption in the administration of the department.[5] Throughout the state, appointed military provosts wielded a virtually unaccountable authority to make purchases, punish civilians, and confiscate property.

The influx of desperately poor refugees and runaways greatly intensified class tensions in the city. Even in St. Louis County, the level of martial activities had the effect of "abolishing many of the schools in this section." Concerned parents who could do so, moved back into the city, as did John Straszer, a carpenter and contractor who came in from Manchester because of "the movements of bodies of armed men." The conditions of those physically beyond the suburbs (or, racially, beyond the whites) provided even greater motives for seeking the protection of the city or joining those "emigrating to Illinois and other States." In the absence of any clear precedents, the army provided refugees with rations and fuel, the quartermaster's office contributed to housing, and the quasi-official Western Sanitary Commission raised money for incidental expenses.[6] Minimizing this problem of displaced persons required military successes that would restore them securely to the homes.

Indeed, beneath his identity as a general, a Democrat, or a Catholic, Rosecrans remained the Cincinnati businessman he had been at the war's onset.

Shortly after he took charge in St. Louis, he won the allegiance of the large military contractors and industrialists. One of the most important of these, Giles F. Filley, had transformed his stove-making enterprise into a lucrative industrial ally of the war effort. Remarkably wealthy for the times, Filley daily commuted from the heights of Glendale in St. Louis County.[7] While the support of such gentlemen became politically essential to the Department of Missouri, the Filleys hardly filled the battalions needed to defend the city.

The wartime prosperity enjoyed in the business community never quite trickled down to the work force. In March and April 1864, one craft after another organized and went on strike. When the ship carpenters and caulkers went out for a raise, "the military were called upon to protect the men who accepted the company's terms." After about a week, strikers resumed work at the old rates, but they remained discontented enough to go out again if they seemed likely to get greater support.[8]

What followed could only be described as a strike wave. The tailors went out for more wages, union recognition, and an end to hiring girls as underpaid apprentices, culminating in a mass meeting with speeches in English, German, and French, after which most of the bosses caved. The machinists and blacksmiths also went on strike because the bosses were reducing wages by putting "too many boys in their workshops." The same issue sparked a strike by the new molders' union against Giles and Oliver Filley's Excelsior Stove Works, where labor troubles had been festering for many years. The Filleys not only fired union organizers, but also imported German immigrants to break the strike. When the foreign workers arrived, eighteen of them joined the union, which got them employment elsewhere. Leading Republicans and war contractors, the Filleys also published a "Card-to-the-Public" in the *Republican* and the *Democrat* pleading patriotic motives in trying to break the strike. Through April, stove and hollowware molders, machine molders, brass finishers and molders, carpenters and joiners, ship carpenters and caulkers, brick molders, steam- and gas-pipe fitters, paper hangers, horseshoers, plasterers, painters, tinners, and printers began holding joint meetings in different languages. The national secretary of machinists and blacksmiths addressed a mass meeting in the rotunda of the courthouse threatening a citywide strike.[9]

The conservative businessman Rosecrans was also a general and introduced the military firmly on the side of the capitalists. The labor organizations, he wrote, raised issues that had "no relation to the matter of wages . . . but to the internal management of such establishments." Employers had told the general that these "combinations . . . to prevent journeymen mechanics, apprentices, and laborers from working in manufacturing establishments, except on terms prescribed to the proprietors thereof, by parties not interested therein" might also stop "the military, naval, and transport of the United States." For this reason, Rosecrans closed April with his General Order No. 65 to thwart "this attack upon private rights and the military power of the nation by organizations led by bad men." It promised employers and potential strikebreakers military protection, and banned any attempt "directly or indirectly . . . to deter or prevent any person from working." Finally, it declared such things would "be punished as a military offense," and asked employers to submit "a list, by name, of all who have taken an active part in any combination to control the conduct of any such establishment." When the general "detailed a number of soldiers who were printers to take the strikers places" on newspapers, two of the soldiers protested vigorously.[10]

The Radical Germans were unrelenting in its attacks, and the *Republican* and *Democrat* shared enough of the sentiments to publish translations. The *Neue Zeit* denounced "military arbitrariness" and the *Westliche Post* decried "an attack on the freedom of labor and the right of association." The *Anzeiger des Westens* warned against the "elastic nature" of Rosecrans's proscriptions, correctly likening it to the imposition of martial law on workers. The national labor movement took up the issue as a dangerous precedent. On May 2, Carl Bernays of the *Anzeiger des Westens* sent a copy of the order with a particularly articulate letter to Lincoln. Citing Lincoln's own earlier letter to Oliver D. Filley that he did not want the military to run the churches, Bernays noted that Rosecrans sought "to decide with the sword the greatest social question of the century. And what is 'running churches' compared with 'running' workshops or rather changing the entire character of the industrial life of the American nation."

> We are not half through with the destruction of slavery and we already begin to attack free labor. Out of this war millions and millions have been made and lawfully made by our manufacturers and whilst our armies have all been taken from the working classes and whilst in fine the greater part of taxation is to be paid by them, we overlook their services and sufferings and a military commander forbids them to associate as they use to do for more than half a century in order to improve their condition and to regulate their relations between themselves and their employers.

In America, "slave and free labor have created all the capital," and it would not do to have labor "destroyed totally or partially in order to maintain capital alone."[11]

The most dramatic rallying point for the Radicals, of course, remained slavery. Citing the growing refugee problem across the state, they pointed out that black self-sufficiency would be both cheaper and more humane. They added that this, of course, would require the immediate embrace of emancipationist measures in Missouri. The Radicals also embraced black military service, with an expectation of civil rights to follow. As Benjamin Gratz Brown—Missouri's junior U.S. senator—put it: "freedom and franchise are inseparable."[12]

Real grievances created a broad constituency deeply distrustful of Rosecrans. To be sure, Lincoln instructed Rosecrans and other generals not to "interfere with the legitimate demands of labor," but this did not necessarily affect sentiment on the street, which would be essential to the defense of the city. Rosecrans, in turn, would be hardly eager to draw on the talents of so virulently antislavery and prolabor a figure as Colonel Joseph Weydemeyer, an old Communist League friend of Karl Marx and Friedrich Engels, then organizing the new Forty-first Missouri up at Benton Barracks.[13] None of this bode well with the Confederate army on its way.

The Army of St. Louis

That myth of an Iron County Thermopylae at Pilot Knob had Rosecrans raising a force capable of deflecting Price's army from St. Louis. Indeed, that headquarters worked tirelessly to use the press to convey a sense of security and, inadvertently, shape how later students of history would think about the incident.

The existence of those ten forts with associated rifle pits and redans visually reassured everyone. Installations at either end of those fortifications provided essential support. To the south was the U.S. Arsenal and, at the foot of Chippewa Street, the Marine Hospital with Arsenal Island for quarantined cases of contagious diseases; ten miles downriver sat Jefferson Barracks, the brooding base of the regular army since the American occupation of the territory. To the north—a few blocks beyond Fort Number Nine at Jefferson and Natural Bridge—the city fairgrounds hosted Camp Benton, with five barracks running about 740 by 40 feet with warehouses, stables, and other buildings, including a two-story headquarters at the eastern ends of the grounds. The coordination of all of this came from Rosecrans's general headquarters at Fourth and Washington.[14]

Moreover, Major General Alfred Pleasonton would be on hand to organize it all, just as soon as he returned from his leave back east. After recruitment duties in Delaware and service in the far west, Pleasonton had become one of the architects of the cavalry within the Army of the Potomac, earning considerable disfavor for its shortcomings. Sent to Missouri in March 1864, he had commanded the Central District at Jefferson City until he went east on leave. As news of an invasion crept northward, Rosecrans sent him an urgent telegram at New York's fashionable Fifth Avenue Hotel, and he had finally replied on Tuesday, arriving the next weekend. Rosecrans also called into service those veteran officers, like Frank Blair, then home on sick leave, though Pleasonton himself arrived Friday.[15]

Most accounts credit Rosecrans as having an army of 15,000 to 24,000 men at St. Louis ready to meet Price. Although General John Sanborn was never in St. Louis during the campaign, he recorded his impressions that Rosecrans mobilized a large militia force that increased his 1,500 garrison troops to some 6,500 men and more. The contemporary press added that "considerable bodies of troops are arriving here. Cavalry and infantry are being rapidly assigned to their proper positions—The militia are responding promptly to the call of the commanding general. The citizens generally manifest a strong disposition to organize for local defense." Reporters wrote that they heard the fife and drum everywhere in St. Louis, with a battery "frowning upon Lucas square in the heart of the city." "The blacksmiths' shops have been busy all day shoeing cavalry horses. Ordnance and ammunition is being sent to different points. Everything is being put into fine condition for immediate active service." As the Confederates crept nearer the city, the *New York Tribune* assured readers that Rosecrans was the "master of the situation, and has full details of the strength of Price's army, its organization, and supposed plan of operation."[16]

A defending force of even 15,000 would have required a tenfold multiplication of the numbers in the army's official returns for the end of August. (Interestingly, it published no such returns for September or October.) At the start of September, the Department of Missouri had only three companies of U.S. Veteran Reserves at Jefferson Barracks with a fourth at the Marine Hospital and four batteries of the Second Missouri Light Artillery at "Camp Gamble." Rosecrans had one company of the Fifth MSM Cavalry at Schofield Barracks as his own mounted escort. As well, the subordinate District of St. Louis had troops at Benton Barracks. These included four companies each of the Second Wisconsin and Seventeenth Illinois Cavalry regiments; two from the First MSM Infantry; several from the Eighteenth United States Colored Troops; and the generally unorganized, undrilled, and unarmed recruits of the Fortieth and Forty-first Missouri, as well as a few from the Forty-seventh, Forty-eighth, and Fiftieth. The barracks also housed Federal prisoners paroled by the rebels and awaiting exchange before returning to the field.[17] Assignments elsewhere had reduced the number of effectives in St. Louis to about 1,500 men, as Sanborn's own account confirmed.

None of the components alleged to have multiplied these numbers bears up to any serious questioning. Sanborn credited General Andrew J. Smith's corps as adding 4,500 men to the city's defenses. However, one of Smith's three divisions, that of Mower, was stumbling through the Arkansas woods hundreds of miles away. While the press described the other two as being "in first-rate fighting trim" at St. Louis, they had actually not all arrived at the time they were needed, and some of those that had had gone south with Ewing.[18]

The impressive-sounding "Illinois Provisional Brigade" consisted of troops sent by Governor Richard Yates of that state and organized by Colonel Hugo Wagelin, commanding Ewing's subdistrict for St. Louis. Various sources mention nine Illinois regiments: the Forty-seventh and Sixty-first, as well as the hundred-day regiments: the 132nd, 134th, 136th, 138th, 139th, 140th, and 142nd. In fact, the tiny veteranized Sixty-first Illinois had been sent downriver to protect Randolph County, Illinois, from a rumored Confederate crossing. As late as October, the 132nd and 136th remained at Chicago with the Forty-seventh and 138th back at Camp Butler, the former earmarked as unavailable, and Sanborn himself noted that only five of the nine regiments ever got to St. Louis. However, on the very day the Confederates threatened St. Louis, Colonel Benjamin L. E. Bonneville at Jefferson Barracks reported only "1,516 in the three Illinois 100-day regiments now here." Bonneville added that he had found "much reluctance on the part of two regiments to go," and expected that those in the newly arrived 140th likely felt the same way.[19]

That massive supplemental militia represented a serious force. Although often depicted as bumbling bumpkins led by politicians, the militia included many experienced men and officers. The St. Louis division of the EMM served under Brigadier General Edward C. Pike, formerly commanding the Seventh EMM. Brigadier General Madison Miller, commanding the First Brigade, had served as an officer in both the First Missouri and the First Missouri Light Artillery before promotion to colonelcy in the Eighteenth Missouri, which he had led at Shiloh and elsewhere before taking charge of Pike's First Brigade. Brigadier General Christian D. Wolff of the Second Brigade had been in militia service from the onset of the war when his "Citizen Guards" had participated in the Unionist seizure of the city. In charge of the Third Brigade, Brigadier General George F. Meyers had similarly long experience. In fact, one of their problems during the 1864 mobilization was that so many of the militia had joined the volunteer service.[20]

Since it enrolled and mobilized all men of fighting age, the EMM provided a better reflection of the adult male population than the regular army, and its success reflected how well the Union military had managed the local social contract. Members of the local elites and political leaders were evident in the militia, but so were labor figures. The twenty-seven-year-old New Hampshire-born printer George Henry Stone had led the local Typographical Union before enlisting in one of the first companies raised at the St. Louis Arsenal, which elected him captain. He subsequently fought in most of the major clashes in the state before fighting at Shiloh and Corinth east of the Mississippi, but had returned to the city and served on the staff of the EMM. Stone's Union brother, the twenty-eight-year-old William J. Whitwell, had entered the Ninth EMM as a sergeant two years before taking a commission in mid-September as captain in the Fortieth Missouri. (Another, Private John R. Cummins, of the

Davenport local, had fallen mortally wounded in the second day's fighting by the Fourteenth Iowa in the Arcadia Valley.)[21] Despite all its reasons for mistrusting Rosecrans and the high command, workers had not lost their willingness to serve.

Nevertheless, by the time of the invasion, conditions in St. Louis left the local EMM in even worse shape than the statewide organization. On paper, the city's EMM did truly represent a formidable force. In addition to some fourteen regiments, a battalion, and an independent company, it added a half dozen "regiments" of "City Guards" among those exempted from military service.[22] However, a ward-based company formed with as few as sixty-four enrollees—not all of which would necessarily show up when called out—and this meant regiments that could be much smaller than a volunteer unit. Given the greater turnover of the urban population, enrollees enlisted, moved, or faded away, and the city failed to have the regular mobilizations that kept the EMM viable elsewhere.

The evidence indicates that, as a fighting force, the St. Louis EMM had become moribund. Even at the peak of their service, two years before, the local units had mobilized fewer than 5,000 men, and the relatively unthreatened position of the city meant that the rolls were outdated and the numbers uncertain at any given point. St. Louis actually never needed to implement Rosecrans's policy of phasing out those older regiments in favor of provisional units of battalion-strength—appropriate to protection of the rails, garrisoning outposts, and contesting guerrillas. In April 1864, General Order No. 15 officially dissolved the Sixteenth, Seventeenth, Twenty-second, Twenty-third, and Twenty-fourth EMM, on the grounds that they had never truly organized or functioned.[23]

Pike started sorting this all out as Ewing had taken off for Pilot Knob. On the recommendation of the mayor and "many leading business men of the city," Rosecrans's General Order No. 176 suspended "all public business" as of noon the following day "to enable us to complete the organizations for local defense, and to permit an active force to pursue the enemy." The authorities would arm all employers in the Quartermaster's Department and all exempts, forming them into organizations that would be "completed in forty-eight hours, when business will be resumed." The press reported loyal men "receiving arms from the Government and organizing for the protection of the State." By Friday, September 30, Rosecrans's headquarters assured the public that it had "about 8,000" armed militia on duty at places such as Camp Sheridan, the "site of the former Camp Jackson." The same paper said the mayor of St. Louis remained hopeful that he might be able to report 5,000 soon. However, the state records actually report only 1,306 men serving in the EMM that September across the entire state of Missouri. Although surely underreported, the number tells us nothing about the size of the force at St. Louis.[24]

Despite the gaps in official reports, Pike mentioned ten regiments: the First, Second, Third, Fourth, Tenth, Seventh, Eleventh, Thirteenth, Eighteenth, Eightieth, and Eighty-fifth, However, he did describe several of them as mere "skeleton" organizations. In fact, the orders brigading these regiments in the fall of 1864 provide the only real indication of their existence, and a random search of the service records of the individual enrollees in these regiments seems rarely to credit them with service at all for that year.[25]

The devil lies in the details, and a closer look at the EMM's brigades proves revealing. At the time of the mobilization, Colonel William P. Fenn's First EMM in the west county and Colonel Edward Stafford's Second proved the strongest. The latter included not only enrolled members but "all others who live in Carondolet Township, that can bear a gun," whether "exempt or not, enrolled or not." Authorities would report Colonel W. J. A. Smith's Eighty-fifth EMM "in fine condition," but only days after it had allegedly helped save the city. Another "regiment" (alternatively described as the Eighteenth or the Eightieth) probably consisted mostly of the small number of refugees of the Eightieth EMM from Jefferson County that had joined Pike north of the Meramec River. As late as October 3, an observer described Miller's brigade along the Meramec as several hundred men, mostly unarmed.[26]

The rest of the EMM was in no better shape. In Wolff's brigade, Colonel Fred Vahlkamp's Third and Colonel Louis Duestrow's Fourth EMM eventually had some substance but Lieutenant Colonel H. Cleveland's Tenth seems to have amounted to nothing. In Myers's brigade, Colonel George E. Leighton's Seventh EMM responded, such as it was, but Lieutenant Colonel Edward Beckman's Eleventh and Lieutenant Colonel John R. Marcy's Thirteenth seem to have remained nothing more than phantoms. As to the smaller EMM units, service records exist for only seventy-five enrollees in the St. Louis Police Battalion, all in Captain John F. Fealy's single but oddly lettered Company B, which apparently mustered once and that over two years before the invasion. There are no records at all for any individuals serving in a National Guard of St. Louis under a Colonel Parker.[27]

In short, that EMM division of 15,000 in St. Louis had never been more than a mere fantasy. What the records do show is that, as late as mid-October, Rosecrans had only 3,000 of them reporting for duty. At the start of the month—when the Union army desperately needed them—the available EMM most likely numbered no more than an indifferently armed and equipped 1,500 men.

At times, though, Rosecrans seems to have understood the value of placating the Radicals to assure the better defense of the community. When he appointed the anti-abolitionist Frank Blair to command the militia, *Westliches Post* and the Radicals complained of the slight to B. Gratz Brown. When Blair assigned the brigades of Wolf and Myers to the forts in the city, the militia complained that "they serve for nothing," so Rosecrans reassigned them to supplement General Smith's infantry down on the Meramec. Some noisy demonstrations and protests expressed their "great dissatisfaction." When the mayor said he hoped to mobilize 5,000 men for the defense of the city, a radical voice from the crowd protested the exclusion of Brown. It complained that "we have got still to have Blair, unless we have a guarantee. The order in the papers says he is here on sick leave to organize the militia. Why don't he go back to the army where he belongs?" The mayor declined to discuss Blair, but Rosecrans agreed that Brown could mobilize the militia while Pleasonton would command the local defenses.[28]

There seemed to be none of the urgency one might expect under the circumstances. Rosecrans certainly lent a sympathetic ear to the official of the North Missouri Railroad, who complained that militia service and war talk had distracted "all the mechanics of our shops." The general dutifully telegraphed Colonel Arnold Krekel at St. Charles: "Don't get up a stampede without cause." Within hours of the arrival of armed Confederates in St. Louis County, headquarters declared itself so pleased with its preparations "that business will be resumed tomorrow," albeit with the stores (not the factories) closing at 3 p.m. for drill.[29] These priorities carried over into the field, where his orders never destroyed railroad property, including bridges, the capture of which might be of active use to the enemy.

Indeed, Rosecrans trusted the business community more than his own men for reliable information. On Wednesday the Confederates raided St. Mary's Landing, just below St. Genevieve on the Mississippi. The information that finally persuaded Rosecrans that a full-scale invasion was underway came from a "reliable citizen" who had actually visited Price at his headquarters, where he met Governor Thomas C. Reynolds, Trusten Polk, "and several other St. Louis Rebels." This finally convinced Rosecrans that the Confederates had a much larger army than the Union command had ever expected, and his source had left "satisfied" that it would move on St. Louis. Rosecrans finally conceded that "the rebels are advancing on Saint Louis," and "could reach Saint Louis from any point in the Meramec Valley."[30] Having ignored his own soldiers and numerous other civilians, his "reliable" source was James Harrison of Choteau, Harrison & Valle, the owners of Iron Mountain, who had dined with the Confederate commanders in the course of looking out for his firm's interest.

Perhaps unconsciously, Rosecrans gambled over the defense of St. Louis. On the surface, he had minimized the size of the enemy army entering Missouri, ignoring information to the contrary until it became absolutely impossible to do so. He had also insisted—with very little evidence and, again, contrary to reports—that the Confederates were moving on Cape Girardeau or Rolla or Jefferson City or anywhere but St. Louis.

Perhaps most peculiarly, the general repeatedly expressed his faith that a mass of infantry was about to catch up to a cavalry force that enjoyed a considerable a head start. Certainly, if General Joseph A. Mower's division would overtake Price's army, the modest military defenses Rosecrans had would be sufficient. "Every hour's delay of the enemy in the Meramec Valley," wrote Rosecrans, "brought Mower nearer, and increased our chances of striking him as it did the security of Jefferson City." With their largely unarmed militia stabilizing the Meramec line, Smith's scouts ventured south as far as Hillsborough, and Merrill's horsemen found the Meramec upstream "fordable at any point" to the west. However, virtually every rumored skirmish to the south seemed to be a sign that Mower's division had arrived to save the day. On Wednesday, it reportedly clashed with the rebels at Cadet Station, near Mineral Point. So, too, when refugees from St. Genevieve reported hearing heavy firing from Pilot Knob, the authorities took it as a sign of Mower's presence.[31]

Then, eyes on both sides watched the skies as well as their maps, hoping that rain would raise the rivers and slow the Confederate movements. The lower reaches of rivers such as the Meramec, Gasconade, Osage, and even the Bourbeuse formed possible natural obstacles to troop movements, but the dry summer had left them fordable where they might not have otherwise been. One Union diarist noted hopefully that it "rained a good shower" over the night of September 26–27, "rained hard" over September 28–29, "continued to rain and drizzle all day" on October 1, and again faced "raining and drizzling weather" October 3. "Rains continue and streams are rising rapidly," wrote General Samuel Curtis from Kansas, who hoped that rising waters might immobilize the Army of Missouri. "I do not see how Price can progress if bridges are destroyed since the rains must have rendered all streams impassable," he added, in apparent unawareness that the Department of Missouri would never do such a thing. Field officers replied that "the streams have raised but little as yet," and the rain stopped on Thursday.[32]

In the end, though, no act of God would substitute itself for one by Mower. And Mower was lost somewhere in the Arkansas Ozarks. Where Rosecrans was remained even less certain.

Spies and Saboteurs

It is almost inescapable that the myth of Federal preparedness became a key defensive strategy, though it seems to have had its origins in self-deception and wishful thinking of all sorts. By the time Price's army approached St. Louis, its recruiters, mail couriers, spies, scouts, and saboteurs had long been slipping in and out of the city. At the onset of the war, such luminaries of the Confederate intelligence operations as Basil W. Duke and John B. Castleman gained their initial training in the city.[33] A key transshipment point for Federal supplies down the river and by rail, and the city remained a vital target for sabotage. No place was more aware of this than Federal headquarters at St. Louis.

Unionists of all sorts later realized Confederate goals as the occupation of St. Louis. One said they hoped to hold it "long enough at least to 'loot' it of all the invaders needed." Another realized the rebels wanted to "occupy Missouri just before the Presidential election, hold the capital and perhaps St. Louis." With metropolitan New York and Philadelphia in a league of their own, the size of American cities dropped precipitously to a class of secondary cities that included St. Louis with Baltimore, Boston, New Orleans, and Cincinnati. Of all these, the only two in the thirteen states claimed by the Confederacy fell early to the Federals. Union strategists had every reason to fear the impact of Price's recovery of one of them after three years of war.[34]

In 1862, a Confederate operative named Emile Longuemare briefly returned to his home in wartime St. Louis. At the time, the Federal authorities stepped up their queries about him and his relatives, but this did not keep him from organizing a meeting in the city at Fifth and Market. It established an Order of American Knights, headed by an inner Sons of Liberty under New Orleans lawyer P. C. Wright, who hoped to rebuild the Democratic Party as a disunionist movement. Beneath Wright, operating heads at the state levels included Charles Lucas Hunt of Missouri.[35]

In September 1863, a year before the invasion, a wave of steamboat burnings afflicted the St. Louis riverfront. The extent to which a centralized Confederate Secret Service planned such attacks remains uncertain, but the loss of millions of dollars in supplies and payroll presents a persuasive pattern of circumstantial evidence. Over the following year, the Federals arrested a number of active agents, including Robert London, "a notorious boat-burner and Rebel mail-carrier."[36]

The scion of the wealthy and powerful St. Louis family, Hunt had been in France and Belgium during the revolutionary upheavals of 1848–49. In the midst of a great conflict within the latter country over the authority of the church, he and his Jesuit mentors, watched incomprehensibly angry demonstrators chanting "*A Bas le Jesuits*" and the destruction of Church property, though acknowledging this to be done mostly "by boys of from 10 to 18 years old generally headed by women." Hunt returned an enemy of a cosmopolitan republicanism he called "European liberty." In the summer of 1864, the authorities brushed aside Hunt's diplomatic credentials from the Belgian government and actually locked him up for a period before paroling him.[37] The concern was an escalating pattern of sabotage.

Moreover, Radicals had every reason to believe that some currents in the Democratic Party favored victory for the secessionists. Although a native of upstate New York, Phineas C. Wright had spent much of his adult life as a lawyer in New Orleans before settling in St. Louis only five years earlier. In the summer of 1864, Rosecrans's provost marshal, Colonel John P. Sanderson, exposed the plans of the Order of American Knights for an armed insurrection and identified Sterling Price as head of the order.[38] It became easy for later scholars to dismiss "the Sanderson Report" because no such rising took place, and most of the concern about shadowy organizations like the Knights of the Golden Circle and the Order of American Knights represented little of substance.

Certainly, a serious Confederate attempt to sabotage the river traffic coincided with the appearance of Price in Missouri. The summer of 1864 brought Confederate operatives from Canada to Chicago, where they expected to spark an insurrection at the Democratic National Convention at the end of August. In his exile at Windsor, Canada, former Democratic congressman Clement L. Vallandigham persuaded Confederate visitors that his party had established a "semi-military Order of the Sons of Liberty" with 175,000 members in Illinois, Indiana, and Ohio and introduced James A. Barrett of St. Louis as their "grand lecturer." They told the rebels that their goal was a vast Northwestern Confederacy, the formation of which would break forever the Union and the war effort on its behalf, and the Confederates proved remarkably credulous, providing the Democrats substantial funding from their coffers, including some $20,000 given Barrett to aid the Democratic campaign in Illinois.[39]

To coordinate action with these Sons of Liberty, Castleman—along with some seventy disguised Confederate soldiers—reached Chicago's Richmond House as the Democrats gathered, along with an estimated 100,000 strangers visiting the city, partly for the convention and many on business. Oddly, he found "little reason to doubt" Copperhead claims that many were Sons of Liberty, *albeit* too disorganized to be of any use to anybody. The Confederates had expected to see 5,000 armed insurgents seize Camp Douglas and free the Confederate prisoners held there, but they apparently believed that no such number was available for the assault. The agents then asked for 500 to help raise the prison at Rock Island, Illinois, but the Sons of Liberty seemed as incapable of providing 500 as 5,000.[40]

When the Chicago plans disintegrated, the agents sent most of the soldiers back south or into Canada, but formed others into detachments that scattered across the region. Already, George B. Eastin took a small force—including John M. Trigg and Henry Sampson—to Louisville. There, on July 1, they torched $1,500,000 in government stores at two warehouses on Main Street between Eighth and Ninth. In part, this was to test their new incendiary devices, the so-called "Greek fire."[41]

After the convention—in late September 1864—Eastin scouted St. Louis, reporting seventy-three steamboats at the waterfront. He sent word to Castleman and the other agents in Illinois that some seventy-three steamboats waited at St. Louis, in the course of bringing military supplies and payroll to the Federal army at Vicksburg. Without specifying the day, Castleman recalled that they gathered at the Olive Street Hotel. After breakfast, they distributed their "Greek fire" and headed for assigned destinations on the riverfront. By 11:30 a.m., he recalled, they found that the devices simply failed to start any fires, quipping that they would have done better with their own matches. At the end of the month, Castleman left for Indiana, where Federal agents arrested him.[42]

Price reported sending his own personal spy north when he left Pocahontas. He wrote that he had "sent an agent into Saint Louis of great intelligence and tact to ascertain the strength of the enemy at that city, with directions to report to me if possible at Potosi." However, the agent could not meet the general's schedule because he came to be "so closely watched." Since this report has a number of mistruths, we cannot assume Price's honesty on this, but Major John N. Edwards, Shelby's adjutant, particularly recalled a Confederate underground in the city. Spies, couriers, recruiters, or blockade runners found John King and Captain William D. Bartle ready to supply "money, pistols, horses, and better than all, information." Edwards believed there to have been "none who excelled these gentlemen in the secrecy of their operation, the munificence of their gifts, and in the indefatigable manner by which they equipped and hurried to the army young men unable to purchase the necessary accouterments."[43]

A particularly likely candidate for Price's spy would have been Arthur C. McCoy. The keeper of a St. Louis hardware store before the war, McCoy served in the MSG and worked as a courier for the Confederates, bringing mail in and out of the city. He also held a commission in Shelby's Fifth Missouri Cavalry, but, during the invasion, rode far ahead of the column. Edwards described him in heroic and romantic terms, uncritically recounting interesting—and unverified—tales by many such individual Confederate soldiers. These included McCoy's duel with a Choctaw angered because McCoy's horse had eaten his, his single-handed courage facing down Union pickets going in and out of the city by way of "Rebel Bend," or forcing Federal officers at gunpoint to cheer Jeff Davis. Since the source for such stories would have been McCoy himself, it raises other questions about the quality of any intelligence he might provide. Later in the raid, he seems to have been working among the scouts in the advance, but may well have been in St. Louis to gauge the possibilities of a Confederate move on the city.[44] Bravery aside, though, his penchant for tall tales about facing long odds may not have made him the wisest choice for the mission. Moreover, McCoy's flamboyance in a city where he was well known would have made it likely that the Federals would have identified him and fed him whatever suited their purposes.

Yet, there were other Confederate agents active in the area during those days. The previous Saturday, September 24, Federal cavalrymen just west of Manchester stopped James Morgan Utz and five other men who wore Federal uniforms and had a wagon, but no papers or passes. They did have, among other things, a cipher book and letters for Confederate officers. The Federals dropped the lot of them into Gratiot Street Prison to where Utz's father had already been removed from his farm between Bridgeton and Florissant. James had been in the MSG and the Confederate army before returning north with the rank of major and an assignment as "special agent." The previous July, Union soldiers in Jefferson County had exchanged fire with another party of five men heading south from the city and recovered a letter in cipher from Utz to Price. In it, Utz told the general that the Federals had jailed Price's liaison to the St. Louis circle and that Utz had a great deal of difficulty even meeting with the man Price had sent to replace him.[45] After his arrest in September, Utz's days as an effective Confederate operative were numbered.

Two days after Utz's arrest, the Federals caught Shelby Cole at Mineral Point. A former Confederate soldier who had earlier burned the Big River bridge, Cole had taken an oath of allegiance but entered the lines without authorization and then tried to make it past the pickets without a pass. During Tuesday's rainy evacuation, the sergeant guarding Cole gave him his coat, but with a desperation hinting he had a schedule, Cole drew a knife, cut the man across both his eyes, seized his musket, and made an unsuccessful dash for safety. The brutal attack only complicated Cole's espionage and the army hanged him in front of the main hotel at DeSoto.[46]

Then, on Wednesday, a particularly audacious band of four thieves robbed August Muegge's store at Cheltenham, four miles from the city. Said to be dressed like "regular officers from the invading army," two of them entered the store and behaved like "old soldiers." They asked whether he held office under the Lincoln administration and he admitted to being the local postmaster, after which one of them leveled a pistol at him. When his wife knocked the gun aside, Muegge dashed out the door. When he got a horse, he hurried off to the militia camp on Olive Street. There were also rumors of such a group taking a house two miles away on the Manchester Road.[47] The authorities did not get around to looking into it on Friday.

In the city's hour of need, Rosecrans had a minuscule force compared to that which he claimed or implied. At that point, his little army consisted in roughly equal parts that of his own garrison troops and recruits, Smith's infantry, some rather unmanageable Illinois troops, and some half-armed enrolled militia. This force, totaling something like 5,700–6,500 men, was spread from Benton Barracks to Jefferson Barracks, and across the fords and bridges from the mouth of the Meramec to Fenton Ferry and beyond. The 12,000 to 13,000 Confederates in the area could probably overrun the Federal defenses at almost any point along the line. As of Friday evening, September 30, elements of all three of Price's divisions had moved toward Pacific.[48] Even as the fighting raged around Atlanta in the Deep South, everything seemed to presage a battle of St. Louis, that would return the battle lines to where they had started three years before.

For several days, Rosecrans had needed to shift his defenses up the Meramec to Pacific, in the direction of the Confederate concentrations in Franklin County. Perhaps, too, Rosecrans's reluctance to shift reflected his own trauma over earlier choices he had made on the battlefield. September 19, the day Price's army entered the state, marked the second anniversary of when Rosecrans had earlier clashed with Price at Iuka. It also marked the first anniversary since the Union general had made that fatal mistake when a larger Confederate army had caught him unaware at Chickamauga, meaning in the local native dialect something like "the river of death." While he stabilized his situation, his staff officers riding behind the lines did not see their own soldiers just beyond a line of timber and reported a gap. Eager to cover a gap that did not really exist, Rosecrans quickly redeployed some of his troops, creating a very real hole in the Union line, which ended in the near destruction of his army. Interestingly, the locals often said that the Meramec, in an Indian tongue, meant "the waters of death."[49] Perhaps every time Rosecrans considered closing the suspected gap in his line on the Meramec, the ghosts of Chickamauga loomed large, conjuring terrifying images of Confederate legions swarming over Missouri's river of death and storming into St. Louis from the south.

Sterling Price *(courtesy Library of Congress)*

James Fagan *(courtesy Library of Congress)*

(Opposite top) Joseph Shelby *(courtesy Library of Congress)*

(Opposite bottom) John Marmaduke *(courtesy Library of Congress)*

William Rosecrans *(courtesy Library of Congress)*

(Opposite top) Thomas Ewing *(courtesy Library of Congress)*

(Opposite bottom) John McNeil *(courtesy Library of Congress)*

William "Bloody Bill" Anderson *(courtesy of the State Historical Society of Missouri)*

(Opposite top) Egbert Brown *(courtesy Library of Congress)*

(Opposite bottom) Clinton Fisk *(courtesy Library of Congress)*

Jefferson City *(courtesy Library of Congress)*

Applying for passes, *Harper's Weekly,* January 18, 1862

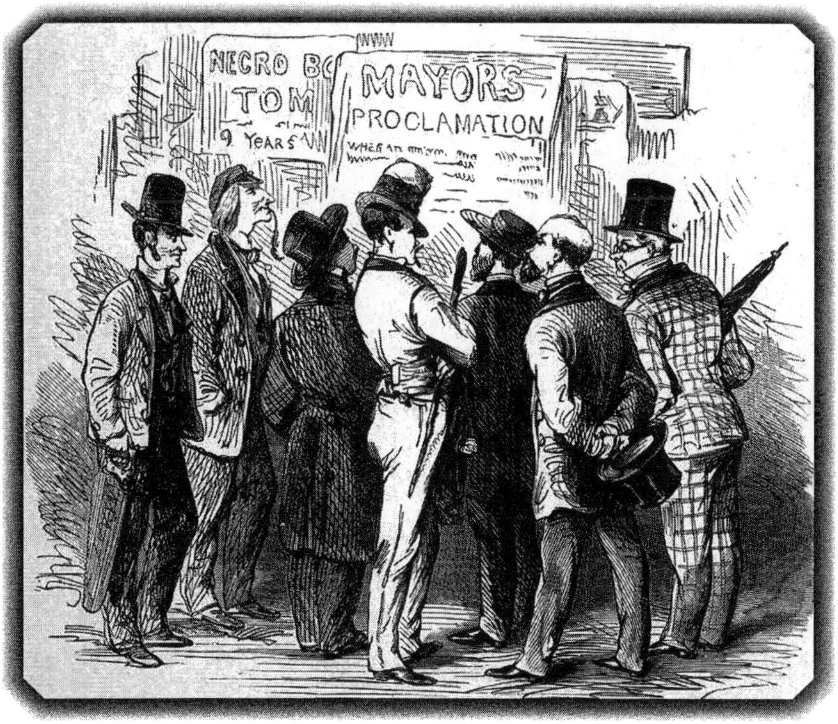

Corner scene in St. Louis, *Harper's Weekly,* June 1, 1861

5

At the Gates of the Metropolis

Pacific and Union

Saturday dawned on a body of armed uniformed Confederates back in St. Louis County for the first time in over three years. Most were almost certainly young Arkansans, hungry and tired after a hard night of rapid marches and short fights. An officer had sent them to destroy track or picket the road toward the city. Although they must have been cautious initially about their assignment, they became more comfortable with their duties after finding no Union defenders in view. The bloodless victors impressed those who remembered the well-dressed, well-financed secessionists who had gone to war three years before.

Saturday, October 1, brought two significant clashes, with related maneuvers and skirmishing. The first decisively severed St. Louis from Jefferson City and marked something of a Confederate high-water mark in the entire Trans-Mississippi war. The other helped force a final decision on the Confederates, as they reached the area of the Missouri River and had to commit to an attack on St. Louis or to turn west. In the course of both, the liberating pretenses of Price's army unraveled, even for many of its leading participants.

Pacific

Shortly after General Thomas Ewing had left St. Louis for Pilot Knob, General Andrew J. Smith's infantry had concentrated south of St. Louis. Initially based at DeSoto, Smith worried that the large Confederate force to his south might get behind him and threaten the city. Deciding that DeSoto was actually "of no importance," he withdrew to a new line of defense along the Meramec River with Colonel L. J. Rankin's Eightieth EMM behind him. As of 3 p.m. Friday, September 30, he reported "all safe at DeSoto" and even sent "a guarded train" that direction from Pevely, carrying mounted scouts, apparently from Colonel Edward Catherwood's Thirteenth Missouri Cavalry. These reported the destruction of three bridges and two or three water tanks, adding that "the rebels infest the entire country south of DeSoto, plundering every body they meet. They have lists of all union men of the country through which they pass, whom it is said they will butcher on sight. They conscript all sympathizers and old men and boys of 15." That Friday night, though, the superintendent of bridges flagged a scout train just above DeSoto, after a night in a cornfield.[1]

The railroader explained that earlier that evening three hundred Arkansans arrived at DeSoto with orders "to destroy the depot at that place, which was effected." The Confederate report implied some resistance in that "the militia who had gathered there in some numbers at the same time scattered." However, the local EMM was then in a brigade in St. Louis, so the Confederates were again blurring the distinctions among soldiers, militia, and civilians. The Arkansans "destroyed some property, and then left without further damage."[2] Price's army had hit a town only forty-two miles from the city.

As something of an afterthought, scouts also began probing to the west of the city. Colonel Lewis Merrill's veteranized Second Missouri Cavalry relocated to Kirkwood and found nothing nearby, but J. F. H. Ruby telegraphed General William S. Rosecrans from the garrison at Pacific that a large rebel force had passed through Richwoods only eighteen miles to the south. Accurately estimating 3,000 Confederates in that area, they sent Lieutenant Jesse Corum, a Potosi officer in the Third MSM Cavalry, with eighty mounted men to cover the roads and rumors that direction. Corum's men rode back into Pacific with the news that the Confederates had sent half of the force at Richwoods to Potosi for more lead, but were asking civilians about directions to—and Federal strength at—Pacific.[3]

A likely participant in Corum's scouting was his Irish-born townsman, Thomas Hanlon Macklind. Educated as a civil engineer, he had come to Missouri in 1856, where he worked on railroad construction until gaining admission to the bar at Potosi just before the war. He had served in various militia units before joining the hated Third MSM Cavalry, serving with other Potosians, Corum and Captain William T. Hunter, the post commander at Pacific. During these tense hours, Macklind likely worried over the fate of the Mineral Point telegraph operator Lousia Volker, to whom he may have already been engaged.[4]

Macklind likely knew that some of his townsmen remained in Confederate hands near where he scouted. On Friday, after marching to and from Caledonia, the nineteen civilian captives from Potosi faced "a proud, conceited-looking man." Asked about his birthplace, Donald Palmer frankly declared himself a Connecticut native and "a full blooded Yankee," but became annoyed when the officer eyed his tattered clothes and asked how long he worked on the railroad or dug in the mines. "You'll do," the official told each of the prisoners. After sending seven Irishmen to an Irish officer, the inspector general assigned the rest to a Captain Smith—probably one William W. Smith, an unattached officer with Fagan's division. As they were moved into line, one of the prisoners asked what they were doing, and the Confederates told them that they were about to made soldiers in Price's army. When asked if they had a choice, an officer replied, "I give you none." Price's recruiters dragooned Missouri civilians down the same path they had taken thousands of other "volunteers" from across the South. When they promised "all the honor due" Confederate soldiers, Palmer quipped: "From this time, we were half-starved, made to perform long marches by night and day, through rain and sleet, and deprived of all comforts and many necessaries."[5]

The Connecticut Confederate made the best of his situation. To escape Smith, he transferred to a different company commanded by one Captain Dark, probably the Captain Joseph N. Dark of Texas usually assigned to Kirby-Smith's headquarters. Palmer thought "a worse man never lived—brutal, cold-blooded, and with about all the vices common to man," but, at least, Dark was not the detested Smith. Determined not to starve, he and six other conscripts formed a mess that learned how to forage and "how to cook bread in the real C.S.A. Style."[6]

Thursday and Friday saw some Federal readjustment of the defenses. Rosecrans asked, "Is our cavalry posted that the enemy cannot pass them by a surprise or forced march into the city?" That Brigadier General Madison Miller's EMM held the line of the Meramec south of the city left General Smith "free to move in the direction of Kirkwood or the city" for redeployment where needed. By 10:55 p.m. Thursday, Smith had all but one of his trains north of the Meramec and, with two brigades on their way to Jefferson Barracks *en route* to points west. However, the old regular army officer never reconciled himself to the new technology available to him. "I hope it will be the last time I ever go soldiering on railroad," Smith complained.[7]

At the forefront of this shift, Brigadier General Edward H. Wolfe's brigade of Smith's infantry had passed supportive citizens along the roadside "with water in buckets, which they handed to the passing soldiers." In the darkness, the soldiers boarded flatcars at Kirkwood. "The night was wet and cold," one later recalled, "and the men suffered considerably." Worse, as the train crept west, it faced unexpectedly crowded eastbound traffic and the last twenty-four miles to Pacific simply dragged. At one point, it even found itself "compelled to wait several miles this side for the downward train."[8]

The Federal authorities had every reason to expect a Confederate attack on Pacific. Friday's *St. Louis Union* reported that such "would not be a surprise." That night, some of the local militia, with a handful of "Merill's Horse," had gone out to strengthen the little outpost at the Moselle bridge southwest of Pacific. At 9 p.m., the sounds of distant gunfire from that direction startled the residents of the town, who heard the shooting escalate "to a loud and incessant roar" over the next hour and a half. Then, "it ceased altogether," and "a big light was seen in the direction of the bridge."[9] From that point, two more small bridges stood between the town and the Confederate advance.

By then, everyone from the most disinterested civilian at Pacific to Rosecrans, at the other end of the telegraph wire, knew the Confederates were about to reach St. Louis County. Probably extrapolating on the news of fighting at the Moselle bridge, the *St. Louis Union* inserted a note of 11 p.m.: "We have every reason to believe that fighting is now going on at Franklin." In fact, the skirmishers on the Moselle were Lieutenant Colonel Robert C. Wood's men sent into the area to slow any Union move against General Jo Shelby's men at St. Clair. The real threat to Pacific came from Brigadier General William Cabell's Arkansas brigade, which Price dispatched to that town from Richwoods. Not particularly concerned with which enemy column was about to seize the town, Hunter telegraphed Rosecrans that the Confederates were "moving in force on this place." Then, the telegraph operator joined most of the other post officials in boarding the last train for St. Louis.[10] Behind, a mere handful of armed Unionists remained to stave off any minor raid.

The garrison had shuttled "all the rolling stock in and near Franklin" toward St. Louis and reversed the last westbound passenger train from the city back to Allenton where it remained until 7 a.m. They also entrusted the books and papers of the post to the ticket agent who planned to leave for the city himself. As the train steamed out, some spotted a body of cavalry approaching, but could not tell whether it was Catherwood's Union regiment or the rebels. The conductor did not want to wait and see, "but pushed on the train for this city."[11] The process made it virtually impossible for the westbound flatcars with Wolfe's brigade of infantry to make much progress.

Saturday morning, between 6 and 6:30 a.m., some 1,500 to 2,000 Confederates with artillery brushed aside "the very small force of Union troops in town together with a small body of militia, scarcely two hundred in all." Cabell immediately set his men to work, burning the depot, the machine shop, the engine house, and the woodsheds. By then, the Confederates had in custody "a large number of railroad laborers with their tools." Cabell later claimed that they tore up "about two miles of the railroad on both sides of Franklin." If true—and his report would not be published until 1900—his men got about thirty-five miles from the city.[12]

Pacific's capture probably forced even the most ardent local critics of the Federal occupation to begin rethinking the matter. Allegedly "piloted into the town by Copperhead citizens," the Confederates not only destroyed the public and railroad property but "thoroughly pillaged" the local stores. They also singled out the homes of prominent Unionists like Dr. E. S. Deweiler for special treatment. Apparently based on the damage, officials of the Western Sanitary Commission thought the Confederates had been "occupying Franklin for a few days." At least, they "killed no one here in cold blood," quipped the *Missouri Democrat*, hopefully and inaccurately.[13]

As elsewhere, the Confederates proved fearsome liberators. In addition to kidnapping a young black boy from his free mother, they seized "about thirty of the citizens" as conscripts. As at Potosi, they assembled every remaining adult white man in town, paroled those in Union service and notified the rest of their conscription, as "the State of Missouri belongs to the Confederate Government." The army exercised no discernible restraint upon those who reserved their "principal animosity" for the Germans. A St. Louis paper said they robbed the "Dutch" mercilessly, but mistakenly reported that they killed none of them. The invaders also conscripted one septuagenarian who marched along with them in sullen obedience, because, as he later explained, the rebels had apparently wanted him to fall out and give them an excuse to murder him; but the old German stubbornly marched fifteen miles until they tired of the game and released him.[14]

Wolfe's brigade finally arrived from Kirkwood later that morning. Their train steamed directly into the enemy guns. When it came to a stop, the Federals detrained "like a swarm of bees, dancing and singing" as they fell into line, "hardly waiting for their officers" and moved forward at the double-quick.[15] Doubtless, the fact that they would remain easy targets at the train helped speed the process.

The Confederates had a very strong position. They had artillery and men "two lines deep" anchored on the bluffs northeast of town and extending "over the meadows and to the woods." The veteranized Fifty-second Indiana formed "at right angles with the road," as Captain William A. Bodkin took a skirmish line forward. Other companies moved along the railroad by the flank until they passed the water tank, then opening "a brisk fire" on the rebels, pushing them "to the back of the town." Later accounts claim rather questionably reported that it took "but one volley" to move Cabell's men from their first position.[16]

The Arkansans quickly took a second position in the town itself. Although Union soldiers back at the train found it impossible to get their artillery off the cars and into action, three pieces of Confederate artillery opened on the Hoosiers, forcing them to hit the ground. They held their position until the Forty-ninth Illinois moved forward on their right, flanking the Confederates from the north. By then, the 117th Illinois had detrained and was running forward to join the battle. Still, it took "several volleys" to push the rebels another half mile west of town.[17]

The fighting continued in this third position long enough for the two Confederate cannons to lob "a dozen or so rounds" into the town. One ball passed through three or four residences and another struck the schoolhouse. After the lines neared and exchanged fire, Cabell's men withdrew "on a wagon road" running west toward Union. Along the way, "some three hundred rebels" hit Gray's Summit, "a place of some dozen houses." There, too, they destroyed "the depot and buildings," leaving along the road within a few miles one broken-down ambulance and some thirty horses wounded and broken down."[18]

Official accounts of the fight at Pacific are as muddled as those of larger battles, particularly as commanders minimized their own losses and exaggerated those inflicted on the enemy. Cabell reported that his brigade "drove them back," which, if it happened, must have represented a brief episode unverified elsewhere, because the Federals held the town by the close. Union reports described merely a few brief exchanges while, decades later, Cabell recalled an engagement of "nearly two hours." He remembered his loss as "small, about two killed, six wounded, eight or ten captured while too much under the influence of liquor, most of whom escaped and returned to their regiments." However, after taking Pacific, the Federals counted nine dead rebels, reported holding "a dozen or so," and estimated having wounded thirty or forty. Reported Federal casualties ranged from half a dozen to eleven wounded, two severely and four named in the *Missouri Democrat* when transported with "others" back to St. Louis that night.[19]

The Confederates' few hours at the vital rail center wrought a physical destruction unprecedented thus far in the campaign. To that point, the Confederates had destroyed sections of the Iron Mountain Railroad, torching the installations from Pilot Knob to DeSoto, and those on the southwestern from Cuba up to Pacific. At Pacific, though, Cabell's brigade not only got the depot, but also the water tanks, the engine house with a stationary engine, a machine shop, and a woodshed. In addition to destroying the track for some distance on either side of the town, his men destroyed a series of vital bridges. These included a 199-foot span over Brush Creek just outside of town; the 525-foot four-span Meramec No. 1 a few miles from Pacific; the 365-foot three-span Meramec No. 2; and the much-discussed Moselle bridge some distance beyond. As stated, Cabell then sent a force up the main line of the Pacific Railroad to burn "the depot at [Gray's] Summit and one or two places on the road," shortly before allegedly paroling his fifteen or twenty prisoners and releasing that "large number of railroad laborers."[20]

All these losses could be—and were—blamed on that troublesome train sitting on the tracks at Allenton, which had delayed the arrival of Smith's infantry, but someone with a view of the larger picture would have put it into a siding or into the nearest rail yard. At about noon, Rosecrans informed Smith that Wolfe's brigade had encountered the enemy at Pacific, but it took until midafternoon for him to suggest that it might be "advisable to send another brigade in train to his assistance, with orders to move carefully so as not to endanger their safety." In fact, when Smith replied that the fighting at Pacific had ended, Rosecrans decided it "would not be advisable to go beyond Kirkwood, and perhaps Gravois road would be far enough to camp your command."[21] In effect, Rosecrans, Smith, and other Federal commanders continued to leave the decision over where the front was to be—at Pacific or elsewhere—in the hands of these low-ranking officers, themselves able to do little more than respond to immediate Confederate initiatives.

Rosecrans found reasons not to move troops quickly into Pacific in his fear that a Confederate mounted force might ford the Meramec around Eureka, getting behind Pacific and moving directly on St. Louis. Those experienced in the perennially undermanned Union military in Missouri had long learned to live with such gaps, relying on extensive scouting to detect enemy movements. Rosecrans's scouts had actually provided him with almost a full day's warning of an attack on Pacific, another advantage he did not take. As Wolfe had steamed to Pacific, Merrill's cavalrymen took the Antire road to Eureka. They moved along a rising river with "not very good" fords into a broad open valley well covered by the rail line, very defensible bluffs north of town, and nearby Union outposts at Big Bend Ford, Meramec Station, and Fenton Ferry. Eureka—"a tavern and railroad station"—sat "on no important line from the south."[22] In short, Merrill thought Eureka and the Federal hold on Pacific secure from that direction.

Moreover, the cost of that inaction still smoldered at Pacific. Amid the charred assets of the Pacific Railroad, one soldier mused at the impact of a mere hour's delay in reaching the town. Although off by a few hours, his point reflected the cost the soldiers knew they would have to pay: "Never before have we so fully realized the value of an hour. That one hour cut off communications with Jefferson City, opened the way of the rebels to the heart of the state, and compelled us to engage in a long and fatiguing march after the plunderers of Price's army."[23] Without the railroad and the telegraph, locating Price's army would now have to rely on horseflesh and shoe leather.

For the duration of the campaign, Union soldiers would look out west from St. Louis into the heart of the state and have no easy means of knowing what was there. Smoke still curled up from the damage at Pacific when the soldiers, militia, and civilians there started at the sound of "cannonading about 2 o'clock." Merrill's experienced ears astutely identified the source as "probably at or in the direction of Union."[24] In the end, staring out quizzically over the hills to the west and awaiting orders to move into dangers of unknown proportions would prove to be good practice for the coming weeks.

Union

Although possibly confusing in the context of the Civil War, Union got its name after an acrimonious dispute over the location of the seat for Franklin County. It grew on the Bourbeuse River about equally distant from the main line of the Pacific railroad at Washington and the southwestern branch at St. Clair. Amos W. Maupin and David Murphy, two Federal heroes from Pilot Knob came from there, but the community had produced its share of men marching with Sterling Price. The town also had the most up-to-date industrial establishment in the county other than a railroad. An impressive three-story brick building on stone foundations housed the new Union roller mills with its recently added steam sawmill, which belonged to John T. Vitt, a lieutenant colonel in the Fifty-fifth EMM.[25]

By 1860, the 16,465 whites in Franklin County had tolerated the presence of nineteen free blacks and owned 1,601 slaves. While this approached the statewide proportion of 11 percent, there were serious internal differences within the country. Washington—the county's main town, up on the Missouri River, some seven miles north of Union—had only twenty-seven slaves owned by seven persons. In such places, talk of destroying the United States to save the institution seemed little short of madness to even the most conservative ears.[26] Early in the war, meetings at Washington and Union to select delegates to the state convention had elected the same Amos Maupin who now found himself making his way ducking rebel patrols as he moved up the tracks northeast from Leasburg. With the war, slavery had been too insignificant locally to keep sentiment from moving quickly toward Radical Unionism.

Guerrilla activities made Unionists trigger happy, including those who filled the Fifty-fourth and Fifty-fifth EMM. Two years earlier, Federals killed Mourton Bournes for resisting arrest, and old Benjamin Horine, one of the three commissioners who had originally established the county seat at Union. September 4, 1863, David Murphy and two other officers had taken the militia out to arrest James Henry Barnes at St. Clair. Ordinarily, nobody there would have paid much heed to the old Virginian whose family, enlarged by eleven slaves, included several sons with Price. Unfortunately, these sons sometimes returned through the lines for a visit and the Barnes farm sat near the southwestern branch of the railroad to the supply base at Rolla. Even a minor bit of sabotage along the tracks could damage the line of supply to all Federal operations to the south and west. The militia subsequently reported the old man shot while trying to escape. True, a grand jury had indicted the perpetrators, but Union officers would not be hanged for killing Confederate sympathizers.[27] From the perspective of perpetrators, they had struck preemptively against a possibly serious threat, but those who shared Barnes's sympathies particularly denounced it bitterly as the murder of an old man by "Hessians" or Tories.

More generally, the Fifty-fourth and Fifty-fifth EMM had a record of loosely interpreting the law when it came to protecting slaveholding. On September 23, 1863, after their officers and men had been implicated in the Barnes incident, the army dissolved both regiments of the local EMM, as part of a statewide purge of emancipationist units. According to the *Franklin County News*, "the Gamble-Schofield dynasty" removed and refused to replace Colonel Daniel Quimby Gale "on account of his Radical Union sentiments."[28] Dissolving the militia it could not control politically seemed a reasonable solution to the immediate problem, but it had long-term implications in terms of defense.

The fall of 1864 had presented Rosecrans no choice but to call up some units. He told them that they "can fight just as well as veterans in a fort," advised them to assemble, meet the enemy, and fire their volleys low aiming to "shoot at the enemy's shins" with the goal of each man inflicting one casualty. This would keep the enemy in "a compact body by attacking the heads of his columns and scattered parties fiercely, and keeping yourself from his grasp."[29] Neither awareness of the invasion's scale nor the disaster that befell the small clusters of local militia at Farmington, Potosi, and other communities ever moved Rosecrans to alter his advice.

While Gale mobilized what he could of what had been the Fifty-fourth and Fifty-fifth EMM at Washington, some detachments had assembled at Union.[30] Although ultimately not documented, command at the county seat likely fell to Captain Andrew Fink, whose small Provisional battalion of the EMM provided all the protection to the county's railroads that had been needed in good times. The son of a veteran of Napoleon's army, the thirty-two-year-old farmer had served as Maupin's deputy sheriff before the war and entered the war a conservative Lutheran Democrat. Nevertheless, the local secessionists cordially hated Fink, and he had little patience for them or their "peculiar institution."

At this point, though, much of his little force seems to have come from parts of Captain Henry Detmer's company of the Fifty-fourth EMM, and Captain Henry Gildehause's of the Fifty-fifth EMM. Detmer had fought earlier in Tennessee with the Fifteenth Missouri, and, like his men, farmed near the tiny village between Washington and Union, then called St. John's for the creek or St. Gertrude's for the Catholic church, though later Polish immigration would lead to its renaming as Krakow. Taking their place with the militia were a number of returned veterans and a few civilians, including the sixty-year-old Virginian Leo Bullock. Maupin's father-in-law, Bullock, "took his rifle, at the approach of the rebels, and bore his part." The little force estimated to be from about 150 to 400—mostly armed farmers—no doubt hoped to prevent the destruction of the mill by a small force of guerrillas. They also hoped to delay any larger enemy advance to allow for the evacuation of Washington or for Washington's reinforcement by the Federal army at St. Louis.

Not surprisingly, the day began, as J. H. Hanneken recalled, "full of rumors."[31] In midmorning, scouts rode into town "with their horses white with foam," announcing the presence of the unexpectedly large Confederate force at St. Clair. At that point, the militia "began erecting breastworks in the woods below Vitts's mill" near the bridge across the Bourbeuse from St. Clair. The works were "made of rails with earth put between the rails. We all worked like beavers. Those who had shovels piled the dirt, and those who had none carried rails."

On Gorg's hill overlooking the bridge south of town, Sallie Jeffries remained apprehensive. The daughter of Achilles W. Jeffries, she belonged to another transplanted Virginia family and had a Confederate brother wounded at Port Hudson who had since gone back east to assist in the defense of Richmond. Her uncle Cuthebert W. Jeffries claimed to dislike secession, but defended southern rights at every turn, and lived close to the Barnes family near St. Clair. "We were for the South," Sallie frankly recalled and saw the EMM simply as "Fink's men," thugs who bullied southern sympathizers and who had murdered Barnes. The family did remain friendly with the southern-born Union colonel Benjamin D. Dean of the Twenty-sixth Missouri, who had led a brigade in the previous year's assault on Missionary Ridge in Tennessee.[32] As the Confederate occupation of Union seemed increasingly likely, Sallie Jeffries took Dean's wife and son into her home and under her protection.

That afternoon, the advance of Price's army turned up on the road from St. Clair opposite the bridge into Union. The press described the Confederate force as 500 and 1,500, the latter far more likely, because parts of two Confederate divisions moved on Union. Years later, Hanneken still recalled the events at the bridge. Captain Detmer gave his orders, "Ready! Fire!" A volley staggered the Confederate column at the bridge. Alerted, the rebels at the head of the column halted, reformed, and tried again only to face another volley from Detmer's line. A third attempt to rush over the bridge also met a volley.[33]

The skirmishing lasted long enough for the Confederates to have deployed several regiments coming off the road and gotten artillery into position, as other accounts indicate. Although Detmer's position protected the mill and the bridge, the rebels simply never needed the bridge to cross the Bourbeuse. Brigadier General John B. Clark Jr.'s regiments under Colonels William Jeffers and Robert Lawther crossed elsewhere, hurrying to the left and right of the Federals, the latter cutting off possible escape to the east and St. Louis. Colonel Sidney D. Jackman's brigade of Shelby's division also formed and joined in the shooting near the bridge. Clark's cannoneers—either Captain H. C. Hynson's Texas battery or Captain S. S. Harris's Missouri guns—forded their artillery over the Bourbeuse and hauled it to the crest of Gorg's Hill south of town.[34] Detmer and his men may have seen the preparations and tried to meet it as best they could.

Moreover, as the Confederates climbed Gorg's Hill, some of the militia went forward to contest them. Sallie Jeffries and the other women and children in the house on the hill listened as the shooting moved in their direction. She saw "Fink's men" as they stopped near the front of the house and tried to interfere with the preparations of the Confederate battery, but the rebels quickly drove them back. Those sheltering in the house listened as the bullets thudded against the walls and roof, followed by the artillery, which surely caused the "cannonading about 2 o'clock" heard at Pacific. When the first cannonballs landed short—one embedding itself in the fence—Jeffries then sent Eliza Harris, one of her slaves, upstairs to wave the yellow curtain out the south window at the gunners, indicating that the Federal skirmishers had pulled back from the house toward the bridge.[35]

The artillery soon got its range and began landing its shots nearer the thinly manned works to which the skirmishers toward the hill had not returned. Hanneken and those near him "imagined that we heard the cannon balls in the trees above our heads." In all probability, other militiamen realized that the cavalry had nearly surrounded them as well. Hanneken recalled that Detmer shouted "'Everybody for himself.' That was the last order given at the Battle of Vitt's Mill. It was obeyed in letter and in spirit. The famous command of Lady Macbeth was also observed, 'Stand not upon the order of your going, but go at once.'"[36] Whether or not Detmer said this, it seems quite plausible that somebody did, and the hearing of it would have been enough for the sorely tested farmers around Hanneken to take it as an order. In addition, the flight toward Washington would permit them to rejoin the bulk of Gale's men.

Jackman saw the militia "taking the alarm." Clark's main body "moved forward rapidly to the attack, routing the enemy," Lawther "observed the Federals falling back. We instantly charged through the town." Jackman's men joined those of Clark in rushing the bridge. The militia scattered, some into the arms of Lawther's cavalry on the St. Charles rock road, which ran toward the Missouri River near Washington, and, particularly those returning from Gorg's Hill, through Union itself. Major John N. Edwards of Shelby's staff blamed Clark for having "permitted the garrison to escape probably because he did not know how to capture it. And why should he? Recently promoted from the infantry, he had little of that sprightliness and dash so essential for a cavalry officer."[37] In reality, those of Shelby's men under Jackman were also present, and nobody really had the time to go around Union and cut off the retreat, but Edwards's fearless obliviousness often served as much to obscure as to celebrate Confederate achievements.

Notwithstanding Hanneken's humorous self-disparaging recollections, a high-ranking Confederate officer thought that the Unionists had shown "considerable pluck and firmness." Greene actually thought a considerable force had "evacuated the place" after "a feeble resistance." Lawther thought "some 400 Federals" engaged; though Clark thought them "some 200 strong." Blurring the distinction between militia and civilians, Confederate reports claimed that they killed somewhere between ten and seventy Federals, and they captured from sixty-five to seventy, though Jackman thought the prisoners "only an inconsiderable number." At a minimum, civilian bystanders saw three or four Confederates killed and half a dozen wounded, but Lawther and Jackman told Clark that they had, respectively, one wounded and one killed. Clark then reported to his superiors that he taken the town without any casualties at all.[38]

EMM resistance at Union had limited results, though it might well have been otherwise. Most immediately, the engagement denied the rebels daylight for any operations against Washington, the Pacific Railroad, and the Missouri River. By the time the invaders had regrouped, Lawther could only move his regiment up the rock road north to South Point on the Missouri River, a few miles east of Washington. The militia won an additional day for Gale to evacuate Washington and for Rosecrans to move his forces west from St. Louis, should he decide to take advantage of the opportunity.[39] However, had Rosecrans moved Smith from St. Louis even a bit earlier, he would have kept Pacific and retained the option of reinforcing Washington by rail forcing a time-consuming concentration of Price's army that would have allowed the rest of the Federal forces to strike west from Pacific.

Price's Decision

For the first time since returning to Missouri, Price concentrated his entire army. "The army again reunited at Union," recalled Major Edwards, and what a collection it was. Louisa Volker had described them as "barefooted, but spurred; others clothed in gaudy-colored curtain damask; all manner of hats and caps; some in Federal uniform, and strapped to their saddles was all kinds of plunder—calico, domestic, shoes, boots, tin pans, bed quilts, etc." Of an earlier encounter with General John S. Marmaduke's men, slaves remembered their tall hats and one said "most of 'em was a-wearin' coonskin caps with de tail a-hangin' down." Another woman assured her cousin, "You never *saw such* a *looking army* as Price had. They were not *half clothed*, and not *over two-thirds* of *them armed*, but O there were *so many*."[40] The impression they left was anything but that of a modern professional military force.

Dr. William McPheeters reached Union the next day, and found it "a pretty little town." The area seemed to him to be "free from Dutch all of whom had fled on our approach, but crowded with soldiers and good southern people who came in to see and welcome Gen. Price and his army." "The town and surrounding country were full of Rebels, the name by which Southern people were called," remembered Jeffries. "All the vacant lots in front of our house were filled with tired loved ones from many places. The night was dark, not a drum or a voice was heard in our part of town." McPheeters described "the alacrity with which the young men join our army," and Edwards claimed that Lieutenant Colonel Alonzo W. Slayback filled his regiment there.[41] None of the Confederates or their sympathizers noted the presence of the previous day's dead or much of what they did not want to see.

A St. Louis newspaperman later opined, "Union has suffered worse, I think, than any other town that rebels have yet visited." Already exasperated by having to fight their way into the town, the rebels found that its two principal stores had already shipped the bulk of their stock to safety. The town had no railroad property to destroy, but it did have the public funds and records of the county, so the Confederates searched for the sheriff and the county treasurer. When they found that the county officers had moved the public funds to safety, they took out their disappointment on the county records. "The debris of the records," wrote the reporter, "are strewn along the road in the track of the rebel for a distance of twelve miles." The scene moved a bugler with the Kansas cavalry to write that "the Rebs have come through this place like a dose of salts."[42]

The Confederates engaged in unprecedented destruction at Union.[43] As expected, the Confederates seized and used Vitt's Mill to grind grain for their own use. In addition, it thoroughly plundered his house, as well as that of Adolph Vitt and took all thirty head of cattle from his nephew, William T. Vitt. The St. Louis *Democrat* listed the most prominent robbery victims, such as Charles and Frederick Reinhardt and Thomas Bruch, but only "a rare exception" avoided that fate on the street and the soldiers "gutted nearly every private residence" in the town. Most victims "added to the crime of Unionism that of being German."

In targeting Unionists, their families and their homes, the Confederates hardly distinguished between the volunteers and the militia. The Reinhardts had been in the Fifty-fifth EMM, Charles serving as its quartermaster, but the area had contributed many men to the hard-fighting Twenty-sixth and Forty-seventh Missouri. Confederates burned several of their homes belonging to their special enemies. They tried to catch William Meyersieck, formerly a sergeant in the Twenty-sixth, but he had taken to the bush after helping to defend the town; when they failed to find him at home, they "burnt his house to the ground." They also torched Bruch's home.

At a house on the edge of town, an Irish railroad worker alternately tried to sleep and to coax information from his guards. He had begun the day walking up the southwestern branch in hopes of reaching Union lines. He had skirted Confederate patrols at Stanton and the "large" numbers at St. Clair, but wound up in custody at Union. When the Confederates tried to conscript him, he "begged off on a plea of a sick family," after which his captors tried to impress him by introducing him to an officer "who he was told was General Price."[44]

Others coming up the southwestern branch had similar experiences. Former sheriff Maupin had made his way from Leasburg, as had Captain Robert L. Lindsay and a handful of other officers, all in hopes of reaching Pacific and getting word to Rosecrans. However, the Confederate presence at Sullivan and St. Clair forced them to veer north toward Union, which they found entirely infested with enemy patrols. At one point, Maupin separated to search for food and found himself chased by rebels from a farmhouse; after getting a bit of a lead on his pursuers, he plunged into a nearby wood, covered himself in the autumn leaves, and eluded capture.[45] Convinced that they were as unlikely to reach Union as Pacific, the officers simply went deeper into the woods and hoped for the best.

In town, Maupin's wife, the former Ada Bullock—Leo Bullock's daughter—encountered Lieutenant Francis Brakett Barnes, the son of old John Henry Barnes. Lieutenant Barnes happily led squads of vindictive Confederates through the streets "spotting" the homes of the most intransigent local Unionists. He gallantly shook Mrs. Maupin's hand, assuring her of his protection, and assigned a "guard" to her home. Before their eyes that "guard" entered the house and began to "break up the furniture, slit the carpet of the parlor into shreds, and destroy everything of value they could lay their hands on." They took all of her clothes and those of their three-year-old child. As a bonus, Barnes's men found and destroyed an oil painting of David Murphy's recently deceased wife, which he had passed on to her friend, Mrs. Maupin. "Thus," wrote a St. Louis paper, "the chivalry sought to appease the anger and mortification they suffered by their defeat at Pilot Knob at the hands, in part, of these two brave officers."[46]

By then, though, Barnes, in particular, was on a spree. He spotted First Lieutenant Moritz Greifeld of the old Franklin County Home Guard. "The ruffian walked deliberately up to him where he was stationed under guard within fifty paces of General Price's headquarters, and shot him through the head, killing him instantly." Almost immediately, Barnes realized that he had just killed the wrong man and wandered off in search of the right one. He apparently did find the man he sought, Henry Boeger of the Fifty-fifth EMM, the newly elected township trustee, reported the next day as having been killed. Greifeld and Boeger may have been "the poor fellows" Private Donald Palmer saw when he reached the courthouse at Union on noon Sunday. There he saw two men "lying dead outside, not the slightest pretense having been made to bury them or to protect them from being devoured by the hogs." Palmer mistakenly thought them casualties incurred "where a few soldiers had made some slight resistance the day before."[47]

There were other killings. Robert Johnson, an old farmer with family in the Twenty-sixth Missouri, happened to be in town that day. After being robbed there, he was stopped again while on his way home, but had nothing left to steal, for which he received a bullet in the front of his head. Sallie Jeffries remembered his killing, adding that he had been "buried west of the fairgrounds near the road" and that, years later, "a big oak tree had grown up in the middle of the grave." Ten miles from town, a Lieutenant Myer had been "last seen in his house in the hands of the rebels." When friends and family found blood there and Myer missing, they assumed that he, too, had been killed. Some days later, Adam Eisenberger lay wounded in his home four miles from town and was not expected to live. Afterward, residents also found the bodies of "several negroes" murdered by the Confederates and, as at Pacific, one of them enslaved a young black boy to accompany the column.[48]

The occupation also provided instances "of the outraging of females by the rebels," a rare ordeal for white women despite the otherwise unrestrained nature of the war. The wife of Corporal Charles G. Schmidt, the absent color-bearer of the Twenty-sixth Missouri "was ravished and her person violated by a number of the fiendish ghouls" to the extent that she was "now nearly dead." Outside of town, a group attacked the wife of one Union soldier but she fled into the woods. Another group entered the home of another demanding whiskey, choked her with a handkerchief around her neck, and threatened to kill her until she convinced them that she had none. Some of Shelby's men assaulted another German woman in her home "not over a square from Price's headquarters" in Union, but "some rebel soldiers less brutal than their fellows" came to her rescue. However the provost guard made no arrests, the locals claiming that they had been "too busy pillaging Union people."[49]

That night, Sallie Jeffries and Mrs. Dean, her Unionist guest hosted Marmaduke, Shelby, and Clark for supper, though Price himself was conspicuous by his absence. The general stayed at the hotel on the square and had likely collapsed with exhaustion in what must have been the best bed he had found in weeks. The campaign had become a difficult ordeal for a man of his age and health, and he had an important decision to make, if he had not made it yet. Afterward, he and others asserted that they had disavowed their hopes for St. Louis back at Pilot Knob and determined at that point to strike at Jefferson City, but he had not moved that way when he had much of his army only two days' march from the state capital, countermarching them east instead. Nor does it make sense that he would have made any final decision to bypass the metropolis until he had to and certainly not before the Saturday date on the proclamation of the Order of American Knights.

That Saturday, back in St. Louis, John H. Taylor, the new supreme commander of the Order of American Knights (OAK) issued a circular aimed at "Sons of Liberty . . . strong in numbers—full 30,000 strong." Claiming that his "absence from the city prevent an earlier issue of this communication," Taylor claimed the authority "to appoint a major-general to command the members called into the military service" and named Price to do so.

> All true knights will yield prompt obedience to the orders and commands of General Price. Meanwhile do all possible damage to the enemy. Seize all arms and munitions of war within your power. Take possession of and hold all important places you can, and recruit as rapidly as possible. If you cannot sustain yourselves fall back upon the army of occupation. In townships and counties where you cannot concentrate on account for the presence of the enemy repair singly or in squads without delay to the army, or to points where your brethren may be marshaling their forces, and in all cases be ready to obey the commands of your chieftain.

Taylor continued, "Already hundreds of militiamen, arms in hand, have taken position beside the brave and gallant soldiers under General Price. In no event permit yourself to be arrayed against your brethren."[50] The proclamation likely mobilized nobody, and, if its primary purpose was to embolden secessionists and demoralize Unionists, it had the opposite effect.

For a while at least, Price himself tarried near Pacific. Near present-day Villa Ridge, a ten-year-old German boy taking corn to a nearby mill fled to the woods with the arrival of Confederate troops. Several of them pursued him and brought him back to a carriage as a possible spy. There he found himself questioned by none other than Sterling Price.[51] The boy went home with a memory of seeing the Confederate general closer to St. Louis than that of any other surviving civilian account.

By late Saturday, though, Price had tested the waters enough to know that he could not see the bottom. If the OAK manifesto provided some measure of the political strength of the Confederate cause in the area, the probe to Pacific had hinted its severe military weakness. The Arkansans had encountered a few regiments of the Sixteenth Corps and Price had no reason to suspect that rest of it was not nearby. Most importantly, the agent Price had sent to St. Louis—the one who had not been able to report as planned at Potosi—most likely turned up during the concentration at Union. "Upon overtaking me," wrote Price much later, "he informed me that I would be pursued by 24,000 men from Saint Louis, 15,000 from Jefferson City, which, with the forces in my front from Kansas, he believed to be the entire force with which I would have to contend."[52]

Price's knowledge of his own army may have been barely better than his grasp of Federal strength. At any given point, it is doubtful whether he knew how many men he had, how many had standard arms, and how many were prepared to fight, and he had trouble commanding what he had. Historians have generally accepted Price's initial report of bringing 12,176 into the state, but have disregarded his later claim to have raised another 5,000 recruits, without counting the thousands of "conscripted" men. At the time Price entered Union, he may well have added some 1,500 in southeast Missouri (replacing the losses between Pilot Knob and Leasburg), and even gained 500 to 1,000 more in proximity to St. Louis, for a total that approached 13,000. Some of the paroled prisoners who straggled into Pacific estimated the Confederate army at about 7,000 men, though they would have seen but part of it. Certainly, Price's army not only recruited but also shed men, both those who longed for a visit home and those who had simply regretted leaving.[53] Whatever its strengths and weaknesses, Price's measure of his own forces rightly raised doubts about what it could achieve by advancing on St. Louis.

Still, if Rosecrans planned to bluff Price with the idea that he had a large Union army at St. Louis, it only worked because Price himself wanted so desperately to be fooled. As the tired old man sat in the shambles of perhaps the most important town he had come to liberate, neither he, Shelby, Reynolds, Thompson, nor anyone else had been able to restrain those members eager to avenge themselves on their Unionist former neighbors for wrongs real or imagined. He could have no reason to believe that he would be able to lead a disciplined and well-ordered Confederate force into St. Louis, and a brutal, vengeful entry into the area would raise against them a city that had many more men of military age than Price's army. Moreover, if Price would make no move on St. Louis, any delay near it allowed the Federal force there to grow ever larger, while his own army and its hangers-on made more enemies.

The hard realities of the campaign seem to have driven Price into deeper levels of denial. Regardless of how extensive the OAK circular may have been, Confederate recruiting in the area hardly encouraged a strike against the city, but Price later explained the problem as volunteers "already pouring in on me so rapidly that I knew I would not be able to protect and feed them, and as it would require that my army should be kept together to protect them on a rapid and dangerous retreat from the State." So, too, Price reported that he decided not to "issue an address to the people calling upon them to rally to me."[54] In short, the reality of the OAK appeal to the people of Missouri went the way of the Confederate artillery on Shepherd Mountain and the long train of murdered prisoners and civilians.

To be fair, of course, the biggest disappearance from the memories of 1864 were the plans of the Confederate high command to follow Price's mounted strike force into Missouri with tens of thousands of well-supplied infantry to secure what had been taken. From where Price sat, he could look south well into Arkansas and see no such support coming up. What had intended to be the advance of a reoccupation had become a large mounted force stranded hundreds of miles from help.

Three

The Secondary Goal

6

The Turning Point

From the Bourbeuse to the Gasconade

By the time General Sterling Price's Confederate army reached the town of Union, it began abandoning the last of its plans to reassert the sovereignty of Missouri against the Federal occupiers. By the time it reached Union, though, its members felt no need to make such a claim by hoisting the Confederate banner over the Franklin County courthouse. Rather, when Private Donald Palmer passed through town, he noted that the building instead "floated our good old flag, union down."[1] Beneath it, the counteroffensive to liberate Missouri from the Yankees took a giant step toward redefining itself mentally as an oversized raid through enemy territory.

When Price's army hit the Missouri River on Sunday, October 2, it had to show its hand as to whether it would challenge the Federal hold on St. Louis or turn west. Its choice, in turn, required responses from Union general William S. Rosecrans and the Department of Missouri, but the Federal high command remained cautious about almost everything other than its reckless deployment of the militia. Unionists, in and out of uniform, engaged in desperate heroics, partly because the state's erstwhile liberators, in frustration, set aside their use of guerilla surrogates to impose a military authority that, for most Missourians, made their very real grievances against Union provost marshals pale in comparison.

Washington

From the Franklin County seat at Union, Price faced north to Washington, on the south bank of the Missouri River some fifty-four rail miles from St. Louis. Founded by the parents of Judge James W. Owen and other transplanted southerners a generation before, Washington had grown to a population of about 1,500. It had ten stores, several brickyards, numerous "mechanics," and a good-sized brewery, half a dozen doctors and teachers, two bankers, an architect, a realtor, a dentist, and six lawyers. The cultural life also flowered with a singing society, a debating society, and a newly organized *Turnerbund*, as well as Presbyterian, Methodist, Lutheran, and Catholic churches. This growth owed less to the southern town fathers than to the thousands of Germans who clustered in northern Franklin County. In the absence of slavery, Unionism not only prevailed but became ardently emancipationist and Radical.

War had shaken the civil authority in Washington, as elsewhere in the state. Local home guards garrisoned the railroad and guarded its bridges, establishing their camp in a field south of Main Street between Jefferson and Lafayette. Soldiers regularly used a building on the east side of Jefferson Street between Third and Fourth Streets as a headquarters and jail. A transient refugee population settled nearby, including many runaway slaves. The town's trustees sometimes failed to muster a quorum, but the previous winter it faced a possible smallpox outbreak among black refugees camped near town, so they sent Dr. John Dugge to vaccinate them. The conservative hierarchy of the state often thought the militia and its community more troublesome than the relatively minor threat of Confederates that near St. Louis, and they had left the militia system dormant for over a year.

The arrival of the Confederate forces left the authorities no option but to remobilize what it could of the militia. Wednesday's telegrams from Rosecrans alerting both Colonel Daniel Quimby Gale and Judge Owen, Amos W. Maupin's former assistant. An unlikely Radical, Gale was the fifty-four-year-old dean of the county's legal profession and the builder of the first brick home in town. However, he had been a Massachusetts born machinist before coming west, and he had an abiding contempt for the arrogance of the slaveocracy that had run his adopted state. On Thursday, Rosecrans had no options to overcoming his conservative reservations and called on Gale to pull together the remnants of the old EMM.[2]

In reality, the Confederates reached Richwoods on the edge of the county before Rosecrans warned Owens, Dugge, and state representative Gert Goebel "to seize the ferry-boats" should Price's army come their way. Captain Amos P. Foster of the Provisional EMM had already called out "all able bodied men here and in this vicinity . . . for immediate self-defense." Goebel and others began alerting the more-isolated residents of the countryside to the possibility of invasion. As well, Captain Julius Wilhelmi seized "one boat and all skiffs" and left standing orders at the waterfront to seize the second ferry when it returned. In short order, they reportedly had both the *Evening Star* and the *Bright Star*, one of the new center-wheelers.[3]

The army had given Gale an absurdly impossible task, as it had the local militias at places such as Potosi. In a matter of a few days, he had to rebuild not only his own Fifty-fourth but also the Fifty-fifth EMM and to amalgamate these with the Provisional companies and "all able-bodied arms-bearing men of Franklin County, Mo. between the ages of eighteen and forty-five." Only partly informed of developments and uncertain of Rosecrans's plans—which could have involved sending reinforcements by train or water—Gale set his men to work as he got them throwing breastworks across the ridge above town along St. John's (now Fifth) Street.[4]

Gale assembled five to six hundred men with their backs to the Missouri River on the north. On Saturday the telegraph to St. Louis went dead, indicating the Confederate presence to the east. Within hours, riders from the south brought news of the Confederate arrival at Union. From this point, Gale's EMM depended exclusively on his couriers. Despite the secessionist proclivities of their superiors, Father J. Martin Seisl and other Jesuit priests in the parishes of Washington, St. Gertrude's, and Union had taken to the road that day as couriers, as their parishioners took up arms for the Federal government.[5]

The local authorities faced a horrific choice, but took the only option they could. The force at Washington would fight, though the St. Louis press described them as "raw militia." However, they had no prospects for reinforcements, "no fortifications, except a temporary breastwork thrown up for the occasion, and no cannon." Worse, if Gale stayed and fought, his men would have no escape if he sent away the town's two ferries, but if he kept them, it risked providing Price's army a means of crossing the river. Gale and Owens agreed that, whether they fought or not, Washington's capture seemed "as certain as anything could be."[6] The only solution would be the town's evacuation, after which the local EMM could bring a modest reinforcement to the Federal force marching west from St. Louis.

Starting at 11 p.m. Saturday, Gale had the ferries shuttling any civilians who wanted to escape to the north bank of the river. A few hours later, Confederate colonel Robert Lawther's advance reached the Missouri River at its South Point only a couple of miles downriver from where hundreds of soldiers and civilians nervously awaited their turn to board the ferries. Part of the militia crossed first and secured the landing site before the boats began shuttling the civilians across. At daybreak, the boats left the last of the militia downstream "well armed but with no commissary stores" at the railroad stop opposite the town of Augusta on the north bank. Returning to Washington for the last trip, the *Bright Star* took on its passengers, including Judge Owens, the *de facto* guardian of the post's records, who boarded with the *Wide Awake* for one last trip.[7]

The channel carried the *Bright Star* quickly downstream a short distance to South Point, the southernmost spot on the Missouri River. Here, Lawther's Confederates opened "a brisk fire of musketry" into the boat from only about thirty yards away. The women and children took shelter in the cabins and stayed on the floor, but between seventy-five and a hundred shots left the boat "much perforated in the cabin and pilot house." The lucky passengers had only one casualty: a railroad bridge builder named Hose Carter, who took a bullet in the head, but the wound proved so shallow that the ball fell from his hat as he removed it.[8] The *Bright Star* had gone only three hundred yards further when the *Wide Awake* came opposite the rebels.

"With no protection other than the window-glass and thin boards of the pilot house," Captain Elijah W. Murphy of the *Wide Awake* steered the boat through a difficult channel. Then, the now-well-prepared enemy "thoroughly riddled" the superstructure of his vessel with gunfire. They continued for half a mile when the *Bright Star* grounded briefly on a sandbar.[9] Nevertheless, their running the gauntlet had denied the Confederates their much-wanted boats.

By 8 a.m., the rest of Clark's brigade had joined Lawther's regiment and marched the last few miles into town. From the boats downriver in the early morning, Owens and his fellow passengers "could see the depot at South Point and Washington in flames." That evening, Colonel Lewis Merrill reported from Pacific that "a bright fire has been burning in the direction of Washington the last hour and is now dying out; looks like the fire of burning buildings." Based on the visibility of the flames from Pacific, the St. Louis papers that day noted the burning of the depots at Washington and South Point.[10] Somewhere in town, fires burned through the day.

Yet, the brief occupation of Washington proved benign compared to that of Union. The unresisting river town hosted only Clark's well-seasoned brigade for a day, while the county seat had contested the occupation and endured the passage of the entire Confederate army with all its hangers-on over several days. Washington even saw acts of genuine gallantry as when Clark ordered soldiers to assist in containing the flames that had leaped from the depot's roof to nearby structures. Finally, there were personal reunions such as that of Confederate sergeant Oscar Quimby Gale with his cousin, the wife of Judge Owens.[11]

Nevertheless, Washington was a large town with rich pickings. Clark and his officers had higher priorities than to control the foraging by their demoralized men, the stragglers, and some of the even more undisciplined camp followers. Indeed, the damage later seemed "principally confined to the stores," as they looted virtually every place of business in town. The nearby brewery alone lost property valued at $11,000, much of it grain that might have slaked the thirst of German militiamen had it not been redirected into the bellies of Confederate horses. After pillaging the stores, they tied ribbons on their bayonets. Paradoxically, the hurried Confederates missed James G. Magann's *Franklin County News*, a Radical paper actively promoting Fletcher's campaign, probably because it had a Bible Dispensary in the front.[12]

Even here, though, some soldiers proved to be trigger happy, particularly in dealing with Germans. One group on southbound Pottery Road west of town killed the young son of the local violin teacher in his own yard; the boy made the mistake of running toward the house at their approach. Others at the riverfront gratuitously fired shots at the refugees who had sheltered across the river in the covered bridge at Quakenbrueck.[13]

The most celebrated local atrocity was the cold-blooded murder of John Henry Uhlenbrock, the local liveryman, a devout Catholic, and "a strong Democrat." The militia had taken his mounts earlier, leaving him only with his own horse. That Sunday, a group of Confederates took the remaining horse from his house while he was going to Mass. Another group accosted him as he was returning, wanting the animal. He referred them to his stable, and the rebels became convinced he had hidden it when they did not find it there. They "marched up to St. John's street to the carding machine," shot him dead, and left the body. The next morning, his head had been "entirely eaten off by the hogs."[14]

The Confederates had sufficient reason to be nervous. The two hundred Federals encountered at Union and the five or six hundred ferried from Washington accounted for only about a fraction of what should have been available to the local EMM. Alone and in small groups of neighbors, many had chosen to remain with their families in the deep woods around northern Franklin County. One group of reported looters showed up at St. Gertrude's Church four miles south of town, but the militia members among the Sunday churchgoers fired on them from the nearby woods, reportedly killing one and driving the rest off.[15]

That afternoon, Rosecrans had confirmation of the Confederates presence at Washington. After Owen reached St. Charles on the *Bright Star* at 4:30, he quickly located the telegraph and reported to Federal headquarters. By then, everything Merrill's men had learned indicated that the Army of Missouri had turned west. General Andrew J. Smith agreed, declaring "the enemy have undoubtedly gone to Jefferson City."[16]

Federal Command Decisions

General Samuel R. Curtis in Kansas read the reality in his maps. He had served only a year after his West Point graduation before taking up civil engineering. War with Mexico had found him the state adjutant general in Ohio, so he took command of a regiment. Moving to Iowa, he entered law, and won elections as mayor of Keokuk and three times to Congress. In 1861, he resigned his seat to take Iowa troops, and quietly went about the business of winning impressive successes when few other Federal commanders had been able to avoid disasters. Like Rosecrans, Curtis had faced Price before. Two and a half years earlier, Curtis had blunted Price's counteroffensive at Pea Ridge, shattering secessionist hopes for Missouri and, inadvertently, making possible a national military reassignment of priorities to the east.

Politics plagued Curtis as much as Rosecrans. After his success at Pea Ridge, he had preceded Rosecrans in heading the Department of Missouri until he fell, the casualty of the explosive political conflicts among Missouri Unionists. Two years later, his command of the Department of Kansas required a balancing among officials, such as Senator Jim Lane or Governor Thomas Carney. These men had built careers on the opportunities presented by the war and war scares, but so mistrusted each other that their cooperation with Curtis turned on whether or not his goals might serve their own agenda. In this case, the facts that Lane stood to gain from an invasion scare and Carney did not muddled Curtis's best efforts to convey the very real threat. Then, even as Price had entered Missouri, Cherokee raiders under Confederate colonel Stand Watie had seized a Federal supply train at Cabin Creek just beyond the Kansas state line, which refocused fears of invasion on the Indian Territory to the south rather than on Missouri to the east. Finally, the wartime misconduct of some Kansas troops in Missouri complicated the cooperation of Union troops and left the Second Colorado Cavalry as the most successful out-of-state unit into western Missouri.

Curtis knew, as he later wrote, that "the crisis as to the direction of the enemy's movement occurred about the 2d of October." Price's army would find that the impassable Missouri River prevented any northern march, making Washington "the turning point." Either Price would have to attack what there was of that massive army Rosecrans claimed to have in St. Louis or a "movement westward towards my department seemed inevitable." As the latter took place, a flustered Curtis asked Rosecrans of Price, "Where are you driving him?"[17] Remarkably, though, the apparently befuddled Federals at St. Louis had not begun to drive anyone anywhere.

The official reports offer no explanation for why that would be the case. Subdistrict commander Lieutenant Colonel Hiram M. Hiller sent very good news from Cape Girardeau. On Sunday, the veteranized and tiny Sixty-first Illinois returned from there "satisfied there has been no rebel force on the river." Hiller reestablished his outposts at Charleston, Bloomfield, and New Madrid and restored telegraph communications, and his scouts as far as the Arkansas line encountered only scattered Confederates. "The rebels have all left this section," he wrote, the only exceptions being their rumored working of lead mines at Hillsboro, and a small force at Fredericktown. Within hours, Dr. Seymour D. Carpenter turned up in St. Louis "under a rebel flag of truce" to arrange for medical supplies to reach the wounded at Pilot Knob, adding ominously that some of the Federal prisoners taken there were being "badly treated." Then, on Monday evening, a tired courier rode into the Cape with news that Major General Joseph A. Mower's lost division had camped some forty-five miles west of town, having exhausted their rations, their horses, and themselves.[18]

The view from the southern defenses of the city confirmed this change. Brigadier General Madison Miller's EMM covered the Meramec from Lemay's Ferry all the way upriver to Fenton, and his scouts to the south "report things quiet and find no enemy this side of Hillsborough, Jefferson County." General Alfred Pleasonton had finally arrived at St. Louis on Sunday, and ordered Lieutenant Colonel Samuel H. Melcher of the Sixth MSM Cavalry to board his horsemen on a well-protected engine and "go as far south as he can with safety." The Federals reoccupied DeSoto, and moved cautiously beyond, two regiments arriving there on Monday to repair the bridge, as Melcher's scouts looked southwest from Fenton Ferry as far as Richwoods.[19] The scouts confirmed that significant enemy forces no longer functioned south of the city with a single exception.

Melcher encountered "some seventy-five citizens" at the Meramec bridge still homeless because of a local Confederate occupation. They reported "considerable number of rebels in and about Potosi, Old Mines, &c. They are robbing indiscriminately of money, watches, &c., occasionally killing." Federals reasonably estimated three to four hundred "intending to remain there until driven out," despite the efforts of one Ben Talvold to conscript a more sizable force.[20]

Nevertheless, General Smith was not taking his infantry west into Franklin County. At the time the Confederates seized Washington on Sunday, Smith was doing his best to concentrate his division at Kirkwood. For a brief instant, the Rosecrans of old—the aggressive fighter of 1861 in western Virginia—mildly nudged Smith to venture west of Kirkwood toward Meramec Station. That evening, as Smith reached Kirkwood *en route* to Meramec Station, Rosecrans even suggested that he take his men still farther, to Pacific.[21]

Such a mood did not last longer than to secure Pacific. Smith got most of his division to Kirkwood around 4 p.m. Sunday. By Monday, General Edward Pike of the EMM had two brigades of militia at Laclede Station on the Pacific Railroad, ready to continue to Pacific once Smith advanced to Gray's Summit. Smith did have his 117th Illinois marching up Manchester Road, but had not yet concentrated all of his infantry at Pacific, much less moved on to Gray's Summit. In fact, as late as Wednesday, most of Smith's men milled about Pacific and Gray's Summit. Back in the city, Rosecrans had sent everyone back to work, though still knocking off early to allow the militia to get together.[22]

Within hours of hearing the guns from Union Saturday afternoon, the ever-reliable Merrill sent scouts and promised to "push reconnaissance out as far as my means will permit both to-night and to-morrow morning." That night, more of his horsemen rode into the void beyond Gray's Summit toward Union and south toward Hillsborough and Richwoods. On Sunday afternoon, Rosecrans asked, "How far have your scouts been towards Washington?" Merrill replied that none had yet returned from the west and southwest, but that a patrol to the south had taken three prisoners in an encounter near Catawissa with "a party of horse-thieves about twenty strong." By Sunday, Merrill thought the Federals well protected against "a strong demonstration, if not a real movement, along the State road towards Saint Louis." "I can hardly believe they intend moving on Saint Louis," added Smith to Rosecrans, "although the direction they are coming might indicate that intention."[23]

When Rosecrans pressed the matter, Merrill responded with an understandable sharpness. After all, in addition to these intelligence operations, he had to cover the approaches to Pacific with "only about 500 cavalry, nearly all of whom have been constantly in the saddle for forty-eight hours scouting, marching, and picketing." Concerned about Price's exact whereabouts in the Bourbeuse Valley, Rosecrans complained that Merrill had been "too cautious" and might allow the rebels to "get the start of us in going towards Jefferson City or Rolla." Rosecrans expected the cavalry to "push after him without hesitation or delay."[24]

Late Sunday night, Merrill and his men provided Rosecrans with reliable information that Price had veered away from St. Louis. That evening, the prisoners and railroad crews taken at Pacific returned from Union. The Confederates had told one Irish railroad worker that they would let him return to Pacific, since they would soon return that way to take the town anyway, and others reported the news from Washington on the river, but the astute laborers had also witnessed the head of their rebel column turning west from Union toward Jefferson City. That night, Merrill's men sent several more prisoners who had evidently been foraging near Catawissa. By 10:30, he became "anxious about my reconnoitering party on the Union road, which should have been back before this," but it reported about an hour later.[25] Indeed, the Union scouts confirmed what the railroad workers had told them, but—unlike Pilot Knob—no industrialist had visited Price in his headquarters to provide Rosecrans information sufficiently "reliable" to him.

The Prisoner's Fate

Almost the entire Confederate army paraded through Union on Sunday. When Palmer and the other "volunteers" arrived from St. Clair around noon, they passed Price, Marmaduke, and Shelby "seated on the piazza of a hotel" opposite the courthouse with Governor Thomas C. Reynolds on horseback nearby. Officers freely told the men that "we were going to march to Jefferson City," formally inaugurate Reynolds, and "hold him in by force of arms."[26]

On Sunday between four and five o'clock, Merrill's scouts found Union so poorly guarded that they simply galloped into town and "sharply attacked the enemy." Costing the Federals one horse killed, this "little skirmish" wounded two rebels, killed another, and made prisoners of "a lieutenant of engineers and a private," both from General John S. Marmaduke's division, the former probably being from Captain James T. Hogane engineer's company. Despite its weak picketing, reported Merrill, "the town was so full of their men that the lieutenant commanding my party considered it prudent to retire with what he had got." Finding that the captured officer had a penchant for drink, Merrill's amiable staff indulged him and subsequently reported with confidence that Price had 12,000 men, "thousands" of conscripts, and no plans to move on Rolla before first dealing with Jefferson City. The talkative prisoner also located the main body of Price's army "camped ten miles out from Union."[27]

To the north, near Washington, Clark's brigade stirred to life along "Massey's Fork" of Dubois Creek, near the brewery south of town. Early that Monday, they headed west out of town. After only a few miles, they reached Miller's Landing, an old riverfront village renamed Miller's Station with the arrival of the railroad, and surveyed only eight years before as New Haven.[28] However, as with Pacific or Franklin, it was still known by its older names.

The Confederates entered the village without resistance, and secession had enough remaining friends in the area to alert Clark's men to the cargo stranded in town. Near the depot, they found three locomotives and about thirty cars. In one, they found "a large amount of clothing" and a cache of new Sharp's rifles, numbering four, six, or eight hundred depending on who was counting. Unionist refugees said they "went directly to the car, showing that they had previous knowledge of its contents." In addition, they looted all the stores, including that of John H. Chambers, who had relocated his business from Rocheport to avoid the guerilla activities there. Chambers lost boots, shoes, clothes, and dry goods. The Confederates found one of the engines disabled, but took the other two with them toward Hermann.[29]

Clark apparently left a small detachment of men to guard their booty, as the rest hurried forward to secure the 230-foot span over Boeuf Creek. Ahead of them, there was another nearly as big over Big Berger, a smaller one at Little Berger, and the massive 750-foot, four-span bridge over the Gasconade River. If possible, they would secure those bridges—and the tracks—before destroying them. At least some of them could look forward to riding in comfort for part of the campaign. More importantly, though, the bridge over the Gasconade might prove essential to the brigade and, possibly, Price's entire army.

Colonel Thomas R. Freeman's brigade of Marmaduke's division spent Sunday night in Union as a rear guard. On Monday morning, Sallie Jeffries watched from her hill south of town as the Army of Missouri trailed off to the west. "I saw the last one go over the Hesselmeyer Hill and disappear from view." At this point, blue-coated cavalry rode into Union and "galloped past and I thought there would be a fight, but they went only to the fairgrounds and turned back." She thought them Colonel Edward Catherwood's Thirteenth Missouri Cavalry, but they were likely Merrill's men. "I never said a word," she continued. "If they had continued their way to the top of the hill a few shots would have been fired anyway."[30] Residents of the battered town had had a hellishly real, if mercifully brief, taste of the war.

The main body of the Army of Missouri started from its camp "ten miles out from Union." That encampment sprawled along roadside fields west and northwest of Union along the St. John's and its tributaries. The divisions of Shelby camped on Jordan Creek and that of General James Fagan along the St. John's and another tributary. Goebel recalled that some passed the night within a mile of his home "a tributary valley" of the small Boeuf Creek.[31] The captured Confederate officer with Merrill's cavalry had surely spent a more comfortable night than most of his comrades.

Other prisoners fared not so well. Raised in the scattered farming population around Boeuf Creek, much of Company I of the Fifty-fourth EMM either did not hear of the orders to report at Washington or did so too late to comply. This was likely its skirmish reported as taking place some fifteen miles west of Union, according to Cabell. On the march, his brigade met Colonel David A. Williams's regiment from Shelby's division. The two units rode along another two or three miles until they encountered "a strong picket." These were "mostly Germans living in that section of the county, belonging to the Home Guards." According to Cabell, the prisoners lost their horses, guns, pistols, saddles, spurs, and other equipage. "I paroled and allowed them to go home," he reported.[32]

In fact, the fate of his captives became one of the sources for the reports of "militiamen shot down in different parts of the county." Most notoriously, Confederate soldiers summarily gunned down Captain Peter Koenig—also known by the anglicized name of King—and an old man, Henry Kosfeld. The rebels also seized and prepared to kill another German, but a neighbor from North Carolina intervened on his behalf. Tuesday morning, after the army broke camp along Boeuf Creek, residents found the bodies of two civilians unidentified except for the papers on their person indicating that they had recently emigrated from Germany.[33]

A Union diarist later passing through the area recorded another incident of the killing and burial of civilians seized and "conscripted" by Price's army. He wrote that his unit had "passed a dead negro in the roadside—also a point where the citizens said Price's Army had killed some 7 or 8 men, who would not agree to go along with them. Some of our boys reported seeing the graves."[34] In this case, the Confederates had permitted burials.

The Confederates had still held some of their prisoners from Pilot Knob at this camp. Captain Franz Dinger later wrote of their experience to Major James Wilson's sister. After their capture, they initially had nothing to eat and were the target of "very insulting language." Their subsequent treatment had been "very bad," receiving "only a little meal and very poor fresh beef with nothing to cook them in, had no blankets and had to sleep on the ground as we were." At one point, they had passed up an opportunity to escape, because they had the impression that they would soon be paroled.[35] That decision surely haunted Dinger in later years.

On Monday morning, October 3, the prisoners could hardly have woken in a less sympathetic area. The area was so thick with families like the Butlers and the Jeffries that it later became known as Jeffriesburg. The nearby farms of Andrew Fink and Herman Gehlert received more than their share of attention, the former loosing "nearly all of his possessions." At the Confederate camp, an "Inspector General"—probably Colonel John T. Coffee and likely the same person who had conscripted Donald Palmer and the civilian prisoners taken at Potosi—rode among the prisoners. Ominously, he ordered every prisoner from the Third MSM Cavalry to take two steps forward. Wilson stepped forward, as did five of his men: Two or three others, realizing what was happening claimed to be from the Fourteenth Iowa. A lad wearing the jacket of an artillery bugler, thinking the Third would be paroled, stepped forward.[36]

The officer then snapped at the Confederates present to "put a double guard over that damned Major" and sent another to the road to wait for Colonel Timothy Reeves. Wilson became insistent, "Sir, what are the charges against us?"[37] He received only silence.

Dinger went to Wilson's side. The major said, "Captain, I have fallen into bad hands and I do not think I will see you again." He passed a pocketbook and papers for his family to Dinger. The two then shook hands and parted.[38]

When the inspector general threatened to hang Dinger, Confederate lieutenant colonel John T. Crisp, also with Shelby's command, hurried to reassure the Federal officer that they would do no such thing. Missouri produced few more ardent Confederates than the North Carolina-born Crisp, a legislator who had helped mastermind the secession of the displaced state government. Afterward, Confederate senator George Graham Vest had tricked Crisp into agreeing to permit sending a civilian to Richmond, but Crisp had a refreshingly pragmatic streak. Once asked to eulogize the Confederate commander killed at Shiloh, Crisp reportedly said, "It is glorious to die for one's country, but I would rather be John T. Crisp alive than General A. Sidney Johnson dead."[39] Although he did quite well in postwar politics, his disconcerting practicality may have contributed to how quickly he faded from the panoply of Missouri Confederate heroes.

The fate of Wilson and his comrades was set when Reeves and his men arrived and took charge of them. He marched them off the road through an abandoned field and over the crest of a low hill, where he told Wilson that General Price had ordered their execution. One of the guards remembered Wilson's looking Reeves straight in the eyes and saying, "You do not mean to say that you are going to shoot us without a trial?" Reves replied, "You have been tried, and such are my orders." The sixteen-year-old bugler, an Arkansan, began to cry, and Reeves's own men appealed to him to spare the boy, but to no avail. As they faced the firing squad, Wilson placed his hat on the ground before them. The first volley dropped all of them except the boy "who stood untouched." Annoyed, Reeves barked orders and a second volley felled the remaining target. The bodies were stripped and left where they fell.[40] Back at the road, other prisoners heard the shots and saw the gun smoke rising from the field.

The political hatreds involved in war atrocities invariably shape their recollection. Fletcher called it a "shameful violation of the rules of war." Other contemporary Unionists claimed that Reeves had taken the prisoners in the presence of Price and his staff, oddly concurring with those apologists for the murder who are no less eager to give it an official sanction by Confederate authorities. Edwards described Wilson's killing as "an act of eminent justice, for he was a common murderer, and entirely destitute of manly and soldierly feelings."[41] This absurdity actually reinforced the groundless wartime Unionist accounts holding the Confederate authorities responsible.

Notwithstanding the lack of evidence, later adherents of the Lost Cause embraced the fiction that Shelby had held a court-martial that convicted Wilson of killing civilians and sentenced him to death. However, Shelby had no connection to the capture or custody of these prisoners, and there is not even the hint of a court-martial in his reports, which Edwards wrote. One wonders when Shelby would have even had time to hold a court-martial since Pilot Knob. Most regrettably, none of the apologetics even attempt to address the murder of the enlisted men whose only crime had been membership in the Third MSM Cavalry, and of an unidentified under-aged civilian southern white boy probably guilty of no more than being a war refugee.

As with other atrocities, they victimized not only the immediate targets of armed violence but the reputation of those who tried to disassociate themselves honorably from the crimes at the time. That is, admirers of the Lost Cause cannot be apologists for this without posthumously silencing those Confederates who opposed it. Setting aside the after-the-fact cover-ups, these executions did not sit at all well with the Confederate enlisted men forced to carry it out nor with the command structure. Another former prisoner himself, Colonel Thomas M. Gunter, commanding the Thirty-fourth Arkansas, bluntly called the murders a "shameful violation of the rules of war." Price and Shelby not only understood Reeves's impulses, but the responsibility of their army to restrain them. While he gave no reason, Colonel Sidney D. Jackman noted that, within hours of the killings, "Colonel Coffee with his regiment was relieved from duty in the brigade by order of Brigadier-General Shelby and directed to report to Major-General Price."[42] For the duration of its history, the Army of Missouri accorded Coffee no responsibility.

Confederate discontent with the course of the campaign had been building steadily. Governor Reynolds and Jeff Thompson, already messmates since Pilot Knob, had taken to riding with Shelby near the front, even over Price's objections. The same day as the murder of Wilson and his six comrades, Reynolds suggested to Price that he combine the units under Coffee and Lieutenant Colonel Alonzo W. Slayback to give Thompson a command. Thompson also turned his mule back over to the quartermaster, because Shelby presented him "a fine large Stallion, which had been brought in by a scout."[43] Things changed, perhaps, but far too slowly to do much good to the unburied corpses in the army's wake.

The flight of civilians from their farms to the woods made the Confederate liberation of Missouri a markedly modern affair. Some left food to placate the invaders in hopes of their sparing the house. However, the raiders generally took everything of value and vandalized what they could not take, even if was of no possible military use. Rebel soldiers found the trunk with the carefully prepared dresses and finery for the upcoming Pries wedding and tore it all to shreds. This was usual and it bore no comparison to the standard conduct of Confederate armies further east.

As the Army of Missouri moved west, the women and children emerged from their hiding places. The scattered members of Ewing's column separated during the long flight to Leasburg turned east to greet the advancing Union column expected from St. Louis. At Rolla, Ewing himself made preparations to return to ride to DeSoto and join the gathering forces outside St. Louis. On Thursday morning, General John McNeil sent for Major Samuel A. Garth and a detachment of the Ninth MSM Cavalry to meet the hero at the Grand Hotel and escort him on to Jefferson City. Instead, Ewing opted to ride to DeSoto and rejoin the troops at St. Louis expected to be actively attacking the invaders.[44] As a result, one of the most effective Federal officers in the campaign would see no more active service in it.

7

The Westward March

From Boeuf Creek to the Osage River

Monday's "heavy cannonading" from Hermann electrified those residents several miles west with Captain Charles D. Eitzen's militia at the Gasconade River bridge. In quieter times, he had made a good living dealing in lumber and iron, though he had faced death at that bridge nine years before when it collapsed beneath the weight of a trainload of luminaries celebrating the opening of the line between St. Louis and Jefferson City. On October 3, Eitzen seemed to be facing death there again, as an overwhelming Confederate force was thought to be bearing down on his small band. Those with Eitzen had probably not enrolled to protect the assets of the Pacific Railroad at the expense of their homes and jobs in Hermann.[1] Meanwhile, the thunderous noise of the fighting at Hermann rolled along the Missouri, startling the Franklin County EMM as far away as Augusta Depot.

The plight of the un-uniformed and unadvised little militia outpost on the Gasconade typified the Federal handling of the invasion. Aside from the unplanned clashes associated with Pilot Knob and Leasburg and from the unavoidable use of a brigade of infantry to retake Pacific, General William S. Rosecrans and the Department of Missouri defended most of the state by clustering isolated garrisons of local militia in the path of an invading army with little or no support. This continued, even as General Sterling Price's Army of Missouri bore down on the state capital at Jefferson City. Success, however, required the same Confederate army unwilling to leave the garrison at Fort Davidson in its rear to turn its back on the largest single Union army in the state.

To the Gasconade River

The course of Price's army raised the possibility of pinning it with its back to an impassable river. Rosecrans and General Samuel R. Curtis in Kansas both knew "Price is on the Union road from Union to Jefferson City," their scouts reported.[2] The Pacific Railroad reached the Gasconade some eighty-eight miles from St. Louis, and the Osage nearly thirty miles farther west with Jefferson City only seven or eight beyond. Both the Gasconade and the Osage Rivers flowed from southwest into south-central Missouri, and then swung north to the Missouri River, each forming a backward "L," the one inside the other. Usually fordable in their upper reaches, both had risen somewhat with the recent rains, making the crossing much trickier and even problematic downstream nearer the Missouri. If Confederates nearer the Missouri River found the downstream crossing of the Gasconade or Osage impassable, a rigorous Federal pursuit from the east would isolate them. However, the Union policy of protecting without ever destroying railroad property would leave the bridges there intact and leave the Confederate army an escape from such a natural trap.

Despite scouting and some good information, the Union high command seems to have remained essentially ignorant of Price's movements. As one officer frankly told General Alfred Pleasonton, the Federal forces "don't know at what point he [Price] will cross the Gasconade." The Confederate army had the artillery and the numbers that required the use of one of the three major crossings of the Gasconade. The main State Road ran west from Union through a tiny crossroads called Cedar Fork, marked a generation later by little more than a grocery with a post office; from here, it continued to the Gasconade at Mount Sterling, a modest little former county seat of several hundred inhabitants. A more northerly road reached the Gasconade at the village of Fredericksburg. Still farther, almost at the Missouri River, was what the locals called the Gasconade Ferry, a third crossing near the bridge of the Pacific Railroad. The Gasconade with its steep bluffs, swift currents, and a deep bottom could be a particularly formidable river. General Andrew J. Smith thought the rainfall sufficient to make it "a very uncertain stream, rising very rapidly and very high."[3] A road south from Hermann connected all three of these routes east of where they crossed the river.

Days before, when General John McNeil warned Rosecrans about the need to defend the lower Gasconade, Rosecrans took the troops from Brigadier General Egbert Benson Brown, who ran the Central District, headquartered at Warrensburg. Brown's troops were spread very thin, across subdistricts organized out of Jefferson City, Lexington, and Kansas City, and garrisons at California, Harrisonville, Independence, Osage City, Pleasant Hill, Sedalia, Tipton, and other posts. Nevertheless, Brown sent his single company of the Forty-fifth Missouri from Jefferson City to the Gasconade, but balked at using Colonel Francis W. Hickox and his Forty-third EMM, which lacked local knowledge, along the upper reaches of the river.[4] Given what the Federal command already knew about the size of the advancing Confederate army, this preoccupation about where to place a few hundred men among these various crossings could not have seemed a plausible defense but merely a test to find where and how many of the enemy they might encounter.

Meanwhile, the most essential things Brown knew about the approaching Confederate force was simply wrong. Rosecrans had repeatedly told his district commanders that Price was moving on Rolla, so Brown clung to that faith through most of Monday, partly because his own communications with Hermann had remained unbroken, even when those sixty horsemen who had thought themselves cut off from Ewing at Leasburg turned up there. Communications with St. Louis became more complicated because the Confederates had cut the line at many points west of Pacific. Brown made do using the telegraph along the North Missouri Railroad with couriers posted to span the frequent cuts in the line through that guerrilla-infested region.[5]

This misinformation from St. Louis may not have been Brown's only reason for not planning a serious challenge to a Confederate crossing of the Gasconade. After having concentrated the troops from his Central District at Jefferson City, he awaited the arrival of General Clinton B. Fisk from the District of North Missouri to reach the capital. Fisk being the senior officer, Brown likely hesitated to take such a major decision and leave the responsibility for its implementation to somebody else. Regrettably, Brown's recognition of the possible value of contesting the crossings with an uncertainty about how seriously he should do so expressed itself in a decision to send the most troublesome regiment of the EMM available to him to protect the crossings and the vague and in the open-ended nature of his orders to them.

For his part, Rosecrans must have been even less eager to mobilize the militia in Gasconade County than in Franklin. What represented one of the strongest centers of Radical Unionism in the state began a generation before. Radical German secularists planned what became Hermann on the high bluffs over the Missouri River some six or seven miles downstream from the mouth of the Gasconade. The distinctive purity of their *Giessener Answanderung Gesellschaft* hardly survived the first years before merging into the wider immigration that included Catholics, Lutherans, and Jews from "the Old Country." Originally, their local economy centered on hauling iron from Meramec Furnace in Crawford County to the Missouri River for shipment to St. Louis. Soon, it became a prosperous center for pine lumber and as much as 200,000 board feet sat at its wharves during the 1850s. The arrival of the railroad closed the eighty-one miles to St. Louis very quickly and its population leaped by 1860 to that of Washington—about 1,500 people without doing much to expand the sparsely populated hinterland. In that year, the county's 433 ballots for Lincoln outpolled all three of his opponents combined.[6] This made Gasconade by far the most Republican of any slaveholding county in the United States.

Nevertheless, the area did not entirely escape fratricidal conflict and the necessity of armed defense. In the dark days after Sumter, Captain Charles C.

Manwaring had helped raise a full ten companies of Home Guards to protect the area from the state authorities, and they continued to function as the local militia into 1863. Manwaring became the state representative, but that did not prevent him, in the spring of 1864, from accompanying a force to arrest some rebels, a case of bravado for which he paid with his life. By then, the Thirty-fourth EMM assumed such duties under Colonel Rudolph Poser, a former officer of the Second Missouri Light Artillery who had resigned the previous year.[7] No less than his predecessor, Poser represented as much of a political officer as a military official, key to maintaining a viable Unionist coalition.

Once called out, the Thirty-fourth EMM proved itself as relentlessly annoying as any conservative might have feared. Poser eventually pulled together 350 men in six companies and sent a seventh under Eitzen to guard the bridge on the Gasconade. The citizens also had a small six-pounder cannon the community used for the Fourth of July and other such events, but it remarkably avoided being called up along with the enrollees. Headquarters ordered Poser to garrison the crossings of the Gasconade, but ultimately issued two contradictory sets of orders, one assigning five companies to Rolla and another placing the entire Thirty-fourth EMM under Jefferson City. Unintimidated, Poser responded bluntly to contradictory orders.[8]

The problem the Gasconade County men had was less political than the low priority on defending their own homes. Couching their complaint in military terms, those who did not wish to abandon Hermann noted that any concentration at Jefferson City or on the Gasconade would leave unguarded the railroad bridges at Little Berger and Cole Creek. Rosecrans ended the argument with a telegram to Brown: "Arrest Colonel Poser if he refuses to obey your orders." Once sustained, Brown showed political tact as well as military wisdom by sending Poser's "entire regiment" with the available two companies of the Forty-fifth Missouri to cover the railroad bridges over the Gasconade as well as the Osage. By Sunday, October 2, though, Poser's militia seemed to be operating almost alone between the state capital and the Confederate army.[9]

The lesser officers and ranks of the militia at Hermann still dragged their feet about leaving their town, partly because of the rumors that "Bloody Bill" Anderson's band prowled just north of the river, and problems certainly persisted there. Two days after Centralia, two men had gone into Danville on the railroad only to be "identified as belonging to Anderson's guerrillas" and were "immediately hung." A few days later, raiders attacked the railroad near Jacksonville in Randolph County. Soon after, guerrillas reportedly derailed the train from Hannibal near Palmyra, then searched the train for soldiers, seized the express containing about $20,000, took a few revolvers from the passengers and compelled the employees to burn all the cars. There had been three soldiers on cars but passengers helped get them into civilian clothes and they "escaped detection."[10]

From the perspective of Jefferson City, though, things seemed relatively under control along the river. An "accidental fire" left the river town of Rocheport "badly scorched," but, on Tuesday, authorities at the capital reported "all quiet as far down as Washington." Probably based on reports from those riverboats reaching the capital, Brown assured Rosecrans that Washington "had not been reoccupied by a single rebel soldier at 6 o'clock this morning." This meant that Price's army had turned west from St. Louis, and most likely marched on Jefferson City. A clear indication that this was so would finally end Rosecran's persistent earlier assurance that Price's goal had been Rolla. To find such information, a telegraph operator set off on a handcar and checked the line to St. Auberts in Osage County.[11]

Still, on Monday, October 3—even as that operator tapped his reassuring message to the outside world—Hermann faced what the local *Volksblatt* rightly called its "day of terror, of worry and unease." Local authorities remained unreconciled to the fact that the military would not protect them, but most of the men had either gone off with the Thirty-fourth EMM or joined the large group of women and children who went out to Graf's Island in the Missouri River to shelter in the caves there. "Most of the inhabitants, fearing the vengeance of the armed enemy fled across the river and camped." For this reason, the St. Louis press could later report, "We did not hear that many citizens were killed." Meanwhile, a handful of discharged veterans, schoolteachers, and others who had not been called up—or who had avoided being called to Jefferson City—decided to defend their homes without the help of the Federal military. This impromptu defense of the town made some sense, even in the absence of the militia. After all, even a token force would be sufficient if the Confederates only sent a handful of guerrillas unwilling or incapable of dealing with any serious resistance.[12] Their deeds became the stuff of local lore.

In the end, more of General John S. Marmaduke's division may have come north to join Brigadier General John B. Clark's brigade on the river after New Haven. Whatever their numbers, the St. Louis road that took them into Hermann from the east negotiated a large bluff that hemmed it against the river. Very late Monday afternoon, when Colonel Colton Greene's Third Missouri Cavalry turned up at the head of this column, a gutsy little band of thirty or forty Unionists began lobbing shots into the enemy's closed ranks, which had neither the room to form a battle line nor a clear line of sight to know what was ahead in the town. Clark described this as "a slight engagement with the enemy," though he and his men actually faced no enemy, the militia being in service elsewhere. The Confederates would have certainly seen this as a technicality, because they had to deploy and move forward cautiously. As they did so, the locals carted their little field piece back to another location and repeated the process before eventually having to toss their little piece into the Missouri and flee to the hills themselves. Having failed to capture the brass six-pounder, Clark officially reported seizing an iron twelve-pounder and destroying it.[13]

The Gasconade

Hours before the capture of Hermann, Captains Eitzen and Francis Onken took the 150 men of their two companies of the Thirty-fourth EMM to their post on the Gasconade railroad bridge. They went "on open Flat-cars in a heavy rain, which rain kept up all day" and they arrived "perfectly drenched," several of the men becoming quite sick, a condition compounded with an understandable worry over Hermann's fate. Almost immediately, the command began to shed lieutenants; one scouted off to the east and another sent to Hermann simply failed to return. Concern over their town's fate increased dramatically at about 6 p.m. when Onken's men on the east side of the bridge and Eitzen's on the west side heard the unmistakable sound of cannon fire from Hermann. Two of the latter threw down their arms and started for town, though Eitzen may well have authorized them as volunteers to shed their only identification as militia and slip back to see what was going on in town.[14] Perhaps the lack of any direct communications with Hermann is only slightly less remarkable than the absence of any official from Jefferson City, or even a telegraph operator since the line back to the state capital remained intact.

Eitzen, the senior captain, also enforced a standard of military conduct far below that to which Onken, the son of a Waterloo veteran, aspired. As the rain fell in torrents about them, the two scouts returned at about 10 p.m. with news of the attack on Hermann, which escalated through the ranks into a realization that the entire town could be burned. Given the Confederate presence in Hermann, their general movement toward the Gasconade, and the absence of any superior from Jefferson City, Eitzen suggested that they fall back to the capital. Eitzen conceded the position to his enthusiastic junior, but Onken held him responsible for the lack of order at the post. When some of the men men drifted off, Eitzen went off in pursuit of them, returning after midnight with only four of them. Still, when Onken recrossed to the east side of the bridge, he found only twenty-six of his own men left. He set these to work removing the rails on the approach to the bridge and throwing them into the river, and sent two scouts for horses, so they could picket the nearest fords, particularly the closest upriver, known as the Gasconade Ferry.[15] Although none of Onken's scouts returned, the men at the bridge saw no sign of Confederates through Monday night.

Remarkably, this little band of militia actually remained at their post through Tuesday and Wednesday, October 4 and 5. Captain James H. Steger, Brown's right-hand man at Jefferson City, personally took a "Locomotive down the railroad to obtain information of the movements of the enemy." At the Gasconade, he "learned of the cannonading" at Hermann. His report gave no indication that the militia he found at the bridge was in considerable turmoil. Meanwhile, Marmaduke had already detached four companies from Lieutenant Colonel Robert C. Wood's battalion to bring forward the train seized at Miller's Landing to the river. Wednesday found them steaming alongside their comrades, who tore up track and burned bridges behind them.[16] The tracks, of course, led directly to the bridge at the Gasconade.

On Wednesday afternoon, the wife of a farmer near the bridge sent word that Price's officers were at her house, but none subsequently turned up at the bridge. Because there is no other indication that "Confederate officers" were in the area at that time, it might be that both were themselves actually Federal scouts in disguise. When the Seventh Kansas Cavalry moved into Missouri from Memphis, one member, William F. Cody, "rode ahead of the command, some considerable distance, to pick up all possible information, concerning Price's movements." To his chagrin, when the future "Buffalo Bill" reached one farm, he found another man "dressed in a gray costume, sitting at a table eating bread and milk." Deciding to bluff, he was shocked to hear the man say: "You little rascal, what are you doing in those 'secesh' clothes?" It turned out to be an old friend, James Butler Hickok. The future "Wild Bill" Hickok scouted for General McNeil out of Rolla and had disguised as a Texas officer with Marmaduke's division. Quietly and quickly, Cody and Hickok shared what they knew and Hickok, saying he would remain with the Confederate army until he could no longer gather information safely, passed on some reports for McNeil to Cody.[17] Exactly where and when this encounter took place is uncertain, but it would explain the strange appearance (and disappearance) of "Confederate officers" with no troops in a farmhouse near the Gasconade.

More reports of mounted rebels continued to reach the bridge. Eitzen asked Onken pointedly whether he proposed to hold the position until surrounded. Onken complained that he did so "within hearing of our men" and even asked for a show of hands whether the men wanted to stay or not. Onken insisted upon holding the bridge, even as more reports arrived of an entire enemy regiment on its way to take the bridge with artillery in support. Nevertheless, when the number of remaining defenders dropped to thirty-four men, Onken had no choice. He sent six with the spare muskets and cartridges to Jefferson City on a hand car, but kept some at his post personally until 10 p.m. "I never would [have] left the Gasconade bridge," he reported, "if my men had staid [*sic*] with me."[18]

At some point, part of Clark's brigade did reach the bridge. Most of them apparently took the road south from Hermann to rejoin the main body of Price's army. Those who had the locomotive with its unusable booty from New Haven took it to Hermann where they destroyed the entire lot. On their way south, almost as an afterthought, they stopped off to burn the Gasconade bridge. Colonel Robert R. Lawther reported that, as ordered, Wood's detachment had already burned it, so his own regiment destroyed that over Bailey's Creek.[19]

To summarize, the Union high command placed a small detachment of militia at a railroad bridge in the face of thousands of Confederates advancing with captured trains. It gave no orders to destroy or abandon the bridge. Unable to see the point of protecting the bridge so the enemy could use it, particularly given the danger to their own homes, the militia tended to melt into the woods. In the end, the Confederates destroyed the trains, burned the bridge, and, after crossing the river, some continued west walking along the tracks.

Toward the Osage

Once west of the Gasconade, the Army of Missouri entered in Osage County on the "neck" between the Gasconade and the Osage Rivers.[20] German immigrants accounted for less than half its relatively small population in 1860. The dominant element remained essentially southern, owning more slaves than anywhere else between the Meramec and the Missouri Rivers. The county had given Breckenridge 308 of its nearly thousand votes, but very few had worked up much enthusiasm for secession.

Indeed, early on, the secessionists in the county could not stop the disturbing local habit of citizens continuing to talk to one another. The area provided its share to the MSG and, later, the Confederate army, but many of those actually returned to their homes early in the war. Some supported efforts to discourage guerrillas by Medora's Home Guard and Colonel Lebbeus Zevely's Twenty-eighth EMM based at Linn. As Price's army approached, Zevely and the militia reported as ordered to Jefferson City, and most of the peace-loving civilians followed or took to the woods. This general, if temporary, abandonment of an already sparsely populated county left interested parties of all sorts as much in the dark as was the Federal army.

On October 4, the advance of Price's army entered Osage County. One column crossed near Howerton's Bluff where Pointer's Creek joined the river. There, they captured a handful of slaveholding Virginians including Sterne White Howerton and his brother John Thomas Howerton. The Confederates decided that the former might be a Union soldier, since he wore blue trousers, so they executed him, even as they conscripted his brother.[21]

Federal reports documented plausible rumors that small detachments and guerrilla bands appeared at different points along the railroad west from the Gasconade through Chamois, Medora, Wallace's Landing, and Dauphine. The Home Guard, the first Unionist troops raised in the area, had functioned primarily as railroad guards, based at Medora. Almost all of Clark's brigade probably crossed the Gasconade River at Fredericksburg and took the road to Lisle on the Osage, but the main body of Price's army reached the Osage by way of the old State Road through Mount Sterling and Linn. One resident remembered how the rebels stole the lamp-burners from private homes along the State Road, fastening them to their belts.[22] Reflecting the persistent Confederate confusion of soldiers and civilians, they regularly spoke of a Neutrality Oath imposed on civilians as a parole used on militia.

The general absence of civilian observers permitted the truly remarkable Battle of Linn. Federal reports clearly locate the Union units in the area, including the Twenty-eighth EMM at Jefferson City. Shelby's aide-de-camp and an old family friend, Captain Oliver Frazer Redd, returned from Linn claiming to have seized arms and paroled "100 prisoners." Given the absence of the militia and the penchant for exaggeration, Redd was likely swearing civilians not to take up arms against the Confederacy, perhaps close enough to the "paroling." Shelby's report—written by Major John N. Edwards at the time—reflected Redd's scout to Linn. A few years later, though Edwards's *Shelby and His Men* chronicled how the Confederates "stormed Linn and captured its garrison of three hundred and seventy-two Federals, scouted the country for miles around, and struck terror into the Dutch and militia, surprised almost into idiocy."[23] Edwards's later account contradicted all the earlier Confederate reports, including his own.

Perhaps Edwards thought there needed to be a Homeric Confederate success, to match the Thermopylae the Federals claimed over Fort Davidson. Alternatively, he may have simply sought to chronicle a victory for Shelby to match what he saw as a botched success for Marmaduke at Union. Whatever his motives, Shelby's entire division passed through—not stormed an enemy garrison at—Linn on Wednesday, October 5. From there, it "marched on Westphalia in a cold and heavy rain, where it was reported a Federal regiment was encamped." At 8 a.m., Shelby's advance reached that town, but found no enemy soldiers. The last phase of this march placed Shelby's men fifteen miles southeast of the state capital, not far from the former garrison of Koeltztown, roughly halfway between Westphalia and Vienna.[24]

Defenders of Jefferson City had several natural lines of defense. The crest running along High Street provided a last ditch, inner line. Several miles beyond, was the Moreau Creek, "a small stream with muddy banks and bad bottom." The Osage River provided an outer line, starting to the east with the impressive 1,122-foot, six-span Pacific Railroad bridge, near the mouth of the Osage at the Missouri and continuing upstream to where the State Road crossed the river some eight miles from the capital. The Federals wisely expected the focus of the Confederate on eight miles of riverfront with four major crossings: Clark's, Bolton's, Prince's, and Castle Rock. Should the rebels strike the Osage farther upstream, it would likely indicate plans to bypass the capital, and nobody expected to be that lucky.

Around 7 a.m. Wednesday, the Confederates showed up where they were least expected. As the *Missouri State Times* noted, the authorities sent to the Pacific Railroad bridge on the Osage on the far left of the outer Union defenses "just men enough to invite an attack, and not enough to afford protection." There, Captain John Sullins had three companies from his Thirty-fourth EMM and one from Zevely's Twenty-eighth EMM. Lieutenant William Berger had about fifty militia at the blockhouse on the east side of the river, where they must have been meeting a steady trickle of their comrades coming by ones and twos from the Gasconade bridge, and daylight brought news that the Confederates had destroyed the nearby village of Loose Creek. Shortly after, Berger's fifty Federals on the far side of the bridge found themselves facing several hundred of Colonel David Shanks's Confederates from Shelby's old "Iron Brigade" sent up from Westphalia. From their blockhouse, Berger's militia killed nine and wounded two rebels according to a Confederate officer. Second Lieutenant William Slinkman exaggerated when he reported about 2,500 rebels, but Union military authorities, who were not present, understated the number as only "about two hundred and fifty, with, as alleged, two pieces of artillery." From the perspective of the mere fifty militiamen, the differences between holding back five times or fifty times their number seemed unimportant. Then, too, Berger surely would have cast a furtive glance back across the river wondering where Sullins's other three companies had gone.[25]

Across the river, Sullins must have wondered where those companies had gone as well. The appearance of the artillery caused "a great panic" among his men. At a certain point, Sullins realized that he was virtually alone to defend the largest single railroad structure in the state. What was far worse, perhaps, nobody had the presence of mind to use the section of the bridge that "should have been drawn" to prevent its passage by men on foot. Supposedly, "only some eight or ten rebels" braved the crossing then torched the stores of J. F. McKiernan and Kenstener, as well as the railroad installations.[26]

The *Richmond Daily Dispatch*, which heard of the event only through northern newspapers, invented a wonderfully comforting coverage for its credulous readers. It inflated the fifty militiamen to two regiments of drafted Federal soldiers. It then continued: "The Missourians turned upon the Yankees, whipped out the force at the post, and when Shelby arrived, they turned themselves, their arms, and everything belonging to the post, over to the Confederate general."[27] Of course, any of the hated Gasconade County "Dutch" attempting to go over would most likely have ended as roadside corpses.

This "big scare" near the capital took its toll on the already limited confidence the Federals had. Poser marched his Thirty-fourth EMM back to the scene within hours and reported "citizens not molested except taking money,

&c., from them." In the absence of any information from his own men, he later told Brown that residents on the west side of the river had seen only about a hundred rebels approaching the blockhouse on the east side and saw "no resistance." Brown passed on the story to the rest of the commanders, describing the captors as "a force of rebels, number unknown" or as "not over 100" to which the blockhouse had surrendered "without firing a gun," while "the guard on this side ran away." Fisk had no reason to doubt the account.[28] All of which begs the question as to why responsibility for protecting such a critical point on the river had been turned over to militia that had repeatedly demonstrated that it was too small, too inexperienced, and too badly officered to make even the most modest kind of defense.

Most importantly, the Confederate forces essentially showed their hand in destroying the bridge. Had they intended to advance on the nearby fords on the lower river, they would not have simply abandoned their hold on the crossing. This simple fact focused the Federal expectations of the Confederate attack near the State Road. From Jefferson City, that road ran southeast into the bluffs, ridges, and hills that deflected the Moreau into a wide loop to the south. It crossed at the far end of that loop and forked into three directions. The eastbound branch reached the Osage about two miles upstream from the railroad, probably that referred to in the reports as Mike Clark's Ford. Another branch passed the farm of Dr. William Bolton near the Moreau and continued on to the river, crossing near Port's Mill to Lisle and continuing to Loose Creek and Linn beyond. The remaining route from the Moreau, the main State Road to St. Louis, ran through Taos, the little village named for the site of Price's New Mexico glory, and hit the Osage at Prince's Ford, sometimes called Shelley's Ford. Four miles farther upstream, the easterly branch of a southbound road from Jefferson City crossed the Osage at Castle Rock.[29]

None of the Union commanders thought that the few thousand troops at Jefferson City would be able to cover adequately the eight miles of the river. Fortunately, the defenders told themselves, Rosecrans's massive army from St. Louis was pressing westward and nipping at Price's heels.

The Pursuit

The absence of Rosecrans and Smith became one of the most conspicuous features of the maneuvers around Jefferson City. The westward dynamic of the invading column brought home the urgency of the situation to Curtis in Kansas, which remained in the path of Price's army. On October 6, Rosecrans assured him that he would have "9,000 infantry up the river to-morrow or next day." Curtis urged him to hurry them forward.[30]

That pursuit remained stalled. Still, Smith described moving his infantry, artillery, and wagons between Pacific and Manchester Road toward Gray's Summit as "impracticable." Despite the Monday appearance of some Confederate scouts along Manchester Road, Union cavalry under Colonel Lewis Merrill and Lieutenant Colonel Samuel Melcher regularly ventured to Union and to Richwoods, reporting Price's army gone. Rosecrans urged their exhausted mounted patrols to "handle the enemy's rear guard of observation so roughly that they will be careful hereafter."[31]

Yet, neither Smith nor Rosecrans had any real desire to find that rear guard. Smith seemed as eager as ever to join the Federal army in Tennessee and marching the opposite direction had few charms for him, and the rest of Rosecrans's army hardly showed a greater interest in moving west. The 138th Illinois did not arrive until Monday, and logical problems plagued any attempt to move the EMM forward. As of Monday, Brigadier General Edward C. Pike had moved that skeletal brigade of EMM at the southern approaches to join his two other brigades waiting at Kirkwood to advance on to Pacific. This, in theory, would allow the Smith's infantry to finish its concentration at Pacific and move west.[32]

Smith dragged his feet through most of this. Brigadier General Edward H. Wolfe's brigade—which had been the first there—reportedly moved on to Gray's Summit and Merrill's cavalry moved its base toward Labadie. On that night, Smith assured Rosecrans that the rest of the infantry would follow Wolfe to Gray's Summit on Tuesday morning, when Pike's EMM would advance to Pacific.[33] It all looked good on paper.

Events repeatedly confirmed Confederate interest in Pacific. That evening, the militia paroled at Union and various railroad laborers trudged into Federal lines, confirming earlier reports about the Confederates turning toward Jefferson City and rumors that they had disposed of "all their captives" before leaving the county seat at Union. While Merrill's horsemen found the roads poor, they reported the railroad "in good order, or very nearly repaired as far as Augusta Station" and guessed that it might be "uninjured as far as South Point" fifteen miles west of their position. "All my cavalry are out on the track of the enemy," he wrote Rosecrans. "I fear I will be broke down again; am scarcely able to walk or ride, but will stick it out as long as I can." Available members of Colonel Thomas P. Herrick's Seventh Kansas Cavalry advanced from Fenton to Eureka to provide some immediate relief in the scouting.[34]

Notwithstanding the intelligence, Smith's schedule for his pursuit fell a full day behind on its very first day. Wolfe's brigade had, in fact, remained at Pacific and, on Tuesday, Colonel William T. Shaw advised their movement to Gray's Summit. Shaw suggested camping south of the railroad along the Meramec rather than near the little village, "as there is no water here." Then, too, for all the earlier rushing, Pike's EMM waited at Kirkwood until late Tuesday afternoon, hoping to hear that Smith had begun to move on from Pacific.[35]

Rosecrans episodically went through the motions of goading ever so gently. He asked, "How are the roads from Franklin to the Summit?" Smith replied, "quite good," and discussed the logistics of such a move. On Tuesday, Smith discussed sending men forward with a train to repair the few places damaged on the tracks to Washington "so that cars can run to that point by 4 pm."[36] Perhaps in presenting Rosecrans the options of going after Price or repairing the railroad, Smith knew his superior's priorities.

Smith also found other reasons. He wanted a hundred large coffee mills for grinding corn in order for his "old troops" to live off the land. While Wednesday brought no clashes with any rebels, he had a brief jurisdictional skirmish when Pike's EMM arrived at Pacific, as ordered, only to find Smith had not moved his infantry out of town to the west. Smith grumbled that the several thousand militia brought "baggage enough for 100,000 men," and complained that they "won't stand marching as old troops."[37] If so, it hardly mattered, since nobody was really marching much of anywhere. The main reason Pacific became crowded was that Smith had decided not to advance.

Despite his periodic suggestions to the contrary, Rosecrans was quite content to have Smith's forces linger at Pacific. At one point, he even discussed whether they should bring McNeil's force up the track to Pacific, a bizarre suggestion for a commander that had been telling McNeil that Price was advancing on Rolla. Rosecrans left the pace of the pursuit to Smith, but couched it in such a way as to minimize his distance from the city. He hinted that any advance did not have to be large, suggesting that he thought it "doubtful if anything is to be gained by moving to-morrow farther than Union." At one point, Rosecrans said, "If you think you can do them [the Confederates] more harm by marching there than by taking steam-boats to Jefferson City do so."[38] At the time, of course, there were no steamboats available.

The most obvious reason for the lack of movement was that Rosecrans and Smith were waiting for General Joseph A. Mower's division. Early in the week, it had turned up near Cape Girardeau with 4,500 infantry, 2,000 cavalry, and 2 six-gun batteries. He even sent an aide-de-camp, Lieutenant Charles Christensen, to Centralia, Illinois, as a liaison. Later, Rosecrans claimed "transports and supply-boats were at once dispatched" and one of the largest steamboat ports in the country should have had whatever was needed to transport Mower's men. In fact, the boats did not leave St. Louis until Wednesday—two days after Mower had showed up—and it became apparent on Thursday that the flotilla Rosecrans sent would have to make at least three trips back and forth between St. Louis and the Cape to move all the men and horses. In the end, a diarist in Smith's infantry reported that it not only remained at Gray's Summit, but had not gotten to within four miles of Union until Friday, October 7.[39] The more of a lead they gave Price's mounted forces, the more pointless any pursuit seemed to the infantry.

Smith did mention on Thursday that he had "advance cavalry scouts on Boeuf Creek" reporting Price's crossing of the Gasconade. However, a Kansas cavalryman noted in his diary that his unit had reached Union October 4, but failed to move until that "big scare about Indians being up at St. Claire" on October 7. Catherwood's cavalry was also at Union and knew enough to ascribe those reports of "large number of Indians" to Confederates moving near St. Clair toward Jefferson City. Rosecrans responded by suggesting that they repair the telegraph to Boeuf Creek and suggested the possibility that Smith should move toward Linn for a convergence with Mower's men in Osage County.[40] In fact, though, the scouts along Boeuf Creek were not actually Smith's.

By Thursday, October 6, the Franklin County EMM had resurfaced. A former town trustee at Union, Captain John W. Maupin, had resigned one army commission to join the new Forty-seventh. On behalf of the St. Louis District, he had gone out to contact Colonel Daniel Quimby Gale's 500 to 600 EMM at Augusta Station, where they had remained stranded since leaving Washington the previous Sunday. On Thursday, Gale's men returned to Washington, reoccupying part of the former militia encampment briefly borrowed by the Confederates. Meanwhile, Maupin used Gale's mounted EMM to scout west, reporting small numbers of Confederates straggling west. St. Louis authorized Maupin to take his boat "as far up the river as you can with safety," and he agreed to do so as far as Miller's Landing or even Hermann.[41] It had almost surely been these scouts, rather than Smith's men, who had ventured to Boeuf Creek.

On the same day, the militia reoccupied Washington, those civilians still fortunate enough to have homes returned to them. All waited in anticipation for their erstwhile rescuers to cross the thirteen empty miles from Gray's Summit. By then, however, the Federal army at St. Louis had given the invaders of the state a "fearful letting alone" for five days and they were not finished doing so. Strangely, one of the otherwise insightful Federal officers later wrote of this campaign that "Price's great fault was slowness."[42] Despite such "slowness," the Confederates had started turning up in force before Jefferson City, even as the Federals waited and discussed coffee grinders, steamboats, and more men.

Rosecrans's own superiors had problems of their own right up to the White House. One Missourian complained to Lincoln that "the slow pace with which Gen Rosecrans moves" would leave the Confederates in the state at the time of the November election. Another warned that "Rebels and Bushwhackers, Bondsmen and Sympathizers will be invoked to aid in defeating the union cause."[43] While these concerns mattered in Washington, the deep split in the ranks of the state's Republicans remained a top priority in terms of the election.

To that purpose, Lincoln sent John George Nicolay, his German-born secretary, to St. Louis. Before he arrived, on October 4 or 5, Secretary William L. Avery of the Union National Committee brought together "the different factions, with a view of bringing about united action, and also to devise measures for a more active campaign. The meeting was well attended, and the talk was conciliatory." When Nicolay arrived, he found things "in a pretty bad tangle, but I think they are gravitating toward an understanding—temporary at least if not permanent—which will unite the vote of all the union men on the electoral and State ticket."[44] Such a unity of purpose had no more compelling reason than the presence of Price's army in the state.

As to Rosecrans, Nicolay did not discuss his own failure to press forward from St. Louis. The general did, however, tell Nicolay that he thought his own role in the battle of Rich Mountain three years earlier had been slighted in the official report of General—and now Democratic presidential candidate—George B. McClellan, and requested a copy so he could refute it. "Without having heard the General say directly that he was for you," wrote Nicolay to Lincoln, "all his language to me leaves no other inference, and I am sure that the foregoing request is made with a view to make a publication that shall assist your election." Nicolay saw no harm resulting from giving him a copy of McClellan's report, "and at the same time it will gratify him and assist the common cause."[45]

At about 4 p.m. Thursday, Captain Francis Onken and the last of the guards from the Gasconade arrived at the Osage from Medora. A mile east of the bridge, they found the handcar abandoned that he had sent with the extra weapons and cartridges. With no sign of his men or the munitions at this point, he assumed the Confederates had taken all of them. When he reached the river, he found the bridge burned. He and his comrades of the Thirty-fourth EMM had returned to Federal lines in a flatboat and a skiff.[46] Clearly, Onken worried that the loss of a few additional guns might prove important in the coming battle.

By then, there were plenty of armed Federals to address the problem, though they were being put to other purposes. The charred timbers of the largest railroad structure in the state—that over the Osage—along "with the depots and mills" capped a week of destruction by the invaders. The Army of Missouri had burned the depots, tanks, and auxiliary structures up the Iron Mountain Railroad, as well as the bridges between them. Up the southwestern branch of the Pacific railroad, the Confederates torched the facilities at Cuba, Bourbon, Stanton, Sullivan, and St. Clair, as well as the much larger bridges, such as that at Moselle, before destroying the massive installations at Pacific on the main line of the railroad. Westward along the main line, the invaders hit Gray's Summit, South Point, Washington, Miller's Landing, Newport, and Hermann, the largest and most expensive bridges yet. These included the spans of 230 feet at Boeuf Creek, 190 at Big Berger, 90 at Little Berger, 160 at Cole Creek, 750 foot over the Gasconade, 110 at Bailey's Creek, and the 1,122-foot, six-span over the Osage.[47] Yet, this very devastation left Smith and Rosecrans a reason to delay going after the Army of Missouri and preventing further destruction.

8

The Capital

From the Osage River to Jefferson City

Thursday and Friday, October 6 and 7, 1864, gave the village of Taos, huddled between the Osage and the Moreau, a mild taste of what earlier befell its namesake. Seventeen years before, events in the pueblo in New Mexico had made Sterling Price's military reputation and provided the Missouri community with its name. Now, thousands of Price's armed Missourians tramped the roads around Taos, banging on its doors, and seizing its food and livestock. What white Missourians had visited upon the native people of the southwest they now visited upon other mostly white Missourians.[1] It will always remain a mystery whether Price himself experienced a flash of political insight or even a moral epiphany.

For days, the Union army had abandoned town after town, leaving any defense and the responsibility for defeat to local militias, without investing so much as clear orders, but such was no option for Jefferson City, the state capital. The overall department commander, General William S. Rosecrans, had used the telegraph to supervise the concentration there of those available Federal forces from both the Central and North Missouri Districts, which forced a heavy reliance on the EMM. The Union army management of the militia system in that part of the state faced very different problems it had in the St. Louis area, but the department's response had been the same, to minimize its mobilization and permit it to fall into disuse. Disorganized and free from the direct command of St. Louis, a handful of desperate Federal officers at Jefferson City gathered everyone they could—and somewhat more than they expected—to challenge the Confederates along the Osage River and the Moreau Creek. At no point in the campaign did Price come nearer physical success.

Jefferson City

Jefferson City sat forty-four rail miles upriver from Hermann and 125 from St. Louis. Jefferson City found the state capitol that dominated the steep bluffs on the south side of the Missouri a mixed blessing. Planned from its inception as the state capital, the little town had faced repeated crises in its development including the 1837 fire that destroyed its first state capitol and periodic visitations of the cholera beginning in 1849. The seasonal moods of the river and its dependence on the presence of the legislature framed the town's potential.[2] The advent of the Pacific Railroad promised an accelerated pace for both the town and the government.

In the years leading to the war, officials and entrepreneurs rushed to finish the railroad. On November 1, 1855, dignitaries of all sorts filed aboard the first train scheduled to run from St. Louis to the capital. Eight miles west from Hermann, it steamed along at twenty-five miles per hour onto the Gasconade bridge. One trestle, built temporarily to allow for the ceremonial train, gave way under the weight and eight coaches dropped to the river, dragging the engine back with them. The accident killed nearly three dozen passengers, injured virtually everybody, and postponed rail service to Jefferson City into 1856. In February 1857, another major accident temporarily severed the line near Miller's Station between Washington and Hermann.[3] None of this did more than delay the transformation of what the locals called "Jeff City" by the Pacific Railroad.

The state capital flourished, despite the national Panic of 1857. Its accelerated commercial life swelled the population to 3,082 and pushed the town's line of construction onto High Street running along the crest of the bluffs. There, substantial new brick structures joined the state capital, which had brooded virtually alone over the landscape for fifteen years. Residents enjoyed the cultivated life of an eastern city, at least during meetings of the assembly, even though, during adjournments it still tended to revert to being an unmanageable river town with a polyglot population.[4]

The secessionists elected to state government in 1860 harnessed the intolerant the knife-wielding and trigger-happy rowdiness of such a community to the repression of suspected Unionists, of which Jeff City actually had many. The Pennsylvania-born printer William H. Lusk and his new wife survived the railroad accident at Miller's Station and he took charge of the *Jefferson Enquirer*, which essentially went under because of its Unionism. Others in town included such perennial iconoclasts as Theron M. Rice, future Greenback-Labor leader, and a Bavarian brewer George Wagner, later leader of the local Workingmen's Union of Coles County. At the onset of the war, such Unionists secretly advised the Federal authorities at St. Louis, and, with the June 1861 Federal occupation, turned to the organization of the city's defenses. By the fall of 1864, the old secessionists were long gone, Rice cutting his way through Georgia with the Twenty-sixth Missouri and Lusk riding with the Tenth Missouri Cavalry somewhere across the Mississippi, while Wagner remained, serving in the militia.[5]

Those years have also rendered largely useless the physical defenses of the city. Early on, Union general John C. Fremont responded to the MSG's siege of Lexington upriver by setting the garrison and large numbers of civilian workers to the construction of unnecessarily immense fortifications. The defensive works ascended the bluffs from the river to High Street, and then crossed the "deep valley" to the south to the next ridge. There, they started digging a line of fortifications, creating a broken patchwork of defenses running three and a half miles parallel to the riverfront.[6] Unneeded for three years, they remained not only incomplete but utterly useless.

All this changed in 1864. Usually headquartered west at Warrensburg, General Egbert Brown's Central District regularly garrisoned Jefferson City with other larger towns. On September 23, Rosecrans had suggested his precautionary concentration at the state capital and, the next day, the governor called out the EMM. Two days later, on September 26, Colonel Francis W. Hickox, a state senator from Moniteau County and former post commander at California, put what he had of his Forty-third EMM to work on the fortifications of the capital. Meanwhile, Brown assembled his scattered forces and started gathering what they might need in the event of a siege. He put "all able-bodied men, white and black" to work on the defenses and organized them into three companies of "Citizens Guards." At least two of the local churches, the Second Baptist and the Episcopalian, prepared to serve as hospitals.[7]

Brown knew he had to abandon Fremont's more expansive but unfinished works on the distant ridge in favor of "a short line." For a week, Brown had soldiers, militia, civilians, and "convicts from the penitentiary" laboring on the works. They numbered "less than 1,000 men at first and never to excede 3,000, including citizens," but had tools for only 800. Fortunately, Captain Edward Louis Berthoud of the Second Colorado arrived to help. Only three years before, the Swiss-born Berthoud had, with the aged Jim Bridger, found a pass through the Continental Divide that bore his name. He and Brown decided to incorporate the older, incomplete works, east and west of town running back north to the river, but establish a new southern line along "the principal business street," High Street. This amounted to three miles of works, anchored by completing "the two partially constructed forts" and adding three new ones. They also cut portholes through the back of the new brick buildings on High Street and some of the private homes on Madison Street. They added supplemental rifle pits "bastions, lunettes and trenches." The plan also required clearing the field of fire by destroying "that portion of the town within the valley between High Street and the hills beyond it," but this demolition consisted "almost entirely of fences" with "a few old out-houses of but little value."[8]

In more ways than one, though, Brown's defenses rested on an impressive bluff. His orders included an impressive array of regimental identifications in his force, but these represented simply the minuscule bits and pieces of partly recruited units and his transplanted garrisons supplemented by the militia and civilian guards. As these entered the capital—aided by the trickle of other reinforcements—he asked St. Louis for nearly 3,000 arms.[9] By the start of October, however, he did not have weapons for almost half of that number.

Of course, not only did Brown turn over the garrison duty in his Central District to the local EMM, but Brigadier General Clinton B. Fisk's District of North Missouri issued similar orders to Brigadier General Joseph Beeler Douglas then at Mexico. With the main telegraph along the Pacific Railroad severed, the troubles all along the North Missouri Railroad between St. Charles and St. Joseph threatened communication between St. Louis and the west. Reports on the new recruits of Colonel David P. Dyer's Forty-ninth, then at Warrenton, incurred the wrath of Rosecrans for behaving in "a most disorderly manner, firing from the cars" and engaging in behavior "worse than savage." Still the trigger-happy newcomers of the Forty-ninth and the remnants of the Thirty-ninth not slaughtered at Centralia were supposed to join the available handful of the Forty-fifth to make a concentration at the capital possible. Rosecrans urged them to seize the ferryboats to keep control of the river.[10]

Monday night, October 3, as the Confederates had moved through Gasconade County, Brown still had a force of only about a thousand men "comprised of companies of unorganized infantry regiments who had never been drilled for an hour." Over the next few days, he and Fisk got together 3,000 men, half being "unorganized infantry volunteers, Enrolled Missouri Militia and citizen guards." Perhaps adding the civilian exempts and those too young or too old for the EMM, most without arms, he might have achieved something like 4,800.[11] This came down to about 2,300 battle-ready effectives to meet four times as many Confederates.

The discomforting realities gradually settled over the Union officers meeting at Tom Price's Virginia Hotel near the capitol. The direct telegraph between St. Louis was down and guerrillas continued to cut the line along the North Missouri Railroad. They adopted an ingenious system of couriers in northern Missouri that dashed between these breaks, but, even so, the dispatches from Jefferson City sometimes had to reach the outside world through such routes as circuitous as Chicago. They used this to find help anywhere they could, asking everybody for reinforcements on Tuesday, for a battery on Wednesday, and for patrol boats for the river on Thursday. Still, from Sunday to Wednesday, they had heard "nothing from Saint Louis." From Fort Leavenworth, General Samuel R. Curtis reported that he, too, had "no news from Saint Louis for several days," and suggested that the garrison should fall back rather than to be "gobbled up by overwhelming numbers." In the end, Brown grumbled that Curtis "does not send any battalions."[12]

For several days, Brown had Colonel John Finis Philips covering the south approaches to the city. The thirty-year-old native Missourian had studied law in Kentucky and practiced at Georgetown, just outside of Sedalia, and he entered the war a Democrat and a conservative. However, he became one of the tried-and-true Federal militia officers of the war. His eight hundred well-supplied men of the Fourth and Seventh MSM Cavalry covered the fords on the Osage River, while scouting east for Prices' army, joined episodically from Jefferson City by newly arrived mounted reinforcements, such as those of Colonel James McFerran and the twenty-eight-year-old Major Alexander W. Mullins from the First MSM Cavalry. Their scouts also scoured Osage County, encountering "light parties of citizens" to provide information east of the capital.[13]

Yet, Brown's troubled little garrison had no reason to expect much more on Monday night, when Fisk rode into town with an escort of two hundred. Missouri district commanders almost never needed to cooperate without the presence of a general from the U.S. volunteer force, and St. Louis headquarters had indicated that one such—Alfred Pleasonton or even Rosecrans himself—had already started for Jefferson City to take charge. More deeply, though, Fisk sensed that Brown and his Central District had done everything possible, and even locating the enemy would best be done by those locals. Fisk, like the St. Louis newspaperman, had "no words but those of commendation." In the end, though Referring to Fisk's older commission as a brigadier general, Rosecrans insisted that "the senior officer must command always," so Fisk would be in charge "until a senior joins you."[14]

Reinforcements

In the end, it may have been the good fortune of the Union cause that none of the saviors from St. Louis arrived in Jefferson City, and that the Confederates severed the telegraph line between St. Louis and Rolla. This left Brigadier Generals John McNeil and John Sanborn to rely upon their own judgments rather than the orders and advice from Rosecrans. After rescuing Thomas Ewing's column at Leasburg, Colonel John Beveridge's Illinoisans and Colonel John E. Phelps's Arkansans had followed the Confederates northeast toward Pacific, encountering only small groups of stragglers.[15] This contradicted the consistently incorrect advice of Rosecrans that Rolla was the Confederate target.

Even as the St. Louis press dutifully reported that calming fiction that Price seemed to be on his way west to Rolla, the scouts working out of that headquarters realized that the Confederates had turned back west away from St. Louis. After Sanborn's men repaired the railroad as far as Cuba, he and McNeil decided to act on their own. "All connection with Saint Louis being cut off," McNeil later reported, "I was compelled to act in the premises without consultation with headquarters." Realizing that Jefferson City might still be in danger, they left Colonel Thomas C. Fletcher in charge of the district, while Sanborn assembled his brigade at Cuba and McNeil at Rolla, both heading north across the Gasconade toward a rendezvous at Vienna.[16]

On Tuesday, October 4, Sanborn soldiers reached Vienna only hours ahead of McNeil. The little village had grown around a grocery at the site of a farmers' exchange that had grown a blacksmith shop, churches, a saloon, and a hotel. Of Maries County's 509 voters, 309 had voted for Breckenridge, mostly due to their largely southern antecedents, for the entire white population owned less than a dozen slaves. The Federals had every reason to suspect that news of their movements might reach Price before the column would arrive at the state capital. As soon as McNeil arrived, the generals decided on a predawn march with Sanborn leading a mounted advance. This entailed "hard traveling for all, particularly the artillery horses, which in ascending some of the clayey hills, would get stuck in the mud," while those who had not been with Ewing chatted with the "bully Leasburg fellows."[17]

Their rapid march got 2,400 to 2,800 men, six field guns, and two mountain howitzers to the Osage River "but a few hours before the enemy." An Illinois cavalry remembered mud "about a foot deep. Going up the bank the horses would slide back in the stream. Many hats were brushed off by low limbs of trees and lost in the mud." Everyone from the pickets at the river to the generals to the civilians in the street saw the unauthorized relief column from Rolla as a godsend, as a real chance at success. As Sanborn's men crossed the Osage, they did not continue into the city, but turned downstream to reinforce Philips, while McNeil continued into the capital.[18]

The Federals continued to close their inner defenses back at the city. Toward the northeastern flank, Colonel Lebbeus Zevely's "German militia"—the Twenty-eighth EMM—covered College Hill, relieving what was left of Colonel Rudolph Poser's Thirty-fourth EMM, which ventured back toward the ruins of the Osage bridge. At the southwest exterior of the line, Lieutenant Colonel Andrew J. Hart's Forty-third EMM moved to Osage near Castle Rock. The mounted mobile forces of the Missouri State Militia Cavalry struggled to cover the crossings between them. Lieutenant Colonel Henry M. Matthews gathered the rest of the Third MSM Cavalry down the Taos Road, strengthening Major Austin A. King's detachment and assuming its command. Philips large body of horsemen concentrated at Bolton Ford, with detachments downstream at Clark's Ford and upstream "as high as Prince's Shoals" just below Castle Rock. He also sent Major George W. Kelley's detachment of the Fourth MSM Cavalry farther downriver. Unable to tell where the Confederates would strike, Philips kept the bulk of his force back where he could deploy them as needed. Brown briefly recalled the EMM from the Osage "for the purpose of being uniformed" in the city and used his reinforcements to strengthen the fords. That small bit of the Forty-ninth Missouri at the capital moved two mountain howitzers to "the first rise south of the penitentiary."[19]

Beneath the orderliness presented by the documents and the newspapers lurks the shadow of a certain seething confusion. These shifts permitted further reconnaissance beyond the Osage by Lieutenant Colonel Daniel M. Draper's Ninth MSM Cavalry, Captain Edward J. Jones's detachment of the Seventeenth Illinois Cavalry, and a small group from the Thirteenth Missouri Cavalry. By Thursday morning, Fisk's scouts at Tuscumbia reported the rebels in force at Linn. Perhaps in an inexplicable retaliation for the Confederate burning of the railroad bridge over the Osage, the apparently panicked Federals themselves torched that over the Moreau, which was safe and secure within their own lines.[20]

Still, the arrival of McNeil and Sanborn provided Jefferson City with a plausible little army. Rosecrans told his superiors that he had arranged the presence there of 4,100 cavalry and 2,600 infantry with "a few citizens and militia," totaling "nearly 8,000" capable of fighting "a strong battle behind intrenchments," if "not very formidable to act offensively against a veteran force." His exaggeration of the garrison's size, of course, minimized his own inaction in its defense. In reality, Fisk had no more than about 7,200, which Sanborn distilled into no more than 6,000 reliable troops.[21] In short, the Federals at the state capital had roughly half the number of Price's army, and that by no virtue of their high command.

Yet, to earthworks of Brown and the initiative of McNeil and Sanborn, Fisk contributed his General Order No. 1, reorganizing the Union forces into brigades. Often misunderstood as an order of battle for the deployment of his forces, Fisk himself described it as a defensive ploy "calculated to convey to the enemy . . . an exaggerated idea of the real force in the city." Experienced soldiers, moreover, reported Fisk "in the saddle constantly" over the next few days, turning up unexpectedly at various points in the line, and described him as being as "cool under fire as the coolest veterans, and that his conduct was calculated to inspire confidence and courage among his men."[22]

The defenders of Jefferson City understood the stakes. McNeil dreaded the impact on the elections of a Confederate claim that Reynolds had been inaugurated as "the constitutional Governor of Missouri" by "this rebel army of occupation." "If Price takes Jefferson City," wrote Brown, "he will have to fight for it." "We shall give Price a good whack if he comes this way," added Fisk. Though outnumbered, he assured headquarters, "we are ready for them." Rosecrans, in turn, assured Curtis in Kansas that the force at Jefferson City "will hurt General Price decidedly."[23]

Still, the Federals at Jefferson City hoped against hope in the arrival of Rosecrans, Pleasonton, Mower, or anyone experienced enough commanding these numbers to do so. When McNeil and Sanborn arrived with news that their scouts or flankers reported Price's army moving on the Osage, Brown had insisted, perhaps largely to himself, that the Confederates "must be further east." As late as Wednesday, Fisk still wondered whether most of Price's men "are in force this side of the Gasconade." This seeming confusion came from the top down, and, on Thursday, Rosecrans confidently told Fisk that "you have not the whole force to contend with yet."[24]

In contrast, many Confederates expected a quick and easy victory followed by a triumphal march into the capital. General Jo Shelby—or, more accurately, his scribe Major Edwards—described the defenders of Jefferson City as "militia utterly worthless for sober fighting." As rather a reflection of his dishonesty as a source, he ventured this opinion after Price's army had already encountered some of them at Pilot Knob. Among the newly arrived defenders of the capital were Battery H, Second Missouri Light Artillery, and some members of the hated Third MSM Cavalry, the "utterly worthless" character of which had been thwarting vastly larger number of Confederates for two weeks.[25]

Over the Osage: October 6

Even as the Union generals reassured one another, the Confederate Army of Missouri concentrated just beyond the fords on the Osage River. The Federals narrowed down the likely locations of an attempted crossing by the Confederates after the latter failed to pursue their success at the railroad bridge. Special Order No. 214 redeployed the Union forces to cover eight miles of fords at the Osage River. McFerran drew his two hundred men of the First MSM Cavalry from Clark's Ford back to the city, though Philips men—having then increased to about 1,500 men—were insufficient to cover the terrain. Fisk sent McNeil to those upriver from Philips with orders "to contest the crossing of the Osage as long as possible and if compelled to do so fall back and form on the west and north side of the Moreau, contesting every inch of ground fiercely against the advance of the enemy."[26]

Shelby studied the problem from the other side of the river. The recent rains left the Osage downriver "a wide and deep stream," difficult enough to cross without the artillery and wagons. From near Bolton's Ford, he heard that the Federals had covered all possible crossings but could not tell how many of them awaited his division. He needed to probe for a weak point, create a breech, and then pour sufficient forces over the river to flank the Federals along the adjacent fords. Just back from the railroad bridge, Colonel David Shanks took charge of finding the most poorly defended crossing.[27]

The fighting "opened at Prince's Ford," according to the *Missouri State Times*. The Confederate advance caught the pickets of Mullins's detachment of the First MSM on the far side of the Osage. Never shy of exaggeration, Edwards described catching "a Federal scout on this side of thirty men and pushing them so hard that they, like the swine possessed of the devil, ran over a steep place and thirteen of them drowned. The rest were captured and killed." The actual number that drowned had been three and four, of whom the press had "not been able to obtain their names." However, two hundred of the Eighth MSM Cavalry and some of Philips's Seventh MSM Cavalry fought alongside Mullins's. In the end, the real breakthrough came upstream where Colonel B. Frank Gordon's Fifth Missouri Cavalry forced a crossing at Castle Rock against Hart's detachment of the Forty-third EMM. Although Union reinforcements poured into the fight there, their numbers proved too thin to prevent the crossing.[28]

As the sound of the artillery from upstream reached Philips, he sent Mullins and his men hurrying upstream to reinforce the outpost. Mullins had not gone half a mile along the river before encountering a large Confederate rebel force. Under the cover of the fight at Castle Rock itself, Colonel Benjamin F. Elliott's Fifth Missouri Cavalry and Lieutenant Colonel David A. Williams's Battalion had forced their way over the river near Bolton's Ford. Edwards, writing on Shelby's behalf, wrote that "the swift and beautiful water was torn into foam-flakes that hurried and danced away to the sea, while the ringing shout of a thousand voices told that the ford was won."[29]

The fight proved desperate and vicious. Second Lieutenant George W. Houts with about ten men from the Seventh MSM Cavalry joined Mullins's company. They flanked the Confederate skirmishers, driving them from "a deep ravine" to occupy it themselves. With their strong position, Mullins stubbornly held his own against the continually growing Confederate numbers, as the brigades of Shanks and Jackman forded the river and started entering the fight. Mullins's men seriously wounded Shanks, and command fell temporarily to Colonel Moses Smith. On his way to the front, the reluctant Private Donald Palmer saw the litter bearing Shanks to the rear. Edwards reported that Shelby's men broke a force that outnumbered them, but Mullins's men reportedly faced so many rebels after fifteen or twenty-five minutes that they threatened his flanks, which "compelled to fall back." Mullins had slowed the advance at a cost of five killed or mortally wounded and three wounded and the handful of men from the Seventh had temporarily lost Houts "severely wounded in the face while bravely resisting the enemy's advance."[30] Throughout, however, officers on both sides reported an intensity of conflict that simply belied the small numbers of the officially acknowledged casualties.

By 11 a.m., both sides had artillery in the field. Within an hour, Shelby's men crossed the Osage under the cover of their guns at Prince's Ferry. While the onslaught had rolled the Federals back from "several fords" both above and below Castle Rock, "the great body of rebels" crossed over Prince's Ford. Facing these converging columns, the Federals could only begin falling back toward the Moreau, hoping only to "fight over every inch of the ground." "Our boys are peppering them already," reported Fisk from the field. "The rebels approached with the most infernal yells, but the Missouri boys are not to be frightened." They fell back with plans to "hold the banks of the Moreau until the last moment." Nevertheless, the Confederates had been "steadily advancing and closing in upon us."[31] Once at the Moreau, the fighting would be only about three or four miles from the last defenses of the state capital.

By 5 p.m., the bulk of Shelby's division had bogged down several miles south of Moreau Creek. Gordon's regiment, which had forded at Castle Rock, fought "a severe engagement of ten minutes' duration" after dark at the Dixon's plantation with an enemy that "fled in great confusion."[32] Given known position of the Federal troops, Gordon's men almost surely encountered scouts or pickets who took to heart the order about delaying actions.

Thursday ended with nervous Federal generals putting their frontline troops into camp around Green Berry's farm, less than four miles from the city. Commanders on both sides claimed to have been pleased at the results of the day. Despite "expending a good deal of artillery ammunition," Fisk described his own casualties as "few" and "inconsiderable." "You are doing well," Rosecrans assured him by telegraph, and Fisk reassured him that the soldiers "toss up their hats for old 'Rosey.'" That said, Fisk, Brown, Sanborn, and McNeil still expected those 9,000 Federals from the St. Louis area to turn up in the rear of Price's army and Fisk declared that he hoped "to hold the enemy at bay, at least until our troops can fall upon his rear." The national press even reported that Rosecrans had audaciously advanced "westward" from Gray's Summit (without informing readers where Gray's Summit was). Rosecrans cultivated such illusions, writing Fisk, "If we can get them between the Meramec and the Osage they will fare badly." In telegraphing Kansas, Fisk included a fervent prayer: "May the good Lord hurry up Smith and Mower."[33]

That very night, the full realization of their situation descended on the four generals managing the little force at Jefferson City. Perhaps because he had experienced a week of terrible advice from Rosecrans about Rolla, McNeil may have become the first to grasp fully the plight of the capital's defenders. Late on Thursday, Rosecrans mentioned that he hoped to get 3,000 of Mower's infantry to rendezvous with Smith near Union and guessed that "our troops will be up in three days." "We are assaulted now," retorted McNeil sharply, "or shall be, by the entire rebel force in the State." He apparently passed the news to Fisk who, at almost eight o'clock, telegraphed Rosecrans fishing for more information, stating, "I trust the troops from below are close upon the foe." In fact, at that time, Smith's infantry had gotten only "to within some four miles of Union," and Mower's exhausted division remained out of touch and somewhere in the Ozarks.[34]

At that point, nobody had time for recriminations. "We have no force pressing the enemy's rear," Fisk told Curtis. "What you do should be done quickly," added Brown. "Telegraph and our communications to the west will probably be cut off to-night." "The story will soon be told," Fisk then telegraphed Rosecrans, adding in a dispatch to the garrison at Macon, "To-morrow they will probably invest us."[35]

That night, generals in Jefferson City held a council of war. They assigned responsibility for the south-facing line, from east to west, to Brown, Sanborn, and McNeil. On the left or eastern end of the Union line, units of Brown's brigade had borne the brunt of Thursday's fighting. In addition to Philips's detachment were Mullins's men, who had not received rations all day and waited at the Moreau bridge "very hungry and worn out." Worse, while the fighting had engaged Philips's attention through the day, his contingent of the Fourth MSM Cavalry under Major Kelley had settled into a position far to his left, almost as far as the mouth of the Osage. Brown quickly ordered Philips to close the gap, moving some troops along an upper road between the Osage and the Moreau.[36] However, as surely as Thursday had been Brown's, Friday belonged to Sanborn covering the center of the Union line.

McNeil's brigade took the western end of the south-facing line, the Union right centered on College Hill. Within McNeil's line, the far right went to Beveridge's Seventeenth Illinois Cavalry, who found that its march from Rolla had reunited it with previously detached companies; it now had 645 men and officers. Toward McNeil's left, Lieutenant Colonel Joseph A. Eppstein's Fifth MSM Cavalry held a makeshift salient, "the southwest corner" of the overall Federal line. Sanborn's brigade held the Federal center with his men posted to contest the rebel advance from the Bolton's and Prince's Fords. McNeil thought Sanborn held "the strongest position on the south side of the town," but sought to ensure his success by sending Captain John Jacob Sutter's section of Battery B, the Second Missouri Light Artillery.[37]

Not that far away, the Army of Missouri spent a hopeful night. Price boarded in the home of the Wallendorfs, a German Unionist family, in Frog Hollow. Family legend recalled the loss of virtually all of their livestock and the general's payment of $27 in Confederate money for their hospitality and troubles. The local paper said that they also hosted Shelby, whose division camped only about six miles short of Jefferson City.[38]

The Moreau: October 7

The next morning, Virginians led both sides. Just as Philips had taken the field on Brown's behalf Thursday, responsibility now fell to Colonel Joseph

Jackson Gravely, a thirty-six-year-old Virginian, who had come to Cedar County, Missouri, before the war. He took the Eighth MSM Cavalry forward to meet the brigade of General William L. Cabell, also a Virginian before coming west to command Arkansas troops.

The Union commanders watched from a house on the hills near town. Starting five miles from the capital, Gravely's Eighth MSM Cavalry had orders "to fall back slowly," with Major William Plumb's detachment of the Sixth MSM Cavalry holding the ford at the Moreau behind it, with orders to hold "at all hazards" until the Union soldiers to the south had forded.[39] Major William B. Mitchell's Seventh Provisional EMM was near enough for any needed support, with the rest of Sanborn's brigade holding the high ground beyond Moreau Creek.

At 7 a.m., Cabell's Confederates appeared in "a great force," but did nothing to upset careful Union plans. Gravely had spent the previous hour stationing "one squadron in the rear of the other" at strategic intervals along the Bolton Ferry road. Each would force the Confederates into a major, time-consuming deployment, and, when the enemy numbers became too great, fall back into the next position.[40] As they did this, it would make each Federal position stronger as the fighting neared the Moreau.

The Confederates first hit Captain William C. Human's company around James Gordon's farm. Cabell's brigade reformed into a large line of battle but, in the end, had to bring up artillery to dislodge the stubborn Federals. Only as the numbers threatened to overwhelm Human's left flank did Gravely order his withdrawal. In a later operation, Cabell took the initiative of ordering a charge against two of Gravely's companies as they were falling back. However, five Union companies hidden "near the edge of the timber" entered the fray, forcing the Confederates once more to wait until they could bring up artillery. Cabell described the day as "a hard fight" and Price called it a "hotly contested battle."[41]

As the fighting neared the Moreau, Lieutenant James M. Murphy had some of the men of the Sixth MSM Cavalry building "temporary breast-works" to protect the ford. Gravely also brought Plumb's Sixth into a line of battle south of the Moreau to cover the crossing of the Eighth. As Gravely's men forded the Moreau, the Confederate advance slammed not only into Plumb's line but Murphy's on opposite banks of the Moreau. As "the guns of Fort Murphy" unleashed an enfilade fire, Gravely's Eighth reformed to protect the crossing of Plumb's men.[42] Meanwhile, Cabell waited for the rest of Fagan's division.

Fisk and Sanborn watched as Gravely managed his withdrawal to rejoin the rest of Sanborn's brigade. Sanborn thought he had "handsomely" commanded the four-hour operation that had "punished the enemy very severely" all along the way. As Gravely's force filed up the bluffs from the Moreau onto "a ridge near the Fair Ground," Plumb's men took and held the ford for "about an hour." This brought the fighting to where the left of Sanborn's brigade abutted the right of Brown's "at a point about a quarter of a mile south of the Fair Grounds." At about 10 a.m. the fighting resumed as the Confederates pushed across the Moreau. Price described the "obstinate resistance" they faced without knowing that some of Brown's dismounted men, including the well-rested horsemen under Philips had begun another skirmish lasting about forty-five minutes.[43]

The Federals grew careless at one point. When Sutter's twelve-pounders moved forward, with two companies of infantry in support, Sanborn thought it was to relieve Gravely's force, and pulled his own cavalry back. Believing this to be a more general withdrawal, the infantry and the artillery then fell back as well, the former in a disordered way. For his part, Sanborn complained later that the "inexperienced" and "badly managed" infantry "broke and fled upon the withdrawal of the cavalry," but the responsibility for not informing them what he was doing rested elsewhere. Confederate reports mentioned this last rear guard action, claiming that the Federals had been "finally routed and forced to seek shelter in their intrenchments."[44]

Nevertheless, the Union position quickly stabilized. Captain Charles H. Thurber's section of Battery L of the Second Missouri Light Artillery rolled into position on the left, and Sutter repositioned his guns at the center, and the Union ranks reformed, before reaching their last line of defense on the High Street ridge. Price's Confederates advanced about a mile beyond Berry Springs (along the present-day Greenberry Road), to the crest of the second ridge from the river.[45]

Between noon and one o'clock, Price's Army of Missouri demonstrated that it could still present a spectacle of itself. In praising Fagan's handling of the division, Price noted that it occupied high ground adjacent to the Fair Grounds. Cabell's men held the advance of that division. "My brigade," he boasted, "occupied the heights in full view of the city." Alongside them, the rest of Price's men began filing into "a line of battle three or four miles long, east, south and west" of the Federal defenses. Shortly thereafter, Fisk got Rosecrans a telegram he thought might be his last: "the ball is opening earnestly."[46]

From only about a mile away, those Unionists who could watched with amazement. Sanborn's brigade had the best seats. Major William B. Mitchell watched from "the south side of the Moreau, but could not for some time determine who they were." However, Sanborn himself stood among Phelps's Arkansas Unionists observing the enemy "moving in full view down the road" toward them and unfolding their line only "about one mile in our front." Among Brown's men on the left, McFerran, in the rifle pits on the far left of the defenses, saw little, but Philips saw the rebel formation so clearly that he assumed they were in "full view of the line of the rifle pits and earth works." On the right, most of McNeil's brigade missed the show, but Eppstein's soldiers saw enough to brace for an attack they expected to strike them first and hardest.[47] The confusion did not last long.

From "a wooded heights at the left of the Fair-Ground," a rebel battery wheeled into position and opened on the Federal line. Mitchell and his men ducked two or three shells lobbed their direction, noting that they had almost landed in the capital itself. Sanborn described a Confederate battery east of the city, and a Union battery "planted east of the cemetery." The latter likely referred to Thurber's on the Union left, which focused on the Confederate big guns and drove them from its exposed position. Half a century later, residents still remembered that Confederate batteries "sent in a few shells, some of which have not yet exploded, but beyond the excitement caused, little damage was effected."[48] By one o'clock, the artillery of both sides dueled to determine the fate of the day.

At about this time, Shelby's division moved into line west of Fagan's position. Brigadier General M. Jeff Thompson, who had taken charge of Shelby's original Iron Brigade when Shanks had fallen Thursday, moved his men by column "in sight of Jefferson City" to within three miles southwest of the capital. Marmaduke's men had also moved to the front. Lieutenant Colonel J. F. Davies's battalion of Clark's brigade later spent the night "within sight of the enemy's camp-fires at Jefferson City." Price thought his men had marched only "two miles south of the city." Meanwhile, "the batteries in the front south of the capital constantly fired at us, but all of their shot fell short or missed their aim and we had no casualties."[49]

During the early part of the artillery exchange, the Confederates advanced on Sanborn, "halted and then fled back behind the crest of a ridge." Viewing the movements from the left, however, Philips clearly saw this broader shift of Price's army toward the west. Brown warned Fisk of the same movement "beyond the valley in front of General Sanborn," who already realized that the rebels "seemed to shift" before him. Over on the Union right under McNeil, Eppstein's Fifth MSM Cavalry faced "some skirmishing" on the southwestern salient of the Federal defenses, and the day closed as McNeil watched the Confederates "massing their whole force on my front."[50] Just as Brown had fought Thursday and Sanborn Friday, McNeil anticipated Saturday and his men "labored industriously the entire night" in expectations of an enemy attack.

Scouts from both sides moved furtively through the darkness. Phelps's Arkansans skirmished with the enemy into the night and two squadrons of Eppstein's men stumbled onto what looked like the main Confederate encampment five miles southwest of town. Confederate major Washington McDaniels of Colonel Benjamin F. Elliott's First Missouri Cavalry led a small group that took "several prisoners," cut the telegraph, destroyed a water station, tore up track, and burned several smaller railroad bridges "on the streams up the valley of which the railroad leaves the Missouri river." All of this might have taken place at Scott's Station just beyond the western end of the Union defenses, but the Illinois cavalrymen on that part of the line reported only that they "remained in that position." Most likely, this account referred to the Confederate destruction of the bridge at Clark's Station, some six miles west of the city,[51] The Federal defenses and the capital itself remained untouched.

Yet, tall tales invariably found their way into accounts of the fighting there. Private George Rea later told his family about that raid west of town in which Frank James and a handful of rebel superheroes defended a bridge, leaving the Yankee bodies piling about them. The account became "history" in at least one account.[52] Perhaps none of the Confederate myths was as far reaching as the implication that Rosecrans, Smith, or Pleasonton played any great role in thwarting Price's advance on the capital or his capture of it.

The reported casualty figures are simply problematic. Officers on both sides grossly minimized and vaguely reported their own casualties, while exaggerating those inflicted on the enemy. Fisk reported losses "as yet inconsiderable" and Union reports mentioned the loss of only four killed with a number of wounded; they claimed to have inflicted heavy losses on the enemy, "killing and wounding in large number." In fact, at least seven died in the first minutes of the attack at Prince's Ford and the two days of fierce fighting that followed were not bloodless. The *Missouri State Times* named fourteen Union fatalities and casualties at the General Hospital. The Federals likely left some on the field, because citizens mentioned burying two killed near the Moreau and reported hearing of other civilians burying a dead Federal back toward the Osage.[53] Reported disappearances or desertions likely masked more serious casualties, and these were themselves only irregularly reported in some of the units engaged and almost all casualties remained unreported for militia.

The Confederate commanders engaged in even greater fictions on this. They claimed almost no losses, though they must have suffered more than the Federals in two days of attacking an enemy in strong defensive positions. The local paper listed eleven Confederates wounded or captured, including Colonel Shanks, a Major Bowls, and a First Lieutenant Key. The *State Times* mentioned nineteen local men who went off with Price's army, though it is unclear whether they did so as volunteers or conscripts. They included two deserters from the Union's Tenth Missouri Cavalry, Major Lusk's regiment.[54]

In the end, the fighting around Jefferson City had been merely probing to test the strength of the Federal position. Ever helpful, Rosecrans advised Fisk to "secure every thing for an assault" and urged "coolness and determination to slaughter them. The best would be to get them to try two or three terrible assaults." No such attempt followed because Price "received positive information that the enemy were 12,000 strong in the city, and that 3,000 more had arrived on the opposite bank of the river by the North Missouri Railroad."[55] Once more, Price discerned a much-larger enemy than he actually faced, and brushed aside the objections of Governor Reynolds and others who urged an attack.

The Confederates themselves seem to have sensed what was coming. During a lull in the troop movements and skirmishing, Jeff Thompson sat on a stump and mused at the view of the capitol building, not that far distant. It struck him "queer that there should be men there firing at us to keep us away, when we had along with us General Price, a former Governor, and Thomas C. Reynolds, the present Governor, and hundreds who had in their time held seats of honor in the Capitol." Nearby, Reynolds himself had similar thoughts as he looked at the site that had brought him north across hundreds of rugged miles of Arkansas and Missouri countryside, through dozens of broken towns, and through the ranks of thousands of miserable Missourians.[56] The feelings of General—and former governor—Sterling Price can only be imagined.

As Saturday, October 8, began, Federal brigades under Sanborn and McNeil faced what they believed to be the entire Confederate Army of Missouri. When no attack came, a suspicious Sanborn got permission from Fisk to test the strength of the rebels to his front and the dismounted battalion of Phelps's Arkansas Unionists moved forward. They continued mile after nervous mile before going some eight miles from the city and meeting Price's rear guard, where the westbound Springfield Road crossed Moreau Creek. When the rebels placed artillery west of the creek, Phelps sent back for Thurber's guns and, before they arrived, the Confederates withdrew.[57] At this point, Fisk realized that the entire of Price's army had moved southwest down the Springfield Road toward Russellville.

On the outskirts of Jefferson City, Price's expedition became the "raid" it was never intended to be. There, the Army of Missouri surrendered its ambitions about recapturing the state to the pragmatic goal of plundering resources and moving on. The only practical legacy of its earlier plans was that it still dragged behind it five hundred wagons, most picked up along the way, constituting what one Confederate officer described as "a wagon train as long as the tail of Plantamour's comet." As Sam Hildebrand colorfully recalled, after Jefferson City, the Confederate army began "quietly making a blind march in the direction of Idaho."[58] Price's would-be liberation of the state finally seemed to have lost all sense of direction.

For the first time in the nineteen-day history of the campaign, a Union officer ordered the active pursuit of retreating Confederates. The circumstances finally approximated how the Federal authorities wanted to see the rebel presence, as a mere raid. Two self-interested mythologies—formulated and embraced for different reasons by conflicting powers—began to converge.

The process literally made history.

Epilogue

Shaping the Memory of a Civil War Campaign

People who saw the ubiquitous Indian mounds as proof of native brutality and their own civilization responded accordingly to the Confederate invasion. As Sterling Price's army rampaged across the state, rumors terrified whites that savage Indians had returned to exact their terrible revenge. Perhaps because Stand Watie's Cherokee raid near the Kansas line took place the same day that Price's men entered Missouri, some accounts regularly described the latter as including Watie and Indian-agent-turned-Confederate-general Douglas Cooper. Moreover, the "first explicit statement . . . of the organization of Price's Army" in the press mentioned "several regiments of half-breeds and Indians." Later descriptions placed some five thousand Indians following in the wake of Price's army doing the real work of destruction and murder.[1] Clearly, the civilizers of the state were predisposed to attribute the atrocities to the spirits of their fears rather than to their once and future governors.

After passing Jefferson City as well as St. Louis, Confederate concerns would center on avoiding their pursuers, real and imagined. Participants in what had become "Price's raid" would take what they needed immediately and keep moving. This, in turn, changed the requirements of commanders on both sides to present their superiors and the general public a campaign that would not reflect poorly on their legitimacy, credibility, or memory. The original purpose of the campaign had been to influence the November elections, which it did, though not in the way intended. The presence of an active secessionist army in Missouri and the mobilizations to meet it virtually assured an electoral vindication of the Unionists at the polls.

From Reoccupation to Raid

Confederate leaders probably never realized—or wanted to realize—just how close they could have taken their army to its original strategic goals.

General William L. Cabell pulled back from Pacific with the arrival of the Federal brigade of General Edward H. Wolfe. This tactical withdrawal masked the actual balance of power within twenty or twenty-five miles of the town. That is, the rest of his Arkansas division and most of the two Missouri divisions were that at Richwoods, Union, or closer. In contrast, only about a thousand enrolled militia scattered between Kirkwood and various outposts along the Meramec backed Wolfe. How a Confederate push might have gotten would have depended on how quickly General William S. Rosecrans and Federal general Andrew J. Smith could have brought up reinforcements and neither had done very well managing the kind of troop movement with what they had.

It is probably obligatory to address the suggestions of Major John N. Edwards and others that Price's army could have reshaped the outcome of the war had it taken St. Louis. These assume that, once taken, the city would switch its allegiance and cooperatively occupy itself for the Confederacy. This would permit Price's army to use the yet available fleet of steamboats—if not walking on water—to cross the Mississippi and go into a rampage across the presumed howling wilderness that was the Midwest. Assuming such a series of miracles had landed the Army of Missouri in Illinois, the Federal authorities there had military installations, fresh recruits, demobilized veterans, and intact railroads to make short work of Price's force before it got very far.

In reality, of course, residents of St. Louis themselves would have responded in the face of Price's advance from Pacific. The secessionists had not been strong enough to hold the city three years before and many of the most ardent of them had long since left. Contrary to the wishful thinking of Confederate commanders, Missourians' disgust with life under Federal military occupation did not translate into a revival of secessionism. If severely pressed, even Rosecrans would likely turn to the Radicals for help in more completely mobilizing the EMM. Had he not, the appearance of the Confederates on the outskirts of St. Louis would have energized and mobilized the city's Unionists anyway. Those men of military age capable and willing to bear arms in self-defense would have certainly been poorly organized and ill prepared, but their sheer numbers would have created a serious obstacle to Price's subjugation of the city.

Such a response grew from the beliefs and activities of Missouri Confederates themselves. Faith that real Missourians supported secession—and that residents of the state who did not had no business in there—provided Price's army with its *raison d'être*. None of that would have changed as it entered the St. Louis area. No Unionist had reason to believe the Confederates would behave any differently there than Potosi, De Soto, Union, or anywhere else. The same that inspired the fierce defense of Fort Davidson would have informed resistance on a much-larger scale throughout the St. Louis area.

Indeed, the Confederate seizure of St. Louis might well have been a disastrous self-immolation. Those inevitable reprisals against African Americans and the hated "Dutch" would have exactly the opposite effect, and the immensely greater numbers that would be killed in St. Louis would doom Price's ambitions. Had the Confederates the discipline to hold themselves to killing merely even a much-smaller proportion of the prisoners, militia, and civilians slaughtered in smaller communities, one suspects that what would have happened in St. Louis would have made Fort Pillow a mere footnote. Even a brief occupation of the city by Price's army might have cast a national and international spotlight on events there. The initial impact in the North would have replicated that in Missouri, creating a wave of indignation that would have further lengthened the majority for Abraham Lincoln's reelection and intensified the Radical hues of the successful electoral coalition. In fact, Price made difficult choices to protect his army, and his choices likely sought to protect it from the damage to itself that only it could have inflicted.

Rightly or wrongly, Price placed his priority on assuring the survival of his army in the field. Why would he not have believed that the rest of Smith's corps did not lurk just behind Wolfe's brigade at Pacific? That thousands of other volunteers were not there as well? Or that an army of enrolled militia large enough to in itself outnumber the Confederates was not there? More importantly, though, Price himself had to wonder whether he could have held St. Louis and what he would have gained by taking it and not being able to hold it.

Somewhat different concerns informed Price's army as it approached its secondary strategic goal, the state capital at Jefferson City, but the defenders proved to be more desperately energetic. Of course, the fighting there provided a taste of what largely less experienced generals and ill-prepared militia could do with their backs to the wall, or, in this case, the Missouri River. Using a three-to-one requirement for success in such an enterprise, the Confederates had enough to overcome the Federals under Egbert Brown and Clinton B. Fisk. However contemptuous the language of Major Edwards, driving Fisk's little army into their inner defenses would have left thousands of Price's men littering the slopes up to the High Street ridge, and the Union reinforcements brought to the capital by John McNeil and John Sanborn make it rather doubtful whether the Confederates had enough to breach those defenses and take the capital.

More importantly, what would be gained by hurling the bodies of his soldiers against the enemy's strong defensive positions seems questionable, even mad to a modern reader. The Confederate installation of Governor Thomas C. Reynolds for a new term would have actually meant no more at Jefferson City than anywhere else. His predecessor had enjoyed an inauguration there with the mandate of a statewide election behind him, but it did not prevent

Unionists from chasing him out of the state. Reynolds would have had less a chance to stay in Jefferson City than his predecessor with Price's devastated army to defend him and the vastly greater number of Federal forces in or near the state than those which dashed secessionist hopes for Missouri three years before. Without the mandate of a statewide election, Reynolds's inauguration would have meant something only to those who already regarded him as the governor and would continue to do so regardless of what happened in the capital. Conversely, those who disputed his claim to governorship without an election would find his inauguration without one meaningless. While the taking of the state capital would have embarrassed Unionist efforts to reestablish civilian government, it would be hard to argue that it would be worth what would have amounted to the destruction of much of Price's army.

Weeks before the planners of the campaign had gotten an army at the capital, they had to have considered the relative insignificance of that achievement for Missouri and Missourians. Clearly, the symbolic victory they sought would be such primarily in other eyes and for other considerations, such as internal Confederate politics, either state or national, or, perhaps, in hopes of having an impact in terms of international diplomacy. Recognizing the inattention accorded Missouri nationally and internationally in the war news, the value of Reynolds's governorship beyond the government-in-exile he led seems of questionable worth for the lives it would have cost.

Then, too, the Confederate occupation of Jefferson City would have produced the same kind of collateral damage there that it had inflicted elsewhere. Three of the four Union generals at the state capital—Fisk, McNeil, and Brown—had long records of dealing as ruthlessly with secessionists as Major James Wilson, and had no fewer enemies among Price's men. Given its record, it is hard to imagine that none of their enemies would seize the opportunity for retaliation, or that Confederate officers would act to prevent it. In contrast to a meaningless ceremony at the capital, the murder of any prisoners holding a general's rank would have had national and international repercussions. Given his options, then, Price surely made the best possible choice in not attacking the state capital.

However, these decisions left what had been an invasion to play out as a "raid." One measure of this change is that Price, in turning his back on St. Louis and Jefferson City, left far larger and more threatening Union forces to his rear than Thomas Ewing's little column at Pilot Knob. Just as Price had feared earlier, the Federal troops behind him had the option of organizing immediately to harass the rear of his column.

As the Confederates left Jefferson City, General Alfred Pleasonton finally arrived. He had taken the easiest and safest route, by the North Missouri Railroad to Mexico, and the relatively well maintained garrison at Mexico then had only fifty men and no cavalry. From there, he had ridden through Fulton to a point on the river opposite the capital.[2] As fortune had it, Pleasonton arrived after the danger to Jefferson City had passed and General Clinton B. Fisk had already sent a mounted force after Price's rear guard.

Back at St. Louis, the Democratic and conservative *Missouri Republican* dutifully reported a version of events fed it by the Federal headquarters. One might say, as did one Iowa cavalryman, "The care of General Rosecrans at Saint Louis had been chiefly for St. Louis," but the *Republican* story portrayed Rosecrans as the architect for the positive outcome of the campaign: "As soon as Sanborn reached Rolla, he and McNeil were ordered to Jefferson City, as was Fisk." The *Republican* also complained that the district commanders would have done better at Jefferson City had Fisk "sufficient military skill and experience to sally forth and attack Price as he retreated," which he had done. The press supplemented its accounts with fictions, "Fortunately, at this time Pleasonton arrived and assumed command. He sent Sanborn out on the pursuit at once." Other accounts even have Pleasonton reaching the capital in time to save it.[3] In fact, Rosecrans had actually been telling McNeil and Sanborn that Price would attack Rolla, though he discussed with Smith whether to bring them up the tracks to Pacific. Pleasonton got nowhere near the capital, and, for all their shortcomings, the brigadiers there had well organized the city's defense and the pursuit of the enemy.

Nevertheless, Pleasonton immediately took charge. He reorganized the cavalry sent in pursuit of Price into a division under Sanborn with brigades under Colonels John F. Philips, Joseph J. Gravely, and John L. Beveridge. Having brushed aside Fisk's work, Pleasonton would also later arrest and try to court-martial both McNeil and Brown.[4] Although Pleasonton knew better, he allowed Sanborn's mounted Federals pressing the Confederates from the east to continue anticipating the appearance of infantry support from St. Louis.

Whatever sense of urgency ever flickered across the minds of Rosecrans and Smith, it faded the farther west Price got. Rosecrans not only strove to avoid responsibility for any possible reversal, but Smith had been on his way to Tennessee and still viewed every step west of St. Louis as taking him farther from that goal. Both had let the Confederate army get a week's start while they had waited for any news of General Joseph A. Mower's division of Smith's corps. Thereafter, they waited for the piecemeal transport of Mower's men up the Mississippi from Cape Girardeau. Finally, they waited for transports.

The process took time because the material damage the Confederates left in their wake proved impressive. In Franklin County alone, the rebels took several thousand horses and mules and robbed virtually "every house on a route of nearly forty miles," stripping about two-thirds of everything, for a total of $50,000 in damages other than the railroad. By Jefferson City, damage to the railroad ran as high as $300,000. The military authorities assured everyone that the railroad everywhere was already being "rapidly repaired" on the Iron Mountain line and the main course of the Pacific Railroad. On October 10, Thomas C. Fletcher reached Jefferson City from Rolla and reported some 1,500 men at work "repairing the South-West branch of the railroad," predicting that the following day would reestablish the telegraph to St. Louis and have the tracks in order from Rolla to Moselle. In the course of the month, the Department of Missouri reported mobilizing 24,164 EMM, a prodigious amount of manpower almost entirely put to uses other than pursuing Price, such as repairing the assets of the railroads.[5]

Apparently oblivious to the experience of Mower's infantry pursuit of mounted Confederates, the generals at St. Louis gave Price's horsemen the additional advantage of a week's head start before ordering their footsore privates to begin the pursuit. The one-hundred-day Illinois men had flatly refused and had to be sent home. Members of the Fourth Iowa Cavalry recalled that Missouri infantry "encamped near Washington, had refused to go aboard the boats there waiting to carry them up the Missouri to fight Price." The Iowans "deployed into line around three sides of it, the river being on the fourth, and closed in. The Missourians were then seen in their open camp, their arms stacked and themselves idly waiting events." As the cavalry closed on them, "one company fell in and took arms," with the rest following. Soon "all marched sullenly aboard the boats. Whether there was any more trouble from them the cavalry never heard."[6] Regardless of what they did, though, the infantry had no chance of ever catching up with Price's army.

The inertia of Rosecrans and Smith around St. Louis crippled Federal efforts as far as Kansas. There, war scares had become part of the power struggle among factions of Unionists and the relatively conservative governor —reputedly the richest man in the state—balked at mobilizing the militia, partly because of the lack of urgency shown in Missouri where the enemy campaigned. General George Dietzler of the Kansas State Militia reasonably wondered how Price's army could meander for two weeks to the west of Jefferson City "without molestation. No satisfactory explanation has yet been given of this singular effort to find Price and to 'draw him into a trap.' In my judgment it was one of the most extraordinary circumstances in the history of campaigning, and it created so great a distrust among the militia that several became discouraged and returned to their homes."[7]

The Confederates themselves became very aware of the problem. One told the compiler of a later county history that, when Price took his army into Saline County, "many of his men left him and went for a brief furlough to their homes near by. While the army was at camp on the Salt Fork near Kiser's, nearly every soldier had a holiday. The troops scattered in every direction, and went almost where they pleased. The Carroll county men went home, the Lafayette county men went home, the Saline county men went home, the Ray county men went home. What a grand opportunity was here presented to Pleasonton and Rosecrans to capture or destroy Price's entire army!"[8] Of course, the logic of this did nothing to keep a well-run Confederate army in the field either.

Still, during these days, Price's army had a brief taste of being the liberators they had hoped to become. That part of the state had "a very heavy frost" on October 9, when the Confederate advance reached Boonville, where locals *fêted* his exhausted, hungry men. In this, the most secessionist area through which they had gone, Price issued more brave proclamations, appealing for volunteers and promising to stay and fight. In the end, he conscripted the reluctant and marched them with the rest of his army out of the area, which would be left to a Federal reoccupation. As one observer wrote a neighbor in the Union army, "the *conscripts deserted* in large numbers, and the volunteers were *very sorrowful*."[9]

In the end, the policies of the Army of Missouri accepted its role as a mere raid. The lesser standards of success for a raid recast almost any stolen farm wagon as an achievement. In embracing this reality, of course, the Confederate high command remade their campaign to suit the initial description made by Federal officials, who called it a "raid" based on their utter cluelessness as to what was taking place, and kept it because it minimized their own unpreparedness.

With the Missouri River to their north, Price's men trudged westward, with Federal forces closing on them in slow motion both ahead of and behind them. What followed on October 21–23 would have simply destroyed any army aspirations higher than survival. Repeated clashes with the two Federal armies under Generals Samuel R. Curtis and Pleasonton ended as both poured onto the prairies south of Westport, disintegrating most of the Confederate forces on the field. General Jo Shelby's stubborn rear-guard action challenged the Federals, until their numbers reached the point where they shattered Shelby's line as well. Only the exhaustion of the Unionists and their commanders' questionable management and abysmally poor coordination saved Price's army.

The ordeal continued. On October 25, down the state line along Mine Creek south of Trading Post in Kansas, the Federals overwhelmed two of Price's three divisions. There, they captured division commander General John S. Marmaduke and two of Fagan's four brigade commanders, General William L. Cabell and Colonel W. F. Slemons. Among the hundreds of prisoners were regimental commanders Colonels William L. Jeffers and Lee Crandall, Surgeon C. H. Smith, Major John Waddle, and other officers.[10] Still unsatisfied, some of the Federals pressed the remaining Confederates through the day, striking Price's army again at Charlot's Farm on the Marmiton River and yet again on the Little Osage River.

Three days later, Union general James G. Blunt managed to get a small force from Kansas into the path of the retreating Confederates just south of Newtonia. Shelby's relatively intact division gave the Federals the worst of it, pushing them aside and clearing a line of retreat. However, the timely arrival of Sanborn's men kept it from being even worse. So the campaign closed with "a single blow dealt Price at Newtonia by Generals Blunt and Sanborn."[11] By then, the rest of the Union army had seemed to have lost interest and begun turning back to their various assignments.

The retreat of Price's shrinking army assumed an increasingly bedraggled appearance. After it reached Arkansas, part of it made a feint toward Fayetteville. On November 2, Price got his remaining 3,000 men across the Red River around Webber Falls in the Indian Territory and hurried them south toward the safety of Texas. Meanwhile, the Copperhead press in the North reported that Price himself died at Dooley's Ferry in Arkansas. The *New York Herald* eulogized him as having had "a certain dignity of style," and reported that the death "ends his career with some dignity, and will command more regard from his enemies than many of the more prominent rebel leaders who still linger."[12] Those closer to Missouri than Manhattan, on both sides, tended to see things a bit differently.

Burying the Bodies

Any unclouded vision would have seen the likely results of the 1864 campaign before it began. Simply put, secession could have won no more supporters over the three years since 1861, when there were far too few to prevent a Union occupation. True, Federal military had imposed a bureaucratic and often-arbitrary regime upon the state, but it provided a relative level of stability and some protection from the guerrillas, whose work won the Confederacy no new allies.

Neither did the Army of Missouri. According to civilians at Pilot Knob, Potosi, and Richwoods, Reynolds and Price promised the people protection from outrage, particularly against conscription into the rebel army. Nevertheless, "the citizens have been robbed of everything, and the able-bodied men without exception carried off into the Rebel army. The Rebel underlings, when reminded of Price's promise, say they don't care a damn for Price as they are acting under conscription officers appointed by Jeff. Davis."[13] Even his well-wishers realized that the best Price's army could offer would be the imposition of a different militarized regime.

Missouri Confederates had an undoubted record of great personal heroism and combativeness, but the persistent problem of Unionism challenged the most elementary assumptions of their sectional identity and their own identity as defenders of state sovereignty. Despite the nostalgic romanticism implicit in the later "Lost Cause," the problem moved Price's followers to a very modern solution. It inspired redoubled efforts to silence those whose thoughts and deeds did not conform to their idea of what Missourians should be thinking and doing. Ultimately, though, an army fights battles and provides a poor tool for winning the hearts and minds of a people.

Further spurred on by the desire for individual revenge, they turned to marauding and murder as a means to punish the civilian population for not being what their liberators wanted them to be. While those of African and German descent bore the brunt of their rage, English-speaking southern whites, who had opted to stay in the state without actively aiding the Confederacy, disproportionately seemed little else than traitors to the South. While less scrupulous Confederate officers—from Samuel Hildebrand to Timothy Reeves—encouraged such conduct, those few who did not—John T. Crisp and M. Jeff Thompson—simply failed to curtail it.

As a result, the Army of Missouri established a record no other Confederate force of comparable size and importance approached in the history of the war. What transpired at Potosi in 1864 less resembles our sense of the arrival of Robert E. Lee's army in Maryland than the Contra occupation of a Nicaraguan village. Scenes in Union less recalled those of Gettysburg than they foreshadowed that in the streets of Saigon. No Confederate force in the war so systematically and consistently left such a trail of bitterness in their wake.

For more than a month, the army rampaged through the state, regularly killing both prisoners of war and civilians. In addition to "a deliberate attempt to ravish a married woman whose husband is in the Union army," the press reported that "the mutilation of dead bodies and other barbarous practices would fill a column with horrible and disgusting details." The arrival of Confederates among more sympathetic people west of Jefferson City did not mitigate their brutal treatment of Unionists. There, independent bands of bushwhackers joined the column and made the army's self-image as liberators more plausible by moving in advance of it and intimidating the most likely sources of opposition. At Boonville, they told residents that they "*intended* to *kill* and *burn* [out] the Dutch," and actually "*killed twenty-four Germans*, nearly all in *cold blood*."[14] While the presence of Price's soldiers provided secessionist civilians with an excellent opportunity for vengeance, numbers of them intervened to save their Unionist neighbors.

This brutalization did terrorize Unionists, but those terrorized Unionists responded to the ferocity of the Confederate assault with reprisals of their own. Near Sullivan, Union cavalrymen called Dr. John D. Butler from his home, asked his sympathies and, when he professed his loyalties to the South, they gunned him down on his porch. The women of the house, forbidden to move the body, buried him in the garden until kindlier times permitted his removal to the cemetery. A Federal officer at Warrensburg reportedly "saw a man of Southern proclivities sitting beside the fire with his wife, and, drawing his revolver, he shot him dead through the window." Of course, any mounted gunmen in blue uniforms might have been on either side, an ambiguity introduced by the guerrillas.

Still, the biggest Unionist reprisal took place after Mine Creek. Federal soldiers had standing orders to summarily execute any prisoners caught wearing blue. The measure was aimed at discouraging guerrilla operations, but Price's army had captured and distributed hundreds of Federal uniforms to the ranks. On October 25, an indefinite proportion of the hundreds of Confederate prisoners were unceremoniously shot for being taken while wearing bits and pieces of Union uniforms.[15]

The actual killings at Mine Creek seem to have been the work of Kansas troops, but Missouri Unionists were continuing to find reasons for reprisals. Early in October, as the armies approached each other at Jefferson City, Lieutenant Colonel Amos W. Maupin set out to locate those of his comrades taken prisoner at Pilot Knob. Captain Franz Dinger, paroled west of Union, told Maupin that Major James Wilson and others had likely been killed somewhere in the area. Maupin's scouting parties searched along the route of Price's army for bodies. One of these apparently got to within a hundred feet of the bodies, but they were well hidden.[16]

By the time of Mine Creek, Unionist search parties found their dead comrades near the Jeffries farm west of Union, and some thirteen miles southwest of Washington. A local man "gathering persimmons" along St. John's Creek the previous day had stumbled onto the bodies, two already largely decomposed and another one "nearly all torn to pieces." Wilson's body had documents that identified him and the youngest of the corpses wore the distinctive artillery jacket. Colonel George Harry Stone, the chief of staff of General Edward C. Pike's division of the EMM, confirmed the find, writing the authorities from Washington. Others returned that night with lanterns and apparently buried them.[17]

The next day, when fate delivered so many of Price's men into Federal hands, Maupin exhumed, identified, and temporarily reburied the bodies. St. Louis headquarters quickly ordered retaliatory executions and selected the requisite number of enlisted men and Major Enoch O. Wolf, captured on Mine Creek, to stand in for Wilson. Wolf's fellow Masons and others quickly requested and won a stay of execution and a pardon from President Lincoln.[18] The enlisted men, of course, had no such luck.

Neither did James M. Utz. Caught with other Confederate couriers wearing Union uniforms in western St. Louis County, he had joined his father in the

Gratiot Street Prison. The authorities there tried him and sentenced him to hang. His uncle, a judge, hurried to Washington and met Lincoln. Utz, too, got a pardon, but it reached St. Louis too late to save him from the hangman.[19]

On October 26, Captain William "Bloody Bill" Anderson galloped at the head of his men into Richmond, Missouri. The citizens of the EMM he despised unleashed a volley of fire that dropped him from the saddle. Thereafter, the author of the Centralia horrors would terrorize nobody. Press accounts made a point of emphasizing that the Confederate army had taken Anderson and other guerrillas into their service, swearing them in through "rebel recruiting officers sent out by Sterling Price, as attested by [the general's son,] Edwin W. Price."[20]

Hildebrand's luck still held. After Price's army had moved on, Hildebrand had remained behind south of St. Louis to rebuild a guerrilla force. Major Samuel Montgomery of the Sixth Missouri Cavalry caught up with them at Tyler's Mill in St. Francois County. It reported finding "a camp of 300 Rebels under Hildebrand" and killing thirty-one of them. Hildebrand said that Montgomery's men killed only seven of his recruits (along with four civilians) with "the balance missing."[21] Even their names are lost.

War's First Casualty

Price's campaign ended in an inglorious and desperate rear-guard action in Texas, not against the Federals but against the recriminations that followed among other Confederates. Governor Reynolds continued to fume over the strategic failure of the campaign and the misleadership of Price. Several weeks after the army settled into winter quarters, he published an open letter in the *Texas Republican* criticizing Price and his conduct of the operation. On January 6, 1865, Price wrote to General Edmund Kirby-Smith requesting a court-martial to correct the record, and, in short order, made that request public.[22]

A specific version of the campaign of 1864 framed the idea of Confederate Missouri. Participants themselves spent the rest of the war trying to find someone to blame for the disaster. Postwar admirers pretended that it had not been an abject failure, and that the army had waged the campaign honorably and to a worthwhile purpose. In the end, they preferred increasingly to talk about the early days of the war when secession had not taken corporeal form and seemed somehow plausible. Still, the ghosts of 1864 continued to haunt them.

Yet, if truth be the first casualty of modern war, the 1864 campaign left an even more impressive trail of metaphorical corpses. So, too, those who came declined to correct the pervasive lies and falsifications associated with the expedition. Part of this may reflect the predisposition to treat war as a personalized chess game by gentlemen generals. Indeed, even an otherwise nicely done local study could not resist making the groundless assertion that Price's army achieved its goals and "probably extended the war" up to four months, while simultaneously vindicating the response of Rosecrans and the Federal commanders to the invasion.[23] Perhaps the reluctance to address the Missouri campaign of 1864 reflects a reluctance to accept the overt fictions in the sources or to challenge those fictions.

In reality, explicitly false statements—they could not realistically have been mere mistakes of memory—pepper Confederate accounts of the campaign, starting with Price's own official report. He claimed to have decided against putting artillery on Shepherd Mountain because of his unwillingness to risk injury to civilians in the fort, though not only the other sources but also the disabled cannon itself up on the mountain told a different tale. His obsession with the garrison probably came from the desire for revenge among secessionists from that part of the state, and it stalled his approach to St. Louis for five days, which he implausibly explained as a goal he had already decided not to pursue.

These self-justifying misrepresentations permeated Price's command, even in what was initially intended to be strictly internal reports. As we saw in the reports on their own casualties at Union, Confederate regimental officers minimized their own casualties in reporting to brigade commander John B. Clark, who reduced them still further when reporting to his superiors. This would not have been happening if the higher command did not ultimately want to receive self-censored reports, though it seemed to have left them misinformed as to the strength of their own army.

If one can officially make one's own dead and wounded disappear, it required far less to fictionalize the casualties of the enemy. While civilians can count as soldiers, no body count needs sustain the number, and, without paperwork, an unlimited numbers of prisoners can be claimed as captured and paroled. All this set the stage for Major Edwards to set aside his own wartime report with that account of how Shelby's men "stormed Linn and captured its garrison of three hundred and seventy-two Federals." The fictional battle, claimed Edwards, had frightened the entirely nonexistent Unionists present "almost into idiocy."

Price downplayed the importance of his lowering the bar of his own success. Obviously, the sooner in its history the campaign would be judged on the standards of a raid, the better. So, when he wrote his report, he claimed simply that this took place as soon as he came into contact with Federal soldiers. The vital record of his own movements belie this.

These self-serving fictions became history because they jibed nicely with those of the Union commanders. Where Price had sought to cover bad decisions, Rosecrans needed to obscure the fact he had made so few. For a week, he had denied the presence in the state of the largest Confederate army ever to have been there. He did so in the face of considerable and reliable information to the contrary. For another week, he could not clearly estimate its size, location, or the direction of its movement. Throughout, he displayed none of the political flexibility and strategic foresight needed to take the most minimally necessary defensive measures. Finally, when it turned up on the doorstep of St. Louis, the Union commander responded lethargically and, then, hardly at all. Meanwhile, he had placed into the path of the advancing Confederates small defensive units, misinformed by omission or commission, as to the size and the ruthlessness of the enemy or of any overarching Union defensive strategy.

Meanwhile, the Union commanders spoke periodically of "bagging" Price's entire army. Had they acted in a timely, informed, and concerted fashion, they had several opportunities to do so. In practice, however, Federal generalship sought only to avoid risking a defeat that could embarrass the war effort, the Lincoln administration, the department, and, of course, their own careers. Unwilling to risk a major fight unless they had no options, the Union forces could never have bagged much of anything.

Rosecrans rarely ventured far beyond his comforting self-delusion to confront the actual problem they faced. Those who directly faced the large Confederate force that was not supposed to be there revised their views. Nevertheless, while the casualties from the Pilot Knob–Leasburg clashes became among the highest suffered by any Union force in the war, the high command and the press celebrated it as a virtually bloodless triumph over a much-larger foe.

Indeed, basic documentary evidence, such as service records on casualties, is nearly nonexistent, a problem even worse as we look beyond the volunteer forces. The dead and wounded of the militia, the largest single component of the state's defenders, went largely unnoted and uncounted. Ultimately, its survivors would go unpensioned but by the graces of a state government would eventually be in the hands of Democratic "Redeemers" such as Marmaduke. Nobody even attempted to document the total civilian losses, even those who had taken up arms to defend their communities alongside the militia. An impersonally standardized, bureaucratic fashion rendered invisible the most immediate, striking realities of the campaign.

From Bullets to Ballots

The underlying goal of the Confederate fall operations in Missouri had been to sabotage Republican victory in the November elections. One voter wrote the White House that he thought it "the design of the Rebel Price to keep his forces in the State untill after the election for the purpose of carrying the State for McLellan [*sic*] and the rebel ticket."[24] However, the passage of Price's army through the state had precisely the opposite effect.

The return of the Confederacy forced many otherwise reluctant Missourians to vote with their feet, risking life and limb on the issues of the war. Most residents of the area through which the Army of Missouri passed from September 19 through October 7 not only failed to rally to Price's appeal but responded as well to the Unionist call to arms as the ineptness of the authorities permitted. Not only did some of them fight "like Tigers" at Pilot Knob, Leasburg and, later, Jefferson City, but small clusters of determined and half-organized recruits, militia, and civilians from DeSoto to Union contested Price's line of march. Many more chose the passive resistance of flight out of the path of Price's army, evacuating their homes as they had earlier. No army can liberate a people that refuses to be liberated and so persistently behaves as though it is passing through enemy territory.

The realities and the myths of the campaign made political heroes, sometimes unlikely ones. When Lincoln had promoted Ewing, his own father had asked the president, "What did you appoint that brat a brigadier general for?" After news of Pilot Knob reached Washington, Lincoln goaded the senator: "What do you think of your brat now?" Ewing returned to St. Louis to find himself and his men subjects of an impromptu celebration Thursday night, September 29, at the courthouse. The presences of Jim Lane of Kansas and Elisha Baxter of Arkansas gave the "Grand Union Rally" a national character.[25] Often vilified for his General Order No. 11, which depopulated some Missouri border districts to make Kansas more secure, Ewing briefly became one of Missouri's greatest heroes.

The Confederates marched through areas where bitter divisions plagued the Unionists, assuring victory in the November elections for the Radical candidates for governors of Missouri and Kansas, Fletcher and Samuel J. Crawford. At the St. Louis rally for Ewing, speakers repeatedly referred to Fletcher's race against Conservative Tom Price, one warning of "two prices abroad in the State—a high Price and a low Price—the difference a high Price in arms against the Government, and the low Price" running against "the man who is fighting the battles of the country, shut up in a Fort."

As Price's army marched through Missouri, Lincoln's secretary, John Nicolay, arrived in St. Louis, where he found politics "in a pretty bad tangle" though hopeful that Lincoln could "unite the vote of all the union men on the electoral and State ticket." John F. Hume, the editor of the *Missouri Democrat,* assured Nicolay that Fletcher and the Radicals would support Lincoln but needed to do so in such a way as to not alienate the Germans "who in such event would take measures to set up a ticket of their own." Fletcher personally assured Nicolay of his good will as well. Back in Springfield on October 18, Nicolay filed a final report, assuring the president that the divisions "are fast giving way before the change and pressure of circumstances, and the mere lapse of time." On November 2, as the Confederates slogged south across the Arkansas River, another correspondent assured Nicolay that its campaign had "helped our cause," even to the point where the Germans would support a united ticket behind Lincoln.[26] By then, the 1864 campaign made many southern proclivities into Unionists, Unionists into Republicans, and Republicans into Radicals.

Later, the Radicals particularly breathed a sigh of relief at the news Lincoln would quietly relieve Rosecrans. A delegation of them wrote that "we need hardly tell you that outside of the ranks of the Radicals you have very few supporters in Missouri." They urged the appointment of Ewing to the position and warned against sending another military ally of the Conservatives: "the storm will burst out again. Our loyal people will not silently submit to the military rule of any man, whose administration, directly or indirectly, shields or encourages rebels, rebel sympathizers, or Conservatives."[27]

Black suffrage and citizenship did not lag far behind Radical victory. Price's campaign had surely placed more guns in the hands of black Missourians than any other event in the history of the state. It vindicated the raising of the First Missouri Colored, renamed the Sixty-second United States Colored Troops. On May 12–13, 1865, Moses Lax—the brother of Solomon Lax, one of the defenders of Fort Davidson—served in that regiment in the last land battle of the Civil War at Palmito Ranch near Brownsville, Texas.[28] By the war's end, African-Missourians continued a march taken up the previous fall.

Survivors emerged from the wake of the campaign to rebuild their lives. Shortly after the passing of the armies, the telegrapher Louisa Volker married Lieutenant Thomas Macklind and moved to St. Louis. There she studied stenography, and eventually graduated from Women's Medical College.[29] Like many in the state, they moved into the future, happily leaving the turmoil behind them.

By this time, many other antebellum residents of Missouri were simply no longer there. The war had largely depopulated the southwestern quarter of the state and along the Arkansas line. Almost everything south of the Missouri River suffered to one extent or another. Outside of St. Louis and Kansas City, virtually no records survived intact in their own county courthouses. Responsible officers sometimes removed them to safety, but often did not. Life in the central and western districts north of the Missouri River generally experienced even more periodic outbursts of violence characteristic of guerrilla war. Many communities bounced back slowly, some hardly at all.

The state that emerged in the generation after the Civil War was different from its antebellum predecessor in many respects. John Finis Philips and his wartime comrade Thomas Theodore Crittenden formed a partnership with their wartime enemies, Francis M. Cockerell and George Graham Vest, but no broader reconciliation proved necessary. Understandably, perhaps, Price, Jo Shelby, Marmaduke, and others fled to Mexico briefly, but returned to face no repercussions, and former Confederates occupied the full range of Federal offices available to the state.[30] In the end, not all of the vanquished would taste defeat, and not all of the victors would emerge triumphant.

More generally, though, the very success of the Union—and the absence of the common secessionist threat—left those victors who could do so to define what victory would mean. Opposition to secession, a willingness to resist it by force of arms, and the desire to preserve a United States motivated the Federal forces and their supporters. Beyond that, the coalition represented diverse interests, often with severe internal contradictions. The 1864 campaign coincided with the political conflict over the extent to which they wanted to transform the Union for which they were fighting.

Radical victory in 1864 had mixed results, of course. Certainly, their misguided attempt to marginalize the Catholic hierarchy backfired, predictably and perhaps decisively. Moreover, many Radicals who believed that "free labor" meant more than the elimination of slavery. Republican ballots elected Joseph Weydemeyer county auditor, but the veteran Communist League continued to promote the International Workingmen's Association. African American leader James Milton Turner declared, "I contend the mission of the party will not be complete until the word white is stricken from the constitution of every State in this Union and all men placed on perfect equality before the law of the country." By 1872, former Radical congressman John Russell Kelso opted to support Victoria Woodhull and Frederick Douglass for president. Ewing concluded that the country needed a monetary policy more favorable to farmers and workers. His father's law partner, Brittan Armstrong Hill, and wartime Missouri's attorney general, the Radical Robert Franklin Wingate decided a new Greenback Party would be needed to promote it.[31] The meaning of Union victory for Missouri and the nation would be contested for years.

Of course, other interests captured the attention of some. A rather typical Radical leader, the twenty-one-year-old New Englander "Colonel" Charles Eugene Moss had come into the state as a soldier, but became very involved with emancipation, became editor of the *Springfield Missourian* by the fall 1862, and, by 1864, got his commission in Colonel Joseph Weydemeyer's Forty-first Missouri. Moss subsequently joined Fletcher at DeSoto to establish the *Jefferson County Republican* and finally became a prominent citizen of Springfield. In the wake of the war, he and Fletcher joined Madison Miller, Emil Pretorious, and George Knapp as the "Atlantic and Pacific Railroad Company" to extend the southwestern line from Rolla through Springfield into the far Southwest.[32] Issues of race moved quickly to the rear of that fast-moving car.

The 1877 compromise to the disputed presidential election of the previous year ended Federal Reconstruction efforts in the South and coincided with a nationwide general strike. An attempt to slash wages by the major railroads in the country sparked what became an insurrectionary working-class upheaval. Germans and the native born, blacks and whites—including many Civil War veterans—rose up in desperation against the seemingly unchallengeable power of the railroads backed by the newly empowered government. The strikers effectively took control of the city.[33] At this point, the business community enlisted the aid of the military to impose "order" on St. Louis and, with no Lincoln in the White House, former Union general Smith and former Confederate general Marmaduke led the military retaking of the city from its working-class resident.

Never quite Aesop's fox and the hare, the two emerged as Machiavelli's lion and the fox. The civil war—at least for them—had ended.

The triumph of the Union indefinitely postponed the victory expected by the Hills, Turners, and Kelsos, and produced a remarkable historical memory of the Civil War in one of its bloodiest places. Jesse James had received a pardon but chose the life of an outlaw and became a folk hero. Timothy Reeves returned to find Wilson's murder, if not that of the others, hanging over his head, but would be lionized in a community where the postwar Ku Klux Klan had taken up the fight for the old order and its values and die a well-respected Baptist minister in 1885. A few decades later, the men who had ridden with Anderson, Hildebrand, and William C. Quantrill formed associations of their own, seeking and receiving the same respect as the uniformed veterans—and immeasurably more than the militia and civilians—that died at their hands.[34] For most, though, then and now, this is but a local reflection of the war of pomp and honor alleged to have taken place farther east.

As much as anything, that history reflected the extent to which the new postwar Missouri had escaped its wartime experience that made those activities so important. Neither those eager to forget its brutalization nor newcomers to the state had any desire to dwell on these old issues that had come to mean so little. They had crops to bring in, cities to govern, new towns to construct, railroads to build, money to make. The Civil War they chose to remember was largely that imagined to have been fought in Virginia and elsewhere.

For a long time, it just seemed best that way.

Appendix A

Timetable of the Missouri Campaign

August 29–October 8, 1864

Locations in bold refer to the activities involving the Army of the Missouri directly, while italics indicate actions away from the main body of the Confederate forces.

AUGUST

29 **Princeton, Arkansas.** Confederate General Sterling Price assumed command of the expeditionary forces.

SEPTEMBER

2 **DuVall's Bluff, Arkansas.** Having slipped between the Federal garrisons on the Arkansas River, Shelby's column encounters Federal troops.

8 **Glass Village (Appleton), Arkansas.** Cabell's Confederate Arkansas troops clash with some of the Union Third Arkansas Cavalry: prisoners executed.

19 *Army of Missouri enters the state in three columns under Marmaduke, Fagan, and Shelby.*

Doniphan and south to the Current River. Mounted Union reconnaissance of members of the Forty-seventh Missouri and Third MSM Cavalry encounters the advance of Shelby's column, skirmishing repeatedly: town destroyed.

Dallas County. Detachment of Sixteenth Illinois Cavalry clashes with guerrillas.

20 **Vandiver's Farm near Ponder's Mills, Little Black River.** Confederates pursued Federal reconnaissance from Doniphan and attack it: prisoners executed.

Keytesville, Chariton County (?). Confederate recruits raised in expectation of joining Price's army forced the surrender of the small mobilized portion of the Thirty-fifth EMM defending the town: civilians murdered.

20–25 *LaFayette County.* Detachment of the Seventh MSM Cavalry scouting increased guerrilla activity.

22 **Patterson.** Union garrison abandoned, attacked while retreating toward Fort Davidson.

Fredericktown. Shelby's advance reaches the town, passing north.

Longwood, Pettis County. First MSM Cavalry encounters guerrillas.

Sikeston. Detachment of Second MSM Cavalry encountered Jeffer's regiment of Marmaduke's column of Price's army.

Carthage, Jasper County. Detachment of the Eighth MSM Cavalry encounters large force of guerrillas and Confederate recruits.

Centralia, Boone County. Detachment of the Seventeenth Illinois Cavalry encounters guerrillas or Confederate recruiters.

23 *Gosline Lane near Rocheport, Boone County.* Detachment of the Third MSM Cavalry received a reported eleven casualties in clash with guerrillas.

Arrow Rock Road, Saline County (?). Detachment of the Seventh MSM Cavalry scouting increased guerrilla activity.

Blackwater, Cooper County. Battalion of the First MSM Cavalry encounters guerrillas.

24 **Farmington.** Part of Shelby's Confederates fail to overcome members of the Sixty-eighth EMM and Forty-seventh Missouri defending the town.

24 *Fayette, Howard County.* Detachment of the Ninth MSM Cavalry received a reported eight casualties in clash with guerrillas.

Jackson. Attempt of tiny force of the Fifty-sixth EMM to retake the town thwarted by return of Confederate regulars.

25 **Farmington.** Second attack by Shelby's Confederates successfully overrun mixed force defending the town.

Huntsville, Randolph County. EMM and guerrillas.

26 **Arcadia.** Slemon's cavalry, the advance of Fagan's division drove a detachment of the Second MSM Cavalry from the road to Ironton.

Ironton. The Arkansans engaged in two fights, the first to drive garrison members of the Forty-seventh Missouri from town or into the courthouse, and the second as some members of that unit, the Fiftieth Missouri, Third MSM Cavalry, and the Fourteenth Iowa with Battery H of the Second Missouri Light Artillery; reported casualties one hundred for the day.

Shut-in Gap. Confederates retreat, pursued by those Federals who were mounted, but reinforced at the gap by more of Fagan's division.

27 **Ironton Gap, Shepherd Mountain, Pilot Knob, and the village of Pilot Knob.** Union withdrawals from Ironton and, with much fighting, from the surrounding sites into Fort Davidson. Losses on both sides inaccurately reported.

Fort Davidson. Most of Fagan's and Marmaduke's divisions engaged in full frontal assaults on the fort. Losses on both sides reported inaccurately, Confederates being given variously as 800 to 1,500.

Mineral Point. Small garrisons, below town near Big River and railroad bridges, clash with Shelby's men.

Potosi. Elements of Shelby's division overrun defense of the town by members of the Thirty-second EMM and Fiftieth Missouri. Prisoners and civilians killed.

? *Cheltenham* (out Manchester Road from St. Louis). Attack on a store by men believed to be guerrillas or Confederate scouts.

Centralia, Boone County. "Bloody Bill" Anderson temporarily combined various guerrilla bands into a force of several hundred, which took the town on the North Missouri Railroad, murdering furloughed soldiers, veterans, and civilians. When three mounted companies of the new Thirty-ninth Missouri arrived, the guerrillas slaughtered them entirely, inflicting reported casualties for the day of over 150, mostly killed.

28 **Caledonia.** Members of the Third MSM Cavalry in the advance of the Union force escaping Fort Davidson encounter the advance of Shelby's southbound division.

Palmer (earlier known as Webster or Harmony). Marmaduke's advance, pursuing the Union column from Fort Davidson, encounters stragglers, scouts, and others near the town and north toward the Courtois and Huzzah before they flow into the Meramec.

Centralia, Boone County. The Ninth MSM Cavalry clashes with small guerrilla bands.

Polk County. Militia and guerrillas.

29 **Meramec River north to Leasburg.** Half a dozen clashes mark the pursuit by Marmaduke's division of the Federal column from Fort Davidson, joined in the later fights by the arrival of Shelby's division from Potosi.

Leasburg (or Harrison Station). Federal column from Fort Davidson successfully reaches the southwest branch of the Pacific Railroad, though the Confederates quickly isolate them with the destruction of the track and stations up and down the line.

Bourbon. Shelby's Confederates burn the next station northeast (toward St. Louis) from Leasburg to St. Louis.

Cuba. Shelby's Confederates take the next town on the railroad southwest (toward Rolla) from Leasburg, overcoming resistance from citizens and possibly some militia.

30 **Leasburg (or Harrison Station).** Confederates determine not to attack the remnants of the Union column from Fort Davidson, but leave a force that continues skirmishing with it.

Sullivan. Shelby's division, moving quickly northeast from Leasburg and Bourbon, occupies the town.

St. Clair (formerly Traveler's Repose). Elements of the divisions of Shelby and Marmaduke arrive at the town.

Moselle Bridge on southwest branch of the Pacific Railroad. Wood's Confederates from the St. Clair area advance up the line toward Pacific, skirmishing along the way, most seriously where a mixed garrison force, mostly militia, defended the railroad bridge over the Meramec River at Moselle.

DeSoto. Confederate detachment made several attacks on the town, the last by an estimated 300 overwhelmed the EMM and seized the town.

Mount Vernon, Lawrence County. Detachment of the Fifteenth Missouri Cavalry clashes with guerrillas.

Waynesville, Pulaski County. Detachment of Company B, Fifth MSM Cavalry clashes with guerrillas.

October

1 **Pacific (usually referred to by the antebellum name Franklin).** Two engagements, the first as Cabell's brigade, Fagan's division, arrived from

Richwoods, brushing aside the mixed force of civilians and militia left to defend the town. Later in the day, a Union brigade, with the Forty-ninth and 117th Illinois, with the Fifty-second Indiana arrived by train from Kirkwood just outside of Pacific, and fought their way into town. Casualties reported for this two- to three-hour fight are missing or grossly inaccurate. Civilians murdered.

Gray's Summit. Cabell's brigade destroys the depot and related track near the station.

Union. Elements of Marmaduke's and Shelby's division converge on the seat of Franklin County, a designated assembly point for Price's army within striking distance of St. Louis. A mixed force of civilians and parts of the Fifty-fourth and Fifty-fifth EMM resist entry into the town: prisoners and civilians executed.

South Point. Lawther's regiment, Clark's brigade of Marmaduke's division, strikes north from Union in a night march, reaching the Missouri River.

Leasburg (or Harrison Station). Detachment of the Seventeenth Illinois Cavalry relieves and removes the Union force from Ford Davidson.

Lake Springs east of Rolla. Detachment of the Fifth MSM Cavalry clashes with Confederates remaining in the area.

2 **South Point.** Lawther's regiment fires on two steamboats of civilians fleeing nearby Washington, depot burned at South Point.

Washington. The rest of Clark's brigade joins Lawther and occupies this town on the river, finding it largely evacuated, without leaving the Confederates with any means of crossing north of the Missouri. Railroad property destroyed and civilians executed.

Boeuf Creek area. Williams's regiment of Shelby's division and Cavell's of Fagan's encountered isolated members of the Fifty-fifth EMM, skirmishing, and execution of an officer with other prisoners and there were possibly related murders of civilians in the area.

Catawissa. Union cavalry operating out of Pacific clash with Confederate scavengers.

Union. Federal scouts with Confederates at and near the town.

Charleston, Bloomfield, New Madrid. Federals out of Cape Girardeau regarrison.

Hillsborough, Potosi, Old Mines. Confederate forces reported still present.

3 **New Haven (also Miller's Station and formerly Miller's Landing, sometimes Boeuf Creek).** Clark's brigade advances along the south bank of the Missouri River, trains and stores west of Washington.

Hermann. Although abandoned by the Federal authorities and with its Thirty-fourth EMM withdrawn to Jefferson City, civilians and remaining militia organized a defense of the town where the bluff hems the road into town close to the river.

Union. Federal cavalry scouting continue to exchange shots with the last of the Confederates as the latter's rear guard prepares to and leaves town on the State Road toward Jefferson City.

Jeffriesburg. Confederate execution of Major James Wilson and other Federal prisoners.

4 **Richwoods.** Scouts from the Sixth MSM Cavalry encountered Confederates remaining this far east.

Howerton's Bluff. Confederate columns on the way to Linn encounter with civilians.

5 **Loose Creek.** Occupation by Confederates.

Osage River railroad bridge. Detachment from Shelby's division overrun small outpost of the Thirty-fourth EMM and destroy the bridge.

6 **Prince's Ford and Bolton's Ford, Castle Rock on the Osage River south of Jefferson City.** Shelby's men probing for weakest point in Philips's Federal defenses centered on the Sixth MSM Cavalry at these points and up river toward Castle Rock.

Castle Rock on the Osage River. Gordon's regiment forcing a crossing past the Forty-third EMM, the rest of Shelby's division.

Dixon's Plantation. Confederates press and clash with scouts there, north of the Osage River and short of the Moreau.

7 **Moreau Bottom.** Fagan's division replaces Shelby's in pressing the Federals, then holding defensive positions near the Moreau with a battalion of the Eighth MSM Cavalry holding the point against Cabell's division. The Federals gradually retreat up the Berry Springs or Green Berry Road, where batteries of the Second Missouri Light Artillery engage in an artillery duel with the Confederate guns. Other Union units present for the defense of Jefferson City are elements—mostly very small detachments—of the Second Arkansas Cavalry, the Seventeenth Illinois Cavalry, the Fifteenth Missouri Cavalry, the First, Third, Fifth,

Seventh MSM Cavalry, Batteries B, C, and L of the Second Missouri Light Artillery, Forty-fifth and Forty-ninth Infantry; Thirty-fourth, Forty-third EMM.

Scott's Station. Confederate raid west of Jefferson City, the position in advance of those held by the Seventeenth Illinois Cavalry, but there is no indication that the station was garrisoned.

Tyler's Mills on the Big River. Battalion of the Sixth MSM Cavalry encounters Confederates left behind in eastern Missouri.

Appendix B

Organization of Engaged Units

Department of Missouri.
Major General William S. Rosecrans.

Defense of Arcadia Valley and Leasburg.

Fort Davidson. Maj. James Wilson (3rd Missouri State Militia Cavalry), Brig. Gen. Thomas Ewing.

Pilot Knob Garrison. Maj. James Wilson, Capt. Henry B. Milks.
3rd Missouri State Militia[1] Cavalry. (Cos. A, C, D, H, I, K).
2nd Missouri State Militia Cavalry. (Part of Co. L). Capt. Amos P. Wright.
1st Missouri State Militia Infantry. (Either Co. G of H). Capt. John Fessler.

Reinforcements from St. Louis, Brig. Gen. Thomas Ewing.
47th Missouri Infantry. (Cos. A, E. F, G, H, and I). Col. Thomas C. Fletcher.
50th Missouri Infantry [not yet mustered]. Co. F). Capt. Robert I. Lindsay.
14th Iowa Infantry. (Cos. B, C, D, E, and H). Capt. William J. Campbell.
2nd Missouri Light Artillery.

- **Company H** (section of two guns). Capt. William C.F. Montgomery.
- **Company L**. Lieutenant Philip Smiley with section under Lieutenant Morgan Simonton, Battery H.

Unspecified civilian volunteers, including a reported fifty African-Americans.
Garrison artillery pieces. Fielded by infantry, cavalry, militia and civilians, including blacks.

---

* The original MSM units formed early in 1862 and were largely depleted by recruitment as of February 1863 when the "New Third" MSM Cavalry formed, marking the disbanding of the "Old Third" and the building of the new unit with elements of several of the older organizations. The regiment performed its service not as a regiment, but by battalions, companies and smaller detachments, garrisoning various outposts.

Enrolled Missouri Militia nearby in southeast Missouri, but not at Fort Davidson.

56th Enrolled Missouri Militia. Cape Girardeau area; assisted in protecting the Iron Mountain railroad and garrisoning southeastern Missouri; mobilized for defense of Cape Girardeau and actively engaged in Price's invasion (Fall 1864).

80th Enrolled Missouri Militia. Col. L.J. Rankin. Jefferson county; service on the Iron Mountain Railroad; mobilized in Price's invasion (Fall 1864); engaged in defense of DeSoto and, upon surrender, suffered subsequent massacre of prisoners.

Defense of St. Louis (start of October).

***Recruits**, incomplete enrollment and organizaiton .*

40th Missouri Infantry.
41st Missouri Infantry. Col. Joseph Weydemeyer.
47th Missouri Infantry, partial.
48th Missouri Infantry, partial.
49th Missouri Infantry, partial.
50th Missouri Infantry, partial.

16th Army Corps (detachments of First and Third Divisions). Maj. Gen. A.J. Smith.
7th Kansas Cavalry (part). Maj. Francis Malone.

First Division, Brig. Gen. Joseph A. Mower (actually in northern Arkansas and southeast Missouri).

Third Division, Col. David Moore (staggered arrival in St. Louis).

Second Brigade (only partially present). Col. James Isham Gilbert .
14th Iowa Infantry. (most of those present sent to Fort Davidson)
24th Missouri Infantry.
27th Iowa Infantry.
32nd Iowa Infantry.

Third Brigade (only partially present). Col. Edward H. Wolfe
49th Illinois Infantry.
52nd Indiana Infantry.
117th Illinois Infantry.
178th New York Infantry.
3rd Indiana Light Artillery.
9th Indiana Light Artillery.

Enrolled Missouri Militia (St. Louis area).

First Division, *present in some form.* Gen. Edward C. Pike.

First Brigade. Brig. Gen. Madison Miller.
1st Enrolled Missouri Militia. Col. William P. Fenn .
2nd Enrolled Missouri Militia. Col. Edward Stafford.

85th Enrolled Missouri Militia. Col. W. J. A. Smith.

Second Brigade. Brig. Gen. Christian D. Wolff.

3rd Enrolled Missouri Militia. Col. Fred Vahlkamp.

4th Enrolled Missouri Militia. Col. Louis Duestrow.

10th Enrolled Missouri Militia. Lieutenant Col. H. Cleveland.

Third Brigade. Brig. Gen. George F. Meyers.

7th Enrolled Missouri Militia. Col. George E. Leighton.

11th Enrolled Missouri Militia. Lieutenant Col. Edward Beckman.

13th Enrolled Missouri Militia. Col. John R. Marcy.

Units apparently disbanded by 1864, or every only existed on paper.

5th Enrolled Missouri Militia.
6th Enrolled Missouri Militia.
9th Enrolled Missouri Militia.
16th Enrolled Missouri Militia.
12th Enrolled Missouri Militia.
14th Enrolled Missouri Militia.
15th Enrolled Missouri Militia.
17th Enrolled Missouri Militia.
18th Enrolled Missouri Militia.
19th Enrolled Missouri Militia.
20th Enrolled Missouri Militia.
21st Enrolled Missouri Militia.
22nd Enrolled Missouri Militia.
23rd Enrolled Missouri Militia.
24th Enrolled Missouri Militia.
St. Louis County battalion.
St. Louis Police battalion.
Old Guard.
City Post Band.
Independent Cavalry company.
Corps of Detectives.
1st City Home Guards.
2nd City Home Guards.
3rd City Home Guards.
4th City Home Guards.
5th City Home Guards.
6th City Home Guards.

Illinois Provisional Brigade, *regiments mentioned as reinforcing the city in early October when Price threatened.* Col. Hugo von Wagelin.

In St. Louis at the time.

134th Illinois Infantry (100-day men).

139th Illinois Infantry (100-day men).

142nd Illinois Infantry (100-day men).

Still en route.

140th Illinois Infantry. (100-day men).

Actually in Camp Butler, Illinois.

47th Illinois Infantry.).

132nd Illinois Infantry. (100-day men).

136th Illinois Infantry. (100-day men).

138th Illinois Infantry . (100-day men).

Actually in Randolph County, Illinois.

61st Illinois Veteran Infantry.

Defense of Jefferson City.

Brig. Gen. Egbert B. Brown, Maj. Gen. Clinton B. Fisk.

Brig Gen. Egbert B. Brown (District of Central Missouri).

45th Missouri Infantry. Parts of Companies F and I. Col. T. A. Switzler.

3rd Missouri State Militia Cavalry (detachment). Lieutenant Col. Henry M. Matthews.

1st Missouri State Militia Cavalry (detachment). Col. James McFerran (arrested Oct. 23), Lieutenant Col. Bazel Lazear.

4th Missouri State Militia Cavalry (detachment). Maj. George W. Kelly.

7th Missouri State Militia Cavalry (detachment). Col. John F. Philips, Lieutenant Col. Thomas T. Crittenden.

28th Enrolled Missouri Militia (Osage county). Col. Lebbeus Zevely.

34th Enrolled Missouri Militia (Gasconade county). Col. Rudolph Poser.

43rd Enrolled Missouri Militia (Coles county). Col. A.J. Hart.

Brig Gen. Clinton B. Fisk, (District of Northern Missouri).

1st Iowa Cavalry (detachment), Maj. John McDermott.

17th Illinois Cavalry (small detachment).

39th Missouri. Mentioned, but very small detachment, if present.

43rd Missouri. Mentioned, but very small detachment, if present.

49th Missouri. Mentioned, but very small detachment, if present.

2nd Missouri Light Artillery.

Company C (one section, two howitzers).

Brig Gen. John McNeil (District of Rolla).

17th Illinois Cavalry (detachment). Col. John C. Beveridge.

5th Missouri State Militia Cavalry, Lieutenant Col. Joseph Eppstein.

9th Missouri State Militia Cavalry (detachment).

2nd Missouri Light Artillery.

Company B (section). Lt. John J. Sutter.

Brig. Gen. John B. Sanborn (District of Southwest Missouri).

2nd **Arkansas Cavalry** (detachment). Col. John E. Phelps.

6th Missouri State Militia Cavalry (detachment). Maj. William Plumb.

8th Missouri State Militia Cavalry (detachment). Col. Joseph J. Gravely.

6th Enrolled Missouri Militia Provisional Battalion. After extensive service, reorganized as a Federal volunteer regiment, the **16th Missouri Cavalry** (detachment). Lt. Col. John F. McMahan.

7th Enrolled Missouri Militia Provisional Battalion [mounted], would become the **15th Missouri Cavalry** (detachment). Maj. William B. Mitchell.

Supplemental troops (District of St. Louis), formerly with Ewing and accompanied McNeil and Sanborn to Jefferson City.

3rd Missouri State Militia Cavalry (detachment). Lt. Col. Henry M. Matthews.

2nd Missouri Light Artillery.

- **Company L** (section of four guns). Capt. Charles H. Thurber.

Uncertain.

4th Missouri State Militia Cavalry (detachment), Maj. George W. Kelly.

Other Relevant EMM.

St. Louis district but cut off from the city.

54th & 55th (actually Provisional) Enrolled Missouri Militia (Franklin county). Col. Daniel Q. Gale.

Central District.

7th Provisional Enrolled Missouri Militia. After extensive service, reorganized as a Federal volunteer regiment, the **15th Missouri Cavalry.**

10th Provisional Enrolled Missouri Militia.

40th Enrolled Missouri Militia (Johnson county).

42nd Enrolled Missouri Militia.

35th Enrolled Missouri Militia.

North Missouri.

33rd Enrolled Missouri Militia (St. Joseph area).

51st Provisional Enrolled Missouri Militia (Carroll and Ray counties).

65th Enrolled Missouri Militia (Carroll county).

70th Enrolled Missouri Militia (Howard and Monroe counties).

Rolla.

63rd Enrolled Missouri Militia (Crawford county). Col. Isaac S. Warmouth.

Army of Missouri.
Major General Sterling Price.

Fagan's Division. Maj. Gen. James F. Fagan.
Cabell's Brigade. Brig. Gen. William L. Cabell.
Monroe's Cavalry. Col. James C. Monroe.
Gordon's Cavalry. Col. Anderson Gordon.
Morgan's Cavalry. Col. Thomas J. Morgan.
Hill's Cavalry. Col. John F. Hill.
Gunter's Cavalry Battalion. Lt. Col. Thomas M. Gunter.
Harrell's Cavalry Battalion. Lt. Col. John M. Harrell.
Witherspoon's Cavalry Battalion. Maj. James L. Witherspoon.
Hughey's Battery. Capt. William M. Hughey.

Slemons' Brigade. Col. William F. Slemons, Col. William A. Crawford.
2d Arkansas Cavalry. Col. W. F. Slemons.
Crawford's Cavalry. Col. William A. Crawford.
Carlton's Cavalry. Col. Charles H. Carlton.
Wright's Cavalry. Col. John C. Wright.

Dobbin's Brigade. Col. Archibald S. Dobbin.
Dobbin's Cavalry. Col. Archibald S. Dobbin.
McGhee's Cavalry. Col. James McGhee.
Witt's Cavalry. Col. Allen R. Witt.
Blocher's Battery (one section). Lt. J. V. Zimmerman.

McCray's Brigade. Col. Thomas H. McCray.
45th Arkansas (mounted). Col. Milton D. Baber.
47th Arkansas (mounted). Col. Lee Crandall.
15th Missouri Cavalry. Col. Timothy Reves.

Unattached.
Lyles' (Arkansas) **Cavalry**. Col. Oliver P. Lyles.
Rogan's (Arkansas) **Cavalry**. Col. James W. Rogan.
Anderson's (Arkansas) **Cavalry Battalion**. Capt. William L. Anderson.

Madmaduke's Division. Maj. Gen. John S. Marmaduke, Brig. Gen. John B. Clark, Jr.
Escort. Company D, Fifth Missouri Cavalry, Capt. D. E. Stallard.
Marmaduke's Brigade. Brig. Gen. John B. Clark, Jr., Col. Colton Greene.
3d Missouri Cavalry. Col. Colton Greene.
4th Missouri Cavalry. Col. John Q. Burbridge.
7th Missouri Cavalry. Col. Solomon G. Kitchen.
Davies' Battalion Cavalry. Lt. Col. J. F. Davies.
8th Missouri Cavalry. Col. William L. Jeffers.

10th Missouri Cavalry. Col. Robert R. Lawther.
14th Missouri Cavalry (battalion). Lt. Col. Robert C. Wood.
Hynson's Battery, also described as **Tenth Texas Light Artillery**. Capt. H. C. Hynson.
Harris' Battery. Capt. S. S. Harris.
Engineer company. Capt. James T. Hogane.

Freeman's Brigade. Col. Thomas R. Freeman.
Freeman's Cavalry. Col. Thomas R. Freeman.
Fristoe's Cavalry. Col. Edward T. Fristoe.
Ford's (Arkansas) **Cavalry Battalion**. Lt. Col. Barney Ford.

Shelby's Division. Brig. Gen. Joseph O. Shelby.
Shelby' s Brigade. Col. David Shanks, Col. Moses W. Smith, Brig. Gen. M. Jeff Thompson.
5th Missouri Cavalry. Col. B. Frank Gordon.
11th Missouri Cavalry. Col. Moses W. Smith.
12th Missouri Cavalry. Col. David Shanks.
Elliott's Cavalry. Col. Benj. Elliott.
Slayback's Cavalry Battalion. Lt. Col. Alonzo W. Slayback.
Collins' Battery. Capt. Richard A. Collins.
1st Cavalry Battalion, also described as **1st Indian Brigade** (includes recruits from Indian Territory and Arkansas, as well as Missouri). Maj. Thomas R. Livingston.

Jackman's Brigade. Col. Sidney D. Jackman.
Jackman's Cavalry. Lt. Col. C. H. Nichols.
Hunter's Cavalry. Col. De Witt C. Hunter.
Williams' Cavalry Battalion. Lt. Col. D. A. Williams.
Schnable's Cavalry Battalion. Lt. Col. John A. Schnable.
Collins' Battery (one section). Lt. Jacob D. Connor.

Tyler's Brigade. Col. Charles H. Tyler.
Perkins' Cavalry. Col. Caleb Perkins.
Coffee's Cavalry. Col. John T. Coffee.
Searcy's Cavalry. Col. James J. Searcy.

Unattached.
46th Arkansas (mounted). Col. W. O. Coleman.
Unarmed Missouri "conscripts" assigned to wagon train.

Uncertain.
Clarkson's Cavalry.

Notes

Introduction

1. Estimates of its size around Union run to 15,000 men with "about 5000 camp followers." With a force of 14,000 men joined by 600 guerrillas in Arkansas and 1,500 in southern Missouri, "nearly 2,000 citizens had been pressed into Confederate service." Also 2,000 were ready to join. "The rebel force then cannot be less than 20,000." Some estimates ran as high as 35,000. At the higher levels, accounts indicate a force large enough to be under the command of General Kirby-Smith or include the 5,000 infantry under Magruder said to have entered southern Missouri in the wake of Price. John Benjamin Sanborn, "The Campaign in Missouri in Sept. and October, 1864," 144; "The Missouri Invasion," *Boston Herald*, October 7, 1864, p. 2l; "From Missouri," *New York Tribune*, October 7, 1864, p. 1; "General Price's Movements in Missouri," *Richmond Daily Dispatch*, October 7, 1864, p. 1; "From Missouri," *Richmond Daily Dispatch*, October 10, 1864, p. 1l; for the breakdown, "The Invasion of Missouri," *New York Tribune*, October 11, 1864, p. 1; "The Great Contest. From Missouri," *New York Tribune*, October 12, 1864, p. 1; "Late from the West. The invasion of Missouri. Demonstration on Memphis" (from *Republican*, October 7) *New Orleans Daily Picayune*, October 16, 1864, p. 4; "Price's Invasion of Missouri. Reliable Account of Rosecran's Operations Against the Enemy" (from *Missouri Republican*), *Louisville Daily Journal*, November 2, 1864, p. 1; and *The Civil War in Ripley County, Missouri: A Collection of Historical Stories Published on the Occasion of the Reenactment of Sterling Price's First Engagement in His Invasion of Missouri* (Doniphan: Prospect-News, 1992), 16. Mistakenly, "1,500 fighting men" and 5,000 camp followers were reported in the "Telegraphic News," *Louisville Daily Journal*, October 7, 1864, p. 1.

2. William Forse Scott, "The Last Fight for Missouri," Military Order of the Loyal Legion of the United States, New York, *Recollections of the War of the Rebellion*, Third Series (1907), 292.

3. "From Missouri," Richmond *Daily Dispatch*, October 10, 1864, p. 1, which also repeated the mistaken story in the Union press that General Douglas Cooper was in the invading force. "From Missouri," Richmond *Daily Dispatch*, October 10, 1864, p. 1; "Latest Northern Reports—Glorious Successes of Price's Army," *Charleston Mercury*, October 8, 1864, p. 1.

4. *Catalogue of the Confederate Museum of the Confederate Memorial Literary Society, Corner Twelfth and Clay Streets, Richmond, Virginia* (Richmond, VA: Ware & Duke, Print., 1905). Price and his troops entering the battle of Corinth. Lithograph 24 on the wall of the Missouri Department of the Confederate Memorial Literary Society, 258.

5. John N. Edwards, *Shelby's Expedition to Mexico, an Unwritten Leaf of the War* (Kansas City, MO: Jennie Edwards, Publisher, 1889), 232.

Prologue

1. William Pidgeon's *Traditions of De-Coo-Dah* (New York: Horace Thayer & Co., 1853).

2. For biographical material on Price in this and the following two paragraphs, see Ralph R. Rea, *Sterling Price, the Lee of the West* (Little Rock, AR: Pioneer Press, 1959), 11–12, 13–14, 17–18, 19–22. See also W. L. Webb, *Battles and Biographies of Missourians: or, The Civil War Period of Our State* (Kansas City, MO: Hudson-Kimberly Pub. Co., 1900), 283–93; Robert E. Shalhope, *Sterling Price, Portrait of a Southerner* (Columbia: University of Missouri Press, 1971), and Albert Castel, *General Sterling Price and the Civil War in the West* (Baton Rouge: Louisiana State University Press, 1968). James A. Crutchfield, *Tragedy at Taos: The Revolt of 1847* (Plano: Republic of Texas Press, 1995).

3. Crutchfield, *Tragedy at Taos*, 49–51, 56–57, 65–66, 72–73, 83–85, 90, 110, 105, 106–7, 109–10, 117–18, 118–20, 120–23, 123–24, 126–29, 129–32, (Polk quoted) 136, 137–39, 140, 144; Jacqueline Dorgan Meketa, *From Martyrs to Murderers: The Old Southwest's Saints, Sinners, and Scalawags* (Las Cruces, NM: Yucca Tree Press, 1993), 105, 106, 107–9. Kearney's column was to be followed by the Mormon batallion under Captain Philip St. George Cooke, who would later face his son-in-law, J. E. B. Stuart, across the battlefields of Virginia.

4. Rea, *Sterling Price*, 25–26, 27–29, 31.

5. John N. Edwards, *Shelby and His Men: or, the War in the West* (Cincinnati: Miami Print & Publishing Co., 1867), 15. Edwards also talked of 200,000 voters in the state. For this period in the history of the state, see William E. Parrish, *A History of Missouri, Volume III. 1860 to 1875* (Columbia: University of Missouri Press, 1973).

6. Qtd. Charles K. Mils, *Harvest of Barren Regrets: The Army Career of Frederick William Benteen, 1834–1898* (Glendale, CA: Arthur H. Clark Co., 1985), 13, and see also 11, 12–13.

7. Charles D. Ross, *Civil War Acoustic Shadows* (Shippenburg, PA: White Mane Books, 2001), 94–99.

8. The best overview of this problem is Michael Fellman, *Inside War: The Guerilla Conflict in Missouri during the American Civil War* (Oxford: Oxford University Press, 1990).

9. Certainly this practice explained a certain portion of the many atrocities attributed to Union soldiers and Jayhawkers in the course of the war.

10. Missouri and the western war raise the greatest objection to Mark E. Neely Jr.'s argument in *The Civil War and the Limits of Destruction* (Cambridge, MA: Harvard University Press, 2007). The numbers of engagements are from Frederick H. Dyer, *A*

Compendium of the War of the Rebellion, 3 vols. (New York: T. Yoseloff, 1959), which, like most statistics on the conflict, tend to be less reliable as one looks west.

11. "Jes Lee," p. 227 in the WPA, Missouri Writers Project, in the *Slave Narratives; History of Cole, Moniteau, Morgan, Benton, Miller, Maries and Osage Counties, Missouri from the Earliest Time to the Present, Including a Department Devoted to the Preservation of Sundry Personal, Business, Professional and Private Records; Besides a Valuable Fund of Notes, Original Observations, Etc., Etc.* (Chicago: Goodspeed Publishing Co., 1889), 492, 667.

12. Bryce A. Suderow, *Thunder in Arcadia Valley: Price's Defeat, Sept. 27, 1864* (Cape Girardeau: Center for Regional History and Cultural Heritage, Southeast Missouri State University, 1986), 24. This excellent account of the battle at Pilot Knob also provides good background on the campaign, though Suderow may be in error to accept Kirby-Smith's after-the-fact assessment (largely also a self-assessment) of the campaign as an accurate reflection of his prior judgment (22). For the present, Magruder declined any responsibility for the venture and Kirby-Smith would not twist his arm over the matter without news from Price of his successes in the field.

13. William E. Parrish, "Missouri," in *The Confederate Governors,* ed. W. Buck Yearns (Athens: University of Georgia Press, 1985), 131–32, 133, 136–37, 138.

14. John N. Edwards, *Shelby's Expedition to Mexico, an Unwritten Leaf of the War* (Kansas City: Jennie Edwards, Publisher, 1889), 234. There is no other notice of Shelby's having urged this, but Captain J. Henry Behan urged the measure upon Jefferson Davis, July 23, 1864. *The War of the Rebellion; A Compendium of the Official Records of the Union and Confederate Armies, Published under the direction of the . . . Secretary of War . . .* 70 vol. in 128 (Washington: Government Printing Office, 1880–1901), hereafter cited as *OR,* 41: (pt. 2), 1022–23.

15. Suderow, *Thunder in Arcadia Valley,* 24, 27, 29, 30–31. Jacob C. Thompson, "The Great-Little Battle of Pilot Knob" (M.A. Thesis, Kent State University, 1986) offers some additional material based on sources from Mayor Jack Mayes of Ironton, but puts together an account of the battle very careless as to some major points.

16. Price's army was variously estimated from 8,000 to 35,000, which was repeated by Curtis to George Sykes, October 5, 1864, *OR,* 41: (pt. 3) 650–51. Curtis did not credit the number.

17. Jay Monaghan, *Civil War on the Western Border* (Boston: Little, Brown, 1955), 119, 348; M. Jeff Thompson, *Memoirs,* ed. Donal J. Stanton, Goodwin F. Berquist and Paul C. Bowers (Dayton, OH: Morningside, 1988), 236–38. See also Doris Land Mueller, *M. Jeff Thompson: Missouri's Swamp Fox of the Confederacy* (Columbia: University of Missouri Press, 2007).

18. Thirty-four-year-old Tennessee born Colonel William Fergusen Slemons. Julie Slemons Riegel, *Brigadier General William F. Slemons, C.S.A.* (Independence, MO: for the author, 1992), xx; *Branded as Rebels: a list of bushwhackers, guerrillas, Partisan Rangers, Confederates and Southern sympathizers from Missouri during the war years,* comp. Joanne Chiles Eakin and Donald R. Hale (Lee's Summit, MO: J. C. Eakin & D. R. Hale, 1995), 398.

19. Suderow, *Thunder in Arcadia Valley,* 53.

20. Scott, "The Last Fight for Missouri," 293.

21. Major Dale E. Davis expertly explores the complexities of combining these kinds of forces in "Guerilla Operations in the Civil War: Assessing Compound Warfare during Price's Raid" (M.MAS thesis, U.S. Army Command and General Staff College, Fort Leavenworth, KS, 2004). The experiences of these officers are given in *Branded as Rebels*, alphabetized under their names. For Slayback and Kelly, see *The Bench and Bar of St. Louis, Kansas City, Jefferson City, and Other Missouri Cities. Biographical Sketches* (St. Louis and Chicago: American Biographical Publishing Company, 1884), 387–89, 427–28. For Freeman, *History of Newton, Lawrence, Barry, and McDonald Counties, Missouri* (Chicago: Goodspeed Publishing Co., 1888), 832. For the estimate of recruits, "The Invasion of Missouri," *New York Tribune*, September 29, 1864, p. 1. Ewing described Freeman, with Reeves, as a guerrilla chief. "Gen. Ewing's Account of the Defense of Pilot Knob," *New York Tribune*, October 14, 1864, p. 1.

22. Suderow, *Thunder in Arcadia Valley*, 30 or 31; Abraham H. Ryan, September 7, 8, 1864, in *OR*, 41: (pt. 1) 743, 744.

23. For this and the following paragraph, see William R. Plum, *The Military Telegraph During the Civil War in the United States, an Exposition of ancient and Modern Means of Communications, and of the Federal and Confederate Cipher Systems; Also a Running Account of the War between the States*, 2 vols. (Chicago: Jansen, McClurg & Company, Publishers, 1882), 2: 213, 214–15. Management of the entire telegraph system had just changed hands. Captain Robert Charles Clowry, the new telegraph operator, had an excellent system in place. He inherited this from the New York-born telegrapher, George H. Smith, whose victories, as one historian wrote, "were bloodless." Charles A. Hammann managed the system in Missouri; Plum, *The Military Telegraph*, 215–17, 220.

24. A. W. Reese, Civil War Memoirs, 250, Western Historical Manuscripts Collections, University of Missouri, Columbia.

25. Some 16,170 of the 58,222 Federal soldiers fell while inflicting 20,950 casualties on the 66,326 rebels engaged.

26. James L. McDonough, *Chattanooga—a Death Grip on the Confederacy* (Knoxville: University of Tennessee Press, 1984), 44, 45, 52. Also Michael R. Bradley, *Tullahoma: The 1863 Campaign for the Control of Middle Tennessee* (Shippensburg, PA: Burd Street Press, 2000).

27. Rev. John Rothensteiner, *History of the Archdiocese of St. Louis in its Various Stages of Development from A.S. 1673 to A.D. 1928*, 2 vols (St. Louis: Blackwell Wielandy, 1928), 211, 212, 213.

28. Rothensteiner, *History of the Archdiocese of St. Louis*, 1: 795+, and 2: 44, 100, 240, 417. Kenrick kept Catholic clergy from becoming chaplains in the Federal army, but Father John Bannon left his duties to become a Confederate chaplain. Nevertheless, one former slave recalled that, in terms of honoring marriage among slaves and other considerations, "the Catholic people treated us like as if we was free." "Peter Corn," 85, in the WPA, Missouri Writers Project, in the *Slave Narratives*.

29. "Melinda Murphy," 261, in the WPA, Missouri Writers Project, in the *Slave Narratives*.

30. "Missouri," *New York Tribune*, August 4, 1864, p. 4.

31. Elmo Ingenthron, *Borderland Rebellion: A History of the Civil War on the Missouri-Arkansas Border*, ed. Kathleen Van Buskirk (Branson, MO: Ozarks Mountaineer, 1980), 197.

32. Sanborn, "The Campaign in Missouri in Sept. and October, 1864," 139; *Missouri Troops in Service During the Civil War: Letter from the Secretary of War . . .* (Washington: Government Printing Office, 1902), 53. During the first season of their use in 1862, the EMM mobilized 52,056 men in sixty-nine regiments and three score smaller units, and it eventually grew to eighty-five regiments, sixteen battalions, and thirty-three independent companies, as well as various "citizen guards." For a discussion of the EMM in the *National Tribune,* see William Fergusson of Fifty-First EMM, "Defends the Enrolled Militia. A Comrade Explains Why They Should Not be Spoken of Lightly," November 4, 1897, p. 2; "L.D.Immell, "Missouri in the Civil War," January 15, 1903, p. 2; and, "Missouri Enrolled Militia. Troops Organized to Keep Peace Within the State," July 12, 1906, p. 6. When the attorney general of Missouri excluded militia veterans and their wives and widows from the soldiers' home, its director, Louis Beneke, objected "that the enrolled Missouri militia men performed valuable service and were exposed to all the hardships of war." "The Missouri Soldiers' Home," *National Tribune*, March 16, 1911, p. 4. This often entertaining and informative veteran's publication is now available in a digitized and searchable format through the "Chronicling America" Web site at the Library of Congress. http://chroniclingamerica.loc.gov/.

33. Wiley Britton, *The Civil War on the Border*, 2 vols. (New York: G. P. Putnam's, 1890–91), 2: 458.

34. General Order No. 107, June 28, 1864, in *OR*, 34: (pt. 4) 581–82. He added that "non-action will be considered as a refusal to aid in the work of peace and protection."

35. See Frederick W. Goman, *Up from Arkansas: Marmaduke's First Missouri Raid, Including the Battles of Springfield and Hartville* (n.p.: for the Author, 1999).

36. *Final Report of the Western Sanitary Commission*, 109; "The Invasion of Missouri," *New York Tribune*, September 29, 1864, p. 1; John C. Waugh, *Electing Lincoln: The Battle for the 1864 Presidency,* 2nd ed. (Cambridge, MA: De Capo Press, 2001), 21, 51, 52–53, 57, 119, 195–96; Fike, Diaries, v. 2, September 22, 23, 1864, Western Historical Manuscripts Collections, University of Missouri, Columbia.

37. William L. Avery to John G. Nicolay, November 2, 1864. Abraham Lincoln Papers. Nicolay enumerated, "Fletcher, for instance, the radical candidate for Governor, is entirely in the hands of Frank Blair's chief fugleman, who also is Johnson's prime agent. The Union newspaper, which assails both Knox and Blow favor Johnson. The more respectable portion of the Claybanks, except the office holders, will vote for Knox, who is the Democrat's candidate."

38. "The Invasion of Missouri," *New York Tribune*, September 29, 1864, p. 1; "The Lindell Hotel Riot," St. Louis *Union*, October 1, 1864, p. 1.

39. James S. Rollins to Edward Bates, September 13, 1863. Abraham Lincoln Papers.

40. Five eventually organized in the northern part of the state: the Thirty-ninth Missouri at Hannibal; the Forty-second at Macon; the Forty-third and Forty-fourth at St. Joseph; and the Forty-ninth at Warrenton, Mexico, and Macon. Four came from central Missouri: the Fortieth and Forty-first at St. Louis; the Forty-fifth from Sedalia, Warrensburg, and Otterville; and the Forty-eighth by St. Louis, Jefferson City, and Rolla. Southern Missouri organized two, the Forty-sixth at Springfield and the Forty-seventh at Pilot Knob. One, the Fiftieth, was organized by the state at large.

Chapter 1

1. Martin in Cyrus A. Peterson and Joseph M. Hanson, *Pilot Knob: the Thermopylae of the West* (New York: Neale Publishing Company, 1914), 77–81; *History of Southeast Missouri, Embracing an Historical Account of the Counties of Ste. Genevieve, St. Francois, Perry, Cape Girardeau, Bollinger, Madison, New Madrid, Pemiscot, Dunklin, Scott, Mississippi, Stoddard, Butler, Wayne and Iron . . .* (Chicago: Goodspeed Publishing Co., 1888), 497, 498, 1109.

2. Suderow, *Thunder in Arcadia Valley*, 32–34, 40. Smith initially had only the brigades of Kinney, Gilbert, and Wolfe with three batteries.

3. "An Intercepted Letter—Price Said to be bound for Jefferson City," St. Louis *Union*, September 28, 1864, p. 4; Sanborn to Rosecrans, September 22, 1864, in *OR*, 41: (pt. 3) 309.

4. Suderow, *Thunder in Arcadia Valley*, 30; Rosecrans to Curtis, September 23, F. Steele to Andrews, September 24, 1864, in *OR*, 41: (pt. 3) 333, 339; "Grand Union Rally," St. Louis *Union*, September 30, 1864, p. 1; "Latest News from the Southeast," St. Louis *Union*, October 3, 1864, p. 2; "The Invasion of Missouri," *New York Herald*, September 27, 1864, p. 4; "The Entry of General Price into Missouri," *Richmond Daily Dispatch*, October 3, 1864, p. 1; and, for the skeptical quote, "The Invasion Excitement," *Louisville Daily Journal*, September 30, 1864, p. 1. A. W. Reese wrote of Price's army between 30,000 and 50,000. A. W. Reese, Civil War Memoirs, p. 680, Western Historical Manuscripts Collections, University of Missouri, Columbia. Some of the exaggeration of the numbers may have been the result of typographical carelessness. Price counted 12,000 men and sloppy handwriting would explain how 22,000 got into print instead.

5. "The Invasion of Missouri," *New York Tribune*, September 29, 1864, p. 1; and, "Obituary. Sketch of the Rebel General Price, of Missouri," *New York Herald*, January 8, 1865, p. 1. The officers presented Smith with a sword and belt on September 20. Wolfe had just returned from visiting his home in Indiana. Henry C. Fike, Diaries, 1851–1919, v. 2, September 18, 20, 24, 1864. Western Historical Manuscripts Collections, University of Missouri, Columbia.

6. Mark J. Crawford, "An Eye for an Eye: An episode from Missouri's Civil War," in his *Confederate Courage on Other Fields: Four Lesser Known Accounts of the War Between the States* (Jefferson, NC: McFarland & Company, 2000), 126.

7. *History of Southeast Missouri*, 455, 456.

8. "Guerilla Attack on Caledonia," *Louisville Daily Journal*, September 19, 1864, p. 1; *Final Report of the Western Sanitary Commission, from May 9th, 1864, to December 31st, 1865* (St. Louis: R. P. Studley & Co., 1866), 55. [J. G. Forman,] *The Western Sanitary Commission; a Sketch of Its Origin, history, Labors for the Sick and Wounded of the Western Armies, and Aid Given to Freedmen and Union Refugees, with incidents of Hospital Life* (St. Louis: R. P. Studley & Co., for the Mississippi Valley Sanitary Fair, 1864), 127.

9. United States Adjutant General's Office, *Official Army Register of the Volunteer Force of the United States army for the years 1861, '62, '63, '64, '65*, 8 vols. (Washington: Government Printing Office, 1865–67), 7: 8, 13, 30, 122 on McMurtry, and 14 on Bradley. In addition, Captain Buxton of Company D had earlier officered a company of the Eightieth EMM. Other companies included Captain William J. Buxton's Company B

in Jefferson County; Captain Charles A. Weber's Company C in Perry County; Captain John W. Maupin's Company D guarding bridges on the Iron Mountain Railroad; Captain William P. Adair's Company E in St. Francois County; and Captain Gustavus St. Gem's Company K at Ste. Genevieve.

10. For the pushing of the Federal outposts from Doniphan to the Arcadia Valley, see Suderow, *Thunder in Arcadia Valley*, 36–37, 38–39; Thompson, "The Great-Little Battle of Pilot Knob," 27–28; Ewing to Wilson, September 16, *OR*, s.1, v.41, pt. 1, 214; *History of Southeast Missouri*, 460, 1140; Ira M. Mallory, "Missouri Bush & Prairie. Price's Raid," *National Tribune*, September 6, 1900, p. 8. This represented the third of four articles by Mallory under the general rubric of "Missouri Bush & Prairie," the others being "Preparing for the Field," "Chasing Guerrillas," and "End of the War and Muster-out," August 23 (pp. 1–2), 30 (p. 7), September 13 (pp. 1–2), 1900.

11. *The Civil War in Ripley County, Missouri: A Collection of Historical Stories Published on the Occasion of the Reenactment of Sterling Price's First Engagement in his Invasion of Missouri* (Doniphan: Prospect-News, 1992), 13, 15, including the letter of Sergeant William Neven, October 1903 on 15–16; Crawford, "An Eye for an Eye," 94–97, 114; and Lonnie R. Speer, *War of Vengeance: Acts of Retaliation Against Civil War POWs* (Mechanicsburg, PA: Stackpole Books, 2002), 143–45. See also, *History of Southeast Missouri,* 835, 1072, 378, 379, 454.

12. *The Civil War in Ripley County, Missouri*, 10–11, 13, 26. Mark J. Crawford accords the assertion official standing by referring to "Confederate accounts," but his footnotes ("An Eye for an Eye," n. 95, n. 96, n. 114, p. 163) cited only quite unofficial accounts, to wit: interviews with Mrs. Washington J. Harris, 1881, 1889, in the Dr. John Hume Collection at Missouri Historical Society Library; a 1907 typewritten statement by Dr. Hume; and the unspecified unshared Ponder Family Records of Mr. Jerry Ponder of Mason, Texas, a clan related to Mr. Kittrell. Crawford dismissed the lack of documentation for mass killings as a Federal cover-up. Generally, sources unavailable for discussion among other participants merit more than unquestioning credulity.

13. Shelby, December 1864, Price, December 28, Jackman, November 30, 1864, *OR*, 41: (pt. 1) 652, 671; *The Civil War in Ripley County, Missouri*, 11, 13, 15–16, the former incorrectly giving the date as October 19. His soldiers came from Companies D, I, and Pape's own K of the Third MSM Cavalry, together with some members of Company A of the newly organized Forty-seventh Missouri.

14. *I Acted from Principle: The Civil War Diary of Dr. William M. McPheeters, Confederate Surgeon in the Trans-Mississippi*, ed. Cynthia Dehaven Pitcock and Bill J. Gurley (Fayetteville: University of Arkansas Press, 2002), 220; *The Civil War in Ripley County, Missouri*, 11, 13, 15–16. *Autobiography of Samuel S. Hildebrand, the Renowned Missouri "Bushwhacker" and Unconquerable Rob Roy of America; Being his Complete Confession*, transcribed and compiled by James W. Evans and A. Wendell Keth (Jefferson City, MO: State Times Book and Job Printing House, 1870), 238.

15. Suderow, *Thunder in Arcadia Valley*, 38; Wilson to Ewing, September 20, *OR*, 41: (pt. 1) 454; McPheeters, *I Acted from Principle*, 220; *Autobiography of Samuel S. Hildebrand*, 238; *The Civil War in Ripley County, Missouri*, 11, 16, the former incorrectly gives the date as October 20. For Branstetter's story and his October 3 arrival at Jackson, near Cape Girardeau, see Crawford, "An Eye for an Eye," 128–29.

16. Suderow, *Thunder in Arcadia Valley*, 39; Price, December 28, 1864, *OR*, 41: (pt. 1) 628; *Autobiography of Samuel S. Hildebrand*, 238; and *The Civil War in Ripley County, Missouri*, 16.

17. Wilson, September 20, 1864, *OR*, 41: (pt. 3) 270, 322.

18. "From the Southwest," *Boston Herald*, September 28, 1864, p. 4; "Rebel Invasion of Missouri," *New York Herald*, September 28, 1864, p. 5; F. D. McClanahan, September 20, 1864, *OR*, 41: (pt. 3) 269; *Official Army Register*, 7: 8, with the Second MSM Cavalry, largely consisting of the old Eleventh MSM Cavalry. *OR*, 41: (pt. 1) 453; *History of Southeast Missouri*, 463.

19. Hiller to Ewing, September 22, *OR*, 41: (pt. 1) 628; Ewing to Hiller, September 22, 23, pt. 3, 304, 323, also 303, 305; *History of Southeast Missouri*, 320, 425, 428, 430; and "The Battle of Pilot Knob by One Who Was There," p. 1. Western Historical Manuscripts Collections, University of Missouri, Columbia.

20. *History of Southeast Missouri*, 503, 513, 807–8, but not listed as commissioned in the *Official Army Register*, VII.

21. "Hannah Jones," pp. 214, 217, in the WPA, Missouri Writers Project, in the *Slave Narratives*.

22. For Fredericktown, Suderow, *Thunder in Arcadia Valley*, 40; and Thompson, "The Great-Little Battle of Pilot Knob," 28; *History of Southeast Missouri*, 446; "The Rebel Invasion," St. Louis *Union*, October 3, 1864, p. 1. Apparently in a mistaken reference to Jeffries, the eastern papers reported that Jefferson "a guerilla leader, took possession of Fredericktown." "The Missouri Invasion," *New York Herald*, October 2, 1864, p. 8.

23. "Harriet Casey," pp. 73–74 in the WPA, Missouri Writers Project, in the *Slave Narratives*. *OR*, 41: (pt. 4) 447.

24. "Louis Hill," pp. 184–85, "Jane Parker," p. 24, "Eliza Madison(?)," p. 241, "Wylie Miller," p. 256, in the WPA, Missouri Writers Project, in the *Slave Narratives*.

25. Ewing to Rosecrans, September 25, 26, 1864, *OR*, 41: (pt. 3) 359, 384; *History of Southeast Missouri*, 440–41, 443; Suderow, *Thunder in Arcadia Valley*, 61; "The Capture of Farmington," *St. Louis Daily Missouri Democrat*, September 28, p. 1; Donald M. Palmer, *Four Weeks in the Rebel Army* (New London, CT: D. S. Ruddock, 1865), 3; *Autobiography of Samuel S. Hildebrand*, 238; and "The Missouri Invasion," *New York Herald*, October 2, 1864, p. 8. The Federal commanders name is sometimes given as Hilber.

26. DuBois to Sanborn and Rosecrans to Canby, both October 5, 1864, *OR*, 41: (pt. 3) 646, 633.

27. Evidently, James Kellogg Mills had charge of the brigade including the Fourteenth, Twenty-second, and Thirty-second Iowa and the Twenty-fourth Missouri.

28. *History of Franklin, Jefferson, Washington, Crawford and Gasconade Counties, Missouri* (Chicago: Goodspeed Publishing Co., 1888), 426, 431. Henry C. Fike of the 117th Illinios recalled getting orders around midnight on September 24 "to be ready to move by seven," which kept them "stirring around lively the remainder of the night." They moved to the train around noon. The next morning, some—not Fike's unit—continued on to Pilot Knob. Diaries, v. 2, September 25, 26, 1864, Western Historical Manuscripts Collections, University of Missouri, Columbia.

29. Fletcher, "The Battle of Pilot Knob and the Retreat to Leasburg," 31–33, 32–33; "The Missouri Invasion," *New York Herald*, October 2, 1864, p. 8.

30. *History of Franklin, Jefferson, Washington, Crawford and Gasconade Counties,* 785–86, 245–46.

31. Maupin to Col. James O. Broadhead, December 30, 1863, in *Freedom, a Documentary History of Emancipation, 1861–1867,* ed. Ira Berlin, Freedmen and Southern Society Project (New York: Cambridge University Press, 1982), 236–37.

32. Thompson, "The Great-Little Battle of Pilot Knob," 28.

33. For Ewing's course south, see Suderow, *Thunder in Arcadia Valley,* 36, 41–42, 73; Thompson, "The Great-Little Battle of Pilot Knob," 22; *History of Franklin, Jefferson, Washington, Crawford and Gasconade Counties,* 444.

34. Fletcher, "The Battle of Pilot Knob and the Retreat to Leasburg," 31–33, 32–33; "The Missouri Invasion," *New York Herald,* October 2, 1864, p. 8.

35. Smith to Hanson, Ewing to Hiller, September 24, Smith to Rosecrans, Ewing to Rosecrans, September 25, Smith to DuBois, September 26, 1864, *OR,* 41: (pt. 3) 343–44, 358, 359, 382, 384.

36. Suderow, *Thunder in Arcadia Valley,* 36, 41–42, 73; Smith to Rosecrans, Ewing to Rosecrans, September 25, Smith to DuBois, September 26, 1864, *OR,* 41: (pt. 3) 358, 359, 382.

37. *History of Southeast Missouri,* 454, 455, 456.

38. Ewing to Rosecrans, September 26, 1864, *OR,* 41: (pt. 3) 385.

39. Suderow, *Thunder in Arcadia Valley,* 61; Fletcher, "The Battle of Pilot Knob and the Retreat to Leasburg," 35. "The Battle of Pilot Knob by One Who Was There," p. 3, Western Historical Manuscripts Collections, University of Missouri, Columbia. Lists twenty names "and others whose names we do not remember."

40. "The Battle of Pilot Knob by One Who Was There," p. 1, Western Historical Manuscripts Collections, University of Missouri, Columbia; Gary L. Scheel, *Sixty-Six Miles in Thirty-Nine Hours: the Retreat from Fort Davidson, Pilot Knob to the Battle of Leasburg, September 28 thru October 1, 1864* (n.p.: for the Author, 2002), 21.

41. For the events of the afternoon of September 26, see Suderow, *Thunder in Arcadia Valley,* 61–62, 63–69; Thompson, "The Great-Little Battle of Pilot Knob", 29–30, 31–34, 39; Martin in Peterson and Hanson, *Pilot Knob,* 77–81; *History of Southeast Missouri,* 497, 498, 1109.

42. For the events of the afternoon of September 26, see Suderow, *Thunder in Arcadia Valley,* 61–62, 63–69; Thompson, "The Great-Little Battle of Pilot Knob," 29–30, 31–34; Martin in Peterson and Hanson, *Pilot Knob,* xxx; *History of Southeast Missouri,* 497, 498, 1109.

43. There is no William Shattuck in these units, so this is probably Warren C. Shattuck.

44. For the events of the night of September 26, see Suderow, *Thunder in Arcadia Valley,* 69–77; Thompson, "The Great-Little Battle of Pilot Knob," 33, 36–39, 53–54.

45. Fletcher, "The Battle of Pilot Knob and the Retreat to Leasburg," 35, 36; Carpenter in Bartels, *Iowa Boy Makes Good,* 151, 152, 153. By 1:27 a.m., when Ewing finally got Smith's warning to evacuate Fort Davidson, he had already decided to ignore them.

46. Seymour D. Carpenter from *Genealogical notes of the Carpenter family, including the autobiography and personal reminiscences of Dr. Seymour D. Carpenter,* ed. Edwin Sawyer Walker (Springfield, IL: for the Author, 1907), reprinted as Carolyn M. Bartels,

Iowa Boy Makes Good: Dr. Seymour D. Carpenter, Lieutenant-Colonel in the War for the Union, Medical Director of the Department of Missouri, His Memories (Independence, MO: Two Trails Publishing, 1996), 153; "Late from the West. The invasion of Missouri. Demonstration on Memphis" (from *Republican*, October 7) *New Orleans Daily Picayune*, October 16, 1864, p. 4.

47. Rosecrans to Porter, September 22, Rosecrans to Curtis, September 23, Rosecrans to Pennock, to Halleck, to Governor Hall, September 24, Rosecrans to Gov. Yates, to Smith, September 26, William T. Shaw to Rosecrans, September 27, Rosecrans to Smith, September 29, 1864, *OR*, 41: (pt. 3) 302, 333, 341, 342, 376, 382, 409, 480–81. Even as Price's Army of Missouri crossed into the state at Doniphan, Confederate Cherokees under Stand Watie had seized a Federal supply train at Cabin Creek, just over the Kansas state line in the Indian Territory (later Oklahoma). The ripples of panic certainly reached southwestern Missouri, but they threw Curtis's situation into a real crisis. "The Cabin Creek Disaster" and "From Fort Gibson," Leavenworth *Daily Conservative*, September 27, 29, 1864, both on p. 2.

Chapter 2

1. "The Battle of Pilot Knob by One Who Was There," p. 3, Western Historical Manuscripts Collections, University of Missouri, Columbia.

2. For activities until 2 p.m., see Sunderow, *Thunder in Arcadia Valley*, 79, 81, 82–86, 88–90, 91, 92–94, 97, 158 n. 31, 99, 100–102, 103–5; Thompson, "The Great-Little Battle of Pilot Knob," 44–49, 53–59.

3. Lieutenant Smith Thompson wounded at Pilot Knob on September 27.

4. Many years later, Shelby told I. S. Hurst that Price had ordered him to cut the railroad north of Pilot Knob. Scheel, *Sixty-Six Miles in Thirty-Nine Hours*, 35–36.

5. Carpenter in Bartels, *Iowa Boy Makes Good*, 153; "The Battle of Pilot Knob," St. Louis *Union*, October 4, 1864, p. 1; "Department of Missouri. The Progress of Price's Invasion," *Philadelphia Inquirer*, October 4, 1864, p. 1.

6. "The Battle of Pilot Knob by One Who Was There," p. 3, Western Historical Manuscripts Collections, University of Missouri, Columbia.

7. Fletcher, "The Battle of Pilot Knob and the Retreat to Leasburg," 38–39.

8. "The Battle of Pilot Knob by One Who Was There," p. 3, Western Historical Manuscripts Collections, University of Missouri, Columbia. Civilians began to spin what one historian called "the fantasy" that Confederate sympathizers had been impressed for service in the fort. Fletcher, "The Battle of Pilot Knob and the Retreat to Leasburg," 38.

9. Fletcher, "The Battle of Pilot Knob and the Retreat to Leasburg," 38. Thompson cites this in the text as though real, but wisely questions it in the footnote. "The Great-Little Battle of Pilot Knob," 50–52, notes 80–81.

10. For the assaults on the mid- and late afternoon of September 27, see Sunderow, *Thunder in Arcadia Valley*, 107–8, 108–9, 109, 110–11, 111–15, 123; Thompson, "The Great-Little Battle of Pilot Knob," 54, 62–74. There is no William Shattuck in these units, so this is probably Warren C. Shattuck.

11. "The War in Missouri," *New York Tribune*, September 30, 1864, p. 1; and, "Important from Missouri," *New York Herald*, September 30, 1864, p. 1; "The War in Missouri,"

New York Tribune, October 2, 1864, continuation on p. 8. Charles A. Hills to Dubois from September 26. "The Very Latest from Pilot Knob," St. Louis *Union*, September 30, 1864, p. 1. The telegraph operator is misnamed "Burns" rather than Byrne. For the correct name, see Plum, *The Military Telegraph During the Civil War*, 2: 220; for his service as a thirty-three-year-old in the Eighth EMM, see the State Archives.

12. Carpenter in Bartels, *Iowa Boy Makes Good*, 153.

13. Fletcher, "The Battle of Pilot Knob and the Retreat to Leasburg," 42.

14. Sergeant James C. Steakley and a civilian named Charles Crozat saved the life of one Confederate prisoner.

15. Sunderow, *Thunder in Arcadia Valley*, 115–16.

16. Sunderow, *Thunder in Arcadia Valley*, 116, 125; Fletcher, "The Battle of Pilot Knob and the Retreat to Leasburg," 44.

17. Thompson, "The Great-Little Battle of Pilot Knob," 74, 88; Carpenter in Bartels, *Iowa Boy Makes Good*, 154; Fletcher, "The Battle of Pilot Knob and the Retreat to Leasburg," 43; *The Civil War in Ripley County, Missouri*, 23; "From Missouri," *New York Tribune*, October 4, 1864, p. 1; "Department of Missouri. The Progress of Price's Invasion," *Philadelphia Inquirer*, October 4, 1864, p. 1; "The Invasion of Missouri," *New York Herald*, October 4, 1864, p. 1; "Latest Northern Reports—Glorious Successes of Price's Army," *Charleston Mercury*, October 8, 1864, p. 1; "Gen. Ewing's Account of the Defense of Pilot Knob," *New York Tribune*, October 14, 1864, p. 1; and, "From Missouri," *Baltimore Sun*, October 15, 1864, p. 1. For 1,500 casualties, see "The Invasion of Missouri," *Boston Herald*, September 30, 1864, p. 4. Crawford, "An Eye for an Eye," 118, 119.

18. Crawford, "An Eye for an Eye," 118. In general, see compilations of casualties drawn from various official sources; see Bryce A. Suderow Collections, f. 1, Western Historical Manuscripts Collections, University of Missouri, Columbia.

19. For events of the night of September 27–38, see Sunderow, *Thunder in Arcadia Valley*, 119–20, 121–22, 123–24, 124–25, 126; Thompson, "The Great-Little Battle of Pilot Knob," 76–79.

20. On Slayback, Carpenter in Bartels, *Iowa Boy Makes Good*, 155; Fletcher, "The Battle of Pilot Knob and the Retreat to Leasburg," 44; and "The Battle of Pilot Knob by One Who Was There," p. 3, Western Historical Manuscripts Collections, University of Missouri, Columbia. Among "those unaccountable errors" order for evacuation "bandied about between Gens. Smith and Rosecrans until it was too late." "The War in Missouri," *New York Tribune*, October 2, 1864, continuation on p. 8.

21. Carpenter in Bartels, *Iowa Boy Makes Good*, 154, 155; Fletcher, "The Battle of Pilot Knob and the Retreat to Leasburg," 42–43.

22. Sunderow, *Thunder in Arcadia Valley*, 125, 126, 128. Confederates told the story of a "fascinating lady" who had distracted the young brigadier Dobbins, but Scott regarded it as an excuse for their failure to notice the movement of the Union column. "The Last Fight for Missouri," 311.

23. Sunderow, *Thunder in Arcadia Valley*, 127, 129.

24. "Department of Missouri. The Progress of Price's Invasion," *Philadelphia Inquirer*, October 4, 1864, p. 1.

25. Sunderow, *Thunder in Arcadia Valley*, 128, 129–30; Fletcher, "The Battle of Pilot

Knob and the Retreat to Leasburg," 44–45; Carpenter in Bartels, *Iowa Boy Makes Good*, 155.

26. McPheeters, *I Acted from Principle*, 225; and, Fletcher, "The Battle of Pilot Knob and the Retreat to Leasburg," 46.

27. "The Invasion of Missouri," *New York Herald*, September 29, 1864, p. 5; "The Missouri Invasion," *New York Herald*, October 2, 1864, p. 8; Plum, *The Military Telegraph During the Civil War*, 2: 218.

28. "Summary of Principal Events," *OR*, 41: (pt. 1) 303, and Smith to Rosecrans and Smith to Dubois (two items to each), Col. William T. Shaw to Rosecrans, Ewing to Smith and to Rosecrans (two items), September 27, 1864, (pt. 3) 407–8, 409–10; "The Rebel Invasion," St. Louis *Union*, September 30, 1864, p. 2; Sunderow, *Thunder in Arcadia Valley*, 94–95. Among those heading south were U.S. Army surgeon Dr. Charles H. Hughes. When the Confederates burned the railroad bridge at Big River, he turned around and rejoined Smith. Fletcher, "The Battle of Pilot Knob and the Retreat to Leasburg," Carpenter in Bartels, *Iowa Boy Makes Good*, 152; "The Invasion of Missouri," *Boston Herald*, September 30, 1864, p. 4; "From Missouri," *New York Tribune*, September 27, 1864, p. 1; "The War in Missouri," *New York Tribune*, October 1, 1864, p. 1. Tuesday rebels lost fifty killed at Mineral Point. "The Invasion of Missouri," *Boston Herald*, September 30, 1864, p. 4; for the number of refugees, see *Final Report of the Western Sanitary Commission*, 55. [J. G. Forman,] *The Western Sanitary Commission; a Sketch of Its Origin, history, Labors for the Sick and Wounded of the Western Armies, and Aid Given to Freedmen and Union Refugees, with incidents of Hospital Life* (St. Louis: R. P. Studley & Co., for the Mississippi Valley Sanitary Fair, 1864), 127. Many years later, Shelby told I. S. Hurst that Price had ordered him to cut the railroad north of Pilot Knob. Thought it was sent in support of Ewing and trying to cut him off and returned south at that time. Scheel, *Sixty-Six Miles in Thirty-Nine Hours*, 35–36.

29. *Autobiography of Samuel S. Hildebrand*, 239; "The War in Missouri," *New York Tribune*, September 30, 1864, p. 1; and "The War in Missouri," *New York Tribune*, October 2, 1864, continuation on p. 8.

30. Maggie MacLean, "Louisa Volker," posted at "Civil War Women," http://civilwarwomen.blogspot.com/2006/11/louisa-volker.html (accessed May 31, 2001); Plum, *The Military Telegraph During the Civil War*, 2: 218.

31. "Robert Bryant," pp. 61, 62–63, in the WPA, Missouri Writers Project, in the *Slave Narratives*; "The Missouri Invasion," *New York Herald*, October 2, 1864, p. 8.

32. *History of Franklin, Jefferson, Washington, Crawford and Gasconade Counties*, 462–63, 517, 518, 520–22, 490, 512, 513, 514; Palmer, *Four Weeks in the Rebel Army*, 3–4, 11. There is no service record for Walker in 1864 and no indication of his fate.

33. Palmer, *Four Weeks in the Rebel Army*, 4, 12–13. *History of Franklin, Jefferson, Washington, Crawford and Gasconade Counties*, 515, records the presence in the courthouse of Lieutenant Henry C. Becker, Jones Tennison, David C. Mason, and Peter Weller in addition to those named elsewhere in this account.

34. Palmer, *Four Weeks in the Rebel Army*, 4–5.

35. *History of Franklin, Jefferson, Washington, Crawford and Gasconade Counties*, 513, 514; Palmer, *Four Weeks in the Rebel Army*, 5–6.

36. *History of Franklin, Jefferson, Washington, Crawford and Gasconade Counties*, 514, 515; "The War in Missouri," *New York Tribune*, September 30, 1864, p. 1; Palmer, *Four Weeks in the Rebel Army*, 6–8, 8–10, 12. He had the presence of mind to use a religious tract to hide a ring from his captors. Confederates got Potosi, 30 soldiers and 130 armed citizens. Citizens "fled after the first fire, and the soldiers, save three, were captured and killed by the Rebels." "The county records and a large amount of valuable private property fell a victim to the Rebels." "The War in Missouri," *New York Tribune*, October 2, 1864, continuation on p. 8.

37. A. N. Grissom to Pleasonton, October 2, *OR*, 41: (pt. 3) 561; Palmer, *Four Weeks in the Rebel Army*, 11–12; and, *History of Franklin, Jefferson, Washington, Crawford and Gasconade Counties*, 515, which mistakenly places the event in October but recorded the casualties as Walker, F. M. and Isaac Jameson, and one Grenia, the two Confederate sympathizers killed are named as Thomas Casey and John Roach. For the description, see "From Missouri," *New York Tribune*, October 4, 1864, p. 1; "The Invasion of Missouri," *New York Herald*, October 4, 1864, p. 1. It is a measure of the state of the EMM service records that the material on Walker not only fails to note his death at the hands of the enemy (which is the norm for these records) but even that he performed any service whatsoever during 1864.

38. A. W. Reese, Civil War Memoirs, p. 670, Western Historical Manuscripts Collections, University of Missouri, Columbia. Montgomery, October 5, 8, *OR*, 41: (pt. 1) 455, 456, which refers to "Judge Ransom," surely Ambrose Ransom, who came to Franklin County with the Jeffries family in 1819 and whose house served as the court in the 1820s. *History of Franklin, Jefferson, Washington, Crawford and Gasconade Counties*, 219, 225, 238, 276, 296, 297, and for the postwar murder of one George W. Simms in Washington County, 502.

39. "Frightful Condition of the Western Part of Missouri" [from *St. Louis Democrat*], *New York Herald*, September 29, 1864, p. 5.

40. Brigadier General Clinton B. Fisk, September 27, 1864, Lieutenant Colonel Dennis J. Hynes, September 26, Kerry Owen, September 27, 1864, *OR*, 41: (pt. 1) 415, 416–17, 426–27, 428–29.

41. *History of Boone County, Written and Compiled from the Most Authentic Official and Private Sources, including a History of Its Townships, Towns and Villages . . .* (St. Louis: Western Historical Company, 1882), 437–38, 439–40, 441; Brigadier General Clinton B. Fisk, September 28, 1864. *OR*, 41: (pt. 1) 417–18.

42. Colonel Ed. A. Kuzner (Macon) to Captain G. A. Holloway, September 29, 1864, *OR*, 41: (pt. 1) 443; *History of Boone County*, 441, 452. Among the many, usually repetitive accounts of the Centralia massacre, see the following reminiscences from the *National Tribune*: James M. Russell, "Missouri Guerrillas. Their Horrible Work at Centralia," March 11, 1886, p. 3; E. J. Smith, "Fighting Them Over. What Our Veterans Have to Say About their Old Campaigns. The Centralia Massacre," August 23, 1888, p. 3; Wiley Britton, "Bill Whose Name Anderson. The Guerrillas was a Terror in Missouri," July 31, 1890, p. 1; Edward R. Heaton, "Fighting them Over. Desperate Men. Quantrell and His Band of Guerrillas in the Southwest," July 25, 1895, pp. 1–2; and, Wiley Britton, "The Massacre at Centralia," November 15, 1894, p. 3.

43. For this account of the Centralia massacre over the next four paragraphs, see *History of Boone County*, 441–43, 444–50, 451–54, 456–57.

44. "The Invasion of Missouri," *Boston Herald*, September 30, 1864, p. 4; "Capture of a Train on the North Missouri Railroad" and "Particulars on the Rebel Raid on Centralia," St. Louis *Union*, September 28, 29, 1864, both on p. 1; "The War in Missouri," *New York Tribune*, October 2, 1864, continuation on p. 8; Untitled item, *Louisville Daily Journal*, October 4, 1864, p. 1; and, *History of Boone County*, 458, 461, 462 with casualties listed on 463–64. The *New York Tribune* described the Federal volunteer soldiers defeated there as "militia . . . all raw and badly armed." "The War in Missouri," *New York Tribune*, October 1, 1864, p. 1.

45. "The War in Missouri," *New York Tribune*, October 2, 1864, continuation on p. 8.

46. "The Battle of Pilot Knob by One Who Was There," p. 6, Western Historical Manuscripts Collections, University of Missouri, Columbia. Lists twenty names "and others whose names we do not remember."

47. Thompson, *Memoirs*, 238–39, 241–42, 244–45, 265.

Chapter 3

1. "Alarm at Franklin," *St. Louis Daily Missouri Democrat*, October 3, p. 2; Smith to Rosecrans, September 28, 1864, *OR*, 41: (pt. 3) 445. An entry from 11:20 a.m. impossibly records that Ewing had fallen back from Fort Davidson to the southwest branch of the Pacific Railroad, something which was only known with certainty in St. Louis hours later. It seems likely that Dick went back and altered the original entry. Franklin Archibald Dick, *Troubled State: Civil War Journals of Franklin Archibald Dick*, ed. Gari Carter (Kirksville, MO: Truman State University Press, 2008), 142.

2. Shields and Ewing in Peterson and Hanson, *Pilot Knob*, 227, 249; Thompson, The Great-Little Battle of Pilot Knob, 88–89; *History of Franklin, Jefferson, Washington, Crawford and Gasconade Counties*, 522–23, 524.

3. Campbell in Peterson and Hanson, *Pilot Knob*, 254; *History of Franklin, Jefferson, Washington, Crawford and Gasconade Counties*, 522–23. Fletcher remembered this as being around 9 a.m., and he also recalled the decision to head for Leasburg as one cast in Caledonia. "The Battle of Pilot Knob and the Retreat to Leasburg," 46; Scheel, *Sixty-Six Miles in Thirty-Nine Hours*, 6; Thompson, The Great-Little Battle of Pilot Knob, 85–86, which not only does not jibe with the sources but would also not jibe with the actual time that the mounted Confederate caught up with Ewing's column.

4. Campbell and Wilkinson in Peterson and Hanson, *Pilot Knob*, 254, 257 and n.

5. Palmer, *Four Weeks in the Rebel Army*, 15–17; Scheel, *Sixty-Six Miles in Thirty-Nine Hours*, 6, 7–8; Ross, *Civil War Acoustic Shadows*, xxx. The predawn hours on Thursday brought the prisoners back to Potosi, but took them on twelve miles further north to Criswell, a place little more than a name, which, recalled Donald Palmer, "consisted of a house and store." *History of Franklin, Jefferson, Washington, Crawford and Gasconade Counties*, 738, indicates that the Criswell family had a boardinghouse and owned land extensively in the area, but makes no reference to a town or village by that name. "Latest from the Southeast," St. Louis *Union*, September 28, 1864, p. 1.

6. McPheeters, *I Acted from Principle*, 225; Carpenter in Bartels, *Iowa Boy Makes Good*, 157, 160; and "Late from the West. The Invasion of Missouri. Demonstration on Memphis" (from *Republican*, October 7), *New Orleans Daily Picayune*, October 16, 1864, p. 4; "Department of Missouri. The Progress of Price's Invasion," *Philadelphia Inquirer*, October 4, 1864, p. 1.

7. Lucas in Peterson and Hanson, *Pilot Knob*, 278; Suderow, *Thunder in Arcadia Valley*, 130.

8. Sutton, Schrumm, Steakley, Rowe, and Luc in Peterson and Hanson, *Pilot Knob*, 254–55, 258, 264, 277–78; *History of Franklin, Jefferson, Washington, Crawford and Gasconade Counties*, 525. Lieutenant William D. Counts got a small loaf of bread from a neighboring family and divided it with Sergeant James W. Nations. Scheel, *Sixty-Six Miles in Thirty-Nine Hours*, 9.

9. Ewing and Rowe in Peterson and Hanson, *Pilot Knob*, 250, 277; *History of Franklin, Jefferson, Washington, Crawford and Gasconade Counties*, 538, 578; and Fletcher, "The Battle of Pilot Knob and the Retreat to Leasburg," 47.

10. Scheel, *Sixty-Six Miles in Thirty-Nine Hours*, 9–10.

11. Rowe, Ewing, Sutton, Schrumm, Milks, Steakley, and Lucas in Peterson and Hanson, *Pilot Knob*, 202, 250, 255, 258–59, 261, 264, 265–66, 266–67, 277–78; Scheel, *Sixty-Six Miles in Thirty-Nine Hours*, 12.

12. Plum, *The Military Telegraph During the Civil War*, 2: 218–19; "The Missouri Invasion," *New York Herald*, October 2, 1864, p. 8 (Fort Davidson newsletter, 2000). The former placed Confederate passage through the town as September 28. If so, Shelby's men were in pursuit of Ewing.

13. McPheeters, *I Acted from Principle*, 225; Fletcher, "The Battle of Pilot Knob and the Retreat to Leasburg," 46–47.

14. Scheel, *Sixty-Six Miles in Thirty-Nine Hours*, 10–11. On Harris of Company H, *History of Franklin, Jefferson, Washington, Crawford and Gasconade Counties*, 513. The Captain Cook of the Fiftieth mentioned by Palmer was sick at the time of the formal mustering and did not receive his commission, 512. Dr. Adams described Joshua as a second lieutenant, but the Military Records, State Archives, indicate that he had been commissioned a first lieutenant early in September. For a very muddled account, having Gilliam and David Mason killed on September 27, see http://boards.ancestry.com.au/localities.northam.usa.states.missouri.counties.washington/818/mb.ashx(accessed May 31, 2011), which also ascribed the killing to Reeves and the location at Pacific. Gilliam's wife had lost two nephews and several sons in Tennessee before having another killed at Potosi, and, when the Confederates marched past their farm on Courtois Creek, they killed Solomon's thirteen-year-old son.

15. Milks in Peterson and Hanson, *Pilot Knob*; Scheel, *Sixty-Six Miles in Thirty-Nine Hours*, 13.

16. Ewing, Sutton, Milks, Steakley, and Lucas in Peterson and Hanson, *Pilot Knob*, 250, 258–59, 261–62, 263, 263 and n, 265, 267, 268, 269–71, 279. Reports that the retreating column remained "unmolested until about 20 miles from Harrison's station, when the rebels attacked him in force, but were driven back by artillery with loss." "The Missouri Invasion," *Boston Herald*, October 7, 1864, p. 2.

17. Scheel, *Sixty-Six Miles in Thirty-Nine Hours*, 15, 16, 18, 19–20. Scheel reported that the owners of the Huzzah Valley Resort on Highway 8 claim that their land was the site of this particular rear guard action. When I drove through the area years ago, the site struck me as the likely location of a nineteenth-century ford. Corporal Peter Shrum may have described this action in terms of the bottom of the Meramec, though it may have been a second action.

18. Scheel, *Sixty-Six Miles in Thirty-Nine Hours*, 16–17, 18, 12.

19. Ewing, Milks, and Steakley in Peterson and Hanson, *Pilot Knob*, 251, 264, 274; Colonel Robert R. Lawther, December 6, 1864, *OR*, 41: (pt. 1) 698. "The Battle of Pilot Knob by One Who Was There," p. 4, Western Historical Manuscripts Collections, University of Missouri, Columbia. Lists twenty names "and others whose names we do not remember."

20. Sutton and Milks in Peterson and Hanson, *Pilot Knob*, 256, 263; Scheel, *Sixty-Six Miles in Thirty-Nine Hours*, 15, 21–22, 23, 36.

21. Scheel, *Sixty-Six Miles in Thirty-Nine Hours*, 14, 15, 22, 23; and Ewing, Sutton, Shrumm, Milks, and Lucas in Peterson and Hanson, *Pilot Knob*, 250, 256, 259–60, 264, 271–72, 280; Fletcher, "The Battle of Pilot Knob and the Retreat to Leasburg," 47.

22. Ewing, Milks, and Lucas in Peterson and Hanson, *Pilot Knob*, 250–51, 263n, 286; and, Fletcher, "The Battle of Pilot Knob and the Retreat to Leasburg," 47, 48. "Two other attacks were made, both of which were repulsed." "The Missouri Invasion," *Boston Herald*, October 7, 1864, p. 2. "The Battle of Pilot Knob by One Who Was There," p. 4, Western Historical Manuscripts Collections, University of Missouri, Columbia.

23. Sutton, Shrumm, and Lucas in Peterson and Hanson, *Pilot Knob*, 257, 260–61, 273–74, 274–75; "The War in Missouri," *New York Tribune*, October 2, 1864, p. 1.

24. Scheel, *Sixty-Six Miles in Thirty-Nine Hours*, 17, 23, 24, 25, which extrapolates from this that Shelby believed that they could capture the force. Shelby's arrival is unclear. He recalled having 3,700 on the pursuit, indicating a net gain of at least 350 since leaving Arkansas, but did not have all of them up at the same time.

25. Lucas and Rowe in Peterson and Hanson, *Pilot Knob*, 283, 289, 290; Shattuck in Peterson and Hanson, *Pilot Knob*, 281; *History of Franklin, Jefferson, Washington, Crawford and Gasconade Counties*, 598; Scheel, *Sixty-Six Miles in Thirty-Nine Hours*, 24.

26. Lucas in Peterson and Hanson, *Pilot Knob*, 280, 281, 286; Fletcher, "The Battle of Pilot Knob and the Retreat to Leasburg," 48; Scheel, *Sixty-Six Miles in Thirty-Nine Hours*, 17–18; and "From Missouri," *New York Tribune*, October 7, 1864, p. 1.

27. Shattuck in Peterson and Hanson, *Pilot Knob*, 281. On October 3, about sixty of these mounted men from Fletcher's command did reach Hermann. "The War in Missouri," *New York Tribune*, October 6, 1864, p. 1; "The Missouri Invasion," *Baltimore Sun*, October 6, 1864, p. 1. Ironically, some of the Confederates attacking them near Leasburg must have come close to doing so at Hermann, as they could not have missed each other there by more than a few hours.

28. Scheel, *Sixty-Six Miles in Thirty-Nine Hours*, 24, 25–26, 26–27, 28. Attack disrupted a long overdue meal for James Brown and others who had nabbed an unfortunate yearling who had wandered too near the big kitchen fire, and rebels fired on it.

29. "Alarm at Franklin," *St. Louis Daily Missouri Democrat*, October 3, p. 2; Lucas and Shrumm in Peterson and Hanson, *Pilot Knob*, 283, 297; and, Scheel, *Sixty-Six Miles*

in Thirty-Nine Hours, 24, 26, 28; and William T. Hunter to Rosecrans, September 30, 1864, *OR*, 41: (pt. 3) 513. His name is also given as Currie.

30. *History of Franklin, Jefferson, Washington, Crawford and Gasconade Counties*, 592, 593, 579, also 537, 575, 599, 601, 609; McNeill to DuBois, October 2, 1864, *OR*, 41: (pt. 3) 562. Lucas in Peterson and Hanson, *Pilot Knob*, 283. The rebels also are said to have reached St. James. Brown heard and reported the development late on Friday.

31. Lucas, Rowe, and Shrumm in Peterson and Hanson, *Pilot Knob*, 283, 289–90, 291–92, 293, 297, 298, 290. "A few soldiers and one or two officers took 'French Leave' during the night and worked their way through to St. Louis." "The Battle of Pilot Knob by One Who Was There," p. 6, Western Historical Manuscripts Collections, University of Missouri, Columbia. A few days later, Ewing's servant arrived in St. Louis and reported him back at Harrison Station "fighting like the devil." "The Rebel Invasion," St. Louis *Union*, October 3, 1864, p. 1.

32. Lucas, Rowe, Martin, and Shrumm in Peterson and Hanson, *Pilot Knob*, 283, 284, 289, 290–91, 294–95, 299; Scheel, *Sixty-Six Miles in Thirty-Nine Hours*, 24, 27–28.

33. Lucas, Rowe, and Shrumm in Peterson and Hanson, *Pilot Knob*, 284, 292, 297.

34. *History of Franklin, Jefferson, Washington, Crawford and Gasconade Counties*, 598; Hal D. Sears, *The Sex Radicals: Free Love in High Victorian America* (Lawrence: Regents Press of Kansas, 1977), 28–33; John Steele McCormick, "Moses Harmon, Forerunner of Women's Liberation," (September–October 1972). See also the Moses Harmon Papers, f. 2–13, Western Historical Manuscripts Collection, University of Missouri, Columbia.

35. Wynn and Wilkinson in Peterson and Hanson, *Pilot Knob*, 290, 302, 302n–3n, 307; Fletcher, "The Battle of Pilot Knob and the Retreat to Leasburg," 49; Scheel, *Sixty-Six Miles in Thirty-Nine Hours*, 28, 30; and "The Battle of Pilot Knob by One Who Was There," p. 6, Western Historical Manuscripts Collections, University of Missouri, Columbia.

36. Lucas, Shrumm, and Wilkinson in Peterson and Hanson, *Pilot Knob*, 283, 298–99, 303–4, 304–5; Scheel, *Sixty-Six Miles in Thirty-Nine Hours*, 26–27, 30, 32–33.

37. Wilkinson in Peterson and Hanson, *Pilot Knob*, 305–6, 306–7; Fletcher, "The Battle of Pilot Knob and the Retreat to Leasburg," 49.

38. Wilkinson in Peterson and Hanson, *Pilot Knob*, 306–7; Wynn in Peterson and Hanson, *Pilot Knob*, 296.

39. Rosecrans to Smith, 6,000 at Rolla, September 27, 1864, *OR*, 41: (pt. 1) 408–9, and Halleck to Rosecrans, September 28, Rosecrans to Curtis, September 29, Rosecrans to Smith, September 30, 1864, (pt. 3) 440, 492, and 510. For the expectation that Rolla would be Price's destination, see also: "The Rebel Invasion of Missouri," *Boston Herald*, September 29, 1864, p. 2; "The Invasion of Missouri," *New York Herald*, September 29, 1864, p. 5.

40. Reporting Rosecrans predictions of Rolla, see "The War in Missouri," *New York Tribune*, October 6, 1864, p. 1; "The Missouri Invasion," *Baltimore Sun*, October 6, 1864, p. 1; and "From Missouri," *New York Tribune*, October 7, 1864, p. 1; McNeil to Captain J. F. Bennett, November 26, 1864, *OR*, 41: (pt. 1) 375, and Brown to Hickox, September 25, McNeil to Rosecrans, to Colonel O. D. Greene, C. G. Laurant Special Order No. 148, September 26, 1864, McNeil to Colonel J. V. Du Bois, September 29, McNeil to Rosecrans, October 2, 2 p.m., 1864, (pt. 3) 365, 386, 387, 389, 484, 563.

41. McNeil to Captain J. F. Bennett, November 26, Brigadier General John B. Sanborn, November 13, 1864, *OR*, 41: (pt. 1) 375, 394, and Eppstein to McNeil, October 2, Lieutenant Thomas B. Wright to Eppstein, September 30, 1864, (pt. 3) 563, 850; Sanborn, "The Campaign in Missouri in Sept. and October, 1864," 150–52; "Uncle Fils Hancock," p. 152, in the WPA, Missouri Writers Project, in the *Slave Narratives*.

42. Lewis M. Gross et al, *Past and Present of DeKalb County, Illinois*, 2 vols. (Chicago: Pioneer Pub. Co., 1907), 1: 380, 383.

43. Shrumm in Peterson and Hanson, *Pilot Knob*, 299. Wynn remembered the cavalry coming in from the south (296), but Lucas (287) said they came from the north. Lucas in Peterson and Hanson, *Pilot Knob*, 287.

44. Lucas in Peterson and Hanson, *Pilot Knob*, 288; Scheel, *Sixty-Six Miles in Thirty-Nine Hours*, 31–32.

45. McNeill to DuBois, October 2, *OR*, pt. 3, 562; Mallory, "Missouri Bush & Prairie, Price's Raid," *National Tribune*, September 6, 1900, p. 8; Lucas in Peterson and Hanson, *Pilot Knob*, 288. Lucas described the enemy as having gone off to "somewhere near Jefferson City" while Rowe described the destination as "at or near Pacific" 287, 293. Scheel, *Sixty-Six Miles in Thirty-Nine Hours*, 32, 35, 36.

46. Sanborn, "The Campaign in Missouri in Sept. and October, 1864," 150–51; Lucas, Shrumm, and Wilkinson in Peterson and Hanson, *Pilot Knob*, 288, 299–300, 309–10; Sanborn to DuBois, November 13, *OR*, 41: (pt. 1) 394; Colonel John E. Phelps, November 2, 1864, *OR*, 41: (pt. 1) 401; Scheel, *Sixty-Six Miles in Thirty-Nine Hours*, 32. The armed black civilians who had charge of the prisoner captured at Caledonia brought him safely through to the Federal army, as well. He was last seen chopping wood at Rolla. Scheel, *Sixty-Six Miles in Thirty-Nine Hours*, 21.

47. Scheel, *Sixty-Six Miles in Thirty-Nine Hours.*

48. McNeil to Captain J. F. Bennett, November 26, *OR*, 41: (pt. 1) 375; "From Missouri," *New York Tribune*, October 7, 1864, p. 1; "The Missouri Invasion," *Boston Herald*, October 7, 1864, p. 2; "Telegraphic News," *Louisville Daily Journal*, October 7, 1864, p. 1.

49. "The Battle of Pilot Knob by One Who Was There," p. 5, Western Historical Manuscripts Collections, University of Missouri, Columbia; Scheel, *Sixty-Six Miles in Thirty-Nine Hours*, 35, 36.

50. Lieutenant Colonel Joseph A. Eppstein, November 18, 1864, *OR*, 41: (pt. 1) 382; Eppstein to McNeil, October 3, 1864, *OR*, 41: (pt. 3) 588.

51. *History of Franklin, Jefferson, Washington, Crawford and Gasconade Counties*, 335, 336, 1031; H. G. Keil, "Washington, Missouri, and Price's Missouri Expedition," *Washington Citizen*, October 10, 1913, qtd. Ralph Gregory, *Price's Raid In Franklin County, Missouri* (Washington: Missourian Pub. Co., 1990), 2; Scheel, *Sixty-Six Miles in Thirty-Nine Hours*, 31. Lieutenant Colonel J. F. Davies, December 12, 1864, *OR*, 41: (pt. 1) 695; Colonel Colton Greene, December 18, 1864, *OR*, 41: (pt. 1) 688.

52. *History of Franklin, Jefferson, Washington, Crawford and Gasconade Counties*, 25, 333, 334; Gregory, *Price's Raid In Franklin County, Missouri*, 5; Palmer, *Four Weeks in the Rebel Army*, 19–20; "The Rebel Invasion," St. Louis *Union*, October 3, 1864, p. 1.

53. Qtd. *History of Saline County, Missouri, Carefully Written and Compiled from the Most Authentic official and Private Sources* (St. Louis: Missouri Historical Company,

1881), 309; *Encyclopedia of the History of Missouri: A Compendium of History and Biography for Ready Reference*, ed. Howard L. Conard, 6 vols. (New York, Louisville, St. Louis: Southern History Company, 1901), 6: 329. Part of general entry on the subject, 324–71. D. M. Grissom, "War Between the States," 324–30, supplemented by James O. Broadhead, "Federal History," 330–50, and Samuel M. Kennard and John G. Kelly, "Confederate side," 350–71.

Chapter 4

1. In general, for the development of the city, see James Neal Primm, *Lion of the Valley: St. Louis Missouri* (Boulder, CO: Pruett Publishing Company, 1981). F. Terry Norris, "Where did the Villages Go?: Steamboats, Deforestation, and Archaeological Loss in the Mississippi Valley," *Common Fields: An Environmental History of St. Louis*, ed. Andrew Hurley (St. Louis: Missouri Historical Society Press, 1997), 73–89.

2. For the contemporary look at the city, reflected in these paragraphs, see J. Thomas Scharf, *History of Saint Louis City and County, from the earliest Periods to the Present Day: Including Biographical Sketches of Representative Men* (Philadelphia: L. H. Everts, 1883), 1863–64, 1880, 1881, 1885, 1887, 1895, 1897, 1898, 1902, 1903, 1904, 1906, 1907–8, 1910, 1912, 1924, and Glencoe and Allenton, 1597–98, 1921, 1923, 1924.

3. *History of Franklin, Jefferson, Washington, Crawford and Gasconade Counties*, 317, 323, 324, 325, 326–27.

4. Norma L. Peterson, *Freedom and Franchise: the Political Career of B. Gratz Brown* (Columbia: University of Missouri Press, 1965), 132.

5. Fred A. Shannon, *The Organization and Administration of the Union Army, 1861–1865,* 2 vols. (Cleveland: A. H. Clark Co., 1928), 1: 62–63, 64–65.

6. Thomas, *History of Saint Louis County, Missouri*, 2: 63, 98; [J. G. Forman,] *The Western Sanitary Commission; a Sketch of Its Origin, History, Labors for the Sick and Wounded of the Western Armies, and Aid Given to Freedmen and Union Refugees, with incidents of Hospital Life* (St. Louis: R. P. Studley & Co., for the Mississippi Valley Sanitary Fair, 1864), 126; "The War in Missouri," *New York Tribune*, October 1, 1864, p. 1.

7. William L. Thomas, *History of Saint Louis County, Missouri,* 2 vols. (St. Louis: S. J. Clarke Publishing Co., 1911), 1: 407.

8. *Tenth U.S. Census*, 20: 499, cited "Strikes and Lockouts Occurring in the United States Prior to 1881," *Third Annual Report of the Commissioner of Labor, 1887: Strikes and Lockouts* (Washington: Government Printing Office, 1888), 1048–49. See also Russell M. Nolen, "The Labor Movement in St. Louis Prior to the Civil War" and "The Labor Movement in St. Louis from 1860 to 1890," *Missouri Historical Review* 34 (October 1939): 18–37, and (January 1940): 157–81.

9. For this and the following paragraphs on the strike movement, see Louis S. Gerteis, *Civil War St. Louis* (Lawrence: University Press of Kansas, 2001), 254–57, 366–67; "Address Delivered by William H. Sylvis," *Fincher's Trade Review*, January 14, 1865, p. 25; James C. Sylvis, *The Life, Speeches and Essays of William H. Sylvis* (Philadelphia: Claxton, Remsen & Haffelfinger, 1872), 135. See also Col. Albert G. Beachett, "St. Louis in 1861–5. Life in a Border City During the War," *National Tribune,* April 12, 1888,

p. 1; and *Proceedings of the Sixth Annual Session of the Iron Molders' International Union, in Convention Assembled, at Chicago, Ill, January 4, 1865* (Philadelphia: Printed at the Office of Fincher's Trades' Review, 1865), 7–8.

10. General Order No. 65, April 29, 1864, in *OR*, 34: (pt. 3) 345–46. Walter R. Houf and Russell Nollen on Missouri labor conditions; "President Lincoln and Labor," *Journal of the International Association of Machinists. Published in the Interest of the Machinists' Trade* 5 (July 1893): 244. Michael H. Madden of Pekin, enlisted September 17, 1864, as private, Company K, 146th Illinois, mustered out July 8, 1865. Probably Thomas Gault of the Eighth Missouri, Company A.

11. Gerteis, *Civil War St. Louis*, 257–58, n. 45, 367; "Strikes in St. Louis," *New York Daily Times*, May 8, 1864, p. 6; "Official Tyranny," *Fincher's Trade Review*, May 14, 1864, p. 95; "Address Delivered by William H. Sylvis," *Fincher's Trade Review*, January 14, 1865, p. 25. Bernays to Lincoln, May 2, 1864, Abraham Lincoln Papers at the Library of Congress. Transcribed and Annotated by the Lincoln Studies Center, Knox College, Galesburg, Illinois. Bernays enclosed a copy of Rosecrans's General Order No. 65, issued on April 29, 1864, which prohibited the formation of labor unions in St. Louis. See Lincoln to Oliver D. Filley, December 22, 1863. Bernays's letter is also printed in Bertram W. Korn, "The Jews of the Union," *American Jewish Archives* 13 (1961): 217, cited Gerteis, *Civil War St. Louis*, 258–59, n. 46, 367.

12. Qtd. Norma L. Peterson, *Freedom and Franchise: The Political Career of B. Gratz Brown* (Columbia: University of Missouri Press, 1965), 143; and [J. G. Forman,] *The Western Sanitary Commission*, 95.

13. Gabor S. Boritt, *Lincoln and the Economics of the American Dream* (Memphis: Memphis State University Press, 1978), 220–21; *Missouri Daily Democrat*, April 15, 19, 26, May 4, 22, 31, 1864; Philip S. Foner, *History of the Labor Movement: From Colonial Times to the Founding of the American Federation of Labor* (New York: International Publishers, 1947), 331–33, 354–55; Montgomery, *Beyond Equality*, 100; James C. Sylvis, *The Life, Speeches, Labors & Essays of William H. Sylvis* (Philadelphia: Claxton, Remsen & Haffelfinger, 1872), 133–35; "President Lincoln and Labor," *Journal of the International Association of Machinists. Published in the Interest of the Machinists' Trade* 5 (July 1893): 244.

14. "The War in Missouri," *New York Tribune*, October 1, 1864, p. 1.

15. Rosecrans to Pleasonton, September 22, Francis P. Blair, General Order No. 182, September 28, Francis P. Blair to E. C. Pike, September 29, 1864, *OR*, 41: (pt. 3) 302, 448, 480. The historian of the last, Bryce Suderow, plausibly described it as the "turning point of the invasion." *Thunder in Arcadia Valley*, 134. "The Lindell Hotel Riot," St. Louis *Union*, October 1, 1864, p. 1.

16. Sanborn, "The Campaign in Missouri in Sept. and October, 1864," 147–48; "From Missouri," *New York Tribune*, September 27, 1864, p. 1; "The War in Missouri," *New York Tribune*, October 2, 1864, continuation on p. 8; "The Invasion of Missouri," *New York Tribune*, September 29, 1864, p. 1. Brugioni is also fulsome in his praise of Rosecrans. *The Civil War in Missouri, As seen from the Capital City*, 117. Summarizing the northern press accounts, "Later from the North," *Richmond Daily Dispatch*, October 4, 1864, p. 1.

17. The numbers of the new recruits and draftees probably always looked better on

paper than in reality. Many of the recruits counted in August had been sent elsewhere, of the 2,300 persons drafted in the Fourth and Fifth Wards, only 531 had presented themselves to the provost marshal. Nearly a hundred "furnished substitutes, chiefly negroes, who have likewise been lodged at the Barracks." "Late from the West. The invasion of Missouri. Demonstration on Memphis" (from *Republican*, October 8), *New Orleans Daily Picayune*, October 16, 1864, p. 4.

18. Sanborn, "The Campaign in Missouri in Sept. and October, 1864," 147–48. "The Invasion of Missouri," *New York Tribune*, September 29, 1864, p. 1; and "The War in Missouri," *New York Tribune*, October 1, 1864, p. 1.

19. DuBois to Bonneville, 11:30 a.m., Bonneville to DuBois, 11:55 a.m. and noon, Bonneville to Lieutenant Hannahs, Yates to Rosecrans, Rosecrans' Special orders No. 205, all dated October 1, McDougall to DuBois, October 2, H. E. Paine to Rosecrans, October 3, John M. Palmer to Rosecrans, October 4, *OR*, 41: (pt. 3) 540, 532, 541, 542, 579, 610. As of Saturday, October 1, Yates had yet to send the Forty-seventh, 138th, 132nd, and the 136th. Palmer only offered his assistance on Tuesday. McDougall reported on the eighty veteranized members of the Sixty-first Illinois, which was actually sent to Chester, Illinois. Newspaper accounts smudged reports that "a large number of veterans arrived" with the story that "several Illinois 100-day Regiments have been ordered here." "The Invasion of Missouri," *Boston Herald*, September 30, 1864, p. 4; "The Invasion of Missouri," *New York Tribune*, September 29, 1864, p. 1; "The War in Missouri," *New York Tribune*, October 1, 1864, p. 1; Sanborn, "The Campaign in Missouri in Sept. and October, 1864," 147–48. DuBois to Wagelin, October 2, 12:45 p.m., *OR*, 41: (pt. 3) 444.

20. Van Buren S. Reber of Miller's staff had been in the Second Missouri Light Artillery, while Wolff's staff included Ernest W. Decker, P. F. Zeppenfeld, and Louis Lipman, former members respectively of the First Missouri, the Fifth USRC, and the Eighth Missouri. In terms of regimental commands, 1861 service in the old First USRC united Casper Koehler, Leonard Weindel, and William Waldschmidt of the First EMM, while the Second USRC included John Ruedi, later of the Fourth EMM, and the Third USRC shaped the careers of Colonel George E. Leighton of the Seventh EMM and Colonel Louis Duestrow, Charles Ludwig, and Theodore Kalb of the Fourth EMM. Of these Decker in the First Missouri Light Artillery, Waldscmidt in the Second. *Official Army Register*, 7: (Leighton) 22, (Leighton) 42, (Decker) 57, (Miller) 60, (Waldschmidt) 70, (Weindel, Ludwig) 75, (Ruedi) 81, (Zeppenfeld) 86, (Lipman) 91, (Miller) 104, (Ruedi) 128, (Miller, Meyers, Decker, Koehler, Weindel, Waldschmidt) 385, (Ruedi) 387, (Leighton, Duestrow, Ludwig, Kalb) 388; and (Wolf) Scharf, *History of Saint Louis City and County*, 454. In addition, the First EMM included Lieutenant Colonel Robert C. Allen, who may have been a captain in the Fortieth Missouri and, in 1861, a lieutenant in King's Independent Company, 128, 143. So too Major John McDonald of the First EMM may have been in the Eighth Missouri. 91. For Wold, Thomas, *History of Saint Louis County, Missouri*, II, 186. Rosecrans army of "nearly 20,000 men." Thompson, "The Great-Little Battle of Pilot Knob," 89.

21. The 1860 St. Louis census has only one George H. Stone, the twenty-seven-year-old printer from New Hampshire. Seventh Ward, p. 12. *The Printer* 2 (February 1860): 207, which also notes Whitwell; *Appendix to the House Journal of the Adjourned Session*

of the Twenty-Second General Assembly of Missouri (Jefferson City, MO: J. P. Ament, 1863), 192; United States Adjutant-General's Office, *Official Army Register of the Volunteer Force of the United States Army for the years 1861, '62, '63, '64, '65.* 8 vols. (Washington: Government Printing Office, 1865–67), hereafter cited as *OAR*; Office of Adjutant General Series Title: Record of Service Card, Civil War, 1861–1865, Box 89. Decades later, John W. Barton remembered how he participated in the militia mobilization with "a large number of printers and newspaper employees." Thomas, *History of Saint Louis County*, 1: 104. On Whitwell, see *The Printer* 2 (February 1860): 207. As with any military organization, it combined people of different classes, and it depended heavily on the contentment of those social groups involved. In the county, its leadership drew from the more active of the industrious middle class. Robert C. Allen, a former Brooklyn plasterer with a farm in the western county, commanded a company of the First EMM at Allenton, and a company of the Pacific Battalion. The latter generally served under Major William C. Inks, the founder of Pacific. Thomas, *History of Saint Louis County, Missouri*, I, 98, 100, II, 246–49.

22. General Order No. 275, October 4, *OR*, 41: (pt. 3) 611. Estimate of 17,000, *Missouri Troops in Service During the Civil War: Letter from the Secretary of War* . . . (Washington: Government Printing Office, 1902), 53. The military service records in the State Archives name eighty-five all Company B of St. Louis Police Battalion EMM, but notes no service in 1864 Some in the Eighty-fifth EMM are listed as a St. Louis county battalion with 1864 service.

23. Scharf, *History of Saint Louis City and County*, 439.

24. "The Invasion of Missouri," "Important from Missouri," and "Dissatisfaction with General F. P. Blair in Missouri," *New York Herald*, September 27 (p. 4), 30 (p. 1), October 4 (p. 1), 1864, p. 1; "The Invasion of Missouri," and "The Missouri Invasion," *Boston Herald*, September 28, 30, 1864, both p. 4; "From Missouri," *New York Tribune*, September 27, 1864, p. 1; "The War in Missouri," *New York Tribune*, September 30, October 1, 2, 1864, all p. 1; and *Missouri Troops in Service During the Civil War: Letter from the Secretary of War* . . . (Washington: Government Printing Office, 1902), 53, 60–61. Rosecrans to Callender, DuBois to Miller, September 28, 1864, *OR*, 41: (pt. 3) 442.

25. The Eighteenth and Eighty-fifth EMM were from outside of St. Louis. *Missouri Troops in Service During the Civil War: Letter from the Secretary of War*, the numbers of which explode to 24,164 for October, which were actually serving after the Confederate drive on the city.

26. "Second Regiment E.M.M.—To Arms! To Arms!," *St. Louis Daily Missouri Democrat*, September 28, p. 1; S. H. Melcher to Pleasonton, October 3, *OR*, 41: (pt. 3) 586; Scharf, *History of Saint Louis City and County*, 443.

27. Scharf, *History of Saint Louis City and County*, 443; S. H. Melcher to Pleasonton, October 3, *OR*, 41: (pt. 3) 586. Scharf described the Eighteenth and Eighty-fifth EMM as Franklin County regiments, which they were not.

28. F. Blair to E. C. Pike, September 29, with DuBois revoking the order, September 30, J. F. Bennett, General Order No. 184, September 30, 1864 *OR*, 41: (pt. 3) 480, 508; and, "Dissatisfaction with General F. P. Blair in Missouri," *New York Herald*, October 4, 1864, p. 1; "The Missouri Invasion," *Boston Herald*, September 30, 1864, p. 4; "The War

in Missouri," *New York Tribune*, October 1, 1864, p. 1; Norma L. Peterson, *Freedom and Franchise: The Political Career of B. Gratz Brown* (Columbia: University of Missouri Press, 1965), 132; Carpenter in Bartels, *Iowa Boy Makes Good*, 150. The Second and Third Brigades were said to have had 3,000 on parade September 30. Scharf, *History of Saint Louis City and County*, 1: 443.

29. "The War in Missouri," *New York Tribune*, October 1, 1864, p. 1; J. H. Gamble to Rosecrans, DuBois to Krekel, October 3, 1864, *OR*, 41: (pt. 3) 592. Interestingly enough, it took headquarters less than two hours to respond from the sending of the first telegram. George H. Frost, railroad surveyor, said high wages made workers self-indulgent. George H. Frost to Frank Frost, June 25, St. Louis History Collection, MHS, cited Gerteis, *Civil War St. Louis*, 256 n. 42, 367.

30. Rosecrans, December 7, 1864, *OR*, 41: (pt. 1) 310, DuBois to Smith, September 29, 1864, *OR*, 41: (pt. 3) 444; Rosecrans to Pennock, to Yates, October 1, 1864, with correspondence *OR*, 41: (pt. 3) 510, 513, 531, 532. Although the regular telegraph operator at Pacific, Clinton S. Barrett, was "on leave of absence" at the time, enough information from the southwest was being reliably forwarded to indicate movement that direction. Plum, *The Military Telegraph During the Civil War*, 2: 219, 223. "The War in Missouri," *New York Tribune*, October 2, 1864, pp. 1, 8. "The city is by no means in a state of siege—people come and go as usual—the railroads to the east arrive and depart regularly—the steamboats the same, and no stranger is molested or made afraid on the street. Even the militia guards, which in former times demanded your pass or certificate of exemption on the corners, have not made their appearance. But business is suspended, all stores closed, and organization of companies and regiments progressing rapidly." There is "good evidence that the Rebels have promised themselves a dash into the city."

31. Rosecrans, December 7, 1864, *OR*, 41: (pt. 1) 310; Merrill to DuBois, September 30, Rosecrans to Yates, Smith to Rosecrans, October 1, 1864, *OR*, 41: (pt. 3) 512, 532, 533. On the refugees, "The War in Missouri," *New York Tribune*, October 2, 1864, p. 1. Related to the rash of troubles with steamboats, on Thursday, September 29, 3 p.m. towboat H. S. Dickerson, Captain John Heron boiler explosion five miles above St. Louis sank "in a few minutes." "Late from the West. The invasion of Missouri. Demonstration on Memphis" (from *St. Louis Democrat*, October 8), *New Orleans Daily Picayune*, October 16, 1864, p. 4.

32. Fike, Diaries, v. 2, September 27, 29, October 1, 3, 1864, Western Historical Manuscripts Collections, University of Missouri, Columbia. Not until October 6 was "nice and pleasant weather" reported. Curtis to Brown, October 5, *OR*, 41: (pt. 1) 466, Curtis to Fisk, to Governor Thomas Carney, Fisk to Rosecrans, to Curtis, October 5, Curtis to Brown, October 6, *OR*, 41: (pt. 3) 646–47, 648, 650, 664.

33. Basil Wilson Duke State Troops at Camp Jackson. May 3, 1861. Basil W. Duke, Captain, Company C, 2nd Regiment, Minute Men. Office of Adjutant General Index of service records, Confederate, 1861–1865, Box 99, Reel s730. Basil W. Duke, *Reminiscences of General Basil W. Duke, C.S.A.* (Garden City, NY: Doubleday, Page & Company, 1911), 32–84. See also, *Absalom Grimes, Confederate Mail Runner*, ed. Milo M. Quife (New Haven, CT: Yale University Press, 1926).

34. Thomas C. Fletcher, "The Battle of Pilot Knob and the Retreat to Leasburg," Military Order of the Loyal Legion of the United States, Missouri, *War Papers and Personal Reminiscences*, I (1892), 29; John B. Sanborn, "The Campaign in Missouri in Sept. and October, 1864," Military Order of the Loyal Legion of the United States, Minnesota, *Glimpses of the Nations Struggle*, Third Series (1893), 137; Scott, "The Last Fight for Missouri," 299.

35. William A. Tidwell, James O. Hall, and David Winfred Gaddy, *Come Retribution: The Confederate Secret Service and the Assassination of Lincoln* (Jackson: University Press of Mississippi, 1988), 182–83, 209 n. 31. Mary K. Maule, "A Chapter of Unwritten History," typescript, n.d., Western Reserve Historical Society, Cleveland, Ohio. All from file F 1483 Missouri's Union Provost Marshal Papers: 1861–1866. http://www.sos.mo.gov/archives/provost/ (accessed May 31, 2011).

36. Deb Houdek Rule, "Boat Burners" posted at http://www.civilwarstlouis.com/boatburners/index.htm (accessed May 31, 2011). For his October 4 escape from a transport on the way to the Alton Military Prison, see "The War in Missouri," *New York Tribune*, October 6, 1864, p. 1; "The Missouri Invasion," *Baltimore Sun*, October 6, 1864, p. 1.

37. Charles L. Hunt to Mary C. Hunt, August 8, September 13, October 6, 9, 1847, February 26, March 12 and 16, 1848. Box 2, The Hunt Family Papers. Missouri History Museum Library, St. Louis, MO. See also, John Bartier, "Belgium in 1848," *The Opening of an Era: 1848, An Historical Symposium*, ed. François Fejtö, introduction by A. J. P. Taylor (London: Wingate, 1948; rpt. New York: H. Fertig, 1966), 160–66. J. P. Sanderson signed parole, July 23, 1864. Box 2, The Hunt Family Papers. Missouri History Museum Library, St. Louis, MO. Belgian settlement. Log church of Father Roux on the ridge between the Kansas and Missouri Rivers, 1847. Rothensteiner, *History of the Archdiocese of St. Louis*, 2: 45.

38. John A. Marshall, *American Bastille. A history of the Illegal Arrests and Imprisonment of American Citizens During the Late Civil War* (Philadelphia: Thomas W. Hartley, 1869), 218, 230. Sanborn, "The Campaign in Missouri in Sept. and October, 1864," 145–46; Scott, "The Last Fight for Missouri," 298–99. Frank L. Klement argues that these organizations were essentially the invention of Republican politicians and ascribes this as a "conspiracy theory" to the "paranoid style" in American politics. In this case, the historian's evident assumption that secret societies and conspiracies never exist whitewashes all tangible evidence for the existence of the legendary pro-Confederate fifth-column in the Knights of the Golden Circle and the Order of American Knights. Our presumptions do not constitute a valid reason to discard all such evidence. So, too, it is simply ahistorical to compare the modern, self-serving and fictitious McCarthyite fears of an enemy on the other side of the globe to the nineteenth-century Republican fears of an enemy on the other side of the room. Some historians have used their vastly overstated claims of membership and support to doubt their existence. *Dark Lanterns: Secret Political Societies, Conspiracies, and Treason Trials in the Civil War* (Baton Rouge: Louisiana State University Press, 1984). I discussed the subject thoroughly with some particular reference to Missouri at this time in my Secret Society History of the Civil War (Urbana: University of Illinois Press, 2011).

39. John B. Castleman, *Active Service* (Louisville: Courier-Journal Job Printers Col., Publishers, 1917), 144–45, 158, 170. Frank L. Klement, *The Limits of Dissent: Clement L. Vallandigham and the Civil War* (New York: J. Walter & Co., 1864; rpt. Lexington: University Press of Kentucky, 1970).

40. Castleman to Secretary of War James A. Seddon, September 7, 1864 in *Active Service*, 158–59. A local Confederate agent and steamboat man later recalled the plans of Joseph W. Tucker, Minor Majors, Thomas L. Clark, and Colonel Barrett of Missouri "for burning boats carrying Government freight, transports, and other vessels on the Mississippi, Ohio, and other rivers," as well as "Government hospitals, store-houses, and everything appertaining to the army." He visited Richmond in August 1864 in preparation for more activities. Edward Frazier testimony, June 8. *The Assassination of President Lincoln: Trial of the Conspirators. . .*, comp. Benn Pitman (New York: Moore, Wilstach & Baldwin, 1865), 49–50. See also the *Conspiracy Trial for the Murder of the President, and the Attempt to Overthrow the Government by the Assassination of Its Principal Officers*, ed. Benjamin Perley Poore, 20 vols. (Boston: J. E. Tilton and Company, 1866), 3: 424–31.

41. Castleman, *Active Service*, 159, who described this as the fire on Eighth and Main. Robert E. McDowell, *City of Conflict: Louisville in the Civil War, 1861–1865* (Louisville: Civil War Round Table, Publishers, 1962), 163, though credulous of Felix Stidger's statement that it had been the work of the Sons of Liberty. If Castleman was correct, though, it was actually done by Confederate agents.

42. Castleman, *Active Service*, 159, 173–74. September 26, Monday fire at Mrs. Craig's ropewalk and warehouse believed the work of an incendiary. "Loss of the Fire Monday Night—Supposed Work of an Incendiary," St. Louis *Union*, September 28, 1864, p. 4.

43. Major General Sterling Price, Army Headquarters, Boggy Depot, Choctaw Nation, November 18, 1864. *OR*, 41: (pt. 1) 633; Edwards, *Shelby and His Men*, 416.

44. John N. Edwards, *Noted Guerrillas, or the Warfare of the Border* (St. Louis, MO: Bryan, Brand, 1877), 256, 316–19, and *Shelby and His Men*, 411–12, 414–16.

45. William C. Winter, *The Civil War in St. Louis: A Guided Tour* (St. Louis: Missouri Historical Society Press, 1994), 98–99.

46. "Horrible Hanging Affair," *St. Louis Daily Missouri Democrat*, September 29, p. 1. Likely some relation to Joshua and Jane Cole, Kentuckieans who described themselves after the war as being "in favor of the Union during the late war, although his sympathies were with the South." *History of Franklin, Jefferson, Washington, Crawford and Gasconade Counties*, 856, 875.

47. "A Daring Exploit of Rebels. The Affair at Cheltenham. Attempt to Murder the Postmaster. He Escapes to the City," *Missouri Republican*, October 1, 1864; Scharf, *History of Saint Louis City and County*, 1: 443.

48. Gregory, *Price's Raid In Franklin County, Missouri*, 4; Suderow, *Thunder in Arcadia Valley*, 52. There were 1,500 garrison troops and recruits; 1,500–2,000 of Smith's infantry; 1,200–1,500 unmanageable Illinois troops; and 1,500 half-armed enrolled militia.

49. Thomas, *History of St. Louis County*, 1: 226–27. Scharf, *History of Saint Louis City and County*, 1918. Some 16,170 of the 58,222 Federal soldiers fell while inflicting 20,950 casualties on the 66,326 rebels engaged.

Chapter 5

1. Smith to Rosecrans (two items), Rosecrans to Smith, September 28, Rosecrans to Smith, Smith to Rosecrans (two items), September 29, 1864, *OR*, 41: (pt. 3) 443, 444, 445, 480, 480–81, 481, 482. "Important from Missouri," *New York Herald*, September 30, 1864, p. 1; "The Missouri Invasion," *New York Herald*, October 2, 1864, p. 8; "The War in Missouri," *New York Tribune*, October 2, 1864, p. 1; "Latest News from the Southeast," St. Louis *Union*, October 3, 1864, p. 2; "The Missouri Invasion," *Boston Herald*, September 30, 1864, p. 4; "Department of Missouri. The Progress of Price's Invasion," *Philadelphia Inquirer*, October 4, 1864, p. 1; "From Missouri," *New York Tribune*, October 4, 1864, p. 1; "The Invasion of Missouri," *New York Herald*, October 4, 1864, p. 1; "From Missouri," *New York Tribune*, October 7, 1864, p. 1; "Latest News from the Southeast," St. Louis *Union*, October 3, 1864, p. 2; Smith to Rosecrans (two items), September 29, 1864, *OR*, 41: (pt. 3) 481, 482.

2. Price's report, December 28, 1864, *OR*, 41: (pt. 1) 630, and S. D. Barlow, Smith to Rosecrans, September 30, 1864, *OR*, 41: (pt. 3) 509, 510; *History of Franklin, Jefferson, Washington, Crawford and Gasconade Counties*, 423.

3. Ewing's report, October 20, 1864, *OR*, 41: (pt. 3) 448, Rosecrans to Smith with Smith to Rosecrans, September 29, J. F. H. Rudy and Rosecrans, September 29, 1864, *OR*, 41: (pt. 3) 481, 484; *History of Franklin, Jefferson, Washington, Crawford and Gasconade Counties*, 509. Corum had been a sergeant in Company B of the Washington County battalion of the Six-Month Militia from September 19, 1861, to January 8, 1862, and a second lieutenant in Company C under Captain William T. Hunter of the Twelfth MSM Cavalry, from February 1862 until his October transfer into the Third MSM Cavalry, serving mostly around Ironton. "The War in Missouri," *New York Tribune*, October 1, 1864, p. 1, and "The War in Missouri," *New York Tribune*, October 2, 1864, continuation on p. 8. Mistakenly called "Richmond." "The Invasion of Missouri," *Boston Herald*, September 30, 1864, p. 4.

4. Maggie MacLean, "Louisa Volker," posted at "Civil War Women," http://civilwarwomen.blogspot.com/2006/11/louisa-volker.html (accessed May 31, 2011).

5. Palmer, *Four Weeks in the Rebel Army*, 17–18; McPheeters, *I Acted from Principle*, 225.

6. Palmer, *Four Weeks in the Rebel Army*, 13–14, 19.

7. Rosecrans to Smith, September 27, DuBois to Madison Miller, Rosecrans to Smith, September 28, 1864, *OR*, 41: (pt. 3) 409, 442, 445–46.

8. "Pursuit of Price. Part Taken by the 16th Army Corps," *St. Louis Daily Missouri Democrat*, November 5, 1864, p. 2; "The War in Missouri," *New York Tribune*, October 2, 1864, p. 1; and Fike, Diaries, v. 2, September 29, October 2, 1864, Western Historical Manuscripts Collections, University of Missouri, Columbia.

9. "Grand Union Rally," St. Louis *Union*, September 30, 1864, p. 1; Reports of Rosecrans, December 7, and Price, December 28, *OR*, 41: (pt. 1) 310, 630; "Alarm at Franklin," *St. Louis Daily Missouri Democrat*, October 3, p. 2; "The War in Missouri," *New York Tribune*, October 2, 1864, continuation on p. 8; and, "General Price's Movements in Missouri," *Richmond Daily Dispatch*, October 7, 1864, p. 1.

10. William T. Hunter to Rosecrans, September 30, 1864, *OR,* 41: (pt. 3) 514; McPheeters reported that the Arkansans moved up and drove out the small number of Federals at the St. Francis Station. *I Acted from Principle,* 226; "Grand Union Rally," St. Louis *Union,* September 30, 1864, p. 1; "From the Southwest Branch Road," St. Louis *Union,* October 1, 1864, p. 1. The previous year had seen the paving of the main routes west of Pacific as "rock roads." *Encyclopedia of the History of Missouri,* 2: 511.

11. Rosecrans to Smith, September 30, 1864, *OR,* 41: (pt. 3) 510; "Alarm at Franklin," *St. Louis Daily Missouri Democrat,* October 3, p. 2; "The War in Missouri," *New York Tribune,* October 2, 1864, continuation on p. 8; "General Price's Movements in Missouri," *Richmond Daily Dispatch,* October 7, 1864, p. 1; "Grand Union Rally," St. Louis *Union,* September 30, 1864, p. 1; "From the Southwest Branch Road," St. Louis *Union,* October 1, 1864, p. 1.

12. "From Franklin," *St. Louis Daily Missouri Democrat,* October 2, p. 1; "Neuester von Franklin," St. Louis *Neuer Anzeiger des Westens,* October 3, 1864, p. 1. Cabell, *Report of the Part Cabell's Brigade took,* 6; McPheeters, *I Acted from Principle,* 226, saying that the brigade left town after an hour and went into camp a mile outside of Pacific. The *St. Louis Union* reported that the Army of Missouri raised fourteen companies in Reynolds County.

13. "From Franklin," "The Sacking of Pacific," and "Price's Invasion," *St. Louis Daily Missouri Democrat,* October 2 (1), October 5 (1), and October 8 (1); "The War in Missouri," *New York Tribune,* October 6, 1864, p. 11; *Final Report of the Western Sanitary Commission,* 55. The press accounts name eight store owners whose businesses were plundered.

14. "From Franklin," "The Sacking of Pacific," and "Paroled Prisoners from Price," *St. Louis Daily Missouri Democrat,* October 2 (1), October 5 (1), October 6 (1).

15. Abraham Johnson and the engineer of the train in Peterson and Hanson, *Pilot Knob,* 49 and n.

16. Reports of Captain Eli Mattocks Fifty-second Indiana, Franklin, October 2, *OR,* 41: (pt. 1) 325; "From Franklin," *St. Louis Daily Missouri Democrat,* October 2, p. 1.

17. Reports of Captain Eli Mattocks Fifty-second Indiana, Lieutenant Colonel Jonathan Merrian 117th Illinois, and Colonel Phineas Pease Forty-ninth Illinois, all dated Franklin, October 2, and Price, December 28, pt. 1, *OR,* 41: (pt. ?) 325, 324, 323, 630; "From Franklin," *St. Louis Daily Missouri Democrat,* October 2, p. 1; Gregory, *Price's Raid In Franklin County, Missouri,* 4.

18. "From Franklin," *St. Louis Daily Missouri Democrat,* October 2, p. 1; Cabell, *Report of the Part Cabell's Brigade took,* 6; Merrill to Rosecrans, October 1, 6:30 p.m., *OR,* 41: (pt. 3) 538; and Fike, Diaries, v. 2, October 4, 1864, Western Historical Manuscripts Collections, University of Missouri, Columbia.

19. Reports of Captain Eli Mattocks Fifty-second Indiana, Lieutenant Colonel Jonathan Merrian 117th Illinois, and Colonel Phineas Pease Forty-ninth Illinois, all dated Franklin, October 2, and Price, December 28, *OR,* 41: (pt. 1) 325, 324, 323, 630; "From Franklin," *St. Louis Daily Missouri Democrat,* October 2, p. 1; Gregory, *Price's Raid In Franklin County, Missouri,* 4; Cabell, *Report of the Part Cabell's Brigade took,* 6; and, for the highest Union figure, "Pursuit of Price. Part Taken by the 16th Army Corps," *St.*

Louis Daily Missouri Democrat, November 5, 1864, p. 2. The wounded named were B. S. Bine, Warren Crawford, and Thomas Horrell of Companies F, C, and A, Fifty-second Indiana, and Andrew J. Nash, Company B, 117th Illinois. "About 4 o'clock p.m. heard our brigade had a fight this morning at Franklin." Fike, Diaries, v. 2, October 1, 1864, Western Historical Manuscripts Collections, University of Missouri, Columbia.

20. "Rebel Destruction of Property," *St. Louis Daily Missouri Democrat*, October 8, p. 1; Cabell, *Report of the Part Cabell's Brigade took*, 6.

21. DuBois to Smith, October 1, 1864, *OR*, 41: (pt. 3) 533.

22. Merrill to Rosecrans, October 2, 9 am, *OR*, 41: (pt. 3) 554–55.

23. "Pursuit of Price. Part Taken by the 16th Army Corps," *St. Louis Daily Missouri Democrat*, November 5, 1864, p. 2, by "Occassional."

24. Merrill to Rosecrans, October 1, 6:30 p.m., *OR*, 41: (pt. 3) 538.

25. *History of Franklin, Jefferson, Washington, Crawford and Gasconade Counties*, 296, 297, 299.

26. Ralph Gregory, *Washington, Missouri—the Civil War Years* (n.p.: n.p., 1962), unpaged. For Gale, see *Bench and Bar of St. Louis, Kansas City, Jefferson City, and Other Missouri Cities*, 380–81.

27. *History of Franklin, Jefferson, Washington, Crawford and Gasconade Counties*, 245–46, 233, 246, 488, 989.

28. "Price's Great Raid" and "Colonel Gale" (from the *Franklin County News*), both in *St. Louis Daily Missouri Democrat*, October 18, p. 2.

29. Rosecrans to Sanborn, September 26, Rosecrans to McNeil, September 27, 1864, *OR*, 41: (pt. 3) 391, 412.

30. For the next two paragraphs, see *History of Franklin, Jefferson, Washington, Crawford and Gasconade Counties*, 746–47, 256, 258; "Rebel Barbarities at Union," *St. Louis Daily Missouri Democrat*, October 13, p. 2. The national press described a clash of five hundred rebels with about a hundred "county militia," and Colonel Robert R. Lawther, who fought them, estimated four hundred in his report of December 6, 1864, *OR*, 41: (pt. 1) 698. "From Missouri," *New York Tribune*, October 4, 1864, p. 1; "Department of Missouri. The Progress of Price's Invasion," *Philadelphia Inquirer*, October 4, 1864, p. 1; and "From Missouri," *Richmond Daily Dispatch*, October 10, 1864, p. 1, which also locates Union, Missouri, as forty miles west of St. Louis, twenty south of the Missouri River, and fifty east of Jefferson City.

31. For the next three paragraphs, see Gregory, *Price's Raid In Franklin County, Missouri*, 6, 7–8.

32. James Lee McDonough, *Chattanooga: a Death Grip on the Confederacy* (Knoxville, 1984), 152.

33. See also: Reports of Price, December 28, *OR*, 41: (pt. 1) 630; "The Rebel Invasion," St. Louis *Union*, October 4, 1864, p. 1; Owen to Rosecrans, October 2, *OR*, 41: (pt. 3) 553; "Colonel Gale" (from the *Franklin County News*), both in *St. Louis Daily Missouri Democrat*, October 18, p. 2.

34. Reports of Jackman, November 30, Clark, December 19, and Lawther, December 6, 1864, in *OR*, 41: (pt. 1) 673, 680, 698; *History of Franklin, Jefferson, Washington, Crawford and Gasconade Counties*, 842.

35. Gregory, *Price's Raid In Franklin County, Missouri*, 8.

36. Gregory, *Price's Raid In Franklin County, Missouri*, 6.

37. Reports of Jackman, November 30, and Clark, December 19, *OR*, 41: (pt. 1) 673, 680; Edwards, *Shelby and His Men*, 391.

38. Reports of Jackman, November 30, Lawther (Tenth Missouri Cavalry), December 6, Clark, December 19, and Price, December 28, *OR*, 41: (pt. 1) 673, 698, 680, 630. Also Davies, December 12, 696; "Rebel Barbarities at Union," *St. Louis Daily Missouri Democrat*, October 13, p. 2. Keil's *Directory* is incomplete, having been evidently compiled from roster rolls of October 1864, which therefore did not include the many reported casualties. Consider: There are several justifications for this critique of Keil's listing: (1) Confederate reports on the Vitt's Mill engagement indicate over eighty Federal casualties, including ten or eleven killed. Although Keil listed fatalities, these are conspicuously missing from his list. (2) The list for Company B, Fifty-fourth EMM includes only eighty-two, though many more served in the company. (3) The enclosed copies of service records for several members of Company B excluded from Keil's list demonstrate the incomplete character of his compilation. (4) Note that these records not reflected in Keil's list indicate service by these individuals in 1862 and 1863 but not 1864. The best explanation for this is that these two companies were mustered into service on October 1 with the rest of their regiments but hurried to Vitt's Mill prior to the taking of any October roll. Those subsequently killed and those captured and paroled would not bear arms during the October period of the regiment's service. As a result, when Keil worked on his lists using those October rolls, he inadvertently excluded the casualties of the most important encounter of troops in the county's Civil War history.

39. "Rebel Barbarities at Union," *St. Louis Daily Missouri Democrat*, October 13, p. 2.

40. Gregory, *Price's Raid In Franklin County, Missouri*, 4; Edwards, *Shelby and His Men*, 391; Sanborn, "The Campaign in Missouri in Sept. and October, 1864," 154; Plum, *The Military Telegraph During the Civil War*, 2: 218; A. W. Reese, Civil War Memoirs, p. 750, Western Historical Manuscripts Collections, University of Missouri, Columbia. "Hannah Jones," p. 217, and "Jes Lee," p. 228 in the WPA, Missouri Writers Project, in the *Slave Narratives*. "Dat was de time Marmaduke was a-tryin' to take de Cape."

41. McPheeters, *I Acted from Principle*, 226; Edwards, *Shelby and His Men*, 391; Gregory, *Price's Raid In Franklin County, Missouri*, 8, 9. Without giving the particulars, McPheeters wrote that, at Union, he "witnessed a brutal act of one of our soldiers to another." Earlier talk that Colonel Charles H. Tyler would organize recruits into a new brigade came to naught, though.

42. "Rebel Barbarities at Union," *St. Louis Daily Missouri Democrat*, October 13, p. 2; October 4 entry, William A. Lyman, Diary 1864–1865, Typescript Collections, v. XVII, Item 490, Western Historical Manuscripts Collections, University of Missouri, Columbia.

43. For this and the next paragraph, see "Rebel Barbarities at Union," *St. Louis Daily Missouri Democrat*, October 13, p. 2, naming over half a dozen robbery victims.

44. Merrill to Rosecrans, October 2, 5:39 p.m., *OR*, 41: (pt. 3) 556–57.

45. "Safe Arrival of Colonel Maupin, Captain Schenk and Lieutenant Fletcher," *St. Louis Daily Missouri Democrat*, October 7, p. 1. Others mentioned are Captain E. S.

Schenck, Lieutenant William Fletcher, and Captain Peck (Sgt. Wilbur Peck of Ninth MSM Cavalry?).

46. "Rebel Barbarities at Union," *St. Louis Daily Missouri Democrat*, October 13, p. 2; *History of Franklin, Jefferson, Washington, Crawford and Gasconade Counties*, 786. Ellen Frances Toss, marriage February 2, 1863.

47. Palmer, *Four Weeks in the Rebel Army*, 21.

48. "Rebel Barbarities at Union," *St. Louis Daily Missouri Democrat*, October 13, p. 2; Gregory, *Price's Raid In Franklin County, Missouri*, 9.

49. "Rebel Barbarities at Union," *St. Louis Daily Missouri Democrat*, October 13, p. 2. The "Mrs. Frank Schryvor" was probably the wife of Franz Schreiber of Detmer's Company B of the Fifty-fourth EMM; Schreiber's service record indicates he was then with Gale at Washington.

50. John H. Taylor, To the Members of the Order of American Knights of the State of Missouri, October 1, 1864, *OR*, 41: (pt. 3) 975–76.

51. The author is indebted for this story to Mrs. Thelma Eckelkamp Kline, the granddaughter of that ten-year-old, Johann William Eckelkamp.

52. Major General Sterling Price, Army Headquarters, Boggy Depot, Choctaw Nation, November 18, 1864, *OR*, 41: (pt. 1) 633. These absurdities are still presented as accurate historical information: "In hindsight, it was probably wise that they did not attack Jefferson City which was certainly prepared for them. General Rosecrans in St. Louis had on site then in Jefferson City, General Pleasonton, Smith, Winslow, Mowers, McNeil, Fisk and Brown with about 17,000 troops." http://www.colecohistsoc.org/civilwar2.html (accessed May 31, 2011). Cole County Historical Society.

53. "Department of Missouri. The Progress of Price's Invasion," *Philadelphia Inquirer*, October 4, 1864, p. 1.

54. Major General Sterling Price, Boggy Depot, Choctaw Nation, November 18, 1864, *OR*, 41: (pt. 1) 633.

Chapter 6

1. Palmer, *Four Weeks in the Rebel Army*, 21.

2. *The Bench and Bar of St. Louis, Kansas City, Jefferson City, and Other Missouri Cities. Biographical Sketches, with Steel Engraved Portraits* (St. Louis and Chicago: American Biographical Publishing Company, 1884), 380–81.

3. Julius Wilhelmi to Rosecrans, Rosecrans to Wilhelmi, and to Dugge, Krueger or Owens, all September 38, 1864, *OR*, 41: (pt. 3) 379, 443; Gregory, *Washington, Missouri—the Civil War Years.*

4. Special Orders No. 270, September 24, 1864, *OR*, 41: (pt. 3) 479; *The Centennial Biographical Directory of Franklin County Missouri*, comp. Herman G. Keil (Washington, DC: the Author, 1925; rpt., Washington, MO: Washington Historical Society, 1986), 112, 118, 132, 133; and, Gregory, *Washington, Missouri—the Civil War Years.* Captains Benjamin E. Anderson, Lewis Frazer, and Andrew Fink, as well as Lieutenant Frederick Steines, had active if depleted companies of the Provisional EMM usually defending the railroad.

5. Rothensteiner, *History of the Archdiocese of St. Louis*, 2: 412–13; Owen to Rosecrans, October 2, *OR*, 41: (pt. 3) 553; "Colonel Gale" (from the *Franklin County News*), both in *St. Louis Daily Missouri Democrat*, October 18, p. 2. Unusually, rumors this time downplayed the size of the enemy force, but frankly acknowledged the Federals under Brigadier General Thomas Ewing "severely handled" at Leasburg.

6. "Price's Great Raid," *St. Louis Daily Missouri Democrat*, October 18, p. 2; "The Rebel Invasion," St. Louis *Union*, October 4, 1864, p. 1; "Department of Missouri. The Progress of Price's Invasion," *Philadelphia Inquirer*, October 4, 1864, p. 1; "From Missouri," *New York Tribune*, October 4, 1864, p. 1; and "From Missouri," *New York Tribune*, October 7, 1864, p. 1. At this point, none of the authorities could account for the whereabouts of the Missouri River ferryboat, the *Evening Star*.

7. Owen to Rosecrans, October 2, *OR*, 41: (pt. 3) 553; "Evacuation of Washington," *St. Louis Daily Missouri Democrat*, October 4, p. 1. A young boy at the time, Fred Bihr announced to his father, of the Ninth MSM Cavalry, that he wanted to see the enemy. "Oh, they won't hurt me," he insisted. The soldiers found his warlike chatter and games so annoying that they locked him in the Boley building for safekeeping until it came time to move across the river. When they hurried to the Boley building to release any political prisoners held there, they found Fred Bihr still locked up and forgotten in the final moments of the evacuation; rejoining his mother and the women, he helped to prepare food for the Confederates. Gregory, *Washington, Missouri—the Civil War Years*. No Bihr is listed in the local militia rolls, so it is assumed that this is a reference to the son of Henry Buhr.

8. Gregory, *Price's Raid In Franklin County, Missouri*, 10, and *Washington, Missouri—the Civil War Years*; "Evacuation of Washington," *St. Louis Daily Missouri Democrat*, October 4, p. 1.

9. "Evacuation of Washington," *St. Louis Daily Missouri Democrat*, October 4, p. 1. This is probably why seventy-five to eighty rebels entered Washington and South Point, engaged in burning the place. Reported at Stanton, St. Clair, "The Rebel Invasion," St. Louis *Union*, October 3, 1864, p. 1.

10. Owen to Rosecrans, October 2, and Merrill to Rosecrans, October 2, 8 p.m., *OR*, 41: (pt. 3) 553, 557; "From Franklin," *St. Louis Daily Missouri Democrat*, October 2, p. 1; "Department of Missouri. The Progress of Price's Invasion," *Philadelphia Inquirer*, October 4, 1864, p. 1; "General Price's Movements in Missouri," *Richmond Daily Dispatch*, October 7, 1864, p. 1.

11. Gregory, *Washington, Missouri—the Civil War Years*.

12. "The Damage at Washington," *St. Louis Daily Missouri Democrat*, October 14, 1864, p. 2; Gregory, *Price's Raid In Franklin County, Missouri*, 10, 12–13, and *Washington, Missouri—the Civil War Years*. Among the stores were Henry Willenkamp, H. and C. H. Kahmann, Keiming & Gast(?), Reistrib and Hibler, William Tiemann, H. Lonkamper, L. Wehrmann, Bueker and Noelke, Everts, McDonald and Godejohns, Edward Reichart, and Charles Volker. "The Damage at Washington," *St. Louis Daily Missouri Democrat*, October 14, p. 2.

13. Gregory, *Price's Raid In Franklin County, Missouri*, 10, and *Washington, Missouri—the Civil War Years*.

14. "The Damage at Washington," *St. Louis Daily Missouri Democrat*, October 14, 1864, p. 2; Gregory, *Price's Raid In Franklin County, Missouri*, 10, and *Washington, Missouri—the Civil War Years*.

15. The story among the Alfermanns and Ballmanns families was that William Ballmann of Company B, Fifty-fourth EMM, shot down one of the rebels on the steps of the church.

16. Gregory, *Washington, Missouri—the Civil War Years*; Smith to Rosecrans, Merrill to Rosecrans, October 3, 1864, *OR*, 41: (pt. 3) 581, 582.

17. Report of Curtis, January 1865, *OR*, 41: (pt. 1) 466, and Curtis to Brown, to Fisk, G. A. Hollaway (Fisk) to Curtis, and Curtis to General George Sykes and Ford, all October 2, Curtis to Rosecrans, October 4, *OR*, 41: (pt. 3) 564, 565, 569, 570, 571, 610. See also Sykes to Thomas Moonlight, Moonlight to Plumb, October 3, 1864, 505.

18. Hiller to Rosecrans, McDougall to DuBois, October 2, Mower to Rosecrans, Mack to Hiller with Hiller to Hannahs, October 3, *OR*, 41: (pt. 3) 560, 561, 581, 587; "Department of Missouri. The Progress of Price's Invasion," *Philadelphia Inquirer*, October 4, 1864, p. 1; "The War in Missouri," *New York Tribune*, October 6, 1864, p. 11; and "From Missouri," *Richmond Daily Dispatch*, October 10, 1864, p. 1. See Bartels, *Iowa Boy Makes Good*, 151–54.

19. Melcher to Pleasonton, V. B. S. Reber to Melcher, C. Thompson to Miller, and Miller to Pleasonton, all October 2, Melcher to Pleasonton, Marsh to Hiller, October 3, *OR*, 41: (pt. 3) 559, 560, 586, 587. Franklin Archibald Dick, the provost marshal for St. Louis, was also back east, in his native Philadelphia and was still wondering whether he should return to the city, as late as the morning of September 30. *Troubled State: Civil War Journals of Franklin Archibald Dick*, ed. Gari Carter (Kirksville, MO: Truman State University Press, 2008), 142.

20. Miller to Pleasonton, A. N. Grissom to Pleasonton, October 2, Melcher to Pleasonton, October 3, *OR*, 41: (pt. 3) 560, 561, 586. This may have been Benjamin A. Talbott.

21. DuBois to Smith, October 2, 11:03 a.m., Smith to Rosecrans, October 2, 9:30 p.m., Rosecrans to Smith, October 2, 10:45 p.m., *OR*, 41: (pt. 3) 553, 554.

22. "The Invasion of Missouri," *New York Herald*, October 4, 1864, p. 1; "From Missouri," *New York Tribune*, October 7, 1864, p. 1; Fike, Diaries, v. 2, October 2, 4, 5, 1864, Western Historical Manuscripts Collections, University of Missouri, Columbia. J. Blish Jr. or B. McMurtrie, operators, with A. J. Smith in pursuit. Plum, *The Military Telegraph During the Civil War*, 2: 219.

23. Merrill to Rosecrans, October 1, 6:30 p.m., Rosecrans to Merrill, October 2, 2:04 p.m., Smith to Rosecrans, October 2, 11:20 p.m., Merrill to Rosecrans, October 2, 3 p.m. and 5:39 p.m., *OR*, 41: (pt. 3) 538, 553, 554, 555, 557.

24. Rosecrans to Merrill, October 2, 3:10 p.m., Merrill to Rosecrans, October 2, 3:40 p.m., Rosecrans to Merrill, October 2, 5:25 p.m., *OR*, 41: (pt. 3) 555–56, 556. The editors of the *OR* mistook the Bourbeuse for the "Bourbon" River.

25. Merrill to Rosecrans, October 2, 5:39 p.m., 8 p.m., 9 p.m., 10:30 p.m., 11:45 p.m., *OR*, 41: (pt. 3) 556–57, 557, 558.

26. Palmer, *Four Weeks in the Rebel Army*, 20–21.

27. Merrill to Rosecrans, October 2, 11:45 p.m., October 3, 2:30 p.m., *OR*, 41: (pt. 3)

558, 582; Gregory, *Price's Raid In Franklin County, Missouri.*

28. *History of Franklin, Jefferson, Washington, Crawford and Gasconade Counties*, 330–31.

29. "More About the Capture of the Train at Miller's Landing," *St. Louis Daily Missouri Democrat*, October 6, p. 1; Price, December 28, and Clark, December 19, 1864, *OR*, 41: (pt. 1) 630, 680; *History of Boone County*, 1021.

30. Gregory, *Price's Raid In Franklin County, Missouri*, 8–9.

31. Merrill to Rosecrans, October 2, 11:45 p.m., Rosecrans to Merrill, October 3, 2:15 p.m., *OR*, 41: (pt. 3) 558, 582; Gregory, *Price's Raid In Franklin County, Missouri.*

32. Cabell, *Report of the Part Cabell's Brigade took*, 6–7.

33. Gregory, *Price's Raid In Franklin County, Missouri*, 15; "Colonel Gale" (from the *Franklin County News*) in *St. Louis Daily Missouri Democrat*, October 18, p. 2. Near sunset, Corporal Henry Beckman was still wearing his black clothes from the morning's Lutheran service as he crossed an open field within view of the road suddenly filled with rebels; dropping to the ground, he covered his face and hands and appeared in the distance to be nothing but a stump. The Beckman story comes from my mother, great-uncles, and great-aunts who lived with Beckman, their grandfather.

34. Fike, Diaries, v. 2, October 8, 1864, Western Historical Manuscripts Collection, University of Missouri, Columbia.

35. Franz Dinger to Mrs. Sophia Rinaman, pp. 11, 13–14, in James Wilson Papers, Western Historical Manuscripts Collection, University of Missouri, Columbia.

36. Dinger to Rinaman, p. 14, in James Wilson Papers, Western Historical Manuscripts Collection, University of Missouri, Columbia; *History of Franklin, Jefferson, Washington, Crawford and Gasconade Counties*, 247; *Atlas map of Franklin County, Missouri* (St. Louis, MO: Saint Louis Atlas Publishing Co., 1878), 38, 46; Crawford, "An Eye for an Eye," 110–11, 116. Based on often-flawed press accounts, Lonnie R. Speer's version shared their carelessness of detail regarded as incidental to the main point in his *War of Vengeance*, 3–4, 5, 7, 8. Corporal William W. Gourley, and Privates William C. Groots, William Scaggs, and John W. Shew, taken at Ponder's Farm, and John D. Hallibaugh or Holabaugh.

37. Dinger to Rinaman, p. 14, in James Wilson Papers, Western Historical Manuscripts Collection, University of Missouri, Columbia.

38. Dinger to Rinaman, p. 14, in James Wilson Papers, Western Historical Manuscripts Collection, University of Missouri, Columbia.

39. Dinger to Rinaman, p. 14, in James Wilson Papers, Western Historical Manuscripts Collection, University of Missouri, Columbia; Benjamin Borton, *On the Parallels or Chapters of Inner History: A Story of the Rappahannock* (Wolodstown, NJ: Monitor-Register Print, 1903), 84; Floyd Calvin Shoemaker, *Missouri's Hall of Fame: Lives of Eminent Missourians* (Columbia, MO: Missouri Book Company, 1918), 241–43. See also, Champ Clark, *My Quarter Century of American Politics*, 2 vols. (New York: Harper & Brothers, 1920), 2: 224–25.

40. Crawford, "An Eye for an Eye," 116–17; Gregory, *Price's Raid In Franklin County, Missouri*, 16–17. This happened "for the alleged killing of some of the latter's associates in Arkansas." "Important from Missouri. The Enemy Before the Capital," *New York Tribune*, October 10, 1864, p. 1; "From Missouri," *Richmond Daily Dispatch*, October

10, 1864, p. 1; *The Civil War in Ripley County, Missouri*, 10, 26. After fantasizing about the participants' unconcern with slavery, Speer, in *War of Vengeance,* geographically mislocates the area, called the Jeffries farm the Jeffersons, says unit members identified themselves as from an Illinois rather than an Iowa regiment, and misidentified the officer in charge as John T. Crisp, apparently confusing Coffee with a secessionist named Crisp murdered by Confederates later in the campaign. Speer also writes, bizarrely, that Stone identified one of the bodies as Third MSM Cavalry because of the trim of his artillery uniform.

41. Edwards, *Shelby and His Men*, 389.

42. Carpenter in Bartels, *Iowa Boy Makes Good*, 157. On Gunter, Fletcher, "The Battle of Pilot Knob and the Retreat to Leasburg," 41, and Russell L. Mahan, *Fayetteville, Arkansas in the Civil War* (Bountiful, UT: Historical Byways, 2003), 16, 31, 56–57, 59. Dinger reported that Crisp told him at the time that he knew no more of the charges. Dinger to Rinaman, p. 14, in James Wilson Papers, Western Historical Manuscripts Collection, University of Missouri, Columbia. Jackman, November 30, 1864, *OR*, 41: (pt. 1) 673. For Shelby's alleged convening of a formal military court-martial, see *The Civil War in Ripley County, Missouri*, 10, 26. One wonders if this was behind McPheeters's witnessing "a brutal act of one of our soldiers to another." McPheeters, *I Acted from Principle*, 226.

43. Thompson, *Memoirs*, 238–39; Reynolds to Price, October 3, 1864, *OR*, 41: (pt. 3) 976–77.

44. "Safe Arrival of Colonel Maupin, Captain Schenk and Lieutenant Fletcher," *St. Louis Daily Missouri Democrat*, October 7, p. 1; Smith to Rosecrans, 9 a.m., McNeil to Rosecrans, McNeil's Special Order No. 156, October 3, *OR*, pt. 3, 580, 587, 588. On the third, Surgeon Carpenter would arrive at St. Louis "under a rebel flag of truce" to arrange for medical supplies at Pilot Knob, and would report news that they were prisoners and being "badly treated." The next day, Carpenter wrote Mrs. Ewing. See Bartels, *Iowa Boy Makes Good*, 151–54.

Chapter 7

1. *History of Franklin, Jefferson, Washington, Crawford and Gasconade Counties*, 652, 665, 666, *passim* 677–81, 1081; Maupin to Pleasonton, October 5, *OR*, s.1, 41: (pt. 3) 640.

2. Captain H. Garner to Pleasonton, October 4, *OR*, s.1, 41: (pt. 3) 614.

3. Smith to Rosecrans, Captain H. Garner to Pleasonton, October 4, *OR*, s.1, 41: (pt. 3) 611, 614. On Cedar Fork, Mount Sterling and Fredericksburg, see *History of Franklin, Jefferson, Washington, Crawford and Gasconade Counties*, 342, 632, 643–44, 684.

4. Rosecrans to Brown, DuBois to Brown, Brown to Hickox, September 28, McNeil to DuBois, September 29, 1864, *OR*, 41: (pt. 3) 448, 450, 484. Forty-fifth Missouri. Henry Wilson. Residence was not listed; seventeen years old. Enlisted as a Private (date unknown). He was listed as: * POW 10/7/1864 (place not stated) (Paroled) * Wounded 10/7/1864 (place not stated) (Severe wound in right leg, amputated) He also had service in: "I" Company, Forty-fifth Missouri Infantry.

5. Shattuck in Peterson and Hanson, *Pilot Knob*, 281; Brown to Rosecrans, October 3, *OR*, s.1, 41: (pt. 3) 589.

6. Rev. John Rothensteiner, *History of the Archdiocese of St. Louis*, 2 vols. (St. Louis, MO: by the Author, 1928), II, 408–9; *History of Franklin, Jefferson, Washington, Crawford and Gasconade Counties*, 636, 658, 659–63, 667; Samuel F. Harrison, *History of Hermann, Missouri* (Hermann, MO: Historic Hermann, 1966), 13.

7. *History of Franklin, Jefferson, Washington, Crawford and Gasconade Counties*, 635–36, 652; *Official Army Register*, VII, 85; on Poser, *Appendix to the House Journal of the Adjourned Session of the Twenty-Second General Assembly Missouri* (Jefferson City, MO: State Printers, 1863), 462.

8. Bond to Poser, Poser to Brown, September 29, 1864, *OR*, 41: (pt. 3) 485; "Die Rebellen in Hermann," *Hermann Volksblatt*, October 24, 1864, p. 1.

9. Brown to DuBois, DuBois to Brown, Steger to commander of detachment of the Fortieth Missouri, Steger to Poser, September 30, 1864, Steger to Poser, October 1, Special Order No. 211, October 2, *OR*, 41: (pt. 3) 515, 516, 517, 518, 544, 565. Brown to DuBois, October 11, *OR*, 41: (pt. 1) 345. Companies F and I of the Forty-fifth were at Jefferson City.

10. General developments, Danville, Jacksonville, and Palmyra are noted in "The War in Missouri," "From Missouri," "The War in Missouri," and "From Missouri," *New York Tribune*, October 2 (p. 1 with continuation on p. 8), 4 (p. 1), 6 (p. 11), 8 (p. 1), 1864. See also: "Department of Missouri. The Progress of Price's Invasion," *Philadelphia Inquirer*, October 4, 1864, p. 1; "The Missouri Invasion," *Baltimore Sun*, October 6, 1864, p. 1; "Late from the West. The Invasion of Missouri. Demonstration on Memphis" (from *Democrat*) *New Orleans Daily Picayune*, October 16, 1864, p. 4; "Die Rebellen in Hermann," *Hermann Volksblatt*, October 24, 1864, p. 1.

11. Fisk to Rosecrans, Fisk to Bancroft, October 3, *OR*, s.1, 41: (pt. 2) 591, 592.

12. *History of Franklin, Jefferson, Washington, Crawford and Gasconade Counties*, 652; "Die Rebellen in Hermann," *Hermann Volksblatt*, October 24, 1864, p. 1; and "The Rebel Invasion," St. Louis *Union*, October 3, 1864, p. 1.

13. "Die Rebellen in Hermann," *Hermann Volksblatt*, October 24, 1864, p. 1; *History of Franklin, Jefferson, Washington, Crawford and Gasconade Counties*, 653; Clark, December 19, 1864, *OR*, 41: (pt. 1) 680; Colonel Robert R. Lawther, December 6, 1864, *OR*, 41: (pt. 1) 696; "The Rebel Invasion," St. Louis *Union*, October 3, 1864, p. 1.

14. "The Rebel Invasion," St. Louis *Union*, October 3, 1864, p. 1, also "From the Southwest Branch Road," St. Louis *Union*, October 1, 1864, p. 1; Captain Francis Onken and Captain Charles D. Eitzen, October 6, *OR*, s.1, 41: (pt. 1) 366–67, 368.

15. Onken, *OR*, 41: (pt. 1) 367–68, Eitzen, 368–69; *History of Franklin, Jefferson, Washington, Crawford and Gasconade Counties*, 1110, 1111.

16. Brown to DuBois, October 11, Clark to MacLean, December 19, *OR*, 41: (pt. 1) 345, 680–81; "The Missouri Invasion," *Boston Herald*, October 7, 1864, p. 2; "From Missouri," *New York Tribune*, October 7, 1864, p. 1.

17. Onken and Eitzen, *OR*, 41: (pt. 1) 367; William F. Cody, *The Life of Buffalo Bill* (1878; rpt. London: Senate, 1994), 136–37.

18. Onken and Eitzen, October 6, Clark to MacLean, December 19, *OR*, 41: (pt. 1) 367, 369, 680–81.

19. Clark to MacLean, December 19, *OR*, 41: (pt. 1) 680–81; Colonel Robert R. Lawther, December 6, 1864, *OR*, 41: (pt. 1) 698.

20. For this and the following paragraph, see *History of Cole, Moniteau, Morgan, Benton, Miller, Maries and Osage counties, Missouri*, 665, 670–72.

21. Bryan R. Howerton, "Rebel or Yankee?" *Howerton Heritage*, ed. John F. Howerton and Bryan R. Howerton, 2 (Spring 1997): Posted http://www.howertonheritage.com/HowertonHeritageSpring1997.htm (accessed May 31, 2011).

22. *History of Cole, Moniteau, Morgan, Benton, Miller, Maries and Osage counties, Missouri*, 668.

23. Shelby, December 1864, *OR*, 41: (pt. 1) 653; Edwards, *Shelby and His Men*, 392. See also Daniel O'Flaherty, *General Jo Shelby, Undefeated Rebel* (Chapel Hill: University of North Carolina Press, 1954), 104, 187. McPheeters, who got to the town on October 5 and camped there for the night, made no mention of any fighting there either. While accuracy is questionable when at a distance, muddling developments at Hermann and Newhaven, his diary is pretty good at noting the after effects of smaller encounters, such as that at Union. *I Acted from Principle*, 227. Brugioni repeats Edwards's fictional account in *The Civil War in Missouri, As seen from the Capital City*, 111.

24. Shelby, *OR*, 41: (pt. 1) 654; Fisk to DuBois, October 6, *OR*, 41: (pt. 3) 666; Lieutenant Colonel J. F. Davies, December 12, 1864, *OR*, 41: (pt. 1) 696. At Linn, Dr. William McPheeters stopped to treat a soldier suffering from tetanus from a foot wound inflicted at Pilot Knob. McPheeters, *I Acted from Principle*, 227.

25. "The Rebel Raid—Assault upon Jefferson City—Price's March Westward," Jefferson City *Missouri State Times*, October 15, 1864, p. 2; Poser to Brown, October 6, October 10, Captain John Sullins, October 6, 1864, Brown to DuBois, October 11, Shelby to Lieutenant Colonel L. A. Maclean, December 1864, *OR*, 41: (pt. 1) 365–66, 369–70, 345, 654. Also see *History of Franklin, Jefferson, Washington, Crawford and Gasconade Counties*, 227, 272, 285, 286.

26. Sullins, *OR*, 41: (pt. 1) 370; Brown to DuBois, October 11, *OR*, 41: (pt. 1) 345, which listed the destruction of the Osage bridge on Tuesday night, which would have placed its capture over a day before the seizure of the bridge over the Gasconade; and, "The Rebel Raid—Assault upon Jefferson City—Price's March Westward," Jefferson City *Missouri State Times*, October 15, 1864, p. 2. Shelby reported forty prisoners taken. Some were paroled at Westphalia; others marched to California before being paroled.

27. "From Missouri," *Richmond Daily Dispatch*, October 10, 1864, p. 1.

28. Poser to Brown, Brown to McNeil, Brown to Rosecrans, and two dispatches from Fisk to Rosecrans, all October 5, as well as Fisk to Rosecrans, October 6, *OR*, 41: (pt. 3) 645, 642, 647, 646, 667.

29. Rosecrans, *OR*, 41: (pt. 1) 311; Sanborn, "The Campaign in Missouri in Sept. and October, 1864," 154; and Brugioni, *The Civil War in Missouri, As seen from the Capital City*, 111–12, 126.

30. DuBois to Curtis, and Curtis to Rosecrans, October 6 *OR*, s.1, 41: (pt. 3) 657, 651/657(?). "If you support me it must be by direct movement down the river as quickly as possible." Brown to Curtis, October 4, *OR*, 41: (pt. 1) 466.

31. Smith to Rosecrans, October 2, 11:20 p.m., and Merrill to Rosecrans, Rosecrans to Merrill, October 3, 11 p.m., Melcher to Pleasonton, October 3, 1864, *OR*, s.1, 41: (pt.

3) 554, 581, 582, 586.

32. DuBois to Smith, General Order No. 185, October 2, and Special Order No. 274, Rosecrans to Smith, Smith to Rosecrans, October 3, *OR*, s.1, 41: (pt. 3) 554, 579, 579–80, 580; "From Missouri," *New York Tribune*, October 4, 1864, p. 1; "From Missouri," *New York Tribune*, October 7, 1864, p. 1.

33. Smith to Rosecrans, Rosecrans to Colonel J. K. Mills, Merrill to Rosecrans, October 3, *OR*, s.1, 41: (pt. 3) 580, 581, 582.

34. Merrill to Rosecrans, to Frank S. Bond, Smith to Rosecrans, October 3, *OR*, s.1, 41: (pt. 3) 580, 582, 583; Paul B. Jenkins, *The Battle of Westport* (Kansas City, MO: Franklin Hudson Publishing Co., 1906), 70.

35. J. Hough to Wolfe, Shaw to Wolfe, Pike to Smith, October 4, *OR*, s.1, 41: (pt. 3) 613.

36. Smith to Rosecrans, Rosecrans to Smith, Smith to Rosecrans, October 4, *OR*, s.1, 41: (pt. 3) 611, 612.

37. Smith to Rosecrans, 8:10 a.m., 1 p.m., and 1:30 p.m., October 5, Smith to DuBois, DuBois to Smith 10:25 a.m., 11:12 a.m., October 6, *OR*, s.1, 41: (pt. 3) 636, 658. Fike described the militia as "a set of good-looking men, but not inured to the march." Fike, Diaries, v. 2, October 7, 9, 1864, Western Historical Manuscripts Collection, University of Missouri, Columbia.

38. Rosecrans to Smith, 1:25 a.m. and 7:15, October 5, *OR*, s.1, 41: (pt. 3) 636, 637.

39. Major General William S. Rosecrans, December 7, 1864, *OR,* 41: (pt. 1) 311; Rosecrans to Canby, Rosecrans to Mower, Lieutenant L. O'Reilly to Colonel O. D. Greene, Eno to fleet commanders, October 5, DuBois to Smith, 11:12 a.m., Mower to Rosecrans, Dubois to Mower, 9:35 pm, First Lieutenant C. Thompson to Mower, October 6, *OR*, s.1, 41: (pt. 3) 633, 637, 638, 659, 660; Fike, Diaries, v. 2, October 4, 5, 7, 1864, Western Historical Manuscripts Collection, University of Missouri, Columbia. The flotilla had the capacity of conveying 2,000 men with their gear or 1,000 men with 600 horses.

40. Smith to Dubois 8 a.m. and 9 p.m., Rosecrans to Smith 10:45 p.m., Smith to Shaw 8:15 p.m., October 6, *OR*, s.1, 41: (pt. 3) 658, 659; and William A. Lyman, Diary 1864–1865, October 4, 6, 7, 1864, Typescript Collections, v. XVII, Item 490, Western Historical Manuscripts Collection, University of Missouri, Columbia.

41. Captain John W. Maupin to Marsh, October 3, Maupin to Pleasonton, October 5, Maupin to Marsh, October 6, *OR*, s.1, 41: (pt. 3) 592, 640, 662; *History of Franklin, Jefferson, Washington, Crawford and Gasconade Counties*, 223, 238, 248–49, 250, 422, 423; *The Centennial Biographical Directory of Franklin County Missouri*, comp. Kiel, 125, 300; Gregory, *Price's Raid In Franklin County, Missouri*, 14.

42. Scott, "The Last Fight for Missouri," 314.

43. D. W. Moore to Abraham Lincoln, October 5, 1864, A. G. Beller to Abraham Lincoln, October 8, 1864. Abraham Lincoln Papers.

44. John G. Nicolay to Abraham Lincoln, October 10, 18, 1864. Abraham Lincoln Papers.

45. John G. Nicolay to Abraham Lincoln, October 12, 1864 (Confidential). Abraham Lincoln Papers.

46. Onken, *OR,* 41: (pt. 1) 367, 368; Poser to Brown, October 5, *OR,* 41: (pt. 3) 645.

47. "Rebel Destruction of Property," *St. Louis Daily Missouri Democrat*, October 8, p. 1; "The Missouri Invasion," *Boston Herald*, October 7, 1864, p. 2; Brown to DuBois, October 11, *OR*, 41: (pt. 1) 345. Additional property destroyed included McKernan's warehouse, all the damage done by no more than fifteen rebels who had crossed the bridge. Poser to Brown, October 5, *OR*, 41: (pt. 3) 645. Cole Creek bridge was also destroyed by them "with thirty cars and twenty locomotives." "From Missouri," *New York Tribune*, October 8, 1864, p. 1.

Chapter 8

1. *History of St. Francis Xavier Church, Taos, Missouri, Illustrated 1838–1988* (Taos, MO: St. Francis Xavier Sesquicentennial Committee, 1988).

2. Writer's Program of the Work Projects Administration, *Missouri: the WPA guide to the "Show Me" State, compiled by workers of the Writer's Program of the Work Projects Administration, with a new foreword by Robert A. Archibald and a new introduction by Walter A. Schroeder and Howard W. Marshall* (St. Louis: Missouri Historical Society Press, 1998), 225, 226, 227, 229.

3. WPA, *Missouri*, 228.

4. Brugioni, *The Civil War in Missouri, As seen from the Capital City*, 4–5.

5. *History of Cole, Moniteau, Morgan, Benton, Miller, Maries and Osage counties, Missouri*, 258, 265, 282–84, 307, 865–67 and, for Wagner, 900. Others like Ohio-born Peter Alexander had fought under Price in the MSG, but now took up arms for the Union. On Alexander, *History of Cole, Moniteau, Morgan, Benton, Miller, Maries and Osage counties, Missouri*, 825; *Official Army Register*, 7: 113, 398; and *Bench and Bar of St. Louis, Kansas City, Jefferson City, and Other Missouri Cities*, 26–38.

6. "The Attack on Jefferson City," *St. Louis Daily Missouri Democrat*, October 18, 1864, p. 4; *History of Cole, Moniteau, Morgan, Benton, Miller, Maries and Osage counties, Missouri*, 282, 283–84; "The Attack on Jefferson City," *St. Louis Daily Missouri Democrat*, October 18, 1864, p. 4; Brugioni, *The Civil War in Missouri, As seen from the Capital City*, 34.

7. Brown to DuBois, October 11, *OR*, 41: (pt. 1) 344; "The Attack on Jefferson City," *St. Louis Daily Missouri Democrat*, October 18, 1864, p. 4; Brugioni, *The Civil War in Missouri, As seen from the Capital City*, 126; and Sanborn, "The Campaign in Missouri in Sept. and October, 1864," 153. Missing from all of this are the arming of local blacks, such as took place at Fort Davidson and, to a lesser extent, elsewhere. Probably more than anything else, this defined Jefferson City as a southern community. See also, "The Colored People in Jefferson City and Vicinity—What is to Become of them," Jefferson City *Missouri State Times*, October 15, 1864, p. 2. On Hickox, see *History of Cole, Moniteau, Morgan, Benton, Miller, Maries and Osage counties, Missouri*, 336, 364, 555.

8. Brown to DuBois, October 11, *OR*, 41: (pt. 1) 344–45, 346, and September 30, pt. 3, 515; "The Attack on Jefferson City," *St. Louis Daily Missouri Democrat*, October 18, 1864, p. 4; "From Jefferson City," *St. Louis Daily Missouri Democrat*, October 20, 1864, p. 4; Brugioni, *The Civil War in Missouri, As seen from the Capital City*, 72–73, 114, 126.

9. Brown to DuBois, DuBois to Brown, September 30, 1864, *OR*, 41: (pt. 3) 515, 516, 517.

10. Bond to Poser, September 29, Rosecrans to Dyer, September 30, 1864, Fisk to Rosecrans, to Douglas, October 2, *OR,* 41: (pt. 3) 485, 523, 567, 569; *History of Boone County,* 462–63.

11. Fisk's units included detachments of the Third and Ninth MSM Cavalry, the First Iowa Cavalry, the Seventeenth Illinois Cavalry, and well as of the new Thirty-ninth, Forty-third, and Forty-ninth Missouri, and a section of Battery C of the Second Missouri Light Artillery. Brown to DuBois, October 11, Fisk to DuBois, December 8, Brown to Curtis, October 4, *OR,* 41: (pt. 1) 345, 418, 466, and Brown to Rosecrans, October 5, *OR,* 41: (pt. 3) 642.

12. Brown to Rosecrans, Curtis to Brown, October 5, Fisk to Curtis, October 5, Brown to McNeil, Curtis to Fisk, October 5, Curtis to Brown, Brown to Curtis, Curtis to Rosecrans, DuBois to Curtis, October 6, *OR,* 41: (pt. 3) 642, 646, 647, 648, 657, 664. Built in the 1840s, the hotel had twenty-eight rooms on three floors. *A Naturalist in Indian Territory: the Journals of S. W. Woodhouse, 1849–50,* ed. and annotated by John S. Tomer and Michael J. Brodhead (Norman: University of Oklahoma Press, 1992), 254 n. 50.

13. Steger to Major G. W. Kelly, Philips to Steger, Kelly to Steger, October 1, Kelly to Steger, Steger to G. W. Kelly, Brown to Rosecrans, October 2, Captain A. R. Conklin, Brown to Philips, Fisk to Rosecrans, October 3, *OR,* 41: (pt. 3) 566, 589, 590, 591; McFerran, November 7, and Mullins to Lieutenant T. Doyle, October 8, 1864, *OR,* 41: (pt. 1) 358, 365.

14. Brown to DuBois, October 11, Fisk to DuBois, December 8, *OR,* 41: (pt. 1) 345, 418; "From Jefferson City," *St. Louis Daily Missouri Democrat,* October 20, 1864, p. 4; Brown to Rosecrans 3:20 p.m., DuBois to Brown 9:30 p.m., and Rosecrans to Fisk 6:20 p.m., Brown to Fisk 8:50 p.m., all October 6, *OR,* 41: (pt. 3) 662, 663, 667, 668. Perhaps reflecting this, Sanborn claimed to have had a virtual command at Jefferson City himself, because Fisk "said to me that he had never been under fire, and should depend wholly upon me for everything." "The Campaign in Missouri in Sept. and October, 1864," 155.

15. McNeill to DuBois, October 2, *OR,* 41: (pt. 3) 562.

16. McNeil to Captain J. F. Bennett, November 26, Sanborn to DuBois, November 13, Colonel John E. Phelps, November 2, 1864, *OR,* 41: (pt. 1) 375, 394, 401; Fletcher, "The Battle of Pilot Knob and the Retreat to Leasburg," 49. Also Sanborn, "The Campaign in Missouri in Sept. and October, 1864," 152–53.

17. McNeil to Captain J. F. Bennett, November 26, *OR,* 41: (pt. 1) 376; *History of Cole, Moniteau, Morgan, Benton, Miller, Maries and Osage counties, Missouri,* 612–13, 608–9; Mallory, "Missouri Bush & Prairie. Price's Raid," *National Tribune,* September 6, 1900, p. 8.

18. McNeil to Captain J. F. Bennett, November 26, Sanborn to DuBois, November 13, Fisk, *OR,* 41: (pt. 1) 375, 394, 419. Also Steger to Philips, October 5, *OR,* 41: (pt. 3) 644; Mallory, "Missouri Bush & Prairie. Price's Raid," *National Tribune,* September 6, 1900, p. 8. Sanborn later claimed that, from Castle Rock, they could see "a column of the enemy" closing on the Osage, even as they arrived. "The Campaign in Missouri in Sept. and October, 1864," 153.

19. Brown to McNeil, Steger to McNeil, Special Order No. 214, Special Order No. 214, Poser to Brown, Brown to McNeil, Steger to Philips, Brown to Matthews, A. R.

Conklin to Draper, Steger to Lieutenant Colonel A. J. Hart, October 5, *OR,* 41: (pt. 3) 642, 643, 644, 645, 646; and "Price's Raid—Pacific Railroad," Jefferson City *Missouri State Times*, October 15, 1864, p. 2. Sanborn mistakenly referred to the Forty-ninth as the Forty-first, a regiment back in St. Louis; neither were at regimental strength. "The Campaign in Missouri in Sept. and October, 1864," 155–56.

20. Special Order No. 214, Steger to Philips, Brown to Matthews, October 5, Fisk to DuBois, October 6, *OR,* 41: (pt. 3) 643, 644, 645, 666.

21. Rosecrans, *OR,* 41: (pt. 1) 311; Rosecrans to Halleck, October 6, *OR,* 41: (pt. 3) 657; and Sanborn, "The Campaign in Missouri in Sept. and October, 1864," 155. Brugioni, *The Civil War in Missouri, As seen from the Capital City*, 114–15, is simply wrong on numbers at Jefferson City, even to the point of describing the capital's reinforcement by the Second Colorado and the Seventh Kansas Cavalry there.

22. "From Jefferson City," *St. Louis Daily Missouri Democrat*, October 20, 1864, p. 4.

23. McNeil to J. F. Bennett, November 26, *OR,* 41: (pt. 1) 375; Brown to Rosecrans, Fisk to G. A. Holloway, October 3, Fisk to Rosecrans, October 5, Rosecrans to Curtis, October 6, *OR,* 41: (pt. 3) 589, 591, 647, 657.

24. Brown to Rosecrans, Fisk to Curtis, to Brigadier General James Craig, October 6, *OR,* 41: (pt. 3) 642, 647, 648; Rosecrans to Fisk 12:30, October 6, *OR,* 41: (pt. 3) 665. As a measure of communication among the Federal troops in the state, Charles W. Porter, a Union soldier in southwest Missouri noted the rumors there of Price's appearance at Jefferson City, "but we doubt the report as true." *In the Devil's Dominions: A Union Soldier's Adventures in "Bushwhacker country"* (Nevada, MO: Bushwhacker Museum, Vernon County Historical Society, 1998), October 6, 1864, 168.

25. Scheel, *Sixty-Six Miles in Thirty-Nine Hours*, 32; and, Brugioni, *The Civil War in Missouri, As seen from the Capital City*, 116.

26. Brown to DuBois, October 11, McFerran, November 7, and Mullins to Lieutenant T. Doyle, October 8, *OR,* s.1, 41: (pt. 1) 345, 358, 365; "The Rebel Invasion," St. Louis *Union*, October 4, 1864, p. 1.

27. Shelby to MacLean, December 1864, *OR,* 41: (pt. 1) 654; "From Missouri," *New York Tribune*, October 8, 1864, p. 1.

28. "The Rebel Raid—Assault upon Jefferson City—Price's March Westward," Jefferson City *Missouri State Times*, October 15, 1864, p. 2; Shelby to MacLean, December 1864, *OR,* 41: (pt. 1) 654; Brown to First Lieutenant William T. Clark, October 6, *OR,* 41: (pt. 3) 669; "From Missouri," *New York Tribune*, October 7, 1864, p. 1; "The Missouri Invasion," *Boston Herald*, October 7, 1864, p. 2. Greeley's paper reported falsely that the Confederate drive at Castle Rock had been "prevented by a force of our troops stationed on the opposite side, between whom and the Rebels fighting had occurred, but with what result is not known." "From Missouri," *New York Tribune*, October 8, 1864, p. 1.

29. "The Rebel Raid—Assault upon Jefferson City—Price's March Westward," Jefferson City *Missouri State Times*, October 15, 1864, p. 2; Philips's "Itinerary," McFerran to unknown, November 7, Mullins to Lieutenant T. Doyle, October 8, and Shelby to MacLean, December 1864, *OR,* 41: (pt. 1) 357, 360, 362, 654. Shelby to MacLean, December 1864, *OR,* 41: (pt. 1) 654. Shelby's report of this action by a Federal force exaggerated to be "about one regiment" also claimed to have been outnumbered. Mullins

had his men of the First MSM Cavalry with 150 others from the Eighth. Sanborn, "The Campaign in Missouri in Sept. and October, 1864," 154, says Shanks crossed at Bolton Shoals, six miles below Castle Rock. Brugioni, *The Civil War in Missouri, As seen from the Capital City*, 112.

30. Philips's "Itinerary," Mullins to Lieutenant T. Doyle, October 8, Shelby to MacLean, December 1864, Jackman to Edwards, November 30, *OR*, 41: (pt. 1) 357, 362, 654, 673; Palmer, *Four Weeks in the Rebel Army*, 22. Brugioni mistakenly reported Shanks killed. *The Civil War in Missouri, As seen from the Capital City*, 117. Some days later, Fike noted that they "passed a house where there was a wounded rebel Colonel." Fike, Diaries, v. 2, October 12, 1864, Western Historical Manuscripts Collection, University of Missouri, Columbia.

31. Brown to DuBois, Steger to Philips, Fisk to DuBois, Fisk to Rosecrans 7:30 p.m., Fisk to Curtis, Brown to Rosecrans, to DuBois, to Curtis, October 6, *OR*, 41: (pt. 3) 663, 664, 666, 667, 668, 671.

32. Sanborn to Colonel John V. DuBois, November 13, 1864, and Shelby to MacLean, December 1864, *OR*, 41: (pt. 1) 395, 655; First Lieutenant William T. Clark to Brown, October 6, *OR*, 41: (pt. 3) 669. Sanborn, "The Campaign in Missouri in Sept. and October, 1864," 154, 156.

33. "The Rebel Raid—Assault upon Jefferson City—Price's March Westward," Jefferson City *Missouri State Times*, October 15, 1864, p. 2; Fisk to Curtis, October 7, qtd., *OR*, 41: (pt. 1) 467; Rosecrans to Smith, 7:15, Fisk to Brigadier General J. B. Douglass, to Curtis, October 5, Rosecrans to Fisk, 12:30, Fisk to DuBois, Rosecrans to Fisk, 3:45 p.m., Fisk to Rosecrans, to Curtis, October 6, *OR*, 41: (pt. 3) 637, 649, 647, 665, 666, 667, 668, 671; "The Missouri Invasion," *Boston Herald*, October 7, 1864, p. 2.

34. Rosecrans to McNeil 3:40 p.m., McNeil to Rosecrans 7:45 p.m., Fisk to Rosecrans 7:30, to Curtis, October 6, *OR*, 41: (pt. 3) 662, 667, 671. A Union diarist noted the painfully slow advance as follows: October 8 at Boeuf Creek, and did not march Sunday, October 9 Only at the Gasconade as of October 10, when it crossed to the west side and spent the night "in what was a rebel camp." Fike, Diaries, v. 2, October 7, 8, 9, 10, 1864, Western Historical Manuscripts Collection, University of Missouri, Columbia.

35. Brown to Curtis, Fisk to Rosecrans 7:30 p.m., Fisk to Colonel William Forbes at Macon, Fisk to Curtis, October 6, *OR*, 41: (pt. 3) 664, 667, 670, 671.

36. Brown to Philips, to Fisk, Clark to Brown, Brown to Clark, October 6, *OR*, 41: (pt. 3) 664, 668, 669.

37. McNeil to Captain J. F. Bennett, November 26, 1864, Beveridge, November 17, and Eppstein, November 18, and for Sutter's twelve-pounder Napoleons, Sanborn to Colonel John V. DuBois, November 13, 1864, *OR*, 41: (pt. 1) 376, 379, 382, 395; Fisk to Rosecrans, October 6, *OR*, 41: (pt. 3) 668.

38. Brugioni, *The Civil War in Missouri, As seen from the Capital City*, 112, 121–25; "The Rebel Raid—Assault upon Jefferson City—Price's March Westward," Jefferson City *Missouri State Times*, October 15, 1864, p. 2.

39. Plumb, November 12, Sanborn, November 13, Plumb, November 12, Gravely, November 15, 1864, *OR*, 41: (pt. 1) 395, 408, 412; Sanborn, "The Campaign in Missouri in Sept. and October, 1864," 157. The Federals watched from a house at 1122 Moreau Drive. Brugioni, *The Civil War in Missouri, As seen from the Capital City*, 126.

40. Gravely, November 15, Price, December 28, 1864, *OR,* 41: (pt. 1) 412, 631; Sanborn, "The Campaign in Missouri in Sept. and October, 1864," 156–57; and, Brugioni, *The Civil War in Missouri, As seen from the Capital City*, 118.

41. Gravely, November 15, Price, December 28, 1864, *OR,* 41: (pt. 1) 412, 631; Cabell, *Report of the Part Cabell's Brigade took*, 7; "The Rebel Raid—Assault upon Jefferson City—Price's March Westward," Jefferson City *Missouri State Times*, October 15, 1864, p. 2.

42. Plumb, November 12, Sanborn, November 13, 1864, *OR,* 41: (pt. 1) 395, 408.

43. Philips's "Itinerary," Plumb, November 12, Sanborn, November 13, Gravely, November 15, Fisk to DuBois, December 8, Price, December 28, 1864, *OR,* 41: (pt. 1) 357, 395, 408, 412, 419, 631; Fisk to Rosecrans, 11:15 a.m., October 7, *OR,* 41: (pt. 3) 689; Brugioni, *The Civil War in Missouri, As seen from the Capital City*, 70.

44. Brugioni, *The Civil War in Missouri, As seen from the Capital City*, 70, 118, 119; "The Rebel Raid—Assault upon Jefferson City—Price's March Westward," Jefferson City *Missouri State Times*, October 15, 1864, p. 2; Sanborn, November 13, Price, December 28, 1864, *OR,* 41: (pt. 1) 395, 631. Also present were two companies of the Forty-third under Lieutenant W. H. Hill (Wm. B. Hill of the Forty-third EMM? Or Adjutant Wm. H. Hill of Forty-fifth Missouri).

45. Brugioni, *The Civil War in Missouri, As seen from the Capital City*, 118, 119; "The Rebel Raid—Assault upon Jefferson City—Price's March Westward," Jefferson City *Missouri State Times*, October 15, 1864, p. 2. Dr. McPheeters established a hospital at the home of a Mr. Berry, only three miles from the capital. Counted "10 or 12 of our own wounded and 2 Federals." McPheeters noted one killed, shot in the head. *I Acted from Principle*, 228.

46. Rosecrans, December 7, Price, December 28, 1864, *OR,* 41: (pt. 1) 311, 631; Cabell, *Report of the Part Cabell's Brigade took*, 7; Fisk to Rosecrans, 11:15 a.m. and 1:30 p.m., October 7, *OR,* 41: (pt. 3) 689. The press reported the Confederate drive "spiritedly contested by our Cavalry." "The Invasion of Missouri," *New York Tribune*, October 11, 1864, p. 1.

47. Philips's "Itinerary," McFerran, William B. Mitchell, November 3, Phelps, November 2, Sanborn, November 13, *OR,* 41: (pt. 1) 357, 358, 395, 401, 410.

48. Mitchell, November 3, McNeil, November 26, Fisk to DuBois, December 8, 1864, *OR,* 41: (pt. 1) 376, 410, 419; and, Sanborn, "The Campaign in Missouri in Sept. and October, 1864," 157; *History of Cole, Moniteau, Morgan, Benton, Miller, Maries and Osage counties, Missouri*, 264.

49. Price, December 28, Thompson, November 24, Davies, December 12, 1864, *OR,* 41: (pt. 1) 631, 663, 696.

50. McNeil, Sanborn, Philips's "Itinerary," *OR,* 41: (pt. 1) 376, 395, 401; Brown to Fisk, October 7, *OR,* 41: (pt. 3) 689, 690.

51. Beveridge, November 17, Eppstein, November 18, 1864, Shelby, Thompson, November 24, *OR,* 41: (pt. 1) 382, 655, 663; "Price's Raid—Pacific Railroad," Jefferson City *Missouri State Times*, October 15, 1864, p. 2. Thompson reported that it had "proceeded to the Pacific Railroad and destroyed the water station and several bridges on the stream, up the valley of which the railroad leaves the Missouri River." Two roads went west from Jefferson City, the more southerly to Russellville. The west-

bound railroad, meanwhile, continued through the city upstream as far as Scott's Station, after which the railroad continued due west away from the upstream river bend. The service records of the Illinois horsemen revealed three October 9 anomalies, the desertions of Benjamin Ough and Lansing Shear, and the officially mustering out of Nicholas DePue after only a few day's service. The bridge near Scott's station would be rebuilt by October 11. The Seventeenth Illinois Cavalry also had its own tales of heroism and close brushes at the edges of the line, including the presence of Wild Bill Hickock. See Mallory, "Missouri Bush & Prairie. Price's Raid," *National Tribune,* September 6, 1900, p. 8.

52. Rea, *Sterling Price, the Lee of the West*, xx; Brugioni, *The Civil War in Missouri, As seen from the Capital City*, 119; *Encyclopedia of the History of Missouri: A Compendium of History and Biography for Ready Reference*, ed. Howard L. Conard, 6 vols. (New York, Louisville, St. Louis: Southern History Company, 1901), 6: 329, 324 n. 71. For part of the general entry on the subject in this title, see also D. M. Grissom, "War Between the States," 324–30, supplemented by James O. Broadhead, "Federal History," 330–50, and Samuel M. Kennard and John G. Kelly, "Confederate side," 350–71.

53. Fisk to Rosecrans, 11:15 a.m. and 1:30 p.m., October 7, *OR,* 41: (pt. 3) 689; and, "The Rebel Raid—Assault upon Jefferson City—Price's March Westward," Jefferson City *Missouri State Times*, October 15, 1864, p. 2.

54. "The Rebel Raid—Assault upon Jefferson City—Price's March Westward," Jefferson City *Missouri State Times*, October 15, 1864, p. 2. The two deserters were Henry Buckner and Pallis Scruggs. Confederate casualties mentioned here may have been Sergeant Andrew J. Bowls of Fristoe's cavalry, Captain John B. Bowles of Elliot's Ninth Missouri Cavalry, or Sergeant James M. Bowles of Lawther's Tenth Missouri Cavalry; service records also include those for Corporal Leander Key of Burbridge's Fourth Missouri Cavalry.

55. Rosecrans, Price, December 28, 1864, *OR,* 41: (pt. 1) 311, 631; Rosecrans to Fisk, 6:20 p.m., October 6, *OR,* 41: (pt. 3) 667.

56. Thompson, *Memoirs*, 239.

57. John E. Phelps, November 10, 1864, *OR,* 41: (pt. 1) 401.

58. John N. Edwards, *Shelby's Expedition to Mexico, an Unwritten Leaf of the War* (Kansas City, MO: Jennie Edwards, Publisher, 1889), 234; *Autobiography of Samuel S. Hildebrand*, 240.

Epilogue

1. Plum, *The Military Telegraph During the Civil War*, II, p. 219; "Department of Missouri. The Progress of Price's Invasion," *Philadelphia Inquirer*, October 4, 1864, p. 1; "From Missouri," *New York Tribune*, October 7, 1864, p. 1; "The Great Contest. From Missouri," *New York Tribune*, October 12, 1864, p. 1.

2. Special order No. 277, Dubois to Fisk, Major Frank Bond to commander at Mexico, Lieutenant Colonel S. M. Wirt (at Mexico to Bond, all October 6, *OR*, s.1, 41 (pt. 3) 658, 668, 669, 670.

3. "Price's Invasion of Missouri. Reliable Account of Rosecran's Operations Against the Enemy" (from *Missouri Republican*), *Louisville Daily Journal*, November 2, 1864,

p. 1; Scott, "The Last Fight for Missouri," 314. Jerry Ponder bought into the myth. *The Civil War in Ripley County, Missouri*, 23.

4. "Addenda. Itinerary of the District of Central Missouri, commanded by Brigadier General Egbert B. Brown," xxx.

5. "General Price's Movements in Missouri," *Richmond Daily Dispatch*, October 7, 1864, p. 1; "The Missouri Invasion," *Boston Herald*, October 7, 1864, p. 2; "Important from Missouri. The Enemy Before the Capital," and "The Great Contest. From Missouri," *New York Tribune*, October 10, 12, 1864, both p. 1; "Price's Raid—Pacific Railroad," Jefferson City *Missouri State Times*, October 15, 1864, p. 2; *Missouri Troops in Service During the Civil War: Letter from the Secretary of War* . . . (Washington: Government Printing Office, 1902), 53. "Price's Great Raid," *Daily Missouri Democrat*, October 18, 1864, p. 2.

6. William Forse Scott, *The Story of a Cavalry Regiment: the Career of the Fourth Iowa Veteran Volunteers, from Kansas to Georgia 1861–1864* (New York and London: G. P. Putnam's Sons, 1893), 318.

7. Major General George W. Dietzler, December 15, 1864, *OR*, s.1, 41 (pt.1) p. 615.

8. *History of Saline County, Missouri, Carefully written and compiled from the most authentic official and private Sources* (St. Louis: Missouri Historical Company, 1881), 310.

9. Fike, Diaries, v. 2, October 9, 1864, Western Historical Manuscripts Collection, University of Missouri, Columbia; letter from T. A. Gunnell to A. W. Reese, copied into Reese's Civil War Memoirs, p. 664, Western Historical Manuscripts Collection, University of Missouri, Columbia.

10. "Arrival of Price's Officers in St. Louis" (from St. Louis *Democrat*), *Daily Picayune*, November 11, 1864, p. 1. Notwithstanding the brutalities of the field, the prisoners were handled with all gentlemanly decorum, the privates "sent supperless to Gratiot, having had no rations for two days, while the officers were taken to one of the best hotels in the city and feasted like lords."

11. "Obituary. Sketch of the Rebel General Price, of Missouri," *New York Herald*, January 8, 1865, p. 1.

12. "Obituary. Sketch of the Rebel General Price, of Missouri," *New York Herald*, January 8, 1865, p. 1.

13. "From Missouri," *New York Tribune*, October 7, 1864, p. 1.

14. "From Missouri," *New York Tribune*, October 7, 1864, p. 1; A. W. Reese, Civil War Memoirs, p. 683, Western Historical Manuscripts Collection, University of Missouri, Columbia.

15. "From Missouri," *Richmond Daily Dispatch*, October 10, 1864, p. 1; Gregory, *PRFC*, 2; Lumir F. Buresh, *October 25th and the Battle of Mine Creek*, ed. Dan L. Smith (Kansas City, MO: Lowell Press, 1977), 135–36, 148–49, 233.

16. Statement of A. W. Maupin, in James Wilson Papers in the Western Historical Manuscripts Collection, University of Missouri, Columbia; Maupin to Pleasonton, October 5, *OR*, 41: (pt. 3) 640.

17. For this and the following paragraph, see Statement of Andy J. Brown. Patterson Farm on the Old State Road. The testimony on the murders, the finding of the bodies, James Wilson Papers in the Western Historical Manuscripts Collection, University

of Missouri, Columbia; Stone to Ewing, October 24, as an enclosure with Joseph Darr Jr. to DuBois, October 29, 1864, 1060–61; Speer, *War of Vengeance*, 8; "From St. Louis," *Pittsfield Sun*, October 27, 1864, p. 3.

18. Crawford, "An Eye for an Eye," 119, 125, 131, 132–33; Speer, *War of Vengeance*, 12–13; "Retaliatory Order by Provost Marshal General Darr," *Louisville Daily Journal*, November 2, 1864, p. 1.

19. Thomas, *History of Saint Louis County, Missouri*, 1: 83, 312.

20. Untitled item, *Louisville Daily Journal*, October 4, 1864, p. 1. "Further from the West. Death of the Guerilla Leader, Bill Anderson," *New Orleans Daily Picayune*, November 11, 1864, p. 2. See also, "From Missouri," *New York Tribune*, October 7, 1864, p. 1.

21. "The Invasion of Missouri," *New York Tribune*, October 11, 1864, p. 1; *Autobiography of Samuel S. Hildebrand*, 240; Samuel Montgomery, October 8, 1864, in *OR*, 41: (pt. 1) 456.

22. "Sterling Price vs. Ex-Gov. Reynolds," *New Orleans Picayune*, March 7, 1865, p. 1.

23. Gary L. Scheel, *Sixty-Six Miles in Thirty-Nine Hours: the Rertreat from fort Davidson, Pilot Knob to the Battle of Leasburg, September 28 thru October 1, 1864* (n.p.: for the Author, 2002), iii.

24. D. W. Moore to Abraham Lincoln, October 12, 1864. Abraham Lincoln Papers.

25. "Department of Missouri. The Progress of Price's Invasion," *Philadelphia Inquirer*, October 4, 1864, p. 1; "From Missouri," *New York Tribune*, October 7, 1864, p. 1; "The Missouri Invasion," *Boston Herald*, October 7, 1864, p. 2; "General Price's Movements in Missouri," *Richmond Daily Dispatch*, October 7, 1864, p. 1; "Gen. Ewing's Account of the Defense of Pilot Knob," *New York Tribune*, October 14, 1864, p. 1; Carpenter in Bartels, *Iowa Boy Makes Good*, 160; Scheel, *Sixty-Six Miles in Thirty-Nine Hours*, 23–24. Story told by Thomas Ewing III. Found by Ron Smith of Kansas in the Thomas Ewing Collection in the Library of Congress. (Fort Davidson newsletter, 2000.) "Grand Union Rally," St. Louis *Union*, September 30, 1864, p. 1.

26. John G. Nicolay to Abraham Lincoln, William L. Avery to John G. Nicolay, October 10, 12, 18, November 2, 1864. Abraham Lincoln Papers.

27. C. D. Drake, Wm. McKee, St. Louis mayor James S. Thomas, Chairman J. H. Lightner of the state's Union Executive Committee, ex-congressman Samuel Knox, and Chauncey J. Filley to Abraham Lincoln, November 2, 1864. Abraham Lincoln Papers at the Library of Congress. Transcribed and Annotated by the Lincoln Studies Center, Knox College. Galesburg, Illinois.

28. Fort Davidson newsletter, 2000. He enrolled at Benton Barracks on December 20, 1863, and enlisted in Company D, Sixty-second USCT, age twenty under Captain Looby. December 5, 1863, at PK, mustered in December 14, 1863. Transferred from Company K, mustered out in Brownsville, March 31, 1866. State Archives. Company D at Palmetto Ranch, Company K was not.

29. Maggie MacLean, "Louisa Volker," posted at "Civil War Women," http://civilwarwomen.blogspot.com/2006/11/louisa-volker.html.

30. Alonzon W. Slayback, one of those who had tried to moderate the brutality of 1864, was later killed in the office of the *St. Louis Post-Dispatch* after a dispute with its editor. *Bench and Bar of St. Louis, Kansas City, Jefferson City, and Other Missouri Cities*, 389; Sanborn, "The Campaign in Missouri in September and October, 1864," 154.

31. *Bench and Bar of St. Louis, Kansas City, Jefferson City, and Other Missouri Cities*, 216–17. See also Hill's *Liberty and Law, or Outlines of a New System for the Organization and Administration of Federative Government*, 2nd ed., rev. and enlarged (St. Louis: G. I. Jones and Company, 1880). Turner qtd. in Gary R. Kremer, *James Milton Turner and the Promise of America; the Public life of a Post-Civil War Black Leader* (Columbia: University of Missouri Press, 1991), 45. On Wingate, *Bench and Bar of St. Louis, Kansas City, Jefferson City, and Other Missouri Cities*, 424–25; and J. T. Pratt, *Pen Pictures of the Officers and Members of the House of Representatives of the Twenty-Sixth General Assembly of Missouri* (Jefferson City, MO: Printed for the Author, 1872), 98–99.

32. Application papers, 1884–1901. One folder. R 703. Grand Army of the Republic. John Matthews Post No. 69 (Springfield, Mo.); July 27, 1866. An Act granting Lands to aid in the Construction of a Railroad and Telegraph line from the States of Missouri and Arkansas to the Pacific Coast. By Authority of Congress. The Statutes at Large, Treaties, and Proclamations, of the United States of America. From December, 1865, to March 1867. ed. George P. Sanger, XIV (Boston: Little, Brown, and Company, 1868), 292. Information on individual soldiers is available from their Service Records; family background available on FamilySearch.com, though the material posted anonymously by users of the site is often contradictory and incorrect; and "A Joke on a Carpet-Bagger," *History of Greene County, Missouri*, ed. R. I. Holcombe (1883).

33. For the St. Louis general strike, see David T. Burbank, *Reign of the Rabble: The St. Louis General Strike* (New York: A. M. Kelley, 1966).

34. *The Civil War in Ripley County, Missouri*, 26–27, 40–41. *The Life and Trial of Frank James* (New York: F. Tousey, 1883). The Wide Awake Library: special number, September 28, 1883. At the war's end, the Federal authorities denied Reeves parole because of the Wilson murder. "Gen. M. Jeff Thompson. Surrender of the Poet Laureate of the New Madrid Swamps," *National Tribune*, June 18, 1908, p. 3.

Index

About the Author

Mark A. Lause came naturally to an interest in Price's raid. He was raised in a blue-collar Missouri community in the path of the 1864 campaign. He later found that the movements of the 1960s posed important questions about the role of the people in changing the institutions and practices of their society. Attempting to understand these issues drew him into the serious professional study of history, where most of his work has focused on pioneering new approaches to understanding the Civil War as "the Second American Revolution." Today, he is Senior Professor of American History at the University of Cincinnati. His numerous publications include *Price's Lost Campaign: The 1864 Invasion of Missouri* (University of Missouri Press). Lause resides in Cincinnati with Katherine Allen, his wife of thirty years.